MW00617023

The Suffering Of Man And The Sovereignty Of God
Twenty-Five Selected Sermons from the Book of Job
by Charles Haddon Spurgeon

Edited by Kerry James Allen

Copyright © 2001 by Fox River Press

Published by
Fox River Press
P.O. Box 1094
Oswego, IL 60543
630-554-1847 Voice Mail
815-886-4144 Voice/FAX
kerryjamesallen@yahoo.com

Front cover illustration: "Job and his friends"
Back cover illustration: "Job hearing of his ruin"
Wood-cuttings by Gustav Doré
Covers designed by Jeff Payne
815-462-3689

We welcome your contact, comments, suggestions, and constructive criticisms. Direct them to the address and numbers above. Quantity prices also available.

Publishers Note: These sermons have been selected from The New Park Street Pulpit series and the Metropolitan Tabernacle Pulpit series, originally printed by Passmore and Alabaster, and more recently reprinted by Pilgrim Publications, and are presented here in their entirety, without alteration of sermon titles, Bible texts or versions, or archaic English spelling. Fidelity to the original sermons has been meticulously sought with the exception of the use of a clearer and larger type font (11 point Century Schoolbook).

ISBN 0-9711434-0-4

The

Suffering of Man

and the

Sovereignty of God

Twenty-five
selected sermons
on the Book of Job
from the works of

Charles Haddon
Spurgeon

Fox River Press

Oswego, IL

Table of Contents

Introduction

Job. One small, three letter name that has inspired voluminous writings spanning thousands of years, launched untold numbers of sermons, and encouraged by the millions people who are suffering and bereaved. Job didn't fully comprehend what was happening to him at the time, and he couldn't realize what a spiritual impact he would have for time and eternity, but then, with our limited understanding, none of us really do. As Francis Anderson states:

Men seek an explanation of suffering in cause and effect. They look backwards for a connection between prior sin and present suffering. The Bible looks forwards in hope and seeks explanations, not so much in origins as in goals. The purpose of suffering is seen, not in its cause, but in its result. The man was born blind so that the works of God could be displayed in him (John 9:3). But sometimes good never seems to come out of evil. Men wait in vain. They find God's slowness irksome. They lose heart, and often lose faith. The Bible commends God's self-restraint. The outworkings of His justice through the long processes of history, which sometimes require spans of many centuries, are part of our existence in time. It is easier to see the hand of God in spectacular and immediate acts, and the sinner who is not instantly corrected is likely to despise God's delay in executing justice as a sign that He is indifferent or even absent. We have to be as patient as God Himself to see the end result, or to go on living in faith without seeing it. In due season we shall reap, if we do not faint.[1]

Job's greatest fears[2] and strongest desires[3] were both realized. Looking back, surely any true believer would be willing to endure what Job did to gain the eternal results that are still accruing to his account. Unfortunately, though, as someone said, "We review our lives backward, but live them forward." Childlike trust in the Unseen Hand is our only hope when engulfed in the darkness of pain, separation, and loss.

Spurgeon. His name is now obscure to all but the religious world, yet, he was the mightiest pulpiteer of his day, and is the most prodigious Christian writer in English history. His sermons have been continually in print for one hundred and fifty years, and their popularity shows no signs of waning. Charles Haddon Spurgeon preached no less than eighty-seven sermons on the book of Job during his ministry, and for him, this was no exercise in mere academics. Spurgeon was a sufferer. His bouts with ill health, almost continual pain, and the need for extensive bed rest began in his twenties. His wife Susannah became a semi-invalid in her thirties, and was rarely able to attend his public services. To Spurgeon, the book of Job was both a balm to use personally and apply publicly.

There are no easy answers to the questions of why people suffer, and why a God who can prevent it still allows it, thereby identifying Himself as the great First Cause. With childlike faith in God, Spurgeon, in these, his twenty-five finest sermons on Job, offers explanations and encouragement to those who suffer. As Spurgeon stated, "God had one Son without sin, but no son without sorrow." If the Captain of our salvation was made perfect through suffering, how much more do we need perfecting, and hence, suffering?

Kerry James Allen
Job 36:24

P.S. If you can find it, **Sitting With Job**, edited by Roy B. Zuck, and published by Baker, will yield you some of the most fruitful information on the book of Job found anywhere. It is not a book of sermons as this book is, but rather, a collection of short articles by theologians. It is highly recommended.

---

[1]Francis Anderson, Job: An Introduction and Commentary, Tyndale Old Testament Commentaries (Downers Grove, IL: InterVarsity, 1976), as excerpted in Sitting With Job, edited by Roy B. Zuck
[2]For the thing which I greatly feared is come upon me, and that which I was afraid of is come unto me. Job 3:25
[3]Oh that my words were now written! oh that they were printed in a book! Job 19:23

1

Satan Considering the Saints

"And the LORD said unto Satan, Hast thou considered my servant Job...?"

Job 1:8

How very uncertain are all terrestrial things! How foolish would that believer be who should lay up his treasure anywhere, except in heaven! Job's prosperity promised as much stability as anything can do beneath the moon. The man had round about him a large household of, doubtless, devoted and attached servants. He had accumulated wealth of a kind which does not suddenly depreciate in value. He had oxen, and asses, and cattle. He had not to go to markets, and fairs, and trade with his goods to procure food and clothing, for he carried on the processes of agriculture on a very large scale round about his own homestead, and probably grew within his own territory everything that his establishment required. His children were numerous enough to promise a long line of descendants. His prosperity wanted nothing for its consolidation. It had come to its flood-tide: where was the cause which could make it ebb?

Up there, beyond the clouds, where no human eye could see, there was a scene enacted which augured no good to Job's prosperity. The spirit of evil stood face to face with the infinite Spirit of all good. An extraordinary conversation took place between these two beings. When called to account for his doings, the evil one boasted that he had gone to and fro throughout the earth, insinuating that he had met with no hindrance to his will, and found no one to oppose his freely moving and acting at his own pleasure. He had marched everywhere like a king in his own dominions, unhindered and unchallenged. When the great God reminded him that there was at least one place among men where he had no foothold, and where his power was unrecognized, namely, in the heart of Job; that there was one man who stood like an impregnable castle, garrisoned by integrity, and held with perfect loyalty as the possession of the King of Heaven; the evil one defied Jehovah to try the faithfulness of Job, told him that the patriarch's integrity was due to his prosperity, that he served God and eschewed evil from sinister motives, because he found his conduct profitable to himself. The God of heaven took up the challenge of the evil one, and gave him permission to take away all the mercies which he affirmed to be the props of Job's integrity, and to pull down all the outworks and buttresses and see whether the tower would not stand in its own inherent strength without them. In consequence of this, all Job's wealth went in one black day, and not even a child was left to whisper comfort. A second interview between the Lord and his fallen angel took place. Job was again the subject of conversation; and the Great One, defied by Satan, permitted him even to touch him in his bone and in his flesh, till the prince became worse than a pauper, and he who was rich and happy was poor and wretched, filled with disease from head to foot, and fain to scrape himself with a miserable potsherd, to gain a poor relief from his pain.

Let us see in this the mutability of all terrestrial things. "He hath founded it upon the floods," is David's description of this world; and, if it be founded on the floods, can you wonder that it changes oft? Put not your trust in anything beneath the stars: remember that "Change" is written on the fore-front of nature. Say not therefore, "My mountain standeth firm: it shall never be moved;" the glance of Jehovah's eye can shake thy mountain into dust, the touch of his foot can make it like Sinai, to melt like wax and to be altogether on a smoke. "Set your affection on things above, where Christ sitteth on the right hand of God," and let your heart and your treasure be "where neither moth nor rust doth corrupt, nor thieves break through and steal." The words of Bernard may here instruct us: "That is the true and chief joy which is not conceived from the creature, but received from the Creator, which (being once possessed thereof) none can take from thee: compared with which all other pleasure is torment, all joy is grief, sweet things are bitter, all glory is baseness, and all delectable things are despicable."

This is not, however, our subject this morning. Accept thus much as merely an introduction to our main discourse. The Lord said to Satan, "Hast thou considered my servant Job?"

Let us deliberate, first, *in what sense the evil spirit may be said to consider the people of God;* secondly, *let us notice what it is that he considers about them;* and then, thirdly, *let us comfort ourselves by the reflection that one who is far above Satan considers us in a higher sense.*

I. First, then, IN WHAT SENSE MAY SATAN BE SAID TO CONSIDER THE PEOPLE OF GOD?

Certainly not in the usual Biblical meaning of the term "consider." "O Lord consider my trouble." "Consider my meditation." "Blessed is he that considereth the poor." Such consideration implies good-will and a careful inspection of the object of benevolence with regard to a wise distribution of favour. In that sense Satan never considers any. If he has any benevolence, it must be towards himself; but all his considerations of other creatures are of the most malevolent kind. No meteoric flash of good flits across the black midnight of his soul. Nor does he consider us as we are told to consider the works of God, that is, in order to derive instruction as to God's wisdom and love and kindness. He does not honour God by what he sees in his works, or in his people. It is not with him, "Go to the ant; consider her ways and be wise;" but he goes to the Christian and considers his ways and becomes more foolishly God's enemy than he was before. The consideration which Satan pays to God's saints is upon this wise. *He regards them with wonder, when he considers the difference between them and himself.* A traitor, when he knows the thorough villainy and the blackness of his own heart, cannot help being astounded, when he is forced to believe another man to be faithful. The first resort of a treacherous heart is to believe that all men would be just as treacherous, and are really so at bottom. The traitor thinks that all men are traitors like himself, or would be, if it paid them better than fidelity. When Satan looks at the Christian, and finds him faithful to God and to his truth, he considers him as we should consider a phenomenon—perhaps despising him for his folly, but yet marvelling at him, and wondering how he can act thus. "I," he seems to say, "a prince, a peer of God's parliament, would not submit my will to Jehovah: I thought it better to reign in hell than serve in heaven: I kept not my first estate, but fell from my throne: how is it that these stand? What grace is it which keeps these? I was a vessel of gold, and yet I was broken; these are earthen vessels, but I cannot break them! I could not stand in my glory—what can be the matchless grace which upholds them in their poverty, in their obscurity, in their persecution, still faithful to the God who doth not bless and exalt them as he did me!" It may be that he also wonders at their happiness. He feels within himself a seething sea of misery. There is an unfathomable gulf of anguish within his soul, and when he looks at believers, he sees them quiet in their souls, full of peace and happiness, and often without any outward means by which they should be comforted, yet rejoicing and full of glory. He goes up and down through the world and possesses great power, and there be many myrmidons to serve him, yet he hath not the happiness of spirit possessed by yonder humble cottager, obscure, unknown, having no servants to wait upon her, but stretched upon the bed of weakness. He admires and hates the peace which reigns in the believer's soul.

His consideration may go farther than this. Do you not think that *he considers them to detect, if possible, any flaw and fault in them, by way of solace to himself?* "They are not pure," saith he—"these blood-bought ones—these elect from before the foundations of the world,—*they* still sin! These adopted children of God, for whom the glorious Son bowed his head and gave up the ghost!—even they offend!" How must he chuckle, with such delight as he is capable of, over the secret sins of God's people, and if he can see anything in them inconsistent with their profession, anything which appears to he deceitful, and therein like himself, he rejoices. Each sin born in the believer's heart, cries to him, "My father! my father!" and he feels something like the joy of fatherhood as he sees his foul offspring. He looks at the "old man" in the Christian, and admires the tenacity with which it maintains its hold, the force and vehemence with which it struggles for the mastery, the craft and cunning with which every now and then, at set intervals, at convenient opportunities, it putteth forth all its force. He considers our sinful flesh, and makes it one of the books in which he diligently reads. One of the fairest prospects, I doubt not, which the devil's eye ever rests upon is the inconsistency and the impurity which he can discover in the true child of God. In this respect he had very little to consider in God's true servant, Job.

Nor is this all, but rather just the starting point of his

consideration. We doubt not that *he views the Lord's people, and especially the more eminent and excellent among them, as the great barriers to the progress of his kingdom;* and just as the engineer, endeavouring to make a railway, keeps his eye very much fixed upon the hills and rivers, and especially upon the great mountain through which it will take years labouriously to bore a tunnel, so Satan, in looking upon his various plans to carry on his dominion in the world, considers most such men as Job. Satan must have thought much of Martin Luther. "I could ride the world over," says he, "if it were not for that monk. He stands in my way. That strong-headed man hates and mauls my firstborn son, the pope. If I could get rid of him I would not mind though fifty thousand smaller saints stood in my way." He is sure to consider God's servant, if there be "none like him," if he stand out distinct and separate from his fellows. Those of us who are called to the work of the ministry must expect from our position to be the special objects of his consideration. When the glass is at the eye of that dreadful warrior, he is sure to look out for those who by their regimentals are discovered to be the officers, and he bids his sharpshooters be very careful to aim at these, "For," saith he, "if the standard-bearer fall, then shall the victory he more readily gained to our side, and our opponents shall be readily put to rout." If you are more generous than other saints, if you live nearer to God than others, as the birds peck most at the ripest fruit, so may you expect Satan to be most busy against you. Who cares to contend for a province covered with stones and barren rocks, and ice-bound by frozen seas? But in all times there is sure to be a contention after the fat valleys where the wheat-sheaves are plenteous, and where the husband-man's toil is well requited, and thus, for you who honour God most, Satan will struggle very sternly. He wants to pluck God's jewels from his crown, if he can, and take the Redeemer's precious stones even from the breastplate itself. He considers, then, God's people; viewing them as hindrances to his reign, he contrives methods by which he may remove them out of his way, or turn them to his own account. Darkness would cover the earth if he could blow out the lights; there would be no fruit to shake like Lebanon, if he could destroy that handful of corn upon the top of the mountains; hence his perpetual consideration is to make the faithful fail from among men.

It needs not much wisdom to discern that *the great object of Satan in considering God's people is to do them injury.* I scarcely think he hopes to destroy the really chosen and blood-bought heirs of life. My notion is that he is too good a divine for that. He has been foiled so often when he has attacked God's people, that he can hardly think he shall be able to destroy the elect, for you remember the soothsayers who are very nearly related to him, spoke to Haman on this wise; "If Mordecai be of the seed of the Jews, before whom thou hast begun to fall, thou shalt not prevail against him, but shalt surely fall before him." He knows right well that there is a seed royal in the land against whom he fights in vain; and it strikes me if he could be absolutely certain that any one soul was chosen of God, he would scarcely waste his time in attempting to destroy it, although he might seek to worry and to dishonour it. It is however most likely that Satan no more knows who God's elect are than we do, for he can only judge as we do by outward actions, though he can form a more accurate judgment than we can through longer experience, and being able to see persons in private where we cannot intrude; yet into God's book of secret decrees his black eye can never peer. By their fruits he knows them, and we know them in the same manner. Since, however, *we* are often mistaken in our judgment, *he* too may be so; and it seems to me that he therefore makes it his policy to endeavour to destroy them all—not knowing in which case he may succeed. He goeth about seeking whom he *may* devour, and, as he knows not whom he may be permitted to swallow up, he attacks all the people of God with vehemence. Some one may say, "How can one devil do this?" He does not do it by himself alone. I do not know that many of us have ever been tempted directly by Satan: we may not be notable enough among men to be worth *his* trouble; but he has a whole host of inferior spirits under his supremacy and control, and as the centurion said of himself, so he might have said of Satan—"he saith to this spirit, 'Do this,' and he doeth it, and to his servant, 'Go,' and he goeth." Thus all the servants of God will more or less come under the direct or indirect assaults of the great enemy of souls, and that with a view of destroying them; for he would, if it were possible, deceive the very elect. Where he cannot destroy, there is no doubt that Satan's object is to worry. He does not like to see God's people happy. I believe

the devil greatly delights in some ministers, whose tendency
in their preaching is to multiply and foster doubts and fears,
and grief, and despondency, as the evidences of God's people.
"Ah," saith the devil, "preach on; you are doing my work well,
for I like to see God's people mournful. If I can make them
hang their harps on the willows, and go about with miserable
faces, I reckon I have done my work very completely." My
dear friends, let us watch against those specious temptations
which pretend to make us humble, but which really aim at
making us unbelieving. Our God takes no delight in our
suspicions and mistrusts. See how he proves his love in the
gift of his dear Son Jesus. Banish then all your ill surmisings,
and rejoice in unmoved confidence. God delights to be
worshipped with joy. "O come, let us sing unto the Lord: let us
make a joyful noise to the rock of our salvation. Let us come
before his presence with thanksgiving, and make a joyful
noise unto him with psalms." "Rejoice in the Lord, ye
righteous, and shout for joy all ye that are upright in heart."
"Rejoice in the Lord always, and again, I say, rejoice." Satan
does not like this. Martin Luther used to say, "Let us sing
psalms and spite the devil," and I have no doubt Martin
Luther was pretty nearly right; for that lover of discord hates
harmonious, joyous praise. Beloved brother, the arch-enemy
wants to make you wretched here, if he cannot have you
hereafter; and in this, no doubt, he is aiming a blow at the
honour of God. He is well aware that mournful Christians
often dishonour the faithfulness of God by mistrusting it, and
he thinks if he can worry us until we no more believe in the
constancy and goodness of the Lord, he shall have robbed God
of his praise. "He that offereth praise, glorifieth me," says
God; and so Satan lays the axe at the root of our praise, that
God may cease to he glorified.

Moreover, if Satan cannot destroy a Christian, how often
has he *spoilt his usefulness?* Many a believer has fallen, not to
break his neck—that is impossible,—but he has broken some
important bone, and he has gone limping to his grave! We can
recall with grief some men once eminent in the ranks of the
Church, who did run well, but on a sudden, through stress of
temptation, they fell into sin, and their names were never
mentioned in the Church again, except with bated breath.
Everybody thought and hoped they were saved so as by fire,
but certainly their former usefulness never could return. It is

very easy to go back in the heavenly pilgrimage, but it is very hard to retrieve your steps. You may soon turn aside and put out your candle, but you cannot light it quite so speedily. Friend, beloved in the Lord, watch against the attacks of Satan and stand fast, because you, as a pillar in the house of God are very dear to us, and we cannot spare you. As a father, or as a matron in our midst, we do you honour, and oh!—we would not be made to mourn and lament—we do not wish to he grieved by hearing the shouts of our adversaries while they cry "Aha! Aha! so would we have it," for alas! there have been many things done in our Zion which we would not have told in Gath, nor published in the streets of Askelon, lest the daughters of the uncircumcised should rejoice, and the sons of the Philistines should triumph. Oh may God grant us grace, as a Church, to stand against the wiles of Satan and his attacks, that having done his worst he may gain no advantage over us, and after having considered, and considered again, and counted well our towers and bulwarks, he may be compelled to retire because his battering rams cannot jar so much as a stone from our ramparts, and his slings cannot slay one single soldier on the walls.

Before I leave this point, I should like to say, that perhaps it may be suggested, "How is it that God permits this constant and malevolent consideration of his people by the evil one?" One answer, doubtless, is, that God knows what is for his own glory, and that he giveth no account of his matters; that having permitted free agency, and having allowed, for some mysterious reason, the existence of evil, it does not seem agreeable with his having done so to destroy Satan; but he gives him power that it may be a fair hand-to-hand fight between sin and holiness, between grace and craftiness. Besides, be it remembered, that incidentally the temptations of Satan are of service to the people of God; Fenelon says they are the file which rubs off much of the rust of self-confidence, and I may add, they are the horrible sound in the sentinel's ear, which is sure to keep him awake. An experimental divine remarks, that there is no temptation in the world which is so bad as not being tempted at all; for to be tempted will tend to keep us awake: whereas, being without temptation, flesh and blood are weak—and though the spirit may he willing, yet we may be found falling into slumber. Children do not run away from their father's side when big dogs bark at them. The howlings of the devil may tend to drive us nearer to Christ, may teach us our own weakness, may keep us upon our own watch-tower, and be made the means of preservation from other ills. Let us "be sober, be vigilant, because our adversary the devil, like a roaring lion, goeth about seeking whom he may devour;" and let us who are in a prominent position be permitted affectionately to press upon you one earnest request, namely, " Brethren, pray for us," that, exposed as we are peculiarly to the consideration of Satan, we may be guarded by divine power. Let us be made rich by your faithful prayers that we may be kept even to the end.

II. Secondly, WHAT IS IT THAT SATAN CONSIDERS WITH A VIEW TO THE INJURY OF GOD'S PEOPLE?

It cannot be said of him as of God, that he knoweth us altogether; but since he has been now nearly six thousand years dealing with poor fallen humanity, he must have acquired a very vast experience in that time, and having been all over the earth, and having tempted the highest and the lowest, he must know exceedingly well what the springs of human action are, and how to play upon them. Satan watches and considers first of all *our peculiar infirmities*. He looks us up and down, just as I have seen a horse-dealer do with a horse; and soon finds out wherein we are faulty. I, a common observer, might think the horse an exceedingly good one, as I see it running up and down the road, but the dealer sees what I cannot see, and he knows how to handle the creature just in such quarters and at such points that he soon discovers any hidden mischief. Satan knows how to look at us and reckon us up from heel to head, so that he will say of this man, "His infirmity is lust," or of that other, "He hath a quick temper," or of this other, "He is proud," or of that other, "He is slothful." The eye of malice is very quick to perceive a weakness, and the hand of enmity soon takes advantage of it. When the arch-spy finds a weak place in the wall of our castle, he takes care to plant his battering-ram and begin his siege. You may conceal, even from your dearest friend, your infirmity, but you will not conceal it from your worst enemy. He has lynx eyes, and detects in a moment the joint in your harness. He goes about with a match, and though you may think you have covered all the gunpowder of your heart, yet he knows how to find a crack to put his match through, and much mischief will he do, unless eternal mercy shall prevent.

He   takes care also to consider *our frames and states of mind.* If the devil would attack us when our mind is in certain moods, we should be more than a match for him: he knows this, and shuns the encounter. Some men are more ready for temptation when they are distressed and desponding; the fiend will then assail them. Others will be more liable to take fire when they are jubilant and full of joy; then will he strike his spark into the tinder. Certain persons, when they are much vexed and tossed to and fro, can be made to say almost anything; and others, when their souls are like perfectly placid waters, are just then in a condition to be navigated by the devil's vessel. As the worker in metals knows that one metal is to be worked at such a heat, and another at a different temperature; as those who have to deal with chemicals know that at a certain heat one fluid will boil, while another reaches the boiling-point much earlier, so Satan knows exactly the temperature at which to work us to his purpose. Small pots boil directly when they are put on the fire, and so little men of quick temper are soon in a passion; larger vessels require more time and coal before they will boil, but when they do boil, it is a boil indeed, not soon forgotten or abated. The enemy, like a fisherman, watches his fish, adapts his bait to his prey; and knows in what seasons and times the fish are most likely to bite. This hunter of souls comes upon us unawares, and often we are overtaken in a fault, or caught in a trap through an unwatchful frame of mind. That rare collector of choice sayings, Thomas Spencer, has the following, which is much to the point:—"The camelion, when he lies on the grass to catch flies and grasshoppers, taketh upon him the colour of the grass, as the polypus doth the colour of the rock under which he lurketh, that the fish may boldly come near him without any suspicion of danger." In like manner, Satan turneth himself into that shape which we least fear, and sets before us such objects of temptation as are most agreeable to our natures, that so he may the sooner draw us into his net; he sails with every wind, and blows us that way which we incline ourselves through the weakness of nature. Is our knowledge in matter of faith deficient? He tempts us to error. Is our conscience tender? He tempts us to scrupulosity, and too much preciseness. Hath our conscience, like the ecliptic line, some latitude? He tempts us to carnal liberty. Are we bold spirited? He tempts us to presumption. Are we timorous and distrustful? He tempteth us to desperation. Are we of a flexible disposition? He tempteth us to inconstancy. Are we stiff? He labours to make obstinate heretics, schismatics, or rebels of us. Are we of an austere temper? He tempteth us to cruelty. Are we soft and mild? He tempteth us to indulgence and foolish pity. Are we hot in matters of religion? He tempteth us to blind zeal and superstition. Are we cold? He tempteth us to Laodicean lukewarmness. Thus doth he lay his traps, that one way or other, he may ensnare.

He also takes care to consider *our position among men.* There are a few persons who are most easily tempted when they are alone; they are the subjects then of great heaviness of mind, and they may be driven to most awful crimes: perhaps the most of us are more liable to sin when we are in company. In some company I never should be led into sin; into another society I could scarcely venture. Many are so full of levity, that those of us who are inclined the same way can scarcely look them in the face without feeling our besetting sin set a-going; and others are so sombre, that if they meet a brother of like mould, they are pretty sure between them to invent an evil report of the goodly land. Satan knows where to overtake you in a place where you lie open to his attacks; he will pounce upon you, swoop like a bird of prey from the sky, where he has been watching for the time to make his descent with a prospect of success.

How, too, will he consider *our condition in the world!* He looks at one man, and says, "That man has property: it is of no use my trying such-and-such arts with him; but here is another man who is very poor, I will catch him in that net." Then, again, he looks at the poor man, and says, "Now, I cannot tempt him to this folly, but I will lead the rich man into it." As the sportsman has a gun for wild fowl, and another for deer and game, so has Satan a different temptation for various orders of men. I do not suppose that the Queen's temptation ever will annoy Mary the kitchen-maid. I do not suppose, on the other hand, that Mary's temptation will ever be very serious to me. Probably you could escape from mine—I do not think you could; and I sometimes fancy I could bear yours—though I question if I could. Satan knows, however, just where to smite us, and our position, our capabilities, our education, our standing in

society, our calling, may all be doors through which he may
attack us. You who have no calling at all, are in peculiar
peril—I wonder the devil does not swallow you outright. The
most likely man to go to hell is the man who has nothing to do
on earth. I say that seriously. I believe that there cannot
happen a much worse evil to a person than to be placed where
he has no work; and if I should ever be in such a state, I
would get employment at once, for fear I should be carried off,
body and soul, by the evil one. Idle people tempt the devil to
tempt them. Let us have something to do, let us keep our
minds occupied, for, if not, we make room for the devil.
Industry will not make us gracious, but the want of industry
may make us vicious. Have always something on the anvil or
in the fire.

> "In books, or work, or healthful play,
> I would be busy too,
> For Satan finds some mischief still,
> For idle hands to do."

So Watts taught us in our childhood, and so let us believe in
our manhood. Books, or works, or such recreations as are
necessary for health, should occupy our time; for if I throw
myself down in indolence, like an old piece of iron, I must not
wonder that I grow rusty with sin.

Nor have I done yet. Satan, when he makes his in-
vestigations, notices all *the objects of our affection*. I doubt not
when he went round Job's house, he observed it as carefully
as thieves do a jeweller's premises when they mean to break
into them. They very cunningly take account of every door,
window, and fastening: they fail not to look at the next-door
house; for they may have to reach the treasure through the
building which adjoins it. So, when the devil went round,
jotting down in his mind all Job's position, he thought to
himself, "There are the camels and the oxen, the asses, and
the servants—yes, I can use all these very admirably."
"Then," he thought, "there are the three daughters! There are
the ten sons, and they go feasting—I shall know where to
catch them, and if I can just blow the house down when they
are feasting, that will afflict the father's mind the more
severely, for he will say 'O that they had died when they had
been praying, rather than when they had been feasting and
drinking wine.' I will put down too in the inventory," says the

devil, "his wife—I dare say I shall want her," and accordingly
it came to that. Nobody could have done what Job's wife did—
none of the servants could have said that sad sentence so
stingingly—or, if she meant it very kindly, none could have
said it with such a fascinating air as Job's own wife, "Bless
God and die," as it may be read, or "Curse God and die." Ah,
Satan, thou hast ploughed with Job's heifer, but thou hast not
succeeded; Job's strength lies in his God, not in his hair, or
else thou mightest have shorn him as Samson was shorn!
Perhaps the evil one had even inspected Job's personal
sensibilities, and so selected that form of bodily affliction
which he knew to be most dreaded by his victim. He brought
upon him a disease which Job may have seen and shuddered
at, in poor men outside the city gates. Brethren, Satan knows
quite as much in regard to you. You have a child, and Satan
knows that you idolize it. "Ah," says he, "there is a place for
my wounding him." Even the partner of your bosom may be
made a quiver in which hell's arrows shall be stored till the
time may come, and then she may prove the bow from which
Satan will shoot them. Watch even your neighbour and her
that lieth in your bosom, for you know not how Satan many
get an advantage over you. Our habits, our joys, our sorrows,
our retirements, our public positions, all may be made
weapons of attack by this desperate foe of the Lord's people.
We have snares everywhere; in our bed and at our table, in
our house and in the street. There are gins and trap-falls in
company; there are pits when we are alone. We may find
temptations in the house of God as well as in the world; traps
in our high estate, and deadly poisons in our abasement. We
must not expect to be rid of temptations till we have crossed
the Jordan, and then, thank God, we are beyond gunshot of
the enemy. The last howling of the dog of hell will be heard
as we descend into the chill waters of the black stream, but
when we hear the hallelujah of the glorified, we shall have
done with the black prince for ever and for ever.

III. Satan considered, but THERE WAS A HIGHER CON-
SIDERATION WHICH OVERRODE HIS CONSIDERATION.

In times of war, the sappers and miners of one party will
make a mine, and it is a very common counteractive for the
sappers and miners of the other party to counter-mine by
undermining the first mine. This is just what God does with
Satan. Satan is mining, and he thinks to light the fusee and to

blow up God's building, but all the while God is undermining him, and he blows up Satan's mine before he can do any mischief. The devil is the greatest of all fools. He has more knowledge but less wisdom than any other creature, he is more subtle than all the beasts of the field, but it is well called *subtlety,* not wisdom. It is not true wisdom; it is only another shape of folly. All the while that Satan was tempting Job, he little knew that he was answering God's purpose, for God was looking on and considering the whole of it, and holding the enemy as a man holds a horse by its bridle. *The Lord had considered exactly how far he would let Satan go.* He did not the first time permit him to touch his flesh— perhaps that was more than Job at that time could have borne. Have you never noticed that if you are in good strong bodily health you can bear losses and crosses, and even bereavements with something like equanimity? Now that was the case with Job. Perhaps if the disease had come first and the rest had followed, it might have been a temptation too heavy for him, but God who knows just how far to let the enemy go, will say to him, "Thus far, and no farther." By degrees he became accustomed to his poverty; in fact, the trial had lost all its sting the moment Job said, "The Lord gave, and the Lord hath taken away." That enemy was slain—nay it was buried and this was the funeral oration, "Blessed be the name of the Lord." When the second trial came, the first trial had qualified Job to bear the second. It may be a more severe trial for a man in the possession of great worldly wealth suddenly to be deprived of the bodily power of enjoying it, than to lose all first, and then lose the health necessary to its enjoyment. Having already lost all, he might almost say, "I thank God that now I have nothing to enjoy, and therefore the loss of the power to enjoy it is not so wearisome. I have not to say, "How I wish I could go out in my fields, and see to my servants, for they are all dead. I do not wish to see my children—they are all dead and gone—I am thankful that they are; better so, than that they should see their poor father sit on a dunghill like this." He might have been almost glad if his wife had gone too, for certainly she was not a very particular mercy when she was spared; and possibly, if he had had all his children about him, it might have been a harder trial than it was. The Lord who weighs mountains in scales, had meted out his servant's woe.

Did not the Lord also consider *how he should sustain his servant under the trial?* Beloved, you do not know how blessedly our God poured the secret oil upon Job's fire of grace while the devil was throwing buckets of water on it. He saith to himself, "If Satan shall do much, I will do more; if he takes away much, I will give more; if he tempts the man to curse, I will fill him so full of love to me that he shall bless me. I will help him; I will strengthen him; yea, I will uphold him with the right hand of my righteousness." Christian, take those two thoughts and put them under your tongue as a wafer made with honey—you will never be tempted without express license from the throne where Jesus pleads, and, on the other hand, when he permits it, he will with the temptation make a way of escape, or give you grace to stand under it.

In the next place, the Lord considered *how to sanctify Job by this trial.* Job was a much better man at the end of the story than he was at the beginning. He was "a perfect and an upright man" at first, but there was a little pride about him. We are poor creatures to criticise such a man as Job—but still there was in him just a sprinkling of self-righteousness, I think, and his friends brought it out. Eliphaz and Zophar said such irritating things, that poor Job could not help replying in strong terms about himself that were rather too strong, one thinks; there was a little too much self-justification. He was not proud as some of us are, of a very little—he had much to be proud of, as the world would allow—but yet there was the tendency to be exalted with it; and though the devil did not know it, perhaps if he had left Job alone, that pride might have run to seed, and Job might have sinned; but he was in such a hurry, that he would not let the ill seed ripen, but hastened to cut it up, and so was the Lord's tool to bring Job into a more humble, and consequently a more safe and blessed state of mind. Moreover, observe how Satan was a lacquey to the Almighty! Job all this while was being *enabled to earn a greater reward.* All his prosperity is not enough; God loves Job so much, that he intends to give him twice the property; he intends to give him his children again; he means to make him a more famous man than ever; a man whose name shall ring down the ages; a man who shall be talked of through all generations. He is not to be the man of Uz, but of the whole world. He is not to be heard of by a handful in one neighbourhood, but all men are to hear of Job's patience in the hour of trial. Who is to do this? Who is to fashion the trump of fame through which Job's name is to be blown? The devil goes to the forge, and works away with all his might, to make Job illustrious! Foolish devil! he is piling up a pedestal on which God will set his servant Job, that he may be looked upon with wonder by all ages.

To conclude, *Job's afflictions and Job's patience have been a lasting blessing to the Church of God, and they have inflicted incredible disgrace upon Satan.* If you want to make the devil angry, throw the story of Job in his teeth. If you desire to have your own confidence sustained, may God the Holy Ghost lead you into the patience of Job. Oh! how many saints have been comforted in their distress by this history of patience! How many have been saved out of the jaw of the lion, and from the paw of the bear by the dark experiences of the patriarch of Uz. O arch fiend, how art thou taken in thine own net! Thou hast thrown a stone which has fallen on thine own head. Thou madest a pit for Job, and hast fallen into it thyself; thou art taken in thine own craftiness. Jehovah has made fools of the wise and driven the diviners mad. Brethren, let us commit ourselves in faith to the care and keeping of God—come poverty, come sickness, come death, we will in all things through Jesus Christ's blood be conquerors, and by the power of his Spirit we shall overcome at the last. I would God we were all trusting in Jesus. May those who have not trusted him be led to begin this very morning, and God shall have all the praise in us all, evermore. Amen.

2

Job's Resignation

"Then Job arose, and rent his mantle, and shaved his head, and fell down upon the ground, and worshipped. And said, Naked came I out of my mother's womb, and naked shall I return thither: the LORD gave, and the LORD hath taken away; blessed be the name of the LORD. In all this Job sinned not, nor charged God foolishly." **Job 1:20-22**

Job was very much troubled, and he did not try to hide the outward signs of his sorrow. A man of God is not expected to be a stoic. The grace of God takes away the heart of stone out of his flesh, but it does not turn his heart into a stone. The Lord's children are the subjects of tender feelings; when they have to endure the rod, they feel the smart of its strokes; and Job felt the blows that fell upon him. Do not blame yourself if you are conscious of pain and grief, and do not ask to be made hard and callous. That is not the method by which grace works; it makes us strong to bear trial, but we have to bear it; it gives us patience and submission, not stoicism. We feel, and we benefit by the feeling, and there is no sin in the feeling, for in our text we are expressly told of the patriarch's mourning, "In all this Job sinned not." Though he was the great mourner —I think I might truly call him the chief mourner—of Scripture, yet there was no sin in his mourning. Some there are who say that, when we are heavy of heart, we are necessarily in a wrong spirit, but it is not so. The apostle Peter saith, "If need be ye are in heaviness through manifold trials," but he does not imply that the heaviness is wrong. There are some who will not cry when God chastiseth them, and some who will not yield when God smiteth them. We do not wish to be like them; we are quite content to have the suffering heart that Job had, and to feel the bitterness of spirit, the anguish of soul which racked that blessed patriarch.

Furthermore, Job made use of very manifest signs of mourning. He not only felt sorrow within his heart, but he indicated it by rending his mantle, by shaving off the hair of his head, and by casting himself prone upon the ground, as if he sought to return to the womb of mother-earth as he said that he should; and I do not think we are to judge those of our brethren and sisters who feel it right to wear the common tokens of mourning. If they give them any kind of solace in their sorrow, let them have them. I believe that, at times, some go to excess in this respect, but I dare not pass sentence upon them because I read here, "In all this Job sinned not, nor charged God foolishly." If the crepe should be worn for a very long while, and if the sorrow should be nursed unduly, as others judge, yet we cannot set up a standard of what is right for others, each one must answer for his conduct to his own Lord. I remember the gentleness of Jesus towards mourners rather than his severity in dealing with them; he hath much pity for our weakness, and I wish that some of his servants had more of the same spirit. If you who are sorrowing could be strong, if the weeds of mourning could be laid aside, it might indicate a greater acquiescence in the divine will; but if you do not feel that it should be so with you, God forbid that we should rebuke you while we have such a text as this before us, "Job arose, and rent his mantle, and shaved his head, and fell down upon the ground;" and "in all this Job sinned not."

I want you, however, to notice that mourning should always be sanctified with devotion. It is very pleasant to observe that, when Job had rent his mantle after the Oriental custom, and shaved his head (in a manner which, in his day, was not forbidden, but which under the Mosaic law was prohibited, for they might not cut their hair by way of mourning as the heathen did), and, after the patriarch had fallen down upon the ground, he "worshipped." Not, he grumbled; not, he lamented; much less that he began to imprecate and use language unjustifiable and improper; but he "fell down upon the ground, and worshipped." O dear friend, when thy grief presses thee to the very dust, worship there! If that spot has come to be thy Gethsemane, then present there thy "strong crying and tears" unto thy God. Remember David's words, "Ye people, pour out your hearts,"—but do not stop there, finish the quotation,—"Ye people, pour out your hearts before him." Turn the vessel upside down; it is a good thing to empty it, for this grief may ferment into something more sour. Turn the vessel upside down, and let every drop run out; but let it be before the Lord. "Ye people, pour out your hearts before him: God is a refuge for us." When you are bowed down beneath a heavy burden of sorrow, then take to worshipping the Lord, and especially to that kind of worshipping which lies in adoring God, and in making a full surrender of yourself to the divine will, so that you can say with Job, "Though he slay me, yet will I trust in him." That kind of worshipping which lies in the subduing of the will, the arousing of the affections, the bestirring of the whole mind and heart, and the presentation of oneself unto God over again in solemn consecration, must tend to sweeten sorrow, and to take the sting out of it.

It will also greatly alleviate our sorrow if we then fall into serious contemplations, and begin to argue a little, and to bring facts to bear upon our mind. Evidently Job did so, for the verses of my text are full of proofs of his thoughtfulness. The patriarch brings to his own mind at least four subjects for earnest consideration, out of which he drew great comfort. In like manner, you will do well, not merely to sit still and say, "I shall be comforted," but you must look about you for themes upon which to think and meditate to profit. Your poor mind is apt to be driven to and fro by stress of your sorrow; if you can get anchor-hold of some great clearly-ascertained truths, about which you can have no possible doubt, you may begin to derive consolation from them. "While I was musing," said David, "the fire burned," and it comforted and warmed him. Remember how he talked to himself as to another self, "Why art thou cast down, O my soul? and why art thou disquieted within me? Hope thou in God: for I shall yet praise him, who is the health of my countenance, and my God." There are two Davids, you see, talking to one another, and cheering one another! A man ought always to be good company for himself, and he ought also to be able to catechise himself; he who is not fit to be his own schoolmaster is not fit to be schoolmaster to other people. If you cannot catechise your own heart, and drill a truth into your own soul, you do not know how to teach other people. I believe that the best preaching in the world is that which is done at home. When a sorrowing spirit shall have comforted itself, it will have learned the art of consoling other people. Job is an instance of this kind of personal instruction; he has three or four subjects which he brings before his own mind, and these tend to comfort him.

I. The first is, to my mind, THE EXTREME BREVITY OF LIFE.

Observe what Job says, "Naked came I out of my mother's womb, and naked shall I return thither." He came forth, and he expected to go back to mother-earth, and there to lie. That is Job's idea of life, and a very true one it is, *"I come forth, and I go back again.* One asked a man of God, one day, "Will you tell me what life is?" The man of God stopped just a moment, and then deliberately walked away. When his friend met him, the following day, he said to him, "Yesterday, I asked you a question, and you did not answer it." "But I did answer it," said the godly man. "No," rejoined the other "you were there, and you were gone." "Well, you asked me what life was, and that was my answer. Could I have answered your question better?" He answered and acted wisely, for that is a complete summary of our life here below,—We come, and we go. We appear for a brief moment, and then we vanish away. I often, in my own mind, compare life to a procession. I see you, dear friends, going by me one by one, and vanishing, and others come on behind; but the point that I am apt to forget—and you do the same,—is that I am in the procession, and you are in it, too. We all count all men mortal but ourselves, yet all are marching towards that country from whose bourn no traveler returns.

Well now, because life is so short, do you not see where the comfort comes? Job says to himself, "I came, and I shall return; then why should I worry myself about what I have lost? I am going to be here only a little while, then what need have I of all those camels and sheep?" So, brethren, what God has given us, is so much spending-money on our journey, to pay our own fares, and to help our fellow-travelers; but we do not, any of us, need as much substance as Job had. He had seven thousand sheep. Dear me! what a task it must have been to drive and to feed such a large flock! "And three thousand camels, and five hundred yoke of oxen!" That is, a thousand oxen. "And five hundred she asses, and a very great household." Our proverb says, "The more servants, the more plagues;" and I am sure it is true that the more camels, the more horses, the more cows, the more of such things that a man has, the more there is to look after, and to cause him trouble. So Job seems to say to himself, "I am here for such a little time, why should I be carried away, as with a flood, even when these things are taken from me? I come and I go; let me be satisfied if other things come and go. If my earthly stores vanish, well, I shall vanish, too. They are like myself; they take to themselves wings, and fly away; and by-and-by I too shall take to myself wings, and I shall be gone." I have heard of one who called life, "the long disease of life;" and it was so to him, for, though he did a great work for his Master, he was always sickly. Well, who wants a long disease? "There's the respect that makes calamity of so long life." We want rather to feel that it is not long, that it is short, and to set small store by all things here below, and to regard them as things which, like ourselves, appear but for a time, and soon shall be gone.

Further, Job seems especially to dwell with comfort upon the thought, *I shall return to the earth*, from which all the particles of my body originally came; I shall return thither." "Ah!" said one, when he had seen the spacious and beautiful gardens of a wealthy man, "these are the things that make it hard to die." You recollect how the tribe of Gad and the tribe of Reuben went to Moses, and said, "If we have found grace in thy sight, let this land be given unto thy servants for a possession, and bring us not over Jordan." Of course, they did not want to cross the Jordan if they could get all their possessions on the other side. But Job had not anything this side Jordan, he was cleaned right out, so he was willing to go. And, really, the losses that a man has, which make him "desire to depart, and to be with Christ; which is far better," are real gains. What is the use of all that clogs us here? A man of large possessions reminds me of my experience when I have gone to see a friend in the country, and he has taken me across a ploughed field, and I have had two heavy burdens of earth, one on each foot, as I have plodded on. The earth has clung to me, and made it hard walking. It is just so with this world, its good things hamper us, clog us, cling to us, like thick clay; but when we get these hampering things removed, we take comfort in the thought, "We shall soon return to the earth whence we came." We know that it is not mere returning to earth, for we possess a life that is immortal, we are looking forward to spending it in the true land that floweth with milk and honey, where, like Daniel we shall stand in our lot at the end of the days; therefore, we feel not only resigned to return to the womb of mother-earth, but sometimes we even long for the time of our return to come. A

dear servant of God, whom you would all recognize if I
mentioned his name, was talking with me concerning our
dear departed brother, Hugh Stowell Brown, and he said, "All
the brethren of my age and yours seem to be going home; they
are passing away, the fathers and the leaders are going, and
I could almost wish," he added, "that our Heavenly Father
would put my name down as the next to go." I said that I
hoped the Lord would not do so, but that our brother might be
spared to labour a while longer here; but that, if I might put
in another name, I would plead for my own to go in there
instead of his. Happily, we have nothing to do with the date of
our home-going, it is out of our hands; yet we are glad to feel
that, when the time of our departure shall arrive, it will be no
calamity, but a distinct advancement, for the Master to bid us
to return to the dust whence we came. "Return, ye children of
men," he will say, and we will joyfully answer, "Yes, Father,
here we are, glad to stretch our wings, and fly straight to
yonder world of joy, expecting that even our poor bodies,
by-and-by, at the trump of the archangel, shall come back to
thee, and we shall be like thine only-begotten Son, when we
shall see him as he is."

II. Secondly, Job seems to comfort himself by noticing THE
TENURE OF HIS EARTHLY POSSESSIONS. "Naked," says he,
"came I out of my mother's womb, and naked shall I return
thither."

He feels himself to be very poor, everything is gone, he is
stripped; yet he seems to say, "*I am not poorer now than I was
when I was born.*" I had nothing then, not even a garment to
my back but what the love of my mother provided for me. I
was helpless then; I could not do anything for myself
whatever." One said to me, the other day, "All is gone, sir, all
is gone, except health and strength." Yes, but we had not as
much as that when we were born. We had no strength, we
were too weak to perform the least though most necessary
offices for our poor tender frame. David often very sweetly
dwells upon his childhood, and still more upon his infancy;
and we shall do well to imitate him. Old men sometimes
arrive at a second childhood. Do not be afraid, brother, if that
is your case; you have gone through one period already that
was more infantile than your second one can be, you will not
be weaker then than you were at first. Suppose that you and
I should be brought to extreme weakness and poverty, we

shall neither be weaker nor poorer than we were then. "But I had a mother," says one. Well, there are some children who lose their mother in their very birth; but if you had a mother to care for you then, you have a Father to care for you now; and, as a child of God, you surely feel that your mother was but the secondary agent to watch over you in your weakness; and God who gave that love to her, and moved her to care for you, will be sure to find that same love which flowed out of him into her still stored up in his own bosom, and he will see you through. Do not be afraid, my brother, my sister, the Lord will see you through. It is wonderful that, after God has been gracious to us for fifty years, we cannot trust him for the rest of our lives; and as for you who are sixty, seventy, or eighty years of age, what! has he brought you thus far to put you to shame? Did he bear you through that very weakest part of your life, and do you think he will now forsake you? David said, "I was cast upon thee from the womb," as if then he had none but God to help him; and will not he who took care of us then take care of us even to the end? Ay, that he will; wherefore, let us be of good courage, and let the poverty and weakness of our infancy, as we think of it, cheer us if we are weak and poor now.

Then Job adds, "However poor I may be, I am not as poor as I shall be, for naked shall I return to mother-earth. *If I have but little now, I shall soon have still less.*" We have heard of a rustic who, when dying, put a crown-piece into his mouth, because he said that he would not be without money in another world; but then he was a clown, and everyone knew how foolish was his attempt thus to provide for the future. There have been stories told of persons who have had their gold sewn up in their shrouds, but they took not a penny with them for all their pains. Nothing can be taken with us; we must go back to the earth, the richest as poor as the poorest, and the poorest no poorer, really, than the richest. The dust of great Caesar may help to stop a hole through which the blast blows, and the dust of his slave cannot be put to more ignoble uses. No, poor and weak as we may be, we are not as poor and weak as we shall be by-and-by; so let us just solace ourselves with this reflection. The two ends of our life are nakedness; if the middle of it should not always be scarlet and fine linen, and faring sumptuously every day, let us not wonder; and if it should seem to be all of a piece, let us not be impatient or complaining.

I want you to notice, also, what I think really was in Job's mind, that, notwithstanding that he was but dust at the beginning, and would be dust at the end, yet, still, there was a Job who existed all the while. "I was naked, but *I was*; naked shall I return thither, *but I shall be there.*" Some men never find themselves till they have lost their goods. They, themselves, are hidden away, like Saul, among the stuff; their true manhood is not to be seen, because they are dressed so finely that people seem to respect them, when it is their clothes that are respected. They appear to be somebodies, but they are nobodies, notwithstanding all that they possess. The Lord brought his servant Job to feel, "Yes, when I had those camels, when I had those she asses, when I had those sheep, when I had those men-servants, they were not myself; and now that they are gone, I am the same Job that ever I was. The sheep were not a part of myself, the camels were not a part of myself; I, Job, am here still, lying in my wholeness and integrity before God, as much a servant of Jehovah, in my nakedness, as I was when I wrapped myself in ermine." O sirs, it is a grand thing when God helps us to live above what we have, and above what we have not! Then it is that he brings us to know ourselves as we are, in our God, not dependent upon externals, but maintained and strengthened by food of which the world knoweth nothing, which cometh not from milk of kine. Then are we robed in a garment that cometh not from fleece of sheep, and we possess a life that dependeth not on the swift dromedary, a true existence that is neither in flocks, nor herds, nor pastures, nor fields, but delights itself in God, and stays itself on the Most High. "Naked came I out of my mother's womb, and naked shall I return thither," says Job, but "still it is I, the blessed of God, his same devoted servant, who will trust him to the end." That was good talk for Job's heart, was it not? Though it may not all have been said in words, I doubt not that something like it, or something much better, passed through the patriarch's mind, and thus he solaced himself in the hour of his sorrows and losses.

III. But now, thirdly, and perhaps the most blessed thing, is what Job said concerning THE HAND OF GOD IN ALL THINGS: "The Lord gave, and the Lord hath taken away; blessed be the name of the Lord."

I am so pleased to think that Job recognized *the hand of God everywhere giving.* He said, "The Lord gave." He did not say, "I earned it all." He did not say, "There are all my hard-earned savings gone." "Ah, me!" he might have said, "all the care for those sheep, and the dreadful expense of those camels, and the trouble that I have been at with those oxen; and now they are all gone, it does seem hard." He does not put it so, but he says, "The Lord gave them to me; they were a gift, and though they are gone, they were a gift from him who had a right to take them back, for all he gives is only lent. 'A loan should go laughing home;' and if God lent me these things, and now has called them back, I will bless his name for having let me have them so long."

What a sweet thing it is, dear brothers and sisters, if you can feel that all you have in this world is God's gift to you! You cannot feel that, you know, if you came by it dishonestly. No, it is not God's gift then, and it brings no blessing with it; but *that which is honestly the result and fruit of your cheerful industry,* you may consider has come from God; and if, in addition, you have really sanctified your substance, and have given your fair proportion to help the poor and the needy, as Job did, if you can say that you have caused the widow's heart to sing for joy when you relieved her wants, then all that you have is God's gift. God's providence is man's inheritance, and your inheritance has come to you from God's providence. Look at it all as God's gift; it will sweeten even that little loaf of bread and that tiny pat of butter,—which is all you will have to eat to-day or to-morrow,—if you regard it as God's gift. It will soften that hard bed upon which you lie, wishing that you were somewhat better covered from the cold, if you think of it as God's gift. A slender income will give us much content if we can see that it is God's gift.

Let us not only regard our money and our goods as God's gifts; but also our wife, our children, our friends. What precious gifts they often are! A man is truly rich who has a good help-meet; he is really rich who has godly children about him. Even though they may cost him much care, he is abundantly repaid by their affection; and if they grow up in the fear of the Lord, what a choice gift they are! Let us look at them all as God's gifts; let us not see them or anything else about the house without feeling, "My Father gave me this." Surely it will tend to draw the teeth of every sharp affliction if, while you have enjoyed the possession of your good things, you have seen God's hand in giving them to you.

Alas! some of you do not know anything about God. What you have, is not counted by you as God's gift. You miss the very sweetness and joy of life by missing this recognition of the divine hand in giving us all good things richly to enjoy.

But then, *Job equally saw God's hand in taking them away.* If he had not been a believer in Jehovah, he would have said, "Oh, those detestable Sabeans! Somebody ought to go and cut to pieces those Chaldeans." That is often our style, is it not? —finding fault with the secondary agents. Job has nothing to say about the Sabeans or the Chaldeans, or the wind, or the lightning. "The Lord,"said he, "the Lord hath taken away." I believe that Satan intended to make Job feel that it was God who was at work when his messenger said, "The fire of God is fallen from heaven, and hath burned up the sheep." "Ah!" said Satan, "he will see that God is against him." The devil did not succeed as he thought he had done, for Job could see that it was God's hand, and that took away the sting of the stroke. "The Lord hath taken away." Aaron held his peace when he knew that the Lord had done it, and the psalmist said, "I was dumb with silence, I opened not my mouth, because thou didst it;" and Job felt just that. "It is the Lord, let him do what seemeth him good." Never mind the secondary agents, do not spend your strength in kicking against this bad man or that; he is responsible to God for all the evil he has done, but at the back of these free agents there is a divine predestination, there is an over-ruling hand, and even that which in men is evil may, nevertheless, in another light, be traced up distinctly to the hand of the Most High. "The Lord gave, and the Lord hath taken away."

Will you recollect that with regard to your children? If Job had lost his eldest son alone, he might have needed much grace to say, "The Lord gave him, and the Lord hath taken him away." Job *had* lost his eldest son, but he had lost six more sons, and he had lost his three daughters as well. I have known a mother say, "My two dear boys sickened and died within a week; I am the most tried woman who ever lived." Not quite, not quite, dear friend; there have been others who have excelled you in this respect. Job lost his ten children at a stroke. O Death, what an insatiable archer thou wast that day, when ten must fall at once! Yet Job says, "The Lord hath taken away." That is all he has to say about it: "The Lord hath taken away." I need not repeat to you the story of the gardener who missed a choice rose, but who could not complain because the master had plucked it. Do you feel that it is just so with all that you have, if he takes it? Oh, yes! why should he not take it? If I were to go about my house, and take down an ornament or anything from the walls, would anybody say a word to me? Suppose my dear wife should say to the servant, "Where has that picture gone?" and the maid replied, "Oh, the master took it!" Would she find fault? Oh, no! If it had been a servant who took it down, or a stranger who removed it, she might have said something; but not when I took it, for it is mine. And surely we will let God be Master in his own house; where we are only the children, he shall take whatever he pleases of all he has lent us for a while. It is easy to stand here and say this; but, brothers and sisters, let us try to say it if it should ever come to us as a matter of fact that the Lord who gave should also take away. I think Job did well to call attention to this blessed truth, that the hand of God is everywhere at work, whether in giving or in taking away; I do not know anything that tends more to reconcile us to our present sorrows, and losses, and crosses, than to feel, "God has done it all. Wicked men were the agents, but still God himself has done it. There is a great mystery about it which I cannot clear up, and I do not want to clear it up. God has done it, and that is enough for me. 'The Lord gave, and the Lord hath taken away.'"

IV. Job's last comfort lay in this truth, that GOD IS WORTHY TO BE BLESSED IN ALL THINGS: "Blessed be the name of the Lord."

Dear friends, *let us never rob God of his praise, however dark the day is.* It is a funeral day, perhaps; but should not God be praised, when there is a funeral, as well as when there is a wedding? "Oh, but I have lost everything!" And is this one of the days when there is no praise due to God? Most of you know that the Queen's taxes must be paid; and our great King's revenue has the first claim upon us. Let us not rob our King of the revenue of his praise. "From the rising of the sun unto the going down of the same, the Lord's name is to be praised." "Oh, but I have lost a child!" Yes, but God is to be praised. "But I have lost my mother." Yes, but God is to be praised. "I have a bad headache." Yes, but God is to be praised. One said to me, one evening, "We should have family prayer, my dear sir, but it is rather late; do you feel too tired to conduct it?" "No," I said, "I never was too tired yet to pray with my brethren, and I hope I never shall be." If it is the middle of the night, let us not go to bed without prayer and praise, for we must not rob God of his glory. "There is a mob in the street," but we must not rob God of his glory. "Our goods are getting cheaper and cheaper, and we shall be ruined in the market," but let us not rob God of his glory. "There is going to be, I do not know what, happening by-and-by." Yes, but we must not rob God of his glory.

"Blessed be the name of the Lord." Job means that *the Lord is to be blessed both for giving and taking.* "The Lord gave," blessed be his name. "The Lord hath taken away," blessed be his name. Surely it has not come to this among God's people, that he must do as we like, or else we will not praise him. If he does not please us every day, and give way to our whims, and gratify our tastes, then we will not praise him. "Oh, but I do not understand his dealings," says one. And are you really such a stranger to God, and is God such a stranger to you, that, unless he enters into explanations, you are afraid that he is not dealing fairly with you? O sir, have you known the Lord for twenty years, and cannot you praise him for everything? Brethren, some of us have known him forty years now, perhaps some of you have known the Lord for fifty years; are you always wanting to have chapter, and verse, and explanations from him before you will praise him? No, no, I hope we have gone far beyond that stage.

God is, however, *specially to be praised by us whenever we are moved by the devil to curse.* Satan had said to the Lord concerning Job, "Put forth thine hand now, and touch all that he hath, and he will curse thee to thy face;" and it seemed as if God had hinted to his servant that this was what the devil was aiming at. "Then," said Job, "I will bless him." His wife suggested afterwards that he should curse God, but he would do no such thing, he would bless him. It is usually a wise thing to do the very opposite to what the evil one suggests to you. If he says, "Curse," do you bless. Remember the story of a man who was going to give a pound to some charitable institution. The devil said, "No, you cannot afford it." "Then," said the man, "I will give two pounds; I will not be dictated to in this way." Satan exclaimed, "You are a fanatic." The man replied, "I will give four pounds." "Ah!" said Satan, "what will your wife say when you go home, and tell her that you have given away four pounds?" "Well," said the man, "I will give eight pounds now; and if you do not mind what you are at, you will tempt me to give sixteen." So the devil was obliged to stop, because the more he tempted him, the more he went the other way. So let it be with us. If the devil would drive us to curse God, let us bless him all the more, and Satan will be wise enough to leave off tempting when he finds that, the more he attempts to drive us, the more we go in the opposite direction.

This is all meant to be sweet, cheery talk to suffering saints; how I wish that everybody here had an interest in it! What will some of you do, what are some of you doing, now that you have lost all,—wife dead, children dead, and you are growing old, yet you are without God? O you poor rich people, who have no interest in God, your money must burn your souls! But you poor, poor, poor people, who have not anything here, and have no hope hereafter, how sad is your case! May God, of his rich mercy, give you even a little common-sense, for, surely, common-sense would drive you to him! Sometimes, in distributing temporal relief, we meet with persons who have been out of work, and full of trouble, and have not had bread to eat, and we say to them, "Did you ever cry to God for help?" "No, sir, we never prayed in all our life." What are you at? Here is a child, crawling about a house, shivering for want of bread and clothes. "Did you never ask your father for anything?" "No, never." Come, friend, did God make you, or did you grow without him? Did God create you? If he made you, he will have respect unto the work of his hands. Go and try him, even on that low ground. Go and seek his face even as his creature, and see whether he does not help you. O unbelief, to what madness dost thou go, that even when men are driven to starvation, they will not turn to God! O Spirit of God, bless the sons of men! Even through their fears, and sorrows, and losses, bless them, and bring them in penitence to the Saviour's feet, for his dear name's sake! Amen.

3

Fifteen Years After!*

"The LORD gave, and the LORD hath taken away; blessed be the name of the LORD." **Job 1:21**

O r, as some read it, "The Lord giveth, and the Lord taketh away; blessed be the name of the Lord." So that the text is not only concerning the past, but it may rightly be considered as relating to the present also. Some of the rarest pearls have been found in the deepest waters, and some of the choicest utterances of believers have come from them when God's waves and billows have been made to roll over them. The fire consumes nothing but the dross, and leaves the gold all the purer. In Job's case, I may truly say, with regard to his position before God, he had lost nothing by all his losses, for what could be purer and brighter gold than this which gleams before us from our text, revealing his triumphant patience, his complete resignation, and his cheerful acquiescence in the divine will? "The Lord giveth, and the Lord taketh away; blessed be the name of the Lord."

There are two points to which I ask your earnest attention while we meditate upon this subject. The first is the exhortation drawn from the text,—*learn to see the Lord's hand in everything,* in giving and in taking; and, secondly,— and this is a harder lesson,—*learn to bless the Lord's name in everything,* in giving and in taking.

I. First, LET US LEARN TO SEE THE LORD'S HAND IN EVERY-THING. Our whole history seems to be divided, as our text divides itself, into a beholding of God's hand in giving, and then a beholding of it in taking.

---

* In retaining all of the original wording of Spurgeon's sermons, including the titles he gave them, a word of explanation is in order about this sermon: This sermon was preached on February 11, 1869, but was not published until January 31, 1907, which was exactly fifteen years after Spurgeon's homegoing, hence the title.

We are then, first of all, to behold God's hand as a giving hand. If we are believers, all the comforts and mercies that we have are to be viewed by us as coming from the hand of our gracious Heavenly Father. Job confessed that the Lord had given him the camels, and the sheep, and the oxen, and that the Lord had given him his seven sons and three daughters; everything which he had ever possessed he looked upon as having been the gift of God. Job did not say, "I worked hard to obtain all that stock that I have now lost." He did not complain, "I spent many weary days and many anxious nights in accumulating all those flocks and herds that have been stolen from me." He did not ascribe any of his wealth either to his own wit, or to his own industry, but he said of it all, "The Lord gave it to me." In his mind's eye, he took an inventory of all that he once had, and of all that he had lost, and he said of the whole, "It was all the Lord's gift to me."

Now, beloved, whatever may be the possessions which you have at the present time, whatever may be the number of those who are the comfort of your life, husband or wife, parents or children, kinsfolk of any sort,—say of all of them, "The Lord gave them to me;" and, as a Christian, *learn the wisdom of never ascribing any earthly comfort to any earthly source.* The worldling may not always be able to say what Job said concerning his possessions. Some of what he has may not have been obtained honestly; the Lord did not give any of that to him. Some of what he has may turn out to be a curse rather than a blessing; but the believer in Christ may say, with the utmost truthfulness, with regard to all that he has, "It is all the gift of my loving and tender Heavenly Father."

And, brethren, there is associated with this fact that all our possessions are God's gifts, the remembrance that *they are all undeserved gifts.* They are gifts in the fullest sense of the word, the gifts of God's grace. They are not given to us because we have merited them, for we have never deserved even the least of all the mercies which the Lord hath so bountifully bestowed upon us. We may say of the whole river of his favour, which flows continually side by side with us as we journey along the pathway of our pilgrimage, that there is not a drop of it which comes to us of debt or by law, but all comes through the free gift of God's grace. All that we have, over and above what would have been our portion in the pit of hell, is the gift of God's mercy towards us. It is of the Lord's mercy, and because his compassions fail not, that we are not consumed. Every believer can truly say, with Job, "'The Lord gave,' yes, the Lord gave even to me, an unworthy one who sat as a beggar at his gate, and received from his own hand countless tokens of his infinite lovingkindness."

And I may add, with regard to these gifts, that *they have been given to us with wondrous kindness and thoughtfulness on God's part.* Some here, I think, will have to say that they have found themselves provided for by God's forestalling their wants. He has gone before them in the way of his providence, and mysteriously cleared a path for them. Before they have felt the pinch of poverty, the pinch has been averted. There are others of God's servants here, who have sometimes been brought very low, yet they can bear witness that, hitherto, their bread has always been given to them, and their waters have been sure; and while God's mercy comes to us very sweetly when forestalling our need, there is equal sweetness if it comes when the need has been felt. No food is so palatable as that which has hunger for its sauce. To know what it is to be poor, will make us more grateful if God ever gives us abundance. But time would fail me to tell all the love and care of God towards each one of us, every day of our lives, and to recount how he not only continues but even multiplies his favours. It is impossible for us to count them, for they are more in number than the hairs of our head, or the sand on the seashore, or the stars in the midnight sky.

Now, as everything we have is freely and graciously given to us by God, this should make us feel, in the first place, that *this truth sweetens all that we have.* I daresay there is many a little thing in your house that is of no great value in itself, but it was given to you by someone who was very dear to you. How much a child values that Bible that was given to her by her mother, who wrote her name in it! Many a man has, in his house, things which an auctioneer would appraise at a very small amount, but which the owner prizes very highly because they were given to him by someone whom he greatly esteemed, and who gave them to him as a token of his love. In like manner, look at the bread on the table of a believer as a love-token from God. The Lord gave it to him; and if there were upon his table nothing but that bread, it would be a token of God's gracious condescension in providing for his

needs. Let us learn to look thus at everything that we receive
in this life, for such a view of it will sweeten it all. We shall
not then begin to calculate whether we have as much as
others have, or as much as our own whims or wishes might
crave; but we shall recognize that all we have comes from the
hand and heart of our Heavenly Father, and that it all comes
to us as a token of our Father's love, and with our Father's
blessing resting upon it.

This fact should also *prevent any believer from acting
dishonestly in his daily avocations,* or even from wishing to
obtain anything that is not his own by right. All of you, who
belong to God, have what God has given you; so mind that you
do not mix with it anything that the devil has given you. Do
not go into any worldly enterprise, and seek to gain
something concerning which you could not say, "The Lord my
God gave it unto me." Men of the world will engage in such
transactions, and they will say that you are not as sharp as
you might be because you will not do the same. But you have
a good reason for refusing to gain even a shilling upon which
you cannot ask God's blessing. A sovereign, dishonestly
procured, though it might gladden your eyes for a little while,
and help to fill your purse, would certainly bring a curse with
it, and you do not want that. You would not like to have to
confess to yourself, concerning anything you possessed, "I
dare not tell my Heavenly Father how I got it, though he
knows; and I dare not ask his blessing upon it, nor do I think
he would ever give it to me. He will probably turn it into a
rod, and sharply scourge me for having dared to use such
unholy means to get what I ought not to have even wished to
possess." Some of God's people might have been very happy if
they had not been greedy and grasping. He that hasteneth to
be rich will soon find that he will fall into many snares and
abundant temptations. It is an evil thing when people cannot
be content although they have enough for all their necessities,
for even the world's proverb says that "enough is as good as a
feast." Yet many stretch out their arms, like wide-encircling
seas, and try to grasp in them all the shore. Such people,
sooner or later, begin to rob others right and left, and very
many of them come down to poverty and the Bankruptcy
Court, disgraced and dishonoured. Let it not be so with you,
beloved, but be ye content with such things as ye have,
whether God gives you little or much; and, above all things,

pray that you may have nothing but what he gives you, nothing in your house or shop but what comes in at the front door in the light of day, nothing but what may be seen coming in if any eye should be watching. That man is truly happy who can say of all his substance, be it little or be it much, "The Lord gave it to me."

Further, as it is the Lord who gives us all the wealth that we possess, *how very foolish are those people who are proud of possessing a little more of this world's wealth than others have!* There are some, who seem to be thoroughly intoxicated by the possession of a larger income than their neighbours enjoy. They even seem to fancy that they were made of better material than was used in the creation of ordinary mortals. Did not a broad grin appear on the faces of many aristocrats when someone said, in Parliament, that we were all made of the same flesh and blood? Of course, all those, who were in their right senses, knew that it was true; but insanity in high places seemed to be moved to utter contempt at the bare mention of such a thing. When a man is poor, unless he has brought his poverty upon himself by extravagance, or idleness, or his own wrongdoing, the man is a man for all that, and none the worse man for being poor. Indeed, some of the best of men have been as poor as their Lord was. I have known many, who have been very poor, yet who have been the excellent of the earth, in whom a true saint of God might well take delight. There always will be various ranks and conditions among men, and there is a certain respect which is due from one to another which should never be withheld where it is rightly due; but, at the same time, whenever a man begins to say that, because God has given him more than he has given to another, therefore he will despise his poorer brother and look down upon him, it must be dishonouring and displeasing to God, and it is extremely likely that he will turn round, and make the proud man bite the dust. How often those, who have held their heads so very high, have been rolled in the mire, and how easily that might be made to come to pass with others!

A further inference arising out of this truth that God gives us all that we have, is that *it ought never to be difficult for us to give back to God as much as ever we can.* As he has given us all that we have, it is but right that we should use it to his glory; and if, under the rule of his grace, and under the gospel, he does not so much claim a return from us as a matter of right, but leaves our liberality to be aroused by the love which constrains us, rather than by the law which compels us; yet let us not give God less because he gives us more. Under the Mosaic dispensation, the Jew gave his tenth by compulsion, but let us willingly give to God more than that, and not need to be constrained to do it, except by the sweet constraint of love. Do I owe every penny that I have in this world to the bounty of God's hand? Then, when God's cause and God's poor are in need, let no one have to beg of me to give to them. I always feel ashamed when I hear people say that we are "begging for God's cause." God's cause has no need to be a beggar from those who would be beggars if it were not for God's grace. Oh, no, no; it must never be so! We ought to be like the children of Israel in the wilderness, who gave so generously towards the building and furnishing of the tabernacle that Moses had to restrain their liberality, for they had already given "much more than enough for the service of the work, which the Lord commanded to make." Let us try to imitate the liberality which God has manifested toward us in the gift of his well-beloved Son, and in all the covenant blessings which come to us through him. All those who have received so much from God should count it their privilege and delight to give back to him all that they can.

These reflections might suffice for this part of the subject, but I shall add one more. *"The Lord gave;"—then we must worship the Giver, and not his gifts.* How can we so degrade ourselves as to worship that which God has given to us? Yet you know that many make idols of their gold, their lands, their husbands, their wives, their children, or their friends. It is no unusual thing for a little child to be the god of the family; and wherever that is the case, there is a rod laid up in store in that house. You cannot make idols of your children without finding out, sooner or later, that God makes them into rods with which he will punish you for your idolatry. "Little children, keep yourselves from idols," was the injunction of the loving apostle John, and he wrote thus in love, because he knew that, if God sees us making idols of anything, he will either break our idols or break us. If we really are his people, he will, in some way or other, wean us from our idols, for he wants our love to be given wholly to himself; so it is best for us to keep the creature in its right place, and never to let the joys or comforts of this life usurp God's rightful position in our hearts. God has been pleased so to fashion the world that it should always be under our feet; and, as Christians, we should always keep it there. The dearest thing we have on earth should ever be estimated by us at its proper value as a gift from God but as nothing more than that; and never be allowed to occupy our heart's throne, which should always be reserved for the Lord alone.

But now we are to think, for a while, of the Lord's hand taking away from us as well as giving to us. Job said, "The Lord gave, *and the Lord hath taken away.*" Some of you have come to this service very sad and heavy of heart because that dear child of yours is dead. Well, I do not blame you for sorrowing over your loss, but I pray you also to remember that it is the Lord who hath taken your child away from you. You say that it was the fever that took away your dear one, and perhaps that was the immediate cause of your child's death; but if you can realize that the fever was only the instrument in God's hand to remove the dear little one from your care to his own, surely you will dry your tears. And as for that substance of yours, which has almost melted away under the fiery trial to which it has been subjected, so that poverty seems now to stare you in the face, you will be able to bear even that when you remember that it is the Lord's hand that has taken away what his hand had first given.

So long as we look at the secondary causes of our trouble, we see reasons for sorrow; but *when our faith can pierce the veil, and see the Great First Cause, then our comfort begins.* If you strike a dog with a stick, he will try to bite the stick, because he is a dog; but if he knew better, he would try to bite you, and not the stick. Yet that is the way that we often act with the troubles that come to us; we fly at the second causes, and so are angry and petulant with them; but if we would always recollect that it is God who taketh away, as well as God who gives;—that he is at the back of all our trials and troubles;—that his hand weighs out our share of grief, and measures our portion of pain, then we should not dare to rebel and bewail; but, like David, we should say, "I was dumb, I opened not my mouth; because thou didst it;" even if we could not set up higher still, and say, with Job, "The Lord giveth, and the Lord taketh away; blessed be the name of the Lord."

Further, *when once we know that God has done anything, that fact forbids any question concerning it.* It must be right because he did it. I may not be able to tell why, but God knows why he did it. He may not tell me the reason; but he has a reason, for the Lord never acts unreasonably. There never was any action of his, however sovereign or autocratic it might appear to be, but was done "after the counsel of his own will." Infinite wisdom dictates what absolute sovereignty decrees. God is never arbitrary, or tyrannical. He does as he wills, but he always wills to do that which is not only most for his own glory, but also most for our real good. How dare we question anything that God does?

My dear sister, rest assured that it is better that you should be a widow, and seek to glorify God in your widowhood. My dear young friend, believe that it is better that you should be an orphan; otherwise, God would not have taken away your parents. It is better that you, dear friends, should lose your eyes; it is better that you should be poor, or diseased, or else the Lord would not let you be so, for "no good thing will he withhold from them that walk uprightly." If health and wealth were good things for you, God would let you have them. If it were a good thing for saints never to die, they never would die. If it were a good thing for them to go to heaven at once, they would go there at once. If you are walking uprightly, you my know that you have all things, which, all things considered, would be good for you. Some things, which might be good in themselves, or good for others, might not be good for you; and, therefore, the Lord in love withholds them from you. But, whatever he gives, or takes away, or withholds, raise no questions concerning it, but let it be sufficient for you that the Lord hath done it.

Besides, *when we know that the Lord takes away our possessions, the knowledge that they are his effectually prevents us from complaining.* Suppose you are a steward to a certain nobleman, and that his lordship has been pleased to entrust you with ten thousand pounds of his money. By-and-by, he withdraws it from your charge, and invests it somewhere else. Well, it never was your money; you might have complained if it had been. But you are only a steward, and if your lord pleases to withdraw his own money, are you going to be out of temper with your master because he does what he wills with his own? Suppose you have a banker,—

and we are, as it were, the Lord's bankers,—and suppose that, a week or two ago, you paid into the bank a thousand pounds, or more, and the clerks or those in authority were pleased to take charge of your money. But suppose that you went to the bank to-day, and drew it all out; they did not get angry with you. You would not like to have a banker who was only civil to you when you were paying in money; and if we are God's bankers, he sometimes puts his treasure into our keeping, and sometimes takes it out; but it is not our treasure any more than our money is the banker's when we entrust it to his care. It is on deposit with us, and we ought to be paying to God good interest upon it. Whatever God has given to us, he never gave it as our own freehold. It was always on a lease;—a lease, too, that had to be renewed every moment; for, if God chose to cancel it, he could do so whenever he pleased. How dare we then complain?

To use another figure, our position is like that of a nurse, into whose care a mother placed her babe, and the nurse dandled the child, and was glad to have the charge of it; but when she had to return it to its mother, she cried over the loss of the little darling. Yet it was not the nurse's child, given to her to keep; it was only hers to nurse. So it was with your children whom God has taken home to himself; they were not yours to keep. The Lord put each one of them, for a while, into your charge, and said to you, "Christian mother, take this child, and nurse it for me, and I will pay thee thy wages;" so, when he called the child back to himself, why should you complain as though he had wronged you? Or, to use another illustration, which has been frequently employed in this connection,—a gardener had been specially careful in tending one particular rose, which was very fair to look upon; but, when he went, one morning, to his favourite rose-bush, he found that the flower, of which he had taken such care, was gone. He was very vexed, for he thought that some bad boy had stolen into the garden, and taken away his best flower. He was complaining very bitterly of his loss, when someone said, "The master has been down in the garden this morning, and he has been admiring this rose-bush, and he has taken away that fine bud of which you were so proud." Then the gardener was delighted that he had been able to grow a flower that had attracted his master's notice; and, instead of mourning any longer, he began to rejoice. So should it be with

anything upon which we have set our hearts. Let each one of
us say to our Master, "My Lord, if it pleases thee to take it, it
pleases me to lose it. Why should I complain because thou
hast taken from me what is really thine own?"

> "If thou shouldst call me to resign,
> What most I prize,—it ne'er was mine;
> I only yield thee what was thine:
> Thy will be done!"

II. The second part of my discourse must be briefer than the
first part, yet it is equally important. It is this, LEARN TO
BLESS THE LORD'S NAME IN EVERYTHING. Learn to ring the
bells of his praise all day long; and, for the matter of that, all
night long too.

First, *bless the name of the Lord when he reveals his hand in
giving.* "Ah!" you say, "that is an easy thing to do." So it ought
to be, my brethren and sisters in Christ, and it is a neglect of
our duty when we do not do it. We come down to our breakfast
in the morning, rejoicing in health and strength, and we go
out to our day's engagements, yet, I hope not without
thankfulness that we are in health, and that we have food to
eat, and raiment to put on. We are out all day, and things
prosper with us, but I trust that we do not accept all this as a
matter of course, but that we praise the Lord for it all the day
long; and then, when we go home again at night, and God is
still with us, I hope we do not fall asleep before we again
praise him. John Bunyan used to say that the very chickens
shame us if we are ungrateful, for they do not take a drink of
water without lifting up their heads, as if in thankfulness for
the refreshing draught. If we, who are the Lord's children, do
not bless him for the mercies which so constantly come to us
from him, we are of all people the most ungrateful. Oh, for a
grateful frame of mind, for I am sure that is a happy frame of
mind. Those who are determined to murmur, and to complain
of God's dealings with them, are sure to find plenty of things
to complain of; while those who are of a thankful spirit will
see reasons and occasions for gratitude in everything that
happens. Do you remember a touching story, told some years
ago, of a poor mother with her two little fatherless children?
On a cold winter's night, they discovered an empty house, into
which they went for shelter. There was an old door standing
by itself, and the mother took it, placed it across a corner of

the room, and told the children to creep behind it so as to get
a little protection from the cold wind. One of the children said,
"Oh mother, what will those poor children do that haven't got
any door to set up to keep out the wind?" That child was
grateful even for such a poor shelter as that; yet there are
some, who have thousands of greater blessings than that, and
yet do not see God's hand in them, and do not praise him for
them. If that has been the case with any of us, let us turn over
a new leaf, and ask God to rule it with music lines, and then
let us put on them notes of thanksgiving, and say to the Lord,
with David, "Every day will I bless thee; and I will praise thy
name for ever and ever;" or say, with one of our old poets,—

> "My God, I'll praise thee while I live,
>   And praise thee when I die,
> And praise thee when I rise again,
>   And to eternity."

Praising God is one of the best ways of keeping away
murmuring. Praising God is like paying a peppercorn rent for
our occupation of our earthly tenement. When the rent is not
paid, the owners generally turn the tenants out, and God
might well do so with us if he were like earthly landlords. If
we are not grateful to him for all the bounties which we
constantly receive from him, he may make the stream to stop,
and then what should we do? Ungrateful mind, beware of this
great danger! Thankfulness is one of the easiest virtues for
anyone to practise, and certainly it is one of the cheapest; so
let all Christians especially comply with the apostolic
injunction, "Be ye thankful." It is a soul-enriching thing to be
thankful. I am sure that a Christian man, with gratitude for
a small income, is really richer than the man who lives a
graceless life, and is plentifully endowed with worldly wealth.
David spoke truly when he said, "A little that a righteous man
hath is better than the riches of many wicked." So, let others
do as they will, we say, "Give us, Lord, whatever thou wilt,
whether it be little or much, so long as thou dost give with it
the light of thy countenance, our souls shall be abundantly
content."

Thus are we to bless the name of the Lord for all that he
gives us.

But, *it is a much more difficult thing to bless the name of the
Lord for what he takes away from us;* yet, difficult as it is, I

venture to say that many believers, who have forgotten to praise God while he was giving to them, have not forgotten to praise him when he was taking away from them. I do not know how thankful Job had been before this trying period in his history, but I do know that his trials brought out this expression of his thankfulness; it is his first recorded praise to God. Some of us need to lie a little while upon a sick-bed in order to make us thankful for having had good health for so long; and we need to be brought low, and to have our spirits depressed, in order to make us grateful that we have had such cheerful spirits, and been blessed with so many comforts. It is not natural or easy for flesh and blood to praise God for what he takes away; yet this painful experience often wakes up the gratitude of the Christian, and he who forgot to praise the Lord before makes up for it now.

Brethren, praise is God's due when he takes as well as when he gives, for there is as much love in his taking as in his giving. The kindness of God is quite as great when he smites us with his rod as when he kisses us with the kisses of his mouth. If we could see everything as he sees it, we should often perceive that the kindest possible thing he can do to us is that which appears to us to be unkind. A child came home from the common with her lap full of brightly shining berries. She seemed very pleased with what she had found, but her father looked frightened when he saw what she had got, and anxiously asked her, "Have you eaten any of those berries?" "No, father," replied the child, to his great relief; and then he said to her, "Come with me into the garden;" and there he dug a hole, put the berries in, stamped on them, and crushed them, and then covered them with earth. All this while, the little one thought, "How unkind father is to take away these things which pleased me so much!" But she understood the reason for it when he told her that the berries were so poisonous that, if she had eaten even one of them, she would in all probability have died in consequence. In like manner, sometimes, our comforts turn to poison, especially when we begin to make idols of them; and it is kind on the part of God to stamp on them, and put them right away from us, so that no mischief may come to our souls. Surely that child said, "Thank you, father, for what you have done; it was love that made you do it;" and you also, believer, can say, "Thank God for my sickness, for my poverty, for that dead child of mine, for my widowhood, for my orphanhood,—thank God for it all. It would have been ruinous to me to have left me unchastened. Before I was afflicted, I went astray; but now have I kept his word. Blessed be his name for all that he has done, both in giving and in taking away."

It is a grand thing when we do not judge God's dealings with us simply by the rules of reason. From the first moment when the love of God is revealed to us, right on to the hour when we shall be in the presence of the Father in glory, we may depend upon it that there is infinite love in every act of God in taking from us, just as much as in giving to us. Jesus said to his disciples, "As the Father hath loved me, so have I loved you." The Father always loved Jesus with infinite love, —he loved him as much when he was on the cross as he did when he was on his throne. And, in like manner, Jesus always loves us with an unchanging love,—a love which can never fail us. He loves us as much in the furnace of affliction as he will love us when we shall be with him in glory; so let us bless his name, whether he gives or takes away. I invite every mourning soul here to bless God's name at this moment.

"Ah!" says one, "I wish I could get a little more happiness to sustain me under my many trials." Well, let me just remind you of the poor widow woman who went out to gather a few sticks to make a fire, that she might bake some cakes for herself and her son. When the prophet Elijah met her, what did he say to her? He told her to make him a little cake first, and afterwards, he added, "make for thee and for thy son. For thus saith the Lord God of Israel, The barrel of meal shall not waste, neither shall the cruse of oil fail, until the day that the Lord sendeth rain upon the earth. And she went and did according to the saying of Elijah: and she, and he, and her house, did eat many days. And the barrel of meal wasted not, neither did the cruse of oil fail, according to the word of the Lord, which he spake by Elijah." Notice that he said to the woman, "Make me a little cake first;" and God seems to say to you, "Praise me first, and then I will bless you." Say, as Job did a little later in his history, "Though he slay me, yet will I trust in him." I believe it marks the turn of the tide, with a saint, when he can say to the Lord, with good old John Ryland,—

> "Thee, at all times, will I bless;
> Having thee, I all possess."

The sky soon begins to clear when the Christian begins to say, "The Lord's will be done;" "not as I will, but as thou wilt." This is a sign that the chastisement has had its due effect; the rod will probably be put away now. Ye mourning souls, take down your harps from the willows and sound forth at least a note or two to the praise of the Lord your God. Praise him with such notes as these: "Truly God is good to Israel, even to such as are of a clean heart...I will not fret myself because of him who prospereth in his way, because of the man who bringeth wicked devices to pass...O my God, I believe that all things are working together for my good, and that thou art my gracious Heavenly Father, full of compassion, and over-flowing with love." If you talk like this, Christian, and mean what you say, it will be a blessing to yourself, a comfort to others, and an honour to your God.

As I speak thus, I am reminded that these comforting truths belong only to true believers; and as I send you away, I dare not put the words of my text into all your mouths, for, alas! some of you cannot see our Father's hand in anything that happens to you. You are without a parent, except that wicked one of whom Christ said to the Jews, "Ye are of your father the devil, and the lusts of your father ye will do." Yet, remember, you who cannot claim God as your Father, that the door of his grace is not yet shut. He is still willing to receive you; if you will come to him, confessing your sins, and seeking mercy through the precious blood of Jesus, he is both able and willing to give you a new heart and a right spirit, to save you here and now, and to adopt you at once into his family. Then will you also be able to see his hand both in giving and in taking away, and you also will learn to bless his name at all times. If God the Lord shall deal thus graciously with you, his shall be the praise for ever and ever. Amen.

4

Patient Job, and the Baffled Enemy

"In all this Job sinned not, nor charged God foolishly."
Job 1:22

That is to say, in all this trial, and under all this temptation, Job kept right with God. During all the losses of his estate, and the deaths of his children, he did not speak in an unworthy manner. The text speaks admiringly of "all this;" and a great "all" it was. Some of you are in troubles many; but what are they compared with those of Job? Your afflictions are mole-hills contrasted with the Alps of the patriarch's grief. "All this!" He was suddenly reduced from a peer to a pauper; from a man of great wealth to a person in absolute poverty; from a happy father to a childless mourner. Who can measure or fathom "all this?" Yet, "In all this Job sinned not." Here was the triumph of a gracious spirit. Ah, dear friends! if God could uphold Job in all this, you may be sure that he can support *you*. Look to him for this divine support.

"All this" also alludes to all that Job did, and thought, and said. He was full to bursting with swelling grief, he shaved his head, and rent his garments, and he lifted up his voice unto the Lord his God; but "In all this Job sinned not." He rose up, for he was a man of action, a man of a sensitive and a powerful mind, a man of poetic energy, who could not fail to express his emotions in striking symbols; but "In all this Job sinned not." This is a great deal to say of a man when you see him in the extreme of trial. If in patience he can possess his soul when all the arrows of affliction are wounding him, he is a man indeed.

May we ourselves so live that it may be said of us in the end, "In all this he sinned not. He swam through a sea of trouble. The roll of his life-story is written within and without with lamentations; but in all this he did not dishonour the name of his Lord. He did and said many things; but in them all he was patient, resigned, obedient, and never uttered a rebellious word." Let us think of the wonderful case of Job in a practical way; desiring the Holy Spirit to make us like him.

I. Our first head shall be, IN ALL OUR AFFAIRS THE MAIN THING IS, NOT TO SIN. It is not said, "In all this Job was never spoken against," for he was spoken against by Satan in the presence of himself; and very soon he was falsely accused by men who should have comforted him. You must not expect, dear friend, that you will pass through this world, and have it said of you in the end, "In all this no one ever spoke against him." I heard say of one man, "He was a man who never had an enemy." I ventured to add, "nor a friend." He has no friend who never had a foe. Those who secure zealous lovers are pretty sure to call forth intense adversaries. A man who is such a chip in the porridge that he never offends, is pretty sure to be equally flavourless in the other direction. The trimmer may dodge through the world without much censure; but it will seldom be so with an out-and-out man of God. Because he is not of the world, the world will hate him. The blessed and holy Lord Jesus was slandered to the utmost. God, the ever-blessed, was himself libelled in Paradise itself by an old servant, who had turned into an old serpent; and, therefore, you must not wonder if you are abused also. To go through life without calumny is not a thing to be expected; but it is anxiously to be desired that we may go through every phase of joy or of sorrow without falling into sin.

Neither is it a chief point for us to seek to go through life without suffering, since the Lord's servants, the best of them, are ripened and mellowed by suffering. Amos, the herdsman, was a bruiser of sycamore figs—a kind of fig that never ripened in Palestine unless it was struck with a rod, and thus was bruised. I fear me, there are very few of the godly who will fully ripen without affliction. The vine bears but little fruit unless it makes the acquaintance of the knife, and is sternly pruned. I fear that much fruit will seldom be forthcoming without much tribulation. A high character might be produced, I suppose, by continued prosperity; but it has very seldom been the case. Adversity, however it may appear to be our foe, is our true friend; and, after a little acquaintance with it, we receive it as a precious thing, the prophecy of a coming joy. It should be no ambition of ours to traverse a smooth path without thorn or stone. Rather let us ask—

> "Shall Simon bear the cross alone,
>   And all the rest go free?
> No, there's a cross for every one,
>   And there's a cross for me."

Dear friends, I think also that it should not be our ambition to go through the world without sadness of heart. It is true that heaviness of heart is worse than bodily suffering: "A wounded spirit who can bear?" Some persons, however, seem to endure terrible trouble without much feeling. They are case-hardened, stout-hearted, thick-skinned persons; and truly I have half envied them at times, and almost prayed to lose that sensitiveness which causes fear; but it would be a very doubtful blessing. We need to be tender, that we may feel the slightest touch of God's hand. "Be ye not as the horse, or as the mule, which have no understanding, whose mouth must be held in with bit and bridle, lest they come near unto thee." The apostle says, "Though now for a season, if need be, *ye are in heaviness* through manifold temptations." Many read it as if there were a needs-be for the trial; and so, indeed, there is; but the needs-be in the passage has reference to being in heaviness. If you can bear trial without ever being heavy, it is scarcely a trial to you. "The blueness of a wound cleanseth away evil." It is the ache of the ache, it is the sting of the wasp which works effectively on the heart. If we do not smart under the rod, what is the use of it to us? Therefore I would not have you ask that you may be kept from sadness of soul; but I would have you pray seven times a day from the very bowels of your being, "Lord, keep me from sin." May it be said at the last, of every one of us, that in all this we sinned not!

Remember, if the grace of God prevents our affliction from driving us into sin, then *Satan is defeated*. Satan did not care what Job suffered, so long as he could but hope to make him sin; and he was foiled when he did not sin. He must have regretted that he tried him, when he found that he could not make him sin. I think I hear the fiend muttering, "Give him back his camels; give him back his sheep; if by the loss of these his patience and resignation are made manifest." If he could not extract a rebellious speech from Job, the tempter had lost all his cruel efforts: his malice had spent itself

without result. If he could not make the good man sin, nor
charge God foolishly, he was defeated, and God was glorified.
If in enduring your particular trouble, my dear friend, you do
not fall into sin, you are more than a conqueror over him that
hateth you. The arch-enemy will fly away confounded from
you, if you are able to resist him while darkness covers your
soul. If you conquer him in your hour of grief, you conquer
indeed. May your conflict with Apollyon be like that of
Christian in "Pilgrim's Progress," and to you also may a
monument be erected, bearing this inscription—

> "The man so bravely played the man,
> He made the fiend to fly;
> Whereof a monument I stand
> The same to testify."

If you do not sin while under the stress of heavy trouble,
God will be honoured. He is not so much glorified by
preserving you from trouble, as by upholding you in trouble.
He allows you to be tried that his grace in you may be tested
and glorified. When one Winstanley, years ago, built a
lighthouse on the Eddystone Rock, he said that he was sure
that it would stand any storm that ever blew, and he should
himself like to be in it in the fiercest tempest that ever drove
adown the Channel. It came to pass that he was in his own
erection one night, and there came a tremendous blast, which
swept him and his lighthouse clean away, so that he was
never heard of more. He courted trial because he believed in
his work: God permits trial because he knows that his wisdom
and grace have made us able to bear it. The lighthouse which
was afterwards built on the Eddystone has had all manner of
storms beating upon it, but it has outlived them all; and
therefore its builder's name is held in honour. Even thus our
God is glorified in every trial of his saints, when their grace
enables them to endure with patience. "There," says he, "see
what grace can do, what suffering it can endure, what labours
it can perform!" Grace is like an athlete performing before the
great King and his heavenly court. A cloud of witnesses look
down upon the feats of faith, and note with joy how it
achieves everything which the Lord appoints it to perform. It
even enters into contest with the fiend of hell, and gives him
a signal overthrow; and he that made the athlete, and trained
him for the contest, is honoured thereby. If you do not sin in

your trouble, your endurance of trial will bring glory to God.

Remember, furthermore, that if you do not sin, *you yourself will be no loser by all your tribulations.* Sin alone can injure you; but if you remain steadfast, though you are stripped, you will be clothed with glory; though you are deprived of comfort, you will lose no real blessing. True, it may not seem a pleasant thing to be stripped, and yet if one is soon going to bed, it is of no great consequence. It is no easy thing to part with wealth; but if thereby you are unburdened, the loss is a gain. A child of God may have the knife sharply cutting him, but if it only removes the superfluous wood, it may be of the utmost benefit to the fruitage of the tree; and that is the main thing. If the metal in the pot loses none of its gold, all that it does lose is well lost, and is, indeed, really gained. Though you be reduced in circumstances, what matters it, if you are enlarged in spirit? Though you be sick in body, what matters it, if the soul's health be furthered thereby? To sin would be terrible; to abide in holiness is triumph. In all our affliction may there be no defection. The Lord may send us a ton of trouble, but this will be better than an ounce of sin. Do not let all your prayer run after deliverance from sorrow, but first of all pray, "Let not any iniquity have dominion over me." Seek first the kingdom of God, and obedience to him, and then deliverance shall be added unto you. We are permitted to say, "Lord, keep us from trouble;" but we are commanded to pray, "Deliver us from evil." Should trials come to us, even like those which happened to Job, it shall be well with our souls if our hearts are not drawn or driven into sin.

II. And, now, a second thought arises out of the text. IN ALL TIME OF TRIAL THERE IS SPECIAL FEAR OF OUR SINNING. It is well for the child of God to remember that the hour of darkness is an hour of danger. Suffering is fruitful soil for certain forms of sin. Hence it was needful for the Holy Spirit to give a testimony to Job that, "In all this he sinned not." It looked as if he must sin; but yet he did not sin; and this is recorded by inspiration as a memorable fact. He still held fast his integrity, and bowed before the will of the Lord. Dear friends, if you are approaching a season of trouble, watch and pray that, in entering upon trial, you may not also enter upon sinning. Many have sorely grieved their God by what they have said and done in the hour of sorrow.

For instance, we are apt to *grow impatient*. We murmur

against the Lord. We think our trial is too long, or that prayer is not answered when it ought to be. If God be faithful, why does he not hasten to deliver his child? In the olden time he rode upon a cherub and did fly, yea, he did fly upon the wings of the wind; but why are his chariots now so long in coming? The feet of his mercy seem shod with lead. Petulance and complaining are sins which easily beset those who are severely tried. Men are apt to have bitter thoughts of God when he puts his hand into the bitter box, and brings out the quinine of sorrow. Of the two sexes, women usually carry the prize for patience, especially in bodily sickness. As for us, who are made of rougher stuff, it is to our shame that we are, as a rule, very impatient of pain. We do not so much lose our patience as show that we have none. Job under his first set of trials was not swift to complain; for ye have heard of the patience of Job, which the Holy Spirit takes care to mention in the New Testament.

We are even tempted to *rebellion* against God. I have met with cases in which rebellious words have been uttered, and even spoken again and again. One said in my hearing, "God has taken away my mother, and I shall never forgive him. I can never think of him as a God of love as once I did." Such words will cause a child of God more pain than the loss itself would have occasioned. I heard one say of his dying child, whom I was called in to visit, that he could not believe that God would be so unjust as to take his daughter from him. Indeed, he spoke so rebelliously that I, with all gentleness, but with deep solemnity of soul, admonished him that I feared the Lord would visit him for such proud speeches. It was clear that his child would soon die, and I feared that he would die himself, when the shock came, because he so stoutly quarrelled with the Lord. I said to myself, "A child of God cannot speak in this way about his Father without coming under further chastisement." It came to pass as I expected, and he himself was laid low. Grieved as I was, I was by no means surprised. How can we rebel against God, and hope to prosper in that rebellion? With the froward he will show himself froward; and we shall find out what a world of misery that will bring us. Oh, for grace not only to yield because we must, but because we trust! May we say, "It is the Lord: let him do what seemeth him good!" Before that temptation Job did not fall; for in this respect he sinned not.

We may also sin by *despair*. An afflicted one said, "I shall never look up again. I shall go mourning all my days." Dear friend, why not be cheerful again? Are God's mercies clean gone for ever? Thou art bidden to believe always. "Who is among you that walketh in darkness, and hath no light? let him trust in the name of the Lord, and stay upon his God." In the dark is the place for trust, not for despair. A child that is sullen will probably make for himself ten times more misery than the rod of itself would cause him. Who dares despair while God bids him trust? Come, if you are as poor as Job, be as patient as Job, and you will find hope ever shining like a star which never sets.

Many sin by *unbelieving speeches*. I have repeated one or two naughty things that God's children have said; but Job said nothing of the kind; he bravely said, "The Lord gave, and the Lord hath taken away; blessed be the name of the Lord."

Men have been driven into *a kind of atheism* by successive troubles. They have wickedly argued—"There cannot be a God, or he would not let me suffer so." Beloved, you must not speak as the foolish do; and such speech is sheer folly. Your mouth would be greatly defiled if you were thus to vex the Holy Spirit. Has the Lord saved you, and will you speak against him? I have no time to say more where so much might be added. The Lord preserve us in trying times from sinning either with heart, or hand, or lip.

III. Notice, thirdly, that IN ACTS OF MOURNING WE NEED NOT SIN. Hearken: you are allowed to weep. You are allowed to show that you suffer by your losses. See what Job did. "Job arose, and rent his mantle, and shaved his head, and fell down upon the ground, and worshipped;" and "in all this Job sinned not." The mother wept much over her child, and yet she may not have sinned: a mother's grief and a mother's love are sacred things. When a dear child is mourned over, those may have been not only perfectly natural tears, but even holy tears. The husband lamented sorely when his beloved was taken from him. He was right. I should have thought far less of him if he had not done so. "Jesus wept."

But there is a measure in the expression of grief. Job was not wrong in rending his garment: he might have been wrong if he had torn it into shreds. He was not wrong in shaving his head: he would have erred had he torn out his hair, as some have done whom despair has turned into maniacs. He

deliberately took the razor and shaved his head; and in this
he sinned not. You may wear mourning: saints did so in other
times. You may weep; for it may perhaps be a relaxing of your
strained emotions. Do not restrain the boiling floods. A flood
of tears without may assuage the deluge of grief within. Job's
acts of mourning were moderate and seemly—toned down by
his faith. I wish that Christians did not so often follow the
way of the world at their funerals, but would try to make it
clear that they sorrow not even as others that are without
hope. You may wear black so long that it becomes the ensign
of rebellion against the will of the Lord.

Job's words also, though very strong, were very true:
"Naked came I out of my mother's womb, and naked shall I
return thither." If we say no more than the truth, we may say
it if the tone is not that of murmuring; although perhaps
sometimes it might be better to be altogether silent, like
Aaron, who held his peace. David said, "I opened not my
mouth; because thou didst it." If we cannot maintain a golden
silence, yet let our speech be silver: we must use nothing less
than precious metal.

Job mourned, and yet did not sin; for he mourned, and
worshipped as he mourned. This is what I commend to you
who are mourning at this time. If you must fall on the ground,
worship there before the Lord. If your heart is bowed down,
emulate the holy ones who fall on their faces and worship
God. I believe that some of the truest, purest, sweetest, and
strongest devotion has come to God from hearts that were
breaking with grief. Remember, then, that in acts of
mourning there is not, of necessity, any sin.

IV. But, fourthly, IN CHARGING GOD FOOLISHLY WE SIN
GREATLY. "Job sinned not," and the phrase which explains it
is, "nor charged God foolishly." Here let me say that *to call
God to our judgment-seat at all is a high crime and
misdemeanour.* "Nay but, O man, who art thou that repliest
against God?" Woe unto him that contendeth with his Maker.
The Lord is absolutely sovereign, and he giveth no account of
his matters. We are usurping fools when we pretend to sit in
judgment upon the Judge of all the earth.

In the next place, *we sin in requiring that we should
understand God.* What? Is God under bonds to explain
himself to us? Do we threaten to revolt unless he will put
himself right with us? Blessed be his name, he is inscrutable,

and I am glad to have him so. Do you want your God to explain his dispensations? Are you not content to believe him? The demand for explanation is unbelief. This is, indeed, making yourselves to be wiser than God. Let us bow before him without a question. He is Jehovah, and that ends the matter. He would have his children feel that what he wills is always best. Bow before God, and prostrate your desire, and thought, and judgment before his throne. What he does is wise, and true, and kind; and of this we are sure. We can very easily charge God foolishly, but we had better not charge him at all; for who are we that we should call the Eternal to account?

We charge God foolishly *when we imagine that he is unjust.* "Ah!" said one, "when I was a worldling I prospered; but ever since I have been a Christian I have endured no end of losses and troubles." Do you mean to insinuate that the Lord does not treat you justly? Think a minute, and stand corrected. If the Lord were to deal with you according to strict justice, where would you be? If he were now to call you to account for your sins, and lay bare the naked sword of justice, what would become of you? You would be at once in despair, and very soon in hell. Never charge upon the Lord a failure of justice, for this is to sin with a vengeance.

Some, however, *will bring foolish charges against his love.* "How can he be a God of love if he permits me to suffer so?" You forget that word—"As many as I tenderly love" (for that is the Greek word), "I rebuke and chasten." The more the Lord loves you, the more surely he will rebuke any and every evil that he sees in you. You are so precious to him, that he desires to make you perfect in every good work to do his will. God prizes you much, my sister, or you would not have to be so often ground upon the wheel to take away all excrescences and make the jewel of your soul to shine. "Oh," said a worldling to me when I was in great pain and weakness of body, "is this the way God treats his children? Then I am glad I am not one." How my heart burned within me, and my eyes flashed, as I said that I would take an eternity of such pain as I endured sooner than stand in the place of the man who preferred ease to God. I felt it would be hell to me to have a doubt of my adoption, and whatever pain I might suffer was a trifle so long as I knew that the Lord was my God. Every child of God under such a taunt would feel exceeding jealous for the

honour of his Lord. Beloved, we are willing to take the divine
love with every possible drawback that can be conceived; for
the love of our Father is a weight of glory, and all the sorrows
of time are but "light afflictions," and they last but for a
moment. How sweet to hear the Lord say—

"In love I correct thee thy gold to refine;
To make thee, at length, in my likeness to shine!"

Alas! at times, unbelief charges God foolishly with reference
to *his power*. We think that he cannot help us in some
peculiar trial. Throw to the winds such fears; they are
unworthy of us, and dishonouring to our Lord. Is anything too
hard for the Lord? Through flood and fire he will bring us in
safety.

We may be so foolish as to doubt *his wisdom*. If he be
All-wise, how can he suffer us to be in such straits, and to
sink so low as we do? What folly is this? Who art thou, that
thou wouldst measure the wisdom of God. Shall an owl begin
to compute the light of the sun? or an emmet estimate the
eternal hills? Shall some tiny animalcules, sporting with
myriads of others in a drop of water, begin to trace the bounds
of the sea? What art thou? Who art thou, that thou shouldest
set thy judgment against that of the Lord God Almighty? Less
than nothing; wilt thou censure the Infinite? A worm of the
dust; wilt thou arraign the mighty God? This be far from thee.
Job did not so, for he sinned not, nor charged God foolishly.

V. Lastly—as I must close in haste—TO COME THROUGH
GREAT TRIAL WITHOUT SIN IS THE HONOUR OF THE SAINTS. If
we are tried, and come forth from it naked as when we were
born, we need not be ashamed; but if we come out of it
without sinning, then the greatness of the affliction increases
the honour of our victory. "In all this Job sinned not:" the "all
this" is a part of the glory with which grace covered him.
Suppose that your life was all ease: suppose that you were
brought up tenderly from a child, well educated, left with a
sufficient fortune to gratify every wish, happily married, free
from sickness, lifted above care, grinding labour, and heavy
sorrow: what then? Assuredly you could never be noted for
patience. Who would ever have heard of Job if he had not
been tried? None would have said of him, "In all this Job
sinned not." Only by his patience could he be perfected and
immortalized. Suppose that your record should be: from birth

a sufferer, throughout life a struggler; at home a wrestler, and abroad a soldier and a cross-bearer; and, notwithstanding all this, full of joy and peace, through strong believing: tried to the uttermost, yet found faithful. In such a chronicle there is something worth remembering. There is no glory in being a feather-bed soldier, a man bedecked with gorgeous regimentals, but never beautified by a scar, or ennobled by a wound. All that you ever hear of such a soldier is that his spurs jingle on the pavement as he walks. There is no history for this carpet-knight. He is just a dandy. He never smelt gunpowder in his life; or if he did, he fetched out his scent-bottle to kill the offensive odour. Well, that will not make much show in the story of the nations. If we could have our choice, and we were as wise as the Lord himself, we should choose the troubles which he has appointed us, and we should not spare ourselves a single pang. Who wants to paddle about a duck-pond all his life? Nay, Lord, if thou wilt bid me go upon the waters, let me launch out into the deep. Those who are uplifted to the heavens by the billows, and then go down again to the deeps as ocean yawns, these see the works of the Lord, and his wonders in the deep. Discomforts and dangers make men of us, and then we deal no more with childish things, but with eternal matters. If we had no troubles, we should in the end be dumb for lack of themes to speak upon; but now we are storing up incidents worth the telling to our brethren when we join the family circle before the throne. Tried souls can tell of the infinite mercy and love of God, who helped them, and delivered them. Give me an interesting life, after all; and if it is to be an interesting life, then it must be one that has its full share of trouble, as Job's had. Then shall it be a heaven to hear the verdict of the great Judge: "In all this my servant sinned not."

The honour of a Christian, or, let me say, the honour of God's grace in a Christian, is when we have so acted that we have obeyed in detail, not forgetting any point of duty. "In all this Job sinned not," neither in what he thought, or said, or did; nor even in what he did not say, and did not do: "In all this Job sinned not." We are apt to purpose that we will shut ourselves up in our own room, and never go out into the world again, or attempt to speak or act any more. Surely, that would be a great blank, and a blot upon our lives. No! No! No! We must not say, "I will speak no more in the name of the

Lord." Go on speaking, go on acting, go on suffering. Breast
the wave, Christian! Swim to the other shore; and may God's
infinite mercy be seen in bringing you there! Crowd your life
with action, and adorn it with patience, so that it shall be
said, "In all this he sinned not." God grant us a detailed
obedience, a following of the Lord fully, a perfect working out
of the minute points of service!

I feel that I must add just this. As I read the verse through,
it looked too dry for me, and so I wetted it with a tear. "In all
this Job sinned not, nor charged God foolishly;" and yet I, who
have suffered so little, have often sinned, and, I fear, in times
of anguish, have charged God foolishly. Dear friends, is not
this true of some of you? If so, let your tear follow mine. But
yet the tear will not wash out the sin. Fly to the fountain
filled with blood, and wash therein from sins of impatience,
sins of petulance, sins of rebellion, sins of unbelief. These are
real sins, and they must be washed away in the blood of the
Lamb. Oh, how dear that fountain is to us! how dear to you
who have often to lie in bed and suffer—for you still sin! How
dear to us who have health and strength wherewith to serve
God, for we see sin in our holy things, and we need to be
purged from its defilement. You that go into business every
day, and mix up with all sorts of persons, how much you have
need of daily washing! Come, beloved, let us go together, and
say, "Lord, forgive us."

I should like to say somewhat to some of you who are not
God's people. Suppose I were to sum up your lives, and wrote
it out in this fashion: "Was fond of gaiety; spent many days in
frivolous amusement; was sometimes drunken; occasionally
would use profane language," and so on. How falsely should I
speak if I were to say, "In all this he sinned not!" Why, in all
this you have done nothing else but sin. God has loaded your
tables, and clothed your backs, and kept you in health, and
prolonged your lives, and in all this you have done nothing
else but sin and act towards God foolishly. I want you to
come, then, to that same fountain of which I spake, and cry
to-night, "Wash me, Saviour, or I die." You have been the very
opposite of Job. You have sinned in all your comforts and your
mercies, and have never shown due gratitude to the blessed
God, but have done evil against him. The Lord bring us all to
his feet, and then may he help us in all future troubles to
stand firm, and not to sin. I know that some of you are

entering upon fierce trials. You have the prospect of it on your minds to-night, and sitting here you feel depressed about it. Do not begin to despond, but be doubly diligent in prayer. Be more concerned to be kept from sinning than from suffering, and daily pray, "Lord, if thou wilt lead me by this rough road, yet keep my feet that I stumble not, and preserve me even to the end with garments unspotted from the world! I will ask no more of thee but this one thing. Holy Father, keep me as a dear child, obeying and serving thee, with all my heart, and soul, and strength, till I go up higher to dwell with thee for ever!" May the Lord hear you all in the day of trouble, and preserve you to life's latest hour, without spot and blameless! Then shall he be glorified in you, and you shall have joy. Amen, and Amen.

5

The Sorrowful Man's Question

"Why is light given to a man whose way is hid, and whom God hath hedged in?"   **Job 3:23**

I am very thankful that so many of you are glad and happy. There is none too much joy in the world, and the more that any of us can create, the better. It should be a part of our happiness, and a main part of it, to try to make other people glad. "Comfort ye, comfort ye my people," is a commission which many of us ought to feel is entrusted to us. If your own cup of joy is full, let it run over to others who have a more trying experience. If you yourself are privileged to have the flashing eye, and the elastic step, and the bounding heart, be mindful to speak words of good cheer to such as are in bonds. Feel as if you were bound with them; and try to revive their drooping spirits. That is what I am going to aim at to-night, so you will excuse me if I bid "good-bye" for a while to you joyous ones, and just seek after those who have no such delight as you now possess; but who are, on the contrary, suffering from extreme depression of spirit. Sometimes, we must single out the wounded ones of the flock; that is what I am about to do; yet I feel sure that, while some few will be distinctly sought after, there will be something that may be of use to the many who are in a less sorrowful condition. The ninety-and-nine shall get their full portion although the shepherd goes specially after the lost one.

The question of our text was put by Job when he first opened his mouth in the extreme bitterness of his anguish: "Why is light given to a man whose way is hid, and whom God hath hedged in?" His case was so sad and so trying that life itself became irksome to him. I suppose that by "light" here he means the power to see the light, the life which lives in the light. "Why," he asked in his agony, "is that continued to a man when God hath filled him with sorrow upon sorrow?"

The verses preceding our text are to the same effect: "Wherefore is light given to him that is in misery, and life unto the bitter in soul; which long for death, but it cometh not; and dig for it more than for hid treasures; which rejoice exceedingly, and are glad, when they can find the grave?" The patriarch was weary of living; and perhaps we shall not wonder so much at his pitiful lamentation if we recollect the extreme distress into which he had been brought. He had lost all his property; by stroke upon stroke, all his wealth had been taken away from him. He might have borne that if it had been his only loss; but, close upon the heels of it had come sore bereavement. His happy children, for whom he daily cared, and whom he had tenderly loved, were all destroyed in a moment, while they were feasting in the house of one of their brothers. The calamity seemed all the greater because it came in the very midst of their joys. Then, as if that was not trial enough, Job was himself smitten from head to foot with sore boils. If you have ever seen a person in that condition, I am sure that you must pity him. There is a dear friend of ours, now with God, whom I visited when he was in much the same state as that. Perhaps he had not to endure quite all that Job suffered, but something exceedingly like it had befallen him. The irritation, the pain, and the depression of spirit that come with that particular form of disease, all tend to make us treat very gently the petulant expressions of Job. We may not excuse them, but only he amongst us that is without fault may take up the first stone to cast at him. I will warrant that, if we had suffered as he did, and been brought to poverty, and left childless, and then been tortured as he was from head to foot, and even his wife rendering him no comfort, but, on the contrary, adding to his grief and woe, we might have said even worse things than Job did. For remember, dear friends, that he said nothing against God in the time of his deepest sorrow. He cursed most vehemently the day of his birth, and wished that he had never existed, or that he might speedily pass away to sleep with the generations that are dead; and he used unwise and foolish expressions, but any of us might have used far worse words if we had been in his case, so we will not condemn him, but we will see what lessons we can learn from his experience.

I think that Job's experience teaches us the very small value of temporal things. To have spiritual blessings, and to enjoy them, is one thing; but to have earthly things, and to enjoy them, is quite another thing. You may have an abundance of them, and yet they may be utterly tasteless to you, or they may even be bitter as gall to you, and you may curse the day that gave them to you. I am sure that it is so, because Job speaks thus concerning life, which is the chief of all earthly things. It is true, although Satan said it, "All that a man hath will he give for his life;" yet we may be brought into such a condition that we may wish that we had never been born. Life itself may become so wearisome to us that we may even wish to escape from it, that we may be at rest, as we hope. Job had once enjoyed every comfort that heart could desire, and he still had this blessing of life left to him; but even that had become curdled and soured, the last thing to which a man usually clings had become distasteful and disgusting to him, so that he set no store by it, but longed to get rid of it. O beloved, seek eternal treasures, for there is no moth that can eat them, no rust can mar them, no fermentation or corruption can injure them; but, as for the things of time and sense, if you do possess them, use them as though you had them not, and never make them your gods, for they are but as a shadow that passeth away in a moment. They come, and they are gone; and if you make idols of them, the Lord may permit you still to retain them, but take away from you all power to enjoy them. You may have abundance, and yet not be able to relish even the bread you eat, or the drink that refreshes you. You may have a loss of health, or a loss of all power to be happy, though everything that men think to be the cause of happiness may be laid abundantly at your feet.

With this as a preface, I now come to my text, and ask you to notice, first, *the case which raises the question;* secondly, *the question itself;* and, thirdly, *answers which may be given to the question:* "Why is light given to a man whose way is hid, and whom God hath hedged in?"

I. First, notice THE CASE WHICH RAISES THE QUESTION: "Why is light given to a man whose way is hid, and whom God hath hedged in?"

That is to say, "Why does God permit men to live *when their souls are under deep depression and gloom?* Why does he not let them die at once? When their days are spent in weariness, and their nights yield them neither rest nor refreshment,— when they look upward, and see nothing to give them hope, or onward, and behold nothing but that which is even more dreadful than the present,—why is it that God continues life to those who are in such sad circumstances?" Well, dear friends, if life were not continued to any but those who are bright of eye, and fleet of foot, and joyous of heart, how few would live! And if, the first time that darkness fell upon a man's pathway, he were to be permitted to die, well, then, the whole population of the globe would soon be swept away. If our murmuring and petulance demanded that we should die rather than suffer, then we should soon pass away, and be gone. But that is the case which is supposed in Job's question,—If a man find himself entirely in the dark, if God's presence be completely hidden from him, and he can find no joy in anything whatever, and his spirit is tossed to and fro with worries and perplexities, the question is, "Why does he continue to live?"

Yet, further, the man here described is in such trouble that *he can see no reason for the trouble.* His "way is hid." Job could not perceive, in his own case, any cause for the distress into which he had been plunged. As far as he knew, he had walked uprightly. He had not sinned so as to be now suffering the result of his sin. He had not committed a crime, else he would have understood the punishment when it came upon him. He looked back upon all that he had done, and he could not, at his first glance, see in himself any cause for his affliction. Nor, indeed, dear brethren, was there any cause why all these things should have happened to Job by way of punishment, for the inspired record concerning him is that he was "perfect and upright, and one that feared God, and eschewed evil."

Even the devil himself, who kept a sharp look-out with his malicious eye, could not find any fault whatsoever with which he could charge Job. He deserved the character which God had given to him, though Satan did insinuate that he had acted from interested motives. He asked, "Doth Job fear God for nought?" That question has always seemed to me to be a very crafty one, yet very foolish, for if it could have been proved that Job had feared or served God for nought, then the devil would have said at once that God was a bad master, and that there was no reward for those who served him. But now that he finds God putting a hedge of roses round about Job, and sheltering him on every side, he declares that Job was only pious because he found it profitable. He could find no other fault with him; and even that accusation was not true.

Job, on his part, remembered how he had fed the widow, and succoured the fatherless,—how he had acted justly towards his fellow-creatures in the midst of an unjust generation,—and how, amidst a mass of idolaters, he had worshipped God, and God alone. He had never kissed his hand in adoration to the moon, as she walked along her shining way in all her queenly brightness, nor had he ever bowed himself down to the host of heaven, as nearly all around him had done. He stood alone, or almost alone, in that age, as a true and faithful servant of Jehovah; yet his sorrows and trials were multiplied. And so, his way was hidden, he was hedged in by God, and he could not make it out. You know, dear friends, that it is often a great aggravation of our troubles when we do not know why they come. A man, when he is ill, usually wants to know what is the nature of his disease, and how he came to be attacked by it. When we see a person suffering, we generally ask, "Where did you catch that cold?" or, "What was it that brought on that congestion?" We always like to know the cause of the complaint, and Job wanted to ascertain the reason for his trouble, but he could not find it out, and this rendered it all the more mysteriously grievous to him, and therefore he enquired, "Why do I continue to live, when I have come into such darkness as this?"

It was equally trying to Job that *he did not know what to do.* There seemed to be nothing that he could do. He was stripped of all his earthly possessions. Those ashes where he sat formed his uncomfortable couch, and the sole property that remained to him was a potsherd, with which, in his desperation, he began to scrape himself because of his sore boils. What could he do in such a case as that? There was no physician there to cure him of his sad complaint.

True, there were his three friends; but all that they could do, or, at least, the best thing they did, was to sit still, and say nothing. When they opened their mouths, it was only to pour vinegar into his wounds, and to increase his agony tenfold. What could poor Job do under such circumstances? His very helplessness tended to increase his wretchedness.

Am I addressing anyone who is in that kind of perplexity? I think I hear someone moaning, "I don't know which way to turn. I have done everything I can think of, and I cannot tell what is to come next. I sit in darkness, and can see no light. Why I am brought to this pass, I cannot tell; or what is the reason for it, I cannot make out anyhow. If I could light upon some great and grievous fault which had brought me where I am, I could understand it; but as it is, I am in thick Egyptian night about it all, and I know not what to do. Why does a man continue to live when his way is thus hidden, or hedged up." If that is the way you talk, you are in very much the same sort of plight that the patriarch was in when he uttered the mournful question which forms our text.

What was still worse to Job was that *he could not see any way out of his trouble.* He said that God had hedged him in, not with a hedge of roses, but with a barrier of briars. Whatever he tried to do, he found himself obstructed in doing it. And there are men, now in this world, whose sorrows are the more grievous because everything they do to alleviate their distress seems only to increase it. Their efforts are all fruitless; they are like men who have become entangled in a bog; the more they struggle to get out, the deeper they descend. They strive to their very utmost, but it is all in vain; they rise up early, they sit up late, and they eat the bread of carefulness mingled with their tears; but there is a blight on all that they do. Nothing prospers with them; they are at their wit's end. Then they begin to cry, "Oh, that we had never been born, rather than that we should have been born to such trouble as this! 'Why is light given to a man whose way is hid, and whom God hath hedged in?'"

I have thus stated the case which gave rise to Job's question, and I should not wonder if I have, at the same time, stated the case of some who are here. Do not think it has been a waste of time for any of you to hear this sorrowful description of a very sad condition of heart and mind. If I should only have been describing one such individual, let us all feel sympathy for him or for her, and let us unite in breathing the silent petition, "Lord, bring thy servant out of prison."

II. Now, secondly, we are to consider THE QUESTION ITSELF: "Why is light given to a man whose way is hid, and whom God hath hedged in?" In other words, why is the light of life given to him who is in the darkness of misery?

Well, first, let me say that *it is a very unsafe question for anyone to ask.* Brethren, we are sure to get into mischief as soon as we begin catechising God, and asking "why?" and "wherefore?" Such questioning comes not well from our lips. He is the Potter, and we are the clay in his hands. "Shall the thing formed say to him that formed it, Why hast thou made me thus? Hath not the potter power over the clay, of the same lump to make one vessel unto honour and another unto dishonor?" God's eternal purposes are a great deep, and when we try to fathom them, we utterly fail. Divine Sovereignty is an ocean without a bottom and without a shore, and all we can do is to set our sail, and steer by the chart which he has given us, and all the while believe that, as we sang just now,—

> "E'en the hour that darkest seemeth,
> Will his changeless goodness prove;
> From the mist his brightness streameth,
> God is wisdom, God is love."

Voyaging in that fashion, we shall be safe indeed. But to try to cross such a sea, without rudder, or chart, or compass,— this is a venturesome piece of sailing which we had better not undertake. I tremble whenever I have to think of the wondrous ways of God; I mean, when I have to think of them after the manner of the reasoner, and not after the style of the believer. Well did Milton describe the fallen spirits sitting, in little groups, discussing predestination and the counsels of the Eternal. You know how Paul answers the man who calls in question the dealings of God either in providence or in grace: "Nay but, O man, who art thou that repliest against God?" Job received his answer when the Lord spake to him out of the whirlwind, and said, "Who is this that darkeneth counsel by words without knowledge?" What God said to him was not so much a vindication of the ways of providence, but a revelation of his matchless power as the Creator and the Ruler of the universe; and, though men may not like to hear it, yet there is, in the thunder of God's power, an answer, which, though it may not always answer the sceptic, but ultimately overpower and silence him. As for God's child, he sits down in the shadow of that black cloud which is the canopy of Deity, and he is well content to be still in the presence of the Lord of the whole earth. Imitate him, my brother, and do not keep asking God the why and the wherefore of what he does. It is an unsafe thing to ask such questions.

Next, *it reflects upon God.* In this question of Job, there is really a reflection upon the wisdom of the Almighty. He has given the light of life to a man whose way is hidden, and whom God hath hedged in, yet Job asks, "Why did he do it?" I think that, far too often, we indulge our questionings of divine providence. Is God to stand and answer to you and me for what he does? Is he bound to tell us the reason why he does it? Job's friend Elihu said, "God is greater than man. Why dost thou strive against him? for he giveth not account of any of his matters." If there be his equal anywhere, let him meet him in the field, and they shall speak together; but to us worms of the dust answers shall not be given if we haughtily put questions to him of "what?" and "why?" and "wherefore?" To accept the Lord's will with absolute submission, is after the manner of the Son of God himself, for he prayed, in the hour of his greatest agony, "O my Father, if it be possible, let this cup pass from me: nevertheless not as I will, but as thou wilt." But to cavil, and to question, is after the manner of the prince of darkness, who is ever seeking to dispute the sovereignty of God. Therefore, beloved, let no question of ours reflect upon the Lord's love, or the dispensations of his providence.

Further, we may rest quite certain that *there must be an answer to this question,* a good answer, and an answer in harmony with the character of God. If there are men and women to be found still sitting in the darkness of grief and sorrow, and we ask why they are allowed to continue to live, there is a reply possible to that enquiry, and a reply consistent with boundless grace and infinite compassion; but, mark you, that reply may never be given, or, if it is given, we may be incapable of understanding it. There is much that God does that could not be understood, even by those great men, of modern times, who would fain sit on the throne of the Eternal and judge him,—

> "Snatch from his hand the balance and the rod,
> Rejudge his judgments, be the god of God."

I say that there are some answers, which God might give if he pleased, but which even they could not comprehend with all their wit and wisdom, and you and I must often come to a point where we have to stop and say, "We cannot understand this;" and we shall be still wiser if we add, "Nor do we wish to do so." Brothers and sisters, I, for one, have had enough of searching into reasons; I am perfectly satisfied to accept facts. I am ready to bow my reason before the Lord, and to accept whatever he says. If I do not, how little shall I ever know! What is there that I do really understand? I confess that I see profound mysteries about the commonest phenomena around me; I cannot fully comprehend anything when I get right to the bottom of it. There is, on every hand, a deep which I cannot fathom; how, then, shall I understand the ways of God, and measure him with my finite mind, comparing so many inches with the Infinite, weighing so many ounces against the Omnipotent, and reckoning so many seconds in contrast with the Eternal? No, brethren, for such calculations, you have nothing to measure with; you have nothing to draw with, and the well is deep, yea, bottomless. So, the less of such questions as Job's any of us ask, the better, for, even if we had the answer to them, we might not be able to understand it.

Let me remind you also that, however important this question may seem to be, *it is not the most profitable question.* I have heard of a farmer, whose boy said to him, "Father, the cows are in the corn; however did they get there?" "Boy," he replied, "never mind how they got there; our work is to get them out as soon as we can." That is our main business also, to get the cows out of the corn; how they got there is a matter that can be thought of by-and-by when we have nothing else to do. The origin of evil is a point that puzzles a great many people; but I hope you will not worry your brains over that question; if you do, you will be very foolish. But if you are wise men, you will not trouble yourself so much about the origin of evil, as about how to conquer it, in yourself, and in others. Get the cows out of the corn, and then find out how they got in, if you can, by so doing, prevent their getting in again.

There will be space enough, and time enough, and better light, to discuss these questions when we get up yonder before the throne of the Eternal. If their solution is of any real consequence to us, we shall get them solved then; but, meanwhile, we are colorblind; or, if we are not, it is so dark and so misty here, and we have so many other more pressing matters to attend to, that we had better leave these whys and wherefores, and rely on the infallible wisdom and the infinite love of God. If he has done anything, it is quite certain that it is right and just; yea, if it has come from his dear hand, it is also gracious and kind. There is more sublimity in being like a little child in the presence of the Eternal than there is in trying to ape the Deity, for that is but a mockery,—a thing to be despised;—nay more, it is the greatest insult we can offer to God, and it is a pity and a shame that any of us should so live and act. Put aside everything of the kind, I implore you, and in very truth submit yourselves unto God.

III. But now, in the last place, speaking to the sorrowful person, I want to mention SOME ANSWERS WHICH MAY BE GIVEN TO HIS QUESTION. "Why do I continue to live," asks he, "in such sorrow as this? Why does not God take from me the light of life when he does not permit me to enjoy the light of comfort?"

Supposing that you are a child of God, I will give you one answer which ought to satisfy you, though, perhaps, it will not if your spirit is rebellious. *God wills it.* If you are one of his true children, that is all the answer that you will require; and you will say, with those early Christians, "The will of the Lord be done;" and with your Lord himself, "Not my will, but thine, be done." It was enough for Christ that his suffering was in accordance with the Father's will, so he bowed before him in unquestioning submission; and shall not you, the disciple, be content to fare as your Master did? Will not you be perfectly satisfied with that which satisfied your Lord? It is the will of the Lord; then what need is there of any further question if you are his child?

But supposing that you are an unconverted person, and you say, "I cannot bear to live in such sorrow as this, why is my life prolonged?" the answer is, *"Because of God's mercy to you."* Where would you go to be better off than you are here? You who have no hope in Christ, and yet who say, "I wish I were dead," you know not what you are saying. You wish you were dead? But what would be your portion after death? What! Do you really wish to hear that dread sentence which must be passed upon you if you die unregenerate: "Depart from me, ye cursed, into everlasting fire, prepared for the devil and his angels?" Do you really desire to feel the full weight of divine justice? Ah! I hope that you are not so foolish.

You have spoken in petulance, and do not mean what you have said: It may be hard for you to live, but it would be harder far for you to die, and then to live for ever in a death that never dies. God grant that you may never know that awful doom!

Moreover, the answer to your question is that the Lord spares you *because he would fain save you.* You are kept alive that you may hear again that voice of mercy which says, "Repent ye, and be converted." "Believe on the Lord Jesus Christ, and thou shalt be saved." God comes to you in this time of suffering, that he may stop you in your sin, and make you think. Even to the most careless and giddy among you, during the poignancy of your grief, he says, "Now, my prodigal child, thou hast wasted thy substance in riotous living, thy belly is hungry, and thou hast nothing with which to fill it; arise, and go unto thy Father, for he will receive thee." Come, then, sorrowful one, it may be that thy sorrows will end when thy sins end; certainly, when thou comest to Christ to be forgiven, thou shalt find divine consolation, even if all thy griefs do not at once disappear. Anyhow, it would be better to be whipped all the way to heaven than to be carried down to hell "on flowery beds of ease." Pray this prayer, "O Lord, let me enter into life with one eye and one hand, halt or maimed, rather than, having two eyes and two hands, to be cast into hell!" This is one answer to your question; the Lord lets you live, even though it is in pain and grief, because he has purposes of love and mercy towards you. Therefore, be not anxious to die; but be thankful that you are still permitted to tarry upon gospel ground. Nay, do not be content to tarry there, but fly at once to the God of grace; look this very instant to Jesus, for—

> "There is life for a look at the Crucified One;
> There is life at this moment for thee;
> Then look, sinner—look unto him, and be saved—
> Unto him who was nail'd to the tree."

One believing glance of the eye to him who is the sinner's Substitute, and all transgression is forgiven; therefore, yield yourself unto him, trust to his finished work, and eternal life is yours. And when you have that unspeakable blessing, why need you sorrow more?

As for the child of God, to whom I now again speak, if you

ask, in a timid, childlike way, "Why do I continue to live in such sorrow as I have to endure?" I would, as your brother, try to answer you. First, it may be that all this trouble has come upon you *to let you know what is in you.* None of us know what there is in us until we are put to the test. We are wonderfully sweet-tempered until somebody touches one of our sore places; and then, ah, me! there is not much sweetness of temper left after that. We are remarkably patient until we get a sharp neuralgic pain, perhaps; and then, where is all our boasted patience gone. We are very generous until we ourselves are somewhat pinched, and then we become as tight-fisted as others whom we have condemned. We do not know what is really in us while all goes smoothly and well; but sickness, and sorrow, and bereavement, and poverty, and hunger, will soon let us see what we are. They make a mental or moral photograph of us, and when we look at the picture we say, "Oh, no! that cannot be our likeness;" but we look again and again, and then we say, "Alas! it is even so; but we did not know we were like that. Now we see our faults and our follies. O Lord, thou hast searched us, and tried us, and shown us the wicked ways that are in us; now purge us from them, and make us clean and pure in thy sight!" That is one reason, and a very good reason, for sharp affliction,—to let us see ourselves as we really are.

The next is that, *often, our trials bring us very near to our God.* Your children run down the meadow to play, and they get a good way off from home in the sunny day, as they ramble along gathering their buttercups and daisies; but by-and-by, the sun sets, and night comes on, and now they cry to be at home. Just so; and you, in all your pretty ways of pleasure in your happy home, though you are a child of God, sometimes forget him. Sorrowfully must you remember that sad fact. But now the night comes on, and there is danger all around you; so you begin to cry for your Father, and you would fain be back to fellowship with him; and that is a blessed trouble which brings us near to our God. Christ's sheep ought to be thankful for the ugly black dog that keeps them from going astray, or fetches them back when they have wandered from the Shepherd. Perhaps Christ will call that black dog off when he has answered the Master's purpose, and brought you near his side.

Dear child of God, anything that promotes your

sanctification, or increases your spirituality, is a good thing for you. I have had my share of physical pain, and perhaps more of it than most who are here; and I bless God for it. If it comes again, I ask him for grace to bless him for it then; and now that it has gone for a while, I freely bless him for it, for I cannot tell you all the good that it has wrought in me. Oh! how often a proud spirit has been cut back by affliction and trial, like a vine that is made to bleed, that the clusters that followed the pruning might be all the better and richer! The mown grass is very sweet and fine; and so, often, are believers who have been deeply tried. This tribulation, as Paul says, "worketh patience; and patience, experience; and experience, hope: and hope maketh not ashamed; because the love of God is shed abroad in our hearts by the Holy Ghost which is given unto us." Wherefore, bow humbly before the Lord, my tried and afflicted friend, and see at least some of the reasons why he thus puts you in the dark chamber of tribulation.

Perhaps, dear brother, you are being very greatly tried, more than most people, *to fit you to be an example to others.* The Lord means to make a veteran of you, so you must be the first in the breach, or you must lead the forlorn hope. He puts you on the hardest service because he wants others of his children to be able to learn from you. I do not know that we should ever have heard anything of Job if it had not been for his troubles; he was a most respectable Eastern farmer, with a considerable estate, very much like a great many country gentlemen we have in England, who may be heard of at the Quarter Sessions, or the corn and cattle market, but nothing more will be known of them unless you go to the parish church, and see some memorial of them stuck up there. Job would have been much the same sort of man as that,—an Oriental magnate, who would have lived, and died, and been forgotten; but now his fame will last as long as the world endures, and "ye have heard of the patience of Job." You have all heard of it, and Job is one of the undying names. So it may be with you, beloved. You are, perhaps, to sail through seas of trouble to reach your crown. God means to use you in his service, and make you a blessing to others, and a teacher of others, by passing you again and again through the fire. One of the ancient warriors said, "I cannot use in battle a sword that has not been ofttimes annealed; but give me a Damascus blade that has been so prepared, and I will cut through a coat of mail, or split a man from head to foot at a single stroke. It gets its temper and keenness of edge from having slept with the flames again and again." So must it be with believers. Full often, they are unfit for God to use till they have been sorely tried.

Perhaps, dear friend, the Lord is putting you through all this trouble—(only I hardly like to say it aloud, I must whisper it in your ears somehow),—*because he loves you more than anybody else.* Dear Samuel Rutherford, when he wrote to a lady who had lost, I think, seven children, congratulated her, and said, "I am sure that the Well-beloved has a strong affection for your ladyship, for he will have all your heart. He has taken away all these children that there may not be a nook or a corner for anybody else but for him." So the Lord loves you much, and he is testing you to see whether you can bear his will,—whether you love him so much that you will take up your cross, and deny yourself, just as, sometimes, architects will ask for their work to be put to the severest possible tests. "Yes," they say, "see what it will really bear." No doubt Stephenson felt great joy when the heaviest train went safely across his tubular bridge; and other engineers have said, "Yes, put on as much pressure as you like; it will stand it." Fathers often take delight in the athletic feats of their sons, and princes revel in the brave deeds of their warriors; and so does the Lord delight to see what his people can do, and he often puts upon them more and more, to prove whether they love him so much that they can bear it all for his sake. Did not the Lord do this to let Satan see that Job did love his God, and would still say, "Shall we receive good at the hand of God, and shall we not receive evil?...The Lord gave, and the Lord hath taken away; blessed be the name of the Lord." We cannot tell what a blessing must come from such a state of heart as that.

It is very possible, dear friend, also, that God is putting you through all this trouble *that he may enable you to bear great prosperity.* Job was to have twice as much as he had ever had before, and that was a very great deal, for he said that he washed his steps with butter, and the rock poured him out rivers of oil; but how much richer he was when everything was doubled! Job was hardly fit to manage such a large estate as that until he had been made to see the vanity of it all, and to get nearer to his God. So, dear friends, you are going to be pressed, and squeezed, and tried, in order that you may be fitted to come right out into the front rank, and to be magnified and made much of by the Lord your God. I have noticed this kind of thing happen more than once. I have seen a man suddenly taken from the very dregs of the people, and put up to preach, and he has been popular all at once. Nobody has abused him, nobody has said a word against him; but, before long, he has passed completely out of sight. He could not bear the weight that was put upon him, and gave way. You have seen others, who have been called of God to preach the Word, and they have been abused year after year. They could not say anything that was not perverted; they were called mountebanks, impostors, and I know not what. And then, when happier days came, and almost all men spoke well of them, they could bear it, for they had learnt to despise alike the flatteries and the abuse of men. Now, something like that must happen to all God's servants who are to be greatly honoured. If they are to bear prosperity, they must go through the fire first. Perhaps that is what the Lord is doing with you, my dear friend; if so, be content with your lot.

And, once again, do you not think that the Lord means thus *to make you more like his dear Son than other people are?* Some other Christians have not as much trouble to endure as you have. No; why is it? You know how an artist can, if he likes, dash off a picture. There! A little red, and a little blue, and so on, and it is done; and away it goes! Ay, but when he wants to paint something that will be observed and admired, then he takes more pains. See how he works at every part of it; note what care and what trouble he takes with it. It is the same with the lapidary or the sculptor when he has choice work in hand; and you are, I hope, the kind of material that will pay for cutting and carving; and the Lord is using his chisel upon you more than he does upon most folk. He wants to make you just like his dear Son; so now he is chipping out a thorn-crown, and you must wear it round your brain. He is fashioning the image of his Son out of the block of your renewed nature, and you must patiently bear the blows from his hammer and chisel till that work is done.

Finally, if I cannot tell you why all this trouble falls to your lot, I know it is right, for *the Lord has done it,* and blessed be his name. Aaron held his peace when his two sons died. He got as far as that in submission to the will of the Lord; but it will be better still if, instead of simply holding your peace, you can bless and praise and magnify the Lord even in your sharpest trouble. Oh, may you be divinely helped to do so! Let every troubled soul march out of this place feeling, "It is good for me that I have been afflicted." Rise, dear friend, out of all despondency and despair, shake yourself from the dust, and put on your beautiful garments of praise and joy, remembering that—

> "The path of sorrow, and that path alone,
> Leads to the land where sorrow is unknown."

You can see the tracks of the martyrs along the road you are journeying; better still, you can see the footprints of the Son of God, your Lord and Saviour. Therefore, you may rest assured that you are on the right road, so press bravely forward on it, and, in due time, you will come to that place of which Job said, "There the wicked cease from troubling; and there the weary be at rest;" and you shall be for ever without fault before the throne of God. May he grant this happy portion to you all, for his dear Son's sake! Amen.

6

The Death of the Christian

"Thou shalt come to thy grave in a full age, like as a shock of corn cometh in in his season."   **Job 5:26**

We do not believe all that Job's friends said. They spoke very often as uninspired men, for we find them saying many things that are not true; and if we read the book of Job through, we might say with regard to them, "miserable comforters are ye all," for they did not speak concerning God's servant, Job, the thing that was right. But, nevertheless, they gave utterance to many holy and pious sentences, which are well worthy of regard, as having come from the lips of three men distinguished in their age for their learning, talent, and ability; three grey-headed sires, who from experience were able to speak what they knew. Their mistakes are not to be wondered at, because they had not then that clear, bright, shining light, which we enjoy in these modern times. They had few opportunities to meet together; there were but few prophets in those days who taught them the things of the kingdom. We only marvel that without the light of the gospel revelation they were able to discover so much of the truth as they did. However I must make a remark concerning this chapter, that I cannot but regard it as being in the main, not so much the utterance of the man—who here speaks— Eliphaz the Temanite—but the very word of God; not so much the simple saying of the unwise comforter who upbraided Job, as the speech of the great Comforter who consoles his people, and who only utters the thing that is right. The opinion is justified by the fact that this chapter is quoted by the apostle Paul. Eliphaz says, in the 13th verse, "He taketh the wise in their own craftiness." And we find the apostle Paul in the Corinthians, saying, "As it is written, he taketh the wise in their own craftiness;" thus giving sanction to this passage as having been inspired of God, at all events as being most

certainly truthful. Most certainly the experience of such a
man as Eliphaz is worthy of much regard: and when speaking
of the general condition of God's people, that they are hid
from the scourge of the tongue, "that they are not afraid of
destruction when it cometh," that they laugh at destruction
and famine, and so on, we may accept his words as being
proven by experience, and authenticated by inspiration.
"Thou shalt come to thy grave in a full age, like as a shock of
corn cometh in in his season." Here is a very beautiful
comparison, the comparison of the aged Christian—for that I
take it lies on the surface of the text—to a shock of corn. Go
into the harvest field, and you shall see how much the wheat
reminds you of the aged believer. How much anxiety has been
expended on that field! When the seed first sprung up the
farmer dreaded lest the worm should bite the tender shoots,
and the blade should be devoured, or lest some sharp frost
should consume the infant plant and cause it to wither and
die. And, then, month after month, as the seasons came, how
did he anxiously look towards heaven and long that the rains
might come, or that the genial sunshine might pour out its
vivifying floods of light upon the field. When it has come to
somewhat of maturity, how greatly has he feared lest the
mildew and blast should shrivel up the precious ears. It
stands in the fields now, and in some respects he is freed from
his anxiety. The months of his travail are over. He has waited
patiently for the precious fruits of the soil, but now they are
there. And so with the grey-headed man. How many years of
anxiety have been expended upon him! In his youth how
likely did it seem that he might be smitten down by death,
and yet he has passed safely through youth, manhood, and
age. What varied accidents have been warded from him! How
has the shield of the Providential Keeper been over his head
to keep him from the shafts of the pestilence, or from the
heavy hand of accident that might have smitten his life! How
many anxieties has he had himself! How many troubles has
he passed through! Look upon the hoary-headed veteran!
Mark the scars that troubles have inflicted upon his forehead!
And see, deep written in his breast, the dark mementos of the
sharp struggles and trials he has endured! And now his
anxieties are somewhat over; he is come very nearly to the
haven of rest. A few short years of trial and trouble shall land
him on fair Canaan's coast, and we look upon him with the

same pleasure that the farmer regards the wheat, because the anxiety is over and the time of rest is now approaching. Mark how weak the stem has become! how every wind shakes it to and fro; it is withered and dried! See how the head hangs down to earth, as if it were about to kiss the dust, and show whence it had its origin! So, mark you the aged man; tottering are his steps, "they that look out of the windows are darkened, the grinders cease because they are few, and the grasshopper has become a burden." Yet even in that weakness there is glory. It is not the weakness of the tender blade, it is the weakness of the full ripe corn, it is a weakness that shows its maturity, it is a weakness that gilds it with glory. Even as the colour of the wheat is golden, so that it looks more beauteous than when the greenness of its verdure is on it, so the grey-headed man has a crown of glory on his head. He is glorious in his weakness, more than the young man in his strength, or the maiden in her beauty. Is not a shock of corn a beautiful picture of the state of man, moreover, because very soon it must be taken home? The reaper is coming. Even now I hear the sickle sharpening. The reaper hath well edged it, and he shall soon cut the corn down. See! he is coming across the field to reap his harvest; and then, by-and-by, it shall be carried into the barn and safely housed, no more subject to blight, or mildew, or insect, or disease. There it shall be secured, where no snow can fall upon it, no winds can molest it. It shall be safe and secure; and joyful shall be the time when harvest home shall be proclaimed, and the shock of corn, fully ripe, shall be carried into the farmer's garner. Such is the aged man. He, too, shall soon be taken home. Death is even now sharpening his sickle, and the angels are getting ready their chariot of gold to bear him up to the skies. The barn is built; the house is provided; soon the great Master shall say, "Bind up the tares in bundles to burn, and gather the wheat into my barn."

This morning, we shall consider *the death of Christians in general*; not of the aged Christian merely, for we shall show you that while this text does seem to bear upon the aged Christian, in reality it speaks with a loud voice to every man who is a believer. "Thou shalt come to thy grave in a full age, like as a shock of corn cometh in in his season."

There are four things we shall mark in the text. First, we shall consider that death is *inevitable*, because it says, "Thou *shalt* come." Secondly, that death is *acceptable*, because it does not read, "I will make thee *go* to thy grave," but "thou shalt *come* there." Thirdly that death is always *timely*: "Thou shalt come to thy grave in *full age*." Fourthly, that death to the Christian is always *honourable*, for the promise declareth to him, "Thou shalt go to thy grave in full age, like as a shock of corn cometh in in his season."

I. The first remark, namely, that death, even to the Christian, is INEVITABLE, is very trite, simple and common, and we need scarcely have made it, but we found it necessary, in order to introduce one or two remarks upon it. How hacknied is the thought, that all men must die, and therefore, what can we say upon it? And yet we blush not to repeat it, for while it is a truth so well known, there is none so much forgotten; while we all believe it in the theory and receive it in the brain, how seldom it is impressed on the heart? The sight of death makes us remember it. The tolling of the solemn bell speaks to us of it. We hear the deep-tongued voice of time as the bell tolls the hours and preaches our mortality. But very usually we forget it. Death is inevitable to all. But I wish to make an observation concerning death, and that is, that while it is written, "It is appointed unto all men once to die," yet a time shall come when some Christian men shall not die at all. We know that had Adam never sinned he would not have died, for death is the punishment of sin; and we know that Enoch and Elijah were translated to heaven without dying. Therefore it does seem to follow, that death is not absolutely necessary for a Christian. And, moreover, we are told in Scripture, that there are some who shall be "alive and remain," when Jesus Christ shall come, and the apostle says, "I tell you a mystery—we shall not all sleep, but we shall all be changed in a moment, in the twinkling of an eye, at the last trump." There shall be some who shall be found living, of whom the apostle says, "Then we which are alive and remain shall be caught up together with them in the clouds, to meet the Lord in the air; and so shall we ever be with the Lord." We know that flesh and blood cannot inherit the kingdom; but it is possible that they may be refined by some spiritual process, which shall preclude the necessity of dissolution. Oh! I have thought of that idea very much, and I have wondered whether it should not be possible that some of us might be in that happy number who shall not see death. Even if we are not, there is something very cheering in the thought: Christ did so conquer death that he not only delivers the lawful captive out of the prison, but he saves a band from the jaws of the monster, and leads them by his den unharmed! He not only resuscitates the dead, and puts new life into those that are slain by the fell scythe, but some he actually takes to heaven by a bye-road. He says to death—"Avaunt, thou monster! On these thou shalt never put thy hand! These are chosen men and women, and thy cold fingers shall never freeze the current of their soul. I am taking them straight to heaven without death. I will transport them in their bodies up to heaven without passing through thy gloomy portals, or having been captives in thy dreary land of shades." How glorious is the thought, that Christ has vanquished death; that some men shall not die. But you will say to me, "How can that be? for the body has mortality mingled with its very essence." We are told it is true, by eminent men, that there is a necessity in nature that there should be death, since one animal must prey upon another; and even could all animals be taught to give up their prey, they must feed upon plants, and so devour certain minute insects which had hidden thereon. Death therefore seems to be the law of nature. Be it remembered; that men have already lived far beyond the present allotted term, and it does seem most easy to conceive that the creature, which can subsist a thousand years, could exceed that period. But this objection is not valid, since the saints will not live for ever in this world, but will be removed to a habitation where laws of glory shall supersede laws of nature.

II. And now comes a sweet thought, that death to the Christian is always ACCEPTABLE—"Thou shalt *come* to thy grave." Old Caryl makes this remark on this verse—"A willingness and a cheerfulness to die. Thou shalt *come*, thou shalt not be dragged or hurried to thy grave, as it is said of the foolish rich man, Luke 12. This night shall thy soul be taken from thee. But thou shalt come to thy grave, thou shalt die quietly and smilingly, as it were; thou shalt go to thy grave, as it were upon thine own feet, and rather walk than be carried to thy sepulchre." The wicked man, when he dies, is driven to his grave, but the Christian *comes* to his grave. Let me tell you a parable. Behold two men sat together in the same house: when Death came to each of them. He said to one, "Thou shalt die." The man looked at him—tears suffused his eyes, and tremblingly he said, "O Death, I cannot, I will not die." He sought out a physician, and said to him, "I am sick, for Death hath looked upon me. His eyes have paled my cheeks, and I fear I must depart. Physician, there is my wealth, give me health and let me live." The physician took his wealth, but gave him not his health with all his skill. The man changed his physician and tried another, and thought that perhaps he might spin out the thread of life a little longer. But, alas! Death came and said, "I have given thee time to try thy varied excuses, come with me; thou shalt die." And he bound him hand and foot, and made him go to that dark land of shades. As the man went, he clutched at every side post by the way; but Death, with iron hands, still pulled him on. There was not a tree that grew along the way but he tried to grasp it, but Death said, "Come on! thou art my captive, and thou shalt die." And unwillingly as the laggard schoolboy, who goeth slowly to school, so did he trace the road with Death. He did not *come* to his grave, but Death fetched him to it—the grave came to him.

But Death said to the other man, "I am come for thee." He smilingly replied, "Ah, Death! I know thee, I have seen thee many a time. I have held communion with thee. Thou art my Master's servant, thou hast come to fetch me home. Go, tell my Master I am ready; whene'er he pleases. Death, I am ready to go with thee." And together they went along the road, and held sweet company. Death said to him, "I have worn these skeleton bones to frighten wicked men; but I am not frightful. I will let thee see myself. The hand that wrote upon Belshazzar's wall was terrible because no man saw anything but the hand; but," said Death, "I will show thee my whole body. Men have only seen my bony hand, and have been terrified." And as they went along, Death ungirded himself to let the Christian see his body and he smiled, for it was the body of an angel. He had wings of cherubs, and a body glorious as Gabriel. The Christian said to him, "Thou art not what I thought thou wast: I will cheerfully go with thee." At last Death touched the believer with his hand—it was even as when the mother doth in sport smite her child a moment. The child loves that loving pinch upon the arm, for it is a proof of affection. So did Death put his finger on the man's pulse, and stopped it for a moment, and the Christian found himself by Death's kind finger changed into a spirit; yea, found himself brother to the angels; his body had been etherealized, his soul purified, and he himself was in heaven. You tell me this is only a parable; but let me give you some facts that shall back it up. I will tell you some of the death-bed sayings of dying saints, and show you that, to them, Death has been an agreeable visitant, of whom they were not afraid. You will not disbelieve dying men. It were ill to act the hypocrite's part at such a time. When the play is over men will take off the mask: and so with these men when they came to die—they stood out in solemn unclothed reality.

First, let me tell you what Dr. Owen said—that celebrated prince of Calvinists. While his works are to be found, I am not afraid that men shall lack arguments to defend the Gospel of Free-grace. A friend called to tell Dr. Owen that he had put to press his "Meditations on the Glory of Christ." There was a momentary gleam in his languid eye as he answered, "I am glad to hear it. Oh!" said he, "the long-wished for time has come at last, in which I shall see that glory in another manner than I have ever done, or was capable of doing in this world."

But, you may say, this man was a mere theologian, let us hear a poet speak.

George Herbert, after some severe struggles, and having requested his wife and nieces, who were weeping in extreme anguish, to leave the room, he committed his will to Mr. Woodnott's care, crying out, "I am ready to die—Lord, forsake me not now, my strength faileth; but grant me mercy for the merits of my Lord Jesus. And now, Lord receive my soul." Then he laid himself back and breathed out his life to God. Thus the poet dies. That glorious fancy of his, that might have pictured gloomy things if it had pleased, was only filled with rapturous sight of angels. As he used to say himself, "Methinks I hear the church bells of heaven ringing." And methinks he did hear them when he came near the river Jordan.

"But," you will say, "one was a theologian, and the other a poet—it might have been all fancy." Now learn what an active man, a missionary, said—Brainard.

He said, "I am almost in eternity. I long to be there. My work is done. I have done with all my friends. All the world is now nothing to me. Oh, to be in heaven to praise and glorify

God with his holy angels." That is what Brainard said. He who counted all things but loss for the excellency of the knowledge of Jesus Christ, and went among wild untutored Indians to preach the gospel.

But it is possible you may say, "These were men of ages gone by." Now, you shall have men of modern times.

And first, hear what the great and eminent Scotch preacher, Haldane, said. He raised himself a little, and distinctly repeated these words, "When Christ who is our life shall appear, then we shall appear with him in glory." He was then asked if he thought he was going home. He answered, "Perhaps not quite yet." Mrs. Haldane affectionately said, "Then you will not leave us very soon." He replied with a smile, "To depart and to be with Christ is far better." On being asked if he felt much peace and happiness, he twice repeated, "Exceeding great and precious promises." He then said, "But I must rise." Mrs. Haldane said, "You are not able to get up." He smiled, and answered, "I shall be satisfied when I awake with his likeness." She said, "Is that what rising up you meant?" He replied, "Yes, that is the rising I meant. I must rise!"

And now, what said Howard—the great philanthropist, the man who while possessing true religion, and being the most eminent and distinguished of Christians, would from his plain common sense mode of acting, never be suspected of being a fanatic and an enthusiast? A few days before his death, when the symptoms of his disease began to assume a most alarming appearance, he said to Admiral Priestman, "You endeavour to divert my mind from dwelling on death; but I entertain very different sentiments. Death has no terror for me. I always look forward to it with cheerfulness, if not with pleasure."

But perhaps you may say, "We never knew any of these people. We should like to hear of somebody whom we did know." Well, you shall hear of one whom you have heard me affectionately mention. He was not of our denomination, but he was a very prince in Israel—I refer to Joseph Irons. Many of you heard the sweet and blessed things that proceeded out of his lips, and will perhaps be able to verify what is said of him. At intervals he repeated short portions of Scripture, and select sentences, such as, "How long, Lord?" "Come, Lord Jesus!" "I long to go home, to be at rest." Seeing his dear wife shedding tears, he said, "Do not weep for me; I am waiting for that far more exceeding and eternal weight of glory." After a pause, to recover his breath, he added, "He that has preserved me thus far, will never leave, or forsake me. Fear not: all is well. Christ is precious. I am going home, for I am a shock of corn fully ripe." Now that is a man you did know, many of you. And it proves the fact that I have asserted, that to a Christian, death is acceptable come when it may. I am sure I can say, with many of my brethren, here, that could I now have the greatest favour conferred on me that mortals could desire, I would ask that I might die. I never wish to have the choice given to me; but to die is the happiest thing man can have, because it is to lose anxiety, it is to slay care, it is to have the peculiar sleep of the beloved. To the Christian, then, death must be acceptable.

A Christian has nothing to lose by death. You say he has to lose his friends. I am not so sure of that. Many of you have many more friends in heaven than on earth; some Christians have more dearly beloved ones above than below. You often count your family circle, but do you do as that little girl of whom Wordsworth speaks, when she said, "Master, we are seven." Some of them were dead and gone to heaven, but she would have it that they were all brothers and sisters still. Oh! how many brothers and sisters we have up stairs in the upper room in our Father's house; how many dear ones, linked with us in the ties of relationship, for they are as much our relations now as they were then! Though in the resurrection they neither marry nor are given in marriage, yet in that great world, who has said that the ties of affection shall be severed, so that we shall not even there claim kindred with one another, as well as kindred with Jesus Christ? What have we to lose by death? Come when he may, should we not open the door for him? I would love to feel like that woman who said, when she was dying, "I feel like a door on the latch, ready to be opened to let my Lord in." Is not that a sweet state, to have the house ready, so that it will require no setting in order? When death comes to a wicked man, he finds him moored fast, he snaps his cable, and drives his ship to sea; but when he comes to the Christian, he finds him winding up the anchor, and he says, "When thou hast done thy work and shipped the anchor, I will take thee home." With sweet breath he blows on him, and the ship is wafted gently to heaven, with no regrets for life, but with angels at the prow, spirits guiding the rudder, sweet songs coming through the cordage, and canvass silvered o'er with light.

III. Then thirdly, the Christian's death is always TIMELY— "Thou shalt come to thy grave in a full age." "Ah!" says one, "that is not true. Good people do not live longer than others. The most pious man may die in the prime of his youth." But look at my text. It does not say, thou shalt come to thy grave in old age—but in a "full age." Well, who knows what a "full age" is? A "full age" is whenever God likes to take his children home. There are some fruits you know that are late in coming to perfection, and we do not think their flavour is good till Christmas, or till they have gone through the frost; while some are fit for table now. All fruits do not get ripe and mellow at the same season. So with Christians. They are at a "full age" when God chooses to take them home. They are at "full age" if they die at twenty one; they are not more if they live to be ninety. Some wines can be drunk very soon after the vintage. Others need to be kept. But what does this matter, if when the liquor is broached it is found to have its full flavour? God never broaches his cask till the wine has perfected itself. There are two mercies to a Christian. The first is that he will never die too soon; and the second, that he will never die too late.

First, he will never die *too soon*. Spencer, who blazed out so brilliantly some years ago, preached so wonderfully that many expected that a great light would shine steadily, and that many would be guided to heaven; but when suddenly the light was quenched in darkness, and he was drowned while yet in his youth, men wept, and said, "Ah! Spencer died too soon."

So it has been sung of Kirk White, the poet, who worked so labouriously at his studies. Like the eagle who finds that the arrow that smote him was winged by a feather from his own body, so was his own study the means of his death; and the poet said he died too soon. It was untrue. He did not die too soon; no Christian ever does. But say some, "How useful might they have been had they have lived." Ah! but how damaging they might have been! And were it not better to die than to do something afterwards that would disgrace themselves, and bring disgrace to the Christian character? Were it not better for them to sleep while their work was going on, than to break it down afterwards? We have seen some sad instances of Christian men who have been very useful in God's cause, but have afterwards had sad falls, and have dishonoured Christ, though they were saved and brought back at last. We could almost wish that they had died rather than lived. You don't know what might have been the career of these men who were taken away so soon. Are you quite sure they would have done so much good? Might they not have done much evil? Could we have a dream of the future, and see what they might have been, we should say, "Ah Lord! let it stop while it is well." Let him sleep while the music playeth, there may be hideous sounds afterwards. We long not to keep awake to hear the dreary notes. The Christian dies well: he does not die too soon.

Again, the Christian never dies *too late*. That old lady there is eighty years old. She sits in a miserable room, shivering by a handful of fire. She is kept by charity. She is poor and miserable. "What's the good of her?" says everybody: "she has lived too long. A few years ago she might have been of some use; but now look at her! She can scarcely eat unless her food is put into her mouth. She cannot move; and what good can she be?" Do not you find fault with your Master's work. He is too good a husbandman to leave his wheat in the field too long and let it shale out. Go and see her; and you will be reproved. Let her speak: she can tell you things you never knew in all your life. Or, if she does not speak at all, her silent unmurmuring serenity, her constant submission, teaches you how to bear suffering. So that there is something you can learn from her yet. Say not the old leaf hangeth too long on the tree. An insect may yet twist itself therein, and fashion it into its habitation. O say not the old sear leaf ought to have been blown off long ago. The time is coming when it shall fall gently on the soil; but it remaineth to preach to unthinking men the frailty of their lives. Hear what God says to each of us:—"Thou shalt come to thy grave in full age." Cholera! thou mayest fly across the land and taint the air: I shall die in a "full age." I may preach to-day, and as many days as I please in the week, but I shall die at a full age. However ardently I may labour, I shall die at a full age. Affliction may come to drain my very life's blood, and dry up the very sap and marrow of my being. Ah! but affliction thou shalt not come too soon—I shall die at a full age. And thou waiting-man! and thou tarrying woman! thou art saying, "O Lord, how long? how long? Let me come home." Thou shalt not be kept from thy beloved Jesus one hour more than is necessary, thou shalt have heaven as soon as thou art ready for it. Heaven is ready enough for thee, and thy Lord will say, "Come up higher!" when thou hast arrived at a full age—but never before nor after.

IV. Now the last thing is, that a Christian will die with HONOUR: "Thou shalt come to thy grave like a shock of corn cometh in in his season." You hear men speak against funeral honours, and I certainly do enter my protest against the awful extravagance with which many funerals are conducted, and the absurdly stupid fashions that are often introduced. It would be a happy thing if some persons could break through them, and if widows were not obliged to spend the money which they need so much themselves, upon a needless ceremony, which makes death not honourable, but rather despicable. But, methinks that while death should not be flaunted out with gaudy plumes, there is such a thing as an honourable funeral which every one of us may desire to have. We do not wish to be carried away just as a bundle of tares, we would prefer that devout men should carry us to the grave and make much lamentation over us. Some of us have seen funerals that were very like a "harvest home." I can remember the funeral of a sainted minister under whom I once sat. The pulpit was hung in black, and crowds of people came together; and when an aged veteran in the army of Christ rose up to deliver the funeral oration over his remains, there stood a weeping people lamenting that a prince had fallen that day in Israel. Then, verily, I felt what Mr. Jay must have experienced when he preached the funeral sermon for Rowland Hill, "Howl fir tree, the cedar is fallen," there was such a melancholy grandeur there. And yet my soul seemed lit up with joy, to think it possible that some of us might share in the same affection, and that the same tears might be wept over us when we come to die. Ah! my brethren here, my brethren in office, my brethren in this church, it may somewhat cheer your hearts to know that when you depart, your death will be to us a source of the deepest grief and most piercing sorrow. Your burial shall not be that prophesied for Jehoiakim—the burial of an ass, with none to weep over him; but devout men will assemble and say, "Here

lies the deacon who for years served his Master so faithfully."
"Here lies the Sunday-school teacher,"will the child say, "who
early taught me the Saviour's name;" and if the minister
should fall, methinks a crowd of people following him to the
tomb would well give him such a funeral as a shock of corn
hath when "it cometh in in his season." I believe we ought to
pay great respect to the departed saint's bodies. "The memory
of the just is blessed." And even ye little saints in the church,
don't think you will be forgotten when you die. You may have
no grave-stone; but the angels will know where you are as
well without a grave-stone as with it. There will be some who
will weep over you; you will not be hurried away, but will be
carried with tears to your grave.

But, methinks, there are two funerals for every Christian:
one, the funeral of the *body*; and the other, the *soul*. Funeral,
did I say, of the soul? No, I meant not so; I meant not so; it is
a marriage of the soul; for as soon as it leaves the body the
angel reapers stand ready to carry it away. They may not
bring a fiery chariot as erst they had for Elijah; but they have
their broad spreading wings. I rejoice to believe that angels
will come as convoys to the soul across the ethereal plains. Lo!
angels at the head support the ascending saint, and lovingly
they look upon his face as they bear him upwards; and angels
at the feet, assist in wafting him up yonder through the skies,
and as the husbandmen come out from their houses and cry,
"A joyous harvest home," so will the angels come forth from
the gates of heaven, and say, "Harvest home! harvest home!
Here is another shock of corn fully ripe gathered into the
garner." I think the most honourable and glorious thing we
shall ever behold, next to Christ's entrance into heaven, and
his glory there, is the entrance of one of God's people into
heaven. I can suppose it is made a holiday whenever a saint
enters, and that is continually, so that they keep perpetual
holiday. Oh! methinks there is a shout that cometh from
heaven whenever a Christian enters it, louder than the noise
of many waters. The thundering acclamations of a universe
are drowned, as if they were but a whisper, in that great
shout which all the ransomed raise, when they cry "Another,
and yet another comes;" and the song is still swelled by
increasing voices, as they chant, "Blessed husbandman,
blessed husbandman, thy wheat is coming home; shocks of
corn fully ripe are gathering into thy garner." Well, wait a

little, beloved. In a few years more of you and I shall be
carried through the ether on the wings of angels. Methinks I
die, and the angels approach. I am on the wings of cherubs.
Oh, how they bear me up—how swiftly and yet how softly. I
have left mortality with all its pains. Oh, how rapid is my
flight! Just now I passed the morning star. Far behind me
now the planets shine. Oh, how swiftly do I fly, and how
sweetly! Cherubs! what sweet flight is yours, and what kind
arms are these I lean upon. And on my way ye kiss me with
the kisses of love and affection. Ye call me brother. Cherubs;
am I your brother? I who just now was captive in a tenement
of clay—am I your brother? "Yes!" they say. Oh, hark! I hear
music strangely harmonious! What sweet sounds come to my
ears! I am nearing Paradise. 'Tis e'en so. Do not spirits
approach with songs of joy? "Yes!" they say. And ere they can
answer, behold they come—a glorious convoy! I catch a sight
of them as they are holding a great review at the gates of
Paradise. And, ah! there is the golden gate. I enter in; and I
see my blessed Lord. I can tell you no more. All else were
things unlawful for flesh to utter. My Lord! I am with thee—
plunged into thee—lost in thee just as a drop is swallowed in
the ocean—as one single tint is lost in the glorious rainbow!
Am I lost in thee, thou glorious Jesus? And is my bliss
consummated? Is the wedding-day come at last? Have I really
put on the marriage garments? And am I thine? Yes! I am.
There is nought else now for me. In vain your harps, ye
angels. In vain all else. Leave me a little while. I will know
your heaven by-and-by. Give me some years, yea give me
some ages to lean here on this sweet bosom of my Lord; give
me half eternity, and let me bask myself in the sunshine of
that one smile. Yes; give me this. Didst speak, Jesus? "Yes, I
have loved thee with an everlasting love, and now thou art
mine! thou art with me." Is not this heaven? I want nought
else. I tell you once again, ye blessed spirits, I will see you
by-and-by. But with my Lord I will now take my feast of loves.
Oh, Jesus! Jesus! Jesus! Thou art heaven! I want nought else.
I am lost in thee!

Beloved, is not this to go to "the grave in full age, like as a
shock of corn," fully ripe? The sooner the day shall come, the
more we shall rejoice. Oh, tardy wheels of time! speed on your
flight. Oh, angels, wherefore come ye on with haggard wings?
Oh! fly through the ether and outstrip the lightning's flash!

Why may I not die? Why do I tarry here? Impatient heart, be quiet a little while. Thou art not fit for heaven yet, else thou wouldst not be here. Thou hast not done thy work, else thou wouldst have thy rest. Toil on a little longer; there is rest enough in the grave. Thou shalt have it there. On! on!

> "With my scrip on my back, and my staff in my hand,
> I'll march on in haste thro' an enemy's land.
> Though the way may be rough it cannot be long;
> So I'll smooth it with hope, and I'll cheer it with song."

My dear friends, you who are not converted, I have no time to say anything to you this morning. I wish I had. But I pray that all I have said may be yours. Poor hearts, I am sorry I cannot tell you this is yours now. I would I could preach to every one of you, and say that you all shall be in heaven. But God knoweth there are some of you that are on the road to hell; and do not suppose you will enter heaven, if you go hell's road. Nobody would expect, if he proceeded to the north, to arrive at the south. Nay; God must change thine heart. By simple trust in Jesus, if thou givest thyself up to his mercy, even though the vilest of the vile, thou shalt sing before his face. And methinks, poor sinner, thou wilt say to me, as a poor woman did last Wednesday, after I had been preaching, when I believe everybody had been crying, from the least to the greatest, and even the preacher in the pulpit. As I went down, I said to one, "Are you chaff or wheat?" And she said, "Ah! I trembled to-night, sir." I said to another, "Well, sister, I hope we shall be in Paradise soon." And she replied, "*You* may, sir." And I came to another, and said, "Well, do you think you will be gathered with the wheat?" And she answered, "One thing I can say—if God ever lets me get into heaven I will praise him with all my might. I will sing myself away and shall never think I can sing loud enough." It reminded me of what an old disciple once said; "If the Lord Jesus does but save me he shall never hear the last of it." Let us praise God, then, eternally—

> " While life, or thought, or being lasts,
> Or immortality endures!"

Now may the Three-One God dismiss you with his blessing.

7

Three Blessings of the Heavenly Charter

"Thou hast granted me life and favour, and thy visitation hath preserved my spirit." **Job 10:12**

It is well sometimes to sit down, and take a grateful review of all that God has done for us, and with us, from our first day until now. We must not be like hogs under the oak, that eat the acorns, but never thank the tree, or the Lord who made it to grow. We must not receive the dew, and yet never think of the heaven from which it comes. To be ungrateful, is to be unmanly; to be ungrateful to God, is to commit high treason against the majesty of his goodness. I think that an hour would be well spent, by any person here, in sitting quite alone, and going over his autobiography. Turn over the pages of your diary; if you have none written, turn over the pages of your memory, and think of all that God has done for you from the day when you hung upon your mother's breast until the present moment.

> "Streams of mercy never ceasing,
> Call for songs of loudest praise."

But God does not hear the songs of praise because we let the streams of mercy glide by unnoticed. Far too often, we—

> "Let his mercies lie,
> Forgotten in unthankfulness,
> And without praises die."

We do not even put a tombstone over their graves; but let them lie as dead things, uncared for, forgotten, out of mind.

If there is any time when it is unlikely for us to think of God's mercies, but when it would be specially wise for us to do so, if there is one time more unlikely than another, it is when we are in great trouble. Here is poor Job, covered with sore boils, sitting on a dunghill, scraping himself with a bit of a broken pot, with his children dead, his property destroyed, and even his wife not giving him a word of comfort, and his friends acting in a most unfriendly manner. Now it is that he talks to his God, and says, "Thou hast granted me life and favour, and thy visitation hath preserved my spirit." You are very ill; think of the time when you were well. You are poor; remember when you washed your feet in milk, and your steps with butter, and had more than heart could wish. Friends have forsaken you; recollect when you had plenty of friends. "Oh!" say you, "that will be rubbing salt into the wound." No, no, I trust not. You will remember that you were not always unhappy, that you were not always full of pain; God has spared your life, and given you many favours. If you do not feel that you can bless him for the present moment, yet forget not to bless him for the past; and when you once begin to do that, you will soon find that your praise will overlap the past, and cover the present, if it does not even run into the future. Only begin to praise God, and you will find that he who praises God for mercy will never be long without a mercy for which to praise him. I therefore invite those of you who are sad to-night to think of God's past goodness; and, as I trust that the larger proportion here will not be found in that condition, I urge you to lead the way in taking a happy retrospect to-night of all that God has done for you in providence and grace.

Job gives us here a charter with three blessings in it; "Thou hast granted me life and favour, and thy visitation hath preserved my spirit." These are choice favours; as we dwell upon them, may our hearts gratefully bless God for all that he has done for us!

I. The first blessing of this heavenly charter is LIFE: "Thou hast granted me life."

Well, I think that *we ought to thank God that we have lived at all.* I know the pessimist version of the psalm of life is that, "Tis something better not to be." Perhaps it would have been something better if that gentleman had not been, better, I should think, for his wife and family if they had not had to live with such a miserable creature. But the most of us thank God for our being, as well as for our well-being. We count it something not to be stones, or plants, or "dumb, driven cattle." We are thankful to be intelligent beings, with powers of thought, and capable of mental and spiritual enjoyment.

Truly, O Lord, it is no small thing to be, even to be a man; for what is man? Well, with all his sin, yet as thou didst make him, when he had no sin, he was but a little lower than the angels, and thou didst make him to have dominion over all the works of thy hands. Thou hast made him immortal. Thou hast made him a king; thou hast crowned him with glory and honour: and if he does but know his destiny, and work it out aright, thou hast made him to be glorified with thyself; thou hast made him to stand even higher than the angels now that thou hast redeemed him, for he has tasted of a love which unfallen angels could not know. If you choose to make your being to be your eternal curse, why, you must do it, I suppose; but not without our tears; but if you are rational beings, and use your reason reasonably, you will thank God that you live, and pray that your life may always be a blessing to you.

But *we also thank God that we have lived on in spite of many perils.* There are some here who ought very much to thank God that they live on after the perils through which they have passed. It was something to find ourselves alive after the terrible thunderstorm of the week before last. It is something to be alive after an earthquake, or a tremendous storm at sea, or to be alive in the midst of a pestilence, or alive after a battle, to be alive after some fearful accident, to be alive, I say, when there are so many gates to the grave.

> "The rising morning can't assure
> That we shall end the day;
> For death stands ready at the door
> To take our lives away."

And yet, despite all these things, we are still here. Some of you, not long ago, were very ill; it was thought that you would die; you thought so yourself, you were brought very low; and yet here you are. While others have died, you are still spared. You went hard by the gates of death, and seemed to look into eternity for a while; but you were allowed to pass on, and you are yet among the living, to praise God, as I hope you are doing this very day. Yes, it is God's grace that has granted us life. I find that, in the Hebrew, it reads, "lives" as if we had several lives, as though, if we had not had many lives, we should not have had any life at this moment. But life upon life has come to us, like wave upon wave at sea; and whereas one might have washed us on the shore of death, another has carried us back to the sea of life again, and still we live.

I am addressing some from whom our text asks for gratitude because *they are alive notwithstanding constitutional weakness.* Perhaps from a child you were always feeble. Oftentimes you have said to yourself, "How is it that I have lived? Strong and hearty men and women have died before me; and I, who have been always ailing, find that the creaking door hangs long on its hinges." Well, do not creak more than you can help; but bless God that you are not taken off the hinges. It is really very marvellous how some live even to old age when every day they seem to be on the very verge of departure. We account for their continued life by this fact, that they can say with Job, "Thou hast granted me life." Let us praise God, then, even if we can only do it with a feeble tongue, for it is something still to live.

And I am speaking to a great many here to whom this text should commend itself because *they have lived so long.* I suppose that, in no other place in London, or perhaps in the world, is there so large a number of old men and women gathered together as in this Tabernacle. One is often struck with the snow that lies about this place on the heads of so many. Do not blame us for getting old. We were all young together; and I remember that many here were introduced into the church as young men and young women. Nearly forty years ago they said of me, "He takes into the church a parcel of boys and girls." Well, they have been cured of that fault, if it was a fault, long ago; and now, perhaps, some will complain that they are old. We do not complain; we are so much nearer heaven; but when I look upon some dear friends here, who have passed even their four-score years, who have quite run out their lease, and now are living upon sufferance, as I trust they may for years to come, and when I remember what a poor tottering fabric this tent-body of ours is, I am amazed that we still live on.

> "Our life contains a thousand springs,
> And dies if one be gone;
> Strange that a harp of thousand strings,
> Should keep in tune so long."

Yet it has kept in tune so long, and we ought to bless God to-night, those of us who are somewhere between fifty and a hundred, and others who are somewhere between sixty and two hundred, ought to bless God to-night that they have been spared so long, and say, in the language of the text, "Thou hast granted me life and favour." You need not be frightened about that two hundred that I mentioned; you will not any of you be likely to reach that figure. If any of us live for a century, we shall have done exceedingly well; we may thank God if we do not live as long as that, for, while it is well to live here, it is better for us, after all, before our infirmities multiply, to be up and away to our Father's house above.

Think of this a little longer, "Thou hast granted me life." You have thought of the perils through which you have passed, and the weaknesses that you have survived. Now think, beloved friends, of *the sin which might have provoked God to make an end of such a guilty life.* Am I not speaking to some here who have lived without any thought of God, their Maker? Up till this time, God has fed you, and preserved you in being, and yet you have not even given him a thought. It is a wonderful thing that he should have spared your life in the midst of such wicked ingratitude. Perhaps, my friend,—I hope it is not so,—but perhaps you have been worse than this, and that mouth of yours has uttered blasphemies, and the members of your body have been given over to uncleanness. If you will look back to-night, it will be a wonder to you, that you, perhaps professedly an atheist, possibly a drunkard, it may be setting an ill example to wife and children, and doing evil on all sides, have been spared. One seems to say, "Cut down that upas tree, it drips with poison;" but God puts by the axe, and he still spares you. Did you not this very day imprecate a curse upon yourself, and yet the curse has not come? There was a tract that used to be given away, and which did much good; it was called, "The Swearer's Prayer." If every swearer would look upon his dreadful imprecation as a prayer, for such it is, he might well wonder that God has not, long ago, blasted him, as he has said, like some oak of the forest, that we have seen struck by lightning, standing there with its stag's-horn branches high in the air, a monument of what divine judgment can do. God has granted you life, yet nothing in that life has been pleasing to him, or good for your fellow-men. Thank him that he has not yet cut you down as a cumberer of the ground.

But even if I speak to the best man and woman here, to those who have tried to be useful, and are endeavouring to be holy, yet, dear friends, what poor failures we are after all! There is not one of us who can boast; we have to lay our hands upon our mouths, and bow ourselves into the very dust. Truly, Lord, thou hast let us live, although we have done so little, and done that little so faultily; we can to-night praise thee, and each one say, "Thou hast granted me life."

I might thus continue to show you that our preservation in life is a theme for great gratitude: "Thou hast granted me life." But if we can say this in a higher sense, "Thou hast granted me life," *spiritual life,* how much greater should our gratitude be! I could not even feel the guilt of sin, I was so dead; but thou hast granted me life to repent. I could not look to Jesus as my Saviour, and find rest in him; but thou has granted me life to believe in him. Oh, what a mercy it is to have spiritual life! I do not like to ask you whether you have it; I do not think that that ever ought to be a matter of question with anybody. A man is either alive or dead, and he must know which he is; and however faint and feeble he may be, the very feeling of faintness and feebleness is a sign of life, for the dead man does not even feel that. If, to-night, you have only life enough with which to groan, to weep, and to cry to God, thank God for it, and say, "Thou hast granted me life;" but if you have that little life, do not be satisfied with it. Pray to have life more abundantly, that you may come to joy and peace through believing, that you may have the full assurance of faith, that you may be strong in the Lord and in the power of his might, that you may tread down sin, and may serve the Lord in your day and generation, and bring hundreds and thousands to Christ. Pray that it may be so; and then, as each single increase of power comes to you, sing, in the words of the patriarch, "Thou hast granted me life." Oh, for more life! Do you feel dull and dead tonight? Cry to God to grant you life. Cry for grace, and then, when it comes, gratefully say, "Thou hast granted me life."

II. The second blessing of this heavenly charter is DIVINE FAVOUR: "Thou hast granted me life and favour."

Have you ever thought of the many favours that God has bestowed upon you, even upon some of you who as yet have never tasted of his grace? What a favour it is to many to be *sound in body!* Dear friends are here to-night, who have not seen the light of the sun for many a day. God is gracious to them in their blindness; but do you not think that we ought to praise him for our eyesight? There are many beloved Christian friends, who used to sit on this lower platform, and around here, for although they were deaf, they could hear my voice in the preaching of the gospel, and with great sorrow they have come to me one by one, and said, "I cannot even hear with the trumpet now, I am getting so deaf." Bless God for your ears, if you still have the use of them; and take heed how you hear. Why, there is not a single faculty that God has given but what we ought to be thankful for it! When you see around you those who are crippled, those who are deprived of one limb or one sense, should you not say, "Thou hast granted me life and favour"? They have favours, too, for which to thank God; but you have this particular favour which is denied to them. Do not fail to thank the Lord for it. It is a great mercy to have been born of good and honest parents, and not to be the inheritors of disease, as some are who are born to a life of sorrow by no fault of their own. Be grateful for your ancestry, young man, if you have sprung of good sound stock, and say, "Thou hast granted me life and favour." Do not go and give that body to the devil, I beseech you. Do not go and yourself plunge into vice and sin if God has restrained your ancestors from evil. By his grace, may you also be kept back, and enabled to say, "Thou hast granted me life and favour, and I cannot sin against thy favour"!

I cannot help reminding you here of the great favour of God in the matter of *soundness of mind.* There is a dear friend, who has gladly heard the preaching of the gospel here, but now he has to be confined in an asylum, for it would be dangerous to have him at liberty. There is another, and we often meet with such, who seemed as cheerful and happy as any of us, but he has now sunk into deep despondency. I have often prayed God to let me go anywhere sooner than into an asylum. It seems so dreadful to lose one's reason. Be grateful that you have your senses. Surely you must be lunatics already if you do not bless God that you are not lunatics. There must be a madness in your heart if you do not thank him for sparing you from so terrible a trial. These favours are looked upon as very common things, a sound mind and a sound body; but if they were universal, they would still be mercies for which we ought specially to bless the name of the Lord.

I speak to many here to whom God has also given *a*

comfortable lot in life. You work, and you work pretty hard; but still you are not starved, and you are not ground to death by forced labour. There are many in this house of prayer who ought to be very grateful for the easy circumstances in which they are found. Why am I talking about these things? Why, because I want, by stirring you up to gratitude, to bind you with cords of thankfulness to God! Will you not thank him who has done so much as this for you? If you were suddenly brought into the deepest poverty, and the most painful sickness, and did not know where to lay your heads, you would then reproach yourselves to think that, when your lives were cast in pleasant places, and you had a goodly heritage, you were not more grateful and more obedient to the God of love.

Some here, too, some few, at any rate, have been favoured with *much prosperity.* O self-made men, do not begin to adore yourselves because you made yourselves; for if you made yourselves, you are poor sticks, I know. I would not trust myself to make myself, I should make an awful mess of myself. No, thank God for your prosperity, and devote your wealth to his service, who granted it to you. Grow not purse-proud; be not exalted above measure among your fellow-men. The more you have, the more you owe to God; therefore be humble, and be devoted to him who has treated you with so much favour.

And I may say to-night that, in this congregation, God has given you the favour of *hearing the gospel;* no mean favour, let me remind you. Multitudes, multitudes, multitudes are without it, perishing for lack of knowledge; and there are some who once heard the gospel who are now far removed from the sound of it. Friends who once used to join in our great assembly are now far away in those parts of South America where as yet there is no gospel teaching, or they are far away in the backwoods of America or Canada, or away in the bush in Australia, where, as yet, the message of mercy is not, at any rate, regularly brought to them; and they very much miss the means of grace. Be thankful that you have the gospel at almost every street corner; and if you are willing to hear it, you may hear it.

Still, putting all these things together, they do not come up to this last point, that many of us have received *the favours of saving grace:* "Thou hast granted me life and favour." The highest favours of all God has given to some of us, the favour of being chosen to be his from before the foundation of the world, the favour of being redeemed from among men, the favour of being called out by his effectual grace, the favour of being renewed in the spirit of our minds, the favour of justification, whereby we are made accepted in the Beloved, the favour of full, free, irreversible pardon, whereby our sin is blotted out for ever, the favour of a throne of grace, the favour of answered prayer, the favour of divine providence, which makes all things work together for our good, the favour of the indwelling of the Holy Spirit, who is with us, and shall abide in us for ever. I cannot run over the list of God's favours to his people, for it is too long. Only praise your God, each one of you, as you say tonight, "Thou hast granted me life and favour." Happy people, thrice-happy people, of whom this is true! If we did not praise the Lord, the stones in the street might well cry out against us.

III. The last blessing of the charter, upon which I shall be a little longer, is DIVINE VISITATION: "Thy visitation hath preserved my spirit." Does God ever come to man? Does he not? Yes; but it is a great wonder: "What is man, that thou art mindful of him? And the son of man that thou visitest him?"

May I remind some of you of how much you ought to praise God for his visitation? He visited you, first, *with an arousement and conviction of sin.* I remember when his Spirit came to me while I was yet a child, and made me feel a heavy burden on account of my childish sins. How I wept and cried, when alone, because I had been so guilty before God! And as a youth, that feeling still pursued me wherever I went. God visited me in the night, visited me often in the morning, when I woke up before anybody else, to read Baxter's "Call to the Unconverted," and Alleine's "Alarm," and such-like books, over which I pored again and again, feeling the evil of my sin, and having the sword of the Spirit piercing yet more deeply into my conscience at every page I read. I thank God for those early visitations. If any of you are having them now, quench not the Spirit of God. Be glad to know your real state as sinners while you are yet young. The visitations of God, in the form of conviction, if at first they bring us under bondage, are nevertheless of the utmost value, for by these he preserves our spirit.

After that first experience, there came visitations of

enlightenment and conversion. Can you remember when Jesus first visited you, and brought you up out of the horrible pit, and out of the miry clay? Does not your heart leap within you even now as you are ready to sing,—

> "Happy day! Happy day!
> When Jesus washed my sins away"?

Yes, God's visitations, by revealing Christ to your broken heart, preserved your spirit.

Perhaps since then you have had visitations of another kind. You have had *chastisement,* or you have had *affliction* in the house. God's visitations are sometimes very unwelcome. We dread that he should come to afflict or chastise us; and yet, in looking back upon all such experiences, I think that you can say, "Thy visitation hath preserved my spirit." I saw a young sister, just before this service; and I said to her, "When did you find the Lord?" She replied, "It was when I was very ill." Yes, it is often so; God makes us ill in body that we may have time to think of him, and turn to him. "Thy visitation hath preserved my spirit." What would become of some people if they were always in good health, or if they were always prospering? But tribulation is the black dog that goes after the stray sheep, and barks them back to the Good Shepherd. I thank God that there are such things as the visitations of correction and of holy discipline, to preserve our spirit, and bring us to Christ.

But then, dear friends, we have had other visitations, visitations of *revival and restoration.* Do you not sometimes get very dull and dead? Then you are glad to go and hear a sermon, or you read some godly, soul-stirring book, or you meet with some Christian friend, and you say afterwards, "Well, I do not know how it is, but I seem quite different from what I was; I have made a new departure, I have started off again." I think that some of our friends have need to do that to-night; it will not hurt any of us if we all seem to begin again to-night, and take Jesus Christ into our heart once more, and let him come as he came at the first, and be like a new Christ to us. Let us joy and rejoice in him with our first love and our early delights. Lord, give us that visitation to-night, and revive our spirits! Oh, what visitations of joy he sometimes gives us when he comes very near to us! We do not hardly know how to bear it; we cry when the vessel gets quite full,

"Hold, Lord, I cannot bear more of joy." "Ah!" say you, "we do not know much about that experience." Do you not? Then, pray the Lord to visit you often, that you may know more about it.

The best of all is, *when the Lord visits us, and never goes away;* but stays with us always, so that we walk in the light of his countenance, and go from strength to strength, singing always, "Thy visitation never ended, daily continued, preserves my spirit." You have all heard the phrase, generally used by juries at a coroner's inquest, when a man has died suddenly, "Died by the visitation of God." No doubt some do thus die; but I want you to live by the visitation of God. That is a very different thing, and that is the only way in which we truly can live, by God's visiting us from day to day, so preserving our spirit from the dangers that surround us. Live, then, by the visitation of God.

You are sick, my friend; your heart is sick. Sin, like a grievous disease, is destroying you. The cancer of an evil habit is eating into your very vitals. What is to be done with you? Nothing but that Jesus Christ the Lord should come and give you a gracious visitation, come and look you in the face, and feel your pulse, and lay his hand on your heart, and change it, and make you a new creature; and he will do all that if you send for him. Doctors have a night-bell, you know, and a night-tube, by which they may be called in cases of urgency. Now ring God's night-bell at once, and speak up that tube of prayer, "Lord, I am sick unto death; come and heal me. Come and heal me." Will not somebody in these pews now, without the use of a word, yet say in the silence of his heart, "Lord, I am sore vexed; I am sick unto death with sin; come and heal me"? and Jesus Christ will say, "I will come and heal you." Then will you say, "Thy visitation hath preserved my spirit."

You know how a farm will sometimes get smothered with weeds, and things seem to go all wrong. What is the matter? On enquiry, you find that the farmer has been out on the Continent, he has been away from his farm. Well, then, of course the farm goes wrong; but have him back again, and the farmer's eye does more than his hand; his foot manures the ground wherever he stands; and things soon get on better. Now, if the farm of your nature has fallen into a bad state, you want the Husbandman back; you need the Lord Jesus to come and survey the estate, and give directions as to what is to be done to it. He will soon set the whole place to rights. Yea, if your farm has become like a desert, bare as the palm of your hand, he can come and turn it to fertility; he can make the wilderness like Eden, and the desert like the garden of the Lord. A visitation from the Lord Jesus Christ is what we all want when we are barren and dead.

May we expect it? Yes, he came on a visit here once. We did not see him when he came, but there were some who saw him. You remember how George Herbert quaintly sings of his laying aside his azure mantle, and making the sky with it; and taking off his bright rings, and hanging them up as stars.

> "He did descend, undressing all the way,
> And when they asked what he would wear;
> He smiled, and said as he did come,
> He had new clothes a-making here below."

And poor clothes they were, when he was born of the Virgin, and lived in our inferior clay. He paid us a visit, but men did not let him lodge comfortably. There was no room for him in the inn. It was a sorry entertainment that they gave him, for they pierced his side ere he went away, and he carried with him the marks in his hands and feet that he had received in the house of his friends. Well, but still, having once come, and died on this earth, he knows the way; and as he cannot die again, he will come again; and now, to-night, in spirit, by his Spirit, he will come to you, if you only cry to him, "Come." If you cry to him, "Come," to-night, that will be only the echo of what he says, "Come unto me, all ye that labour and are heavy laden." He cries, "Come," catch up that word, and say, "Come." Echo his "Come" by your own "Come"; and you two will meet before the service is over, though we have reached the last few minutes of it. May your "Come" and Christ's "Come" blend in one! Come, Lord Jesus, even so, come quickly, and set thy poor servants free from the taint of sin, and from the dread of the wrath of God! Yes, you want a visitation from him who has come already; and beside that, he has sent his Holy Spirit to abide until he himself descends from heaven with a shout. The Holy Ghost is here in this assembly now; plead and cry to him for his visitation.

And if my Lord will come anywhere to-night, it is to you who think yourselves unfit for him to come to you, to you who would give your eyes to have him, but scarcely dare to hope that he will ever come to you. The Lord says, "To this man will I look, even to him that is poor and of a contrite spirit, and trembleth at my word." Do you not belong to that kind of people, trembling at God's Word, wishing only that you dared to hope in his mercy? Come now, and cast yourselves on Jesus; come now, and trust yourselves with the great Saviour, who has ascended on high, to give repentance and remission of sins, and who is ready to give both the repentance and the remission to every soul that is willing to have them. If you would have them, they are yours. Believe for eternal life. Believe now. The Lord grant you such a visitation that you may be constrained to believe, for Jesus' sake! Amen and Amen.

8

Comfort From the Future

"Because thou shalt forget thy misery, and remember it as waters that pass away."   **Job 11:16**

Job's misery was extreme, and it seemed as if he could never forget it. He never did forget the fact of it, but he did forget the pain of it. That he had been utterly miserable, would always remain recorded upon the tablets of his memory; but the wretchedness itself would not remain. It would be so entirely removed that it should be as a thing that has been altogether forgotten. Nothing better can happen to our misery than that it should be forgotten in the sense referred to in our text; for then, evidently, it will be clean gone from us. It will be as it is when even the scent of the liquor has gone out of the cask, when even the flavour of the bitter drug lingers no longer in the medicine glass, but has altogether disappeared. So is it with the sorrow that has so effectually gone out of the mind that it is just as though it had never been there.

If anyone here is in misery of any kind,—whether it be misery of physical pain, or misery of want, or misery of soul on account of sin, or the loss of the light of God's countenance,—I can only pray for you, dear friend, that you may speedily forget your misery, and only remember it as waters that pass away. The things goes to be done; it is quite possible, and you may expect it. If you look carefully at the connection of our text, and give earnest attention to the matter, I do not doubt that you will experience this blessed forgetfulness. When we are in pain of body, and depression of spirit, we imagine that we never shall forget such misery as we are enduring. The sharp ploughshare has gone down so deeply that we think it has made a mark in the soul that can never be erased. We seem to lie all broken in pieces, with our thoughts like a case of knives cutting into our spirit; and we say to ourselves, "We never shall forget this terrible experience." And yet, by-and-by, God turns towards us the palm of his hand, and we see that it is full of mercy, we are restored to health, or uplifted from depression of spirit, and we wonder that we ever made so much of our former suffering or depression. We remember it no more, except as a thing that has passed and gone, to be recollected with gratitude that we have been delivered from it, but not to be remembered so as to leave any scar upon our spirit, or to cause us any painful reflection whatsoever. "Thou shalt forget thy misery, and remember it as waters that pass away."

I. I am not going to limit the application of the text to Job and his friends, for it has also a message for many of us at the present time; and I shall take it, first, WITH REFERENCE TO THE COMMON TROUBLES OF LIFE WHICH AFFECT BELIEVING MEN AND WOMEN.

These troubles of life happen to us all more or less. They come to one in one shape, and perhaps he thinks that he is the only man who has any real misery; yet they also come to others, though possibly in another form. There is certainly a cross for every shoulder to bear; Simon must not bear the cross alone, and all the rest go free. There is no road to heaven without its stones, or without its Hill Difficulty; and I think that there are few pilgrims from the City of Destruction who get to the Celestial City without passing through the Valley of Death-shade, and having to fight with giants and even with Apollyon himself. Cowper truly wrote,—

> "The path of sorrow, and that path alone,
> Leads to the land where sorrow is unknown."

There is much joy in true religion. Wisdom's "ways are ways of pleasantness, and all her paths are peace. She is a tree of life to them that lay hold upon her: and happy is every one that retaineth her." But, still, notwithstanding the joy, and in addition to it, there is sorrow; there is misery lurking close by the believer's pathway, and it is ever ready to pounce upon him somewhere between here and heaven. The Lord of the pilgrims was "a man of sorrows and acquainted with grief;" and his disciples must expect to fare even as their Master fared while here below; it is enough for the servant if he be as his Lord.

You, dear friends, who are just now enduring misery,

should seek to be comforted under it. Perhaps you will ask
me, "Where can we get any comfort?" Well, if you cannot draw
any from your present experience, seek to gather some from
the past. You have been miserable before, but you have been
delivered and helped. There has come to you a most
substantial benefit from everything which you have been
called to endure. You must be conscious that, when you think
of your troubles, you can say, with Hezekiah, "O Lord, by
these things men live, and in all these things is the life of my
spirit: so wilt thou recover me, and make me to live." Or you
can say, with the psalmist, "Before I was afflicted I went
astray: but now have I kept thy word." I believe that, very
often, God sends his very choicest love-tokens to us in black-
edged envelopes; and many a time has it happened that the
great rumbling waggons of tribulation have been those which
have brought the heaviest weight of treasure to the doors of
the saints. Do we ever learn much without the rod? I fear we
do not; most of us are quickest learners, I think, when we
smart most. Well, then, if affliction has been profitable in the
past, let us rest assured that it will be so in the future.

Let us gather consolation also from the future. If, as the
apostle truly says, "No chastening for the present seemeth to
be joyous, but grievous," recollect how he goes on to say,
"Nevertheless afterward it yieldeth the peaceable fruit of
righteousness unto them which are exercised thereby." I have
been trying to ring the changes on those two words, during
the last few weeks, while I have been laid aside by illness:
"nevertheless afterward"—"nevertheless afterward"— "nevertheless afterward it yieldeth the peaceable fruit of
righteousness unto them which are exercised thereby." The
apostle James tells us that "the husbandman waiteth for the
precious fruit of the earth, and hath long patience for it, until
he receive the early and latter rain." He does not complain
because his corn is buried under the clods, and covered with
the snow; but he lives upon hope, and rejoices in the future
harvest, pleading the promise, "He that goeth forth and
weepeth, bearing precious seed, shall doubtless come again
with rejoicing, bringing his sheaves with him." In your own
case, dear friend, if you are a believer in the Lord Jesus
Christ, what will happen in the future? For it is with that I
would comfort you at this time. Why, this is what will happen:
"Thou shalt forget thy misery, and remember it as waters

that pass away." How will that be?

Well, first, by *the lapse of time.* Time is a wonderful healer. Hearts, that seem as if they must break when first the trial comes, at last grow quite used to it. Look through the veil of a few minutes, gaze through the longer vista of a few years, and that which seemed dark as tempest wears quite another aspect. Oh, if you, whose hearts seem now almost ready to burst, could but project yourselves only six months ahead, if you could leap forward a year, and then look back, probably even in that time you would almost have forgotten your misery.

Ay, but there is something better than the lapse of years, and that is when, *during a considerable time, you are left without trial.* That is a sharp pain you are now enduring; but what if you should have years of health afterwards? Then you will forget your misery. That is a sad loss which you have been called to suffer, it seems to you to be a crushing disaster, but what if it should be succeeded by years of prosperity? Remember how Job forgot his misery when, in a short time, he had double as much of all that he possessed as he had before. He had back twice the amount of all his former wealth, he had again a smiling family around him, so he might well forget his misery. Year after year, and, perhaps, even to his death,—it was so as far as we know,—Job was again a man who had a hedge made round about him and all that he had, and in the happiness of his later life he might well forget his former misery. Well, now, it is very likely to be so with you after you get through this present struggle; therefore, keep your heart up, believe in God, have confidence in him, and all shall be well. There is wonderfully smooth sailing on ahead for some of you when you are once over this little stretch of broken water. If you can safely pass over this stony portion of the road, it will be good travelling for you all the way to heaven. Recollect that the horses' heads are towards home, you are journeying to your Father's house, so be of good courage, for you shall forget your misery, and only remember it as waters that pass away.

And besides the lapse of time, and an interval of rest and calm, it may be—it probably is the fact with God's people— that *he has in store for you some great mercies.* When the Lord turns your captivity, you will be like them that dream; and you know what happens to men who dream. They wake up;

their dream is all gone, they have completely forgotten it. So will it be with your sorrow. Through God's goodness, you will seem suddenly to wake up out of a dreary dream, and then you will begin to laugh, and soon your mouth will be filled with laughter. You will almost despise your former depression of spirit; and when you see the abundant mercy of God toward you, all your misery shall seem like a dream that has gone, a vision of the night—unsubstantial, unreal,—that has melted into nothingness. Some of you have no idea what is reserved for you; you would not be weeping, but laughing, if you did know what God has in store for you,—I mean, even here below. It is good for us not to be able to read the roll closed by the hand of God; but we may be sure that there are such blessed things in it concerning our future that each believer may well say, "I will not be bowed down by the trials of the present, but my spirit shall rejoice in God, who doeth for me what eye hath not seen, nor ear heard, and what my heart hath never conceived."

Be of good courage, brother, sister, in these dark, dull times, for, mayhap, this text is God's message to thy soul, "Thou shalt forget thy misery, and remember it as waters that pass away." It has been so with many, many, many believers in the past. What do you think of Joseph sold for a slave, Joseph falsely accused, Joseph shut up in prison? But when Joseph found out that all that trial was the way to make him ruler over all the land of Egypt, and that he might be the means of saving other nations from famine, and blessing his father's house, I do not wonder that he called his elder son "Manasseh." What does that name mean? "Forgetfulness"— "for God, said he, hath made me forget all my toil, and all my father's house." Why, sitting on the throne there, feeding the nation, and blessing his father and his brethren, he must have thought that the being cast into the pit, and being sold to the Ishmaelites, and being put into prison, was not worth recollecting, except for gratitude to God that it ever happened as a means to the grand end of helping him up into that position of usefulness. And Joseph is not the only one who has had such an experience as that. Read the Scriptures through, and you will find that those whom God has called and anointed to eminent service have been put, like the blades of Damascus, into the fire, and drawn through the fire again and again, that in the day of battle they might strike on the northern iron and steel, and yet not turn their edge. These servants of the Lord have been prepared for an immortal destiny by desperate griefs; and—

"The deeper their sorrows, the louder they'll sing."

As a woman remembereth no more her travail, for joy that a man is born into the world, so has it happened to the believer in the time of his sorrow; he has forgotten it, cast it all away, because of the greater joy which God has brought out of it. Jabez is the child of sorrow, but he is therefore more honourable than his brethren. The more stormy the sea, the sweeter the haven. The rougher the road on earth, the better the rest above. So, poor tried child of God, believe that this text is intended to be a divine message of comfort to thy heart, "Thou shalt forget thy misery, and remember it as waters that pass away."

Thus much on the first head.

II. I should be greatly rejoiced if, in the second place, I might speak A CHEERING WORD TO POOR SOULS UNDER DISTRESS ON ACCOUNT OF SIN. I mean you who long to be saved, yet cannot understand how it is to come to pass, or who, understanding the plan of salvation, are somehow unable to appropriate it to yourselves. You feel as if you have your eyes bandaged, and your feet fast fixed in the stocks, so that you cannot go to Christ, and cannot even look to Christ, and therefore your souls are full of sorrow. I want you, dear friends, specially to notice what Zophar recommends to a man who has sin upon him. Read the 13th, 14th, 15th, and 16th verses of this chapter: "If thou prepare thine heart, and stretch out thine hands toward him; if iniquity be in thine hand, put it far away, and let not wickedness dwell in thy tabernacles. For then shalt thou lift up thy face without spot; yea, thou shalt be stedfast, and shalt not fear: because thou shalt forget thy misery, and remember it as waters that pass away." I recommend these words to you also; only I have something even better to recommend to you. Does any man here say, "I cannot get peace with God; I am full of misery on account of sin?" I know all about you, friend; I have gone that road, long ago. I have been splashed up to my very eyes in the mire of the Slough of Despond; and I sometimes get a little of its mud in my eyes even now.

Well, now, I exhort you, first of all, to *look to Christ, and lean on Christ.* Trust in his atoning sacrifice, for there alone can a troubled soul find rest. If you say that, somehow, you cannot get peace, then I shall have to ask you to see whether, perhaps, sin may not be lying at the door. To use Zophar's expression, have you prepared your heart? Have you gone to Christ with your whole heart and soul? Have you sought him with all your might? I hope you realize that repentance and faith are very bad things to play with, for such play will damn a man's soul. These are things to be earnestly used in a most solemn undertaking. "The kingdom of heaven suffereth violence" in this matter. We can neither repent nor believe with half our heart; it is our whole soul that is required if salvation is to be ours. Now, hast thou sought the Lord with all thy heart? If thou hast, thou wilt surely find him. I am certain that thou wilt; and then, afterwards, "thou shalt forget thy misery, and remember it as waters that pass away." There was never a man yet who, with all his heart, did seek the Lord Jesus Christ, but sooner or later found him; and if you have been long in seeking, I lay it to the fact that you have not sought with a prepared heart, a thoroughly earnest heart, or else you would have found him.

But, perhaps, taking Zophar's next expression, you have not stretched out your hands toward the Lord, giving yourself up to him like a man who holds up his hands to show that he surrenders. You must come and say, "My opposition is all over; I have no quarrel now with God; I yield unconditionally to him." The word may refer to one who stretches out his hands to grasp whatever may come from God within his reach. He stretches out his empty hands, asking to have them filled; stretches out his entreating hands, pleading that God will bless him. Well now, if you have done that, you shall get a blessing.

Further, you may and you shall forget your misery, provided you fulfil one more condition mentioned by Zophar, and that is, that you are not harbouring any sin: "If iniquity be in thine hand, put it far away, and let not wickedness dwell in thy tabernacles." There is an old-fashioned grace that I am never ashamed to preach, though some, who call themselves evangelists, have folded it up, and put it away in the back cupboard; they never mention this old-fashioned grace, which is called repentance. Now, I learn from the

Scriptures that repentance is just as necessary to salvation as faith is; and the faith that has not repentance going with it will have to be repented of one of these days. A dry-eyed faith is a faith that will save no man. Peter's message was, "Repent ye, therefore, and be converted, that your sins may be blotted out;" and our Lord's own declaration was, "Except ye repent, ye shall all likewise perish." He began his public ministry by crying, "Repent ye, and believe the gospel," which means just this, that if any man is living in sin, it is no use his praying, or pretending to believe, until he gives up that sin. If there is any passion that you are indulging, any lust that is your master,—if you are carrying on a wicked business,—if you are living in wilful transgression of God's law, Christ can save you from your sins, but even Christ cannot save you in your sins. If you will have your sin, you must be lost, so stands God's decree. Christ must, by his grace, separate you from your sin, or else you will be separated from him for ever. I want this to be a very heart-searching word; and therefore I say to any miserable man or miserable woman here,—You shall forget your misery if you give up your sin, and trust in the sin-atoning Saviour. Come, friend, you shall not say that I am flattering you, for I tell you plainly that you must fly for your life from the dearest sin that now lays hold upon you.

"Oh!" you say, "but how am I to do it?" Christ will help you. Trust him to help you. But if you say, "I will trust him to save me," and yet continue to live in sin, he will not save you. That is not the salvation that we preach; we proclaim salvation from sin, for that is the salvation which Jesus came to bring to us. You must, as Zophar said to Job, put your iniquity far away, and you must not let wickedness dwell in your tabernacles; that is to say, in your tents, in your houses. I know some men, who will never get peace of conscience, and rest of heart, while they let their wives live as they do live, and while they allow their children to live as they do live. Some of you will not find mercy for yourselves while you neglect your children's highest welfare as you do. I know some men,—I hope they are good men, but certainly they are not good fathers. They are so peaceful, and gentle, that they never like to utter a word of reproof; their boys and girls may go where they like,—I might almost say that they may go to the devil if they like,—yet their father has not a word to say to them; do you call that proper conduct for a professedly

Christian man? There are some parents, who allow their
children to do such things that God is grieved with them for
their children's sakes; and they will never get peace of mind
till they set their house in order. What! is God coming to live
where there is no family prayer, where there is no care for his
name or his day, where there is no rebuke of open sin? It has
filled me with unspeakable sorrow when I have heard of
Christian parents whose boys swear, and whose girls are
allowed to go where, if they are not ruined, body and soul, it
is little short of a miracle. Oh, do see that you let not
wickedness dwell in your tabernacles, you who are the people
of God, and you who wish to be his, if you would have
Zophar's words to Job fulfilled in your experience, "Then shalt
thou lift up thy face without spot; yea, thou shalt be stedfast,
and shalt not fear: because thou shalt forget thy misery, and
remember it as waters that pass away."

III. Now let me tell you HOW SWEETLY GOD CAN MAKE A
SINNER FORGET HIS MISERY.

The moment a sinner believes in Jesus Christ with true
heart and repentant spirit, God makes him forget his misery,
first, *by giving him a full pardon.* All his sin is forgiven, and
therefore he feels ready to dance for joy, and he soon forgets
his misery. By faith, he gets a sight of the great, pardoning
Lord, and of his atoning blood. He sees the Son of God
suffering and dying for him on the tree, and he is overjoyed at
the revelation of such a wondrous redemption. He claps his
hands, and he forgets his misery.

Next, *he rejoices in all the blessings that God gives with his
grace.* He reads that those whom Christ has pardoned "are
justified from all things," from which they could not be
justified by the law of Moses. He learns that they are clothed
with the robe of Christ's perfect righteousness, and he forgets
his own nakedness while he rejoices that he is so wondrously
clothed. He feeds on the bread of heaven, and forgets his
former hunger. He drinks of the water of life, and forgets his
previous pangs of thirst. He enjoys the liberty of the sons of
God, and he forgets the chains he used to wear as Satan's
slave. He has peace with God, and he forgets the trouble that
was such a burden on his heart. He is so full of joy that there
is no room for sorrow; and if, perchance, the tear of
repentance still lingers in his eye, it is not sullen but sweet
sorrow, and the tear glistens in the sunlight of God's

countenance like the diamond, or like some choice pearl that
slumbers in its shell. Oh, beloved, if you will but come to
Christ, and leave your sin, whatever your misery is, you shall
forget it; or, if you do recollect it at all, it shall only be to
remember it as the snow that has melted and vanished, or as
the rain that has soaked into the earth, "as waters that pass
away."

Now, dear friends, all that I have been saying to the sinner
is quite as applicable to every backsliding child of God. It may
be that some of you who are here are Christians;—that is, you
have trusted in Christ to save you;—but you have got into a
very sad state of heart. You have not half the spiritual life
that you once had, and therefore you do not glorify God as you
once did. It is most grievous to think how many professing
Christians live at a poor dying rate; they seem to be just alive,
or hardly that. Well, dear brother or sister, if you have
become miserable, I am rather glad that you have. That is
part of the way towards a better state of things. When a man
cannot be happy in a backsliding state, he will soon seek to
get out of it. The smart is a part of the cure. Solomon says,
"The blueness of a wound cleanseth away evil"; and the
chastisement which follows sin is often for the healing of the
sinner.

IV. I will bring my discourse to a close with this last
reflection. THIS TEXT WILL COME TRUE TO THE SICKENING,
DECLINING, SOON-DEPARTING BELIEVER.

Ah! dear friend, when first you found out that the complaint
from which you are suffering really was consumption, what a
chill seemed to come over everything! When the physician
said to you, very tenderly but very faithfully, "I fear I cannot
do much for you. I can perhaps give you a little relief, but I
dare not deceive you, for you have an incurable disease;"—
then, although you are a child of God, you endured a great
deal of misery, and spent many long, sleepless nights looking
forward to you scarcely knew what. Are you still in that state,
my dear sister? As you get worse and worse, do your spirits
continue to sink? My dear brother, as you gradually fade
away, does the light seem to fade, too? Well, then, listen. If
thou hast believed in the Lord Jesus Christ, and if thou art
resting alone upon him, recollect that, in a very short time,
"thou shalt forget thy misery, and remember it as waters that
pass away." In a very, very, very short time, your suffering

and sadness will all be over. I suppose the expression, "waters that pass away," signifies those rivers which are common in the East, and which we meet with so abundantly in the South of France. They are rivers with very broad channels, but I have often looked in vain for a single drop of water in them. "Then," perhaps you ask, "what is the use of such rivers?" Well, at certain times, the mountain torrents come rushing down, bearing great rocks, and stones, and trees before them, and then, after they have surged along the river-bed for several days, they altogether disappear in the sea. Such will all the sorrows of life and the sorrows even of death soon be to you, dear friend, and to me also. They will all have passed away, and all will be over with us here. The passage to the grave may be sharp, but it must be short.

> "The road may be rough, but it cannot be long,
> So I'll smooth it with hope, and cheer it with song."

And then, you know, dear friends, those waters that have passed away will never come back again. Water that is spilt upon the ground can never be gathered up again, and it is one of the charms of the heavenly world that our sorrows will never reach us there. No more poverty, no more cold, no more heat, no more sin, no more depression of spirits, no more pain, no more forsaking of friends, no more sorrow of any kind, for "the ransomed of the Lord shall return, and come to Zion with songs and everlasting joy upon their heads: they shall obtain joy and gladness, and sorrow and sighing shall flee away." That is a very beautiful expression: "Sorrow and sighing shall flee away." Here, they keep clinging to us, one on one arm, and the other on the other arm. Sorrow and sighing will come with us wherever we go; and we sometimes say to them, "Now, you might go somewhere else, for we do not want you;" yet they still hold fast to us; but when we get up to the golden gate, no sooner shall the light eternal flash on our eyes than we shall look in vain for our old companions, for they will be gone. "Sorrow and sighing shall flee away"; and lest there should be any trace of their mournful companionship left, we are expressly told that "God shall wipe away all tears from their eyes; and there shall be no more death, neither sorrow, nor crying, neither shall there be any more pain: for the former things are passed away."

Thank God, we shall recollect our sorrows in heaven only to

praise God for the grace that sustained us under them; but we shall not remember them as a person does who has cut his finger, and who still bears the scar in his flesh. We shall not recollect them as one does who has been wounded, and who carries the bullet somewhere about him. In heaven, you shall not have a trace of earth's sorrow; you shall not have, in your glorified body, or in your perfectly sanctified soul and spirit, any trace of any spot, or wrinkle, or any such thing that shall show that you ever had a pang on earth, or even that you ever committed a sin. Some diseases, you know, leave marks on our hands or faces, so that we say to our friends, "Do you see that lump? It was a time of terrible pain that brought that up, and I fear it will not go away." Ah! but, in heaven, there will be no trace of anything like pain or sorrow of any sort. All sorrow and suffering shall be gone, and we shall forget our misery, or only remember it as waters that have passed away, never to come back again.

This is the sum and substance of all that I have been trying to say to you: "Be of good courage, and he shall strengthen your heart, all ye that hope in the Lord." Christian men do not live on the comforts of this world; their inheritance is on the other side of Jordan. If you are like Esau, and can be content with red pottage, well, you may have it; but you will lose the birthright if you do not prize it. But if you are God's true Jacob, you will gladly give up the pottage to get the promise of the future inheritance. Oh, what a blessed thing is the faith that enables the soul to postpone the present in order to obtain that blessed future! For what is the present, after all, but a fleeting show, an empty dream? But the future is eternal and incorruptible, reserved in heaven at the right hand of God, where there are pleasures for evermore.

Now that, by God's mercy, I find myself again in your midst after a season of sore suffering, I desire to forget my miseries, —and some of them have been very sharp ones. I am so glad to be here again, to see you all, and I pray that it may be a long time before I am deprived of the great privilege of speaking to you in the name of the Lord. I bless God to-night, and praise his name in the great congregation; and I ask for every brother and sister that, when your time of misery comes, you may be brought through it all, and come out of the big end of the horn, rejoicing in the cornucopia of God's bounty and blessedness, and praising his name, as I do at this time with all my heart. Oh, may every one of you find this text to be true to you, "Thou shalt forget thy misery, and remember it as waters that pass away"!

The blessing of the Lord be with you all for evermore! Amen.

9

Faith's Ultimatum

"Though he slay me, yet will I trust in Him..." **Job 13:15**

This is one of the supreme sayings of Scripture. It rises, like an alpine summit, clear above all ordinary heights of speech, it pierces the clouds, and glistens in the light of God. If I were required to quote a selection of the sublimest utterances of the human mind, I should mention this among the first: "Though he slay me, yet will I trust in him." Methinks I might almost say to the man who thus spoke what our Lord said to Simon Peter when he had declared him to be the Son of the Highest: "Flesh and blood hath not revealed this unto thee." Such tenacious holding, such immovable confidence, such unstaggering reliance are not products of mere nature, but rare flowers of rich almighty grace. The text contains a precious jewel of grace, fitly set in the purest gold of choice speech; happy is the man upon whose arm it can be worn as an ensign in the day of battle.

It is well worthy of observation that in these words Job answered both the accusations of Satan and the charges of his friends. Though I do not know that Job was aware that the devil had said, "Doth Job fear God for nought? Hast thou not set a hedge about him and all that he hath?" yet he answered that base suggestion in the ablest possible manner, for he did in effect say, "Though God should pull down my hedge, and lay me bare as the wilderness itself, yet will I cling to him in firmest faith." The arch-fiend had also dared to say that Job had held out under his first trials because they were not sufficiently personal; "skin for skin, yea, all that a man hath will he give for his life. But put forth thy hand now and touch his bone and his flesh, and he will curse thee to thy face." In the brave words before us Job most effectually silences that slander by, in effect, saying, "Though my trial be no longer the slaying of my children, but of myself, yet will I trust in him." He thus in one sentence replies to the two slanders of Satan; thus unconsciously doth truth overthrow her enemies, defeating the secret malice of falsehood by the simplicity of sincerity. Job's friends also had insinuated that he was a hypocrite. They inquired of him "Who ever perished, being innocent? or where were the righteous cut off?" They thought themselves quite safe in inferring that Job must have been a deceiver, or he would not have been so specially punished. To this accusation Job's grand declaration of his unstaggering faith was the best answer possible, for none but a sincere soul could thus speak. Will a hypocrite trust in God when he slays him? Will a deceiver cling to God when he is smiting him? Assuredly not. Thus were the three miserable comforters answered if they had been wise enough to see it.

Our text exhibits a child of God under the severest pressure, and shows us the difference between him and a man of the world. A man of the world under the same conditions as Job would have been driven to despair, and in that desperation would have become morosely sullen, or defiantly rebellious! Here you see what in a child of God takes the place of desperation. When others despair he trusts in God. When he has nowhere else to look he turns to his heavenly Father; and when for a time, even in looking to God, he meets with no conscious comfort, he waits in the patience of hope, calmly expecting aid, and resolving that even if it do not come he will cling to God with all the energy of his soul. Here all the man's courage comes to the front, not, as in the case of the ungodly, obstinately to rebel, but bravely to confide. The child of God is courageous, for he knows how to trust. His heart says, "Ay Lord, it is bad with me now, and it is growing worse, but should the worst come to the worst, still will I cling to thee, and never let thee go." In what better way can the believer reveal his loyalty to his Lord? He evidently follows his Master, not in fair weather only, but in the foulest and roughest ways. He loves his Lord, not only when he smiles upon him, but when he frowns. His love is not purchased by the largesses of his Lord's golden hand, for it is not destroyed by the smitings of his heavy rod. Though my Lord put on his sternest looks, though from fierce looks he should go to cutting words, and though from terrible words he should proceed to cruel blows, which seem to beat the very life out of my soul, yea, though he take down the sword and threaten to execute me therewith, yet is my heart steadfastly set upon one resolve, namely, to bear witness that he is infinitely good and just. I have not a word to say against him, nor a thought to think against him, much less would I wander from him; but still, though he slay me, I would trust in him.

What is my text but an Old Testament version of the New Testament, "Quis separabit?"—Who shall separate? Job does but anticipate Paul's question. "Who shall separate us from the love of Christ? shall tribulation, or distress, or persecution, or famine, or nakedness, or peril, or sword? Nay, in all these things we are more than conquerors through him that loved us. For I am persuaded, that neither death, nor life, nor angels, nor principalities, nor powers, nor things present, nor things to come, nor height, nor depth, nor any other creature, shall be able to separate us from the love of God, which is in Christ Jesus our Lord." Was not the same Spirit in both Job and Paul? Is he also in us? If so, we are men indeed, and our speech is with power, and to us this declaration is no idle boast, no foolish bravado, though it would be ridiculous, indeed, if there were not a gracious heart behind it to make it good. It is the conquering shout of an all-surrendering faith, which gives up all but God. I want that we may all have its spirit this morning, that whether we suffer Job's trial or not we may at any rate have Job's close adherence to the Lord, his faithful confidence in the Most High.

There are three things in the text: *a terrible supposition*—"though he slay me"; *a noble resolution*, "yet will I trust in him"; and, thirdly, *a secret appropriateness.* This last will require a little looking into, but I hope to make it clear that there is a great appropriateness in our trusting while God is slaying us—the two things go well together, though it may not so appear.

I. First, then, here is A TERRIBLE SUPPOSITION—"though he slay me." The Lord is here set forth as a slayer of his trusting servant. An idea full of terror. *It is a supposition which in some senses cannot be tolerated for a minute*—"Though he slay me." Here I am, his dear child, one whom he has loved from before the foundation of the world, one for whom he laid down his life upon the cross, one of whom he has said, "I have graven thee upon the palms of my hands." How can he slay me? If he do so, it can only be in a minor sense: as to my best and truest life, it must be safe, for he is its author and guardian, and cannot be its destroyer. Can a mother forget her sucking child, that she should not have compassion on the son of her womb? Could she suffer a child of hers to die while she had power to keep it alive? Would she lay violent hands upon the child of her love and destroy it? God forbid. Neither will God destroy, or suffer to be destroyed, any one of his own dear children. Jesus has solemnly said—"I give unto my sheep eternal life, and they shall never perish, neither shall any pluck them out of my hand." The fairest children of the earth will die, for that which is born of the flesh is flesh, and all flesh is as decaying grass; but the feeblest child of God will live for ever, for the life of God in every degree of it is immortality. Time will put out the sun, the lamp of the moon will grow dim in ages yet to come, but neither time nor age shall quench a solitary spark of heaven-born grace and light. Though faith be but as a grain of mustard seed, it is essentially a living thing, and it is not conceivable that God himself should slay that which is quickened with his life. Though it be imperceptible sometimes even to the possessor of it, and though it should raise many painful questions as to whether it be there at all, yet if it be there, God will preserve it even to the end. Come, child of God, you must not suppose that the Lord will slay you for ever. You must not allow suppositions which would dishonour your God. You may suppose what you like if it be innocent, but you must not suppose that which would blaspheme the divine love, or cast a slur upon God's fidelity to his promise. He may cast you aside for awhile, but he cannot cast you away for ever; he may take away your goods, but not your highest good. He may allow a cloud to rest upon your reputation, a blight to fall upon your usefulness, and a storm to sweep away your happiness, but his mercy is not clean gone for ever, he hath not in anger turned away his heart from you. He has chastened you sore, but he has not given you over unto death. No, you must not interpret the supposition of the text as though it said, "Though he leave me to perish, though he cast me into hell," for that can never be. But I make bold to say that even if the devil were to whisper in your ear that the Lord would finally destroy you, it would be a glorious thing if you could bravely reply, "And if he did I would still trust him." One old saint once used very daring and perhaps unjustifiable, language when he said, in ecstacy of love, "if God casts me into hell, I will hold so fast by him that he shall go there too; I will not let him go, and hell itself will be no hell to me while he is there." Beloved, say in your soul—Though the Lord should condemn me, I will not rebel, but confess that he is just; though he should refuse to hear my prayers, yet he is an infinitely good and blessed God, and I will praise him still. But, beloved, it cannot be that God should slay or condemn a believer, and you need not tolerate the supposition. Blessed be his name, he hath not cast away the people whom he did foreknow, neither has one soul that trusted in him ever been forsaken.

The terrible supposition before us is inclusive of all possible ills. "Though he slay me." He means that if every form of evil up to actual death should come upon him, yet would he trust in God. Though he should lose all that he had in flock or field, in purse or portion, yet would he trust. In Job's case away went the oxen and the asses, away went the sheep, away went the camels, and away went all the servants, and each time as the messenger came breathlessly running in, he said, "I only am left alone to tell thee." At last the worst news of all came, for all his children were taken away at a stroke. All was gone, for his wife was as good as lost also, since she went over to the enemy, and said, "Curse God and die." Well saith Job, "Though my troubles have left me bare of all but life, though nothing remains to me but this dunghill and the broken potsherd with which I scrape my sores, yet will I trust in the Lord." Oh, it was bravely said!

In this resolve, as we have seen, he includes not only all losses of property, but all bereavements of friends; and I should like you Christian people to look this in the face. Perhaps the Lord may suddenly take away from you the dearest object of your heart's affection—your husband or your wife; can you trust him then? The almost idolised children may be removed one by one, and leave sad vacancies within your heart. O fond wife, the beloved of your soul may pass away in the prime of his manhood, the brother may be cut down as the green herb, and the sister fade as a flower. Parents, children, brethren, any and all of these may be put far from you, and you may find yourselves as lone trees, whereas now you are surrounded by a kindred forest. You may be the last of the roses, left alone, scarcely blooming, but bowing your head amid the heavy showers of sorrow which drench you to the soul. Now, believer, if you are in such a deplorable case as that, can you still say, "If the Lord should go even further than this, should his next arrows penetrate my own lacerated heart, even then, as I bleed to death, I will kiss his hand"?

Job included in his supposition all kinds of pain. We can hardly imagine the bodily agony of Job when he was covered with sore boils from the sole of his foot unto his crown. None could approach him, the disease was so foul, neither could he endure to be touched. Yet he says, "Though I have all these boils, and even should they grow worse, so that the pains I now endure should become unendurable, and should I suffer the very anguish of death itself, yet still would I put my trust in my God. Neither poverty, loneliness, nor fierce torment shall make me forsake the Lord, nor shall all put together cause me to doubt him." What a victory of faith is this!

Job at that time also suffered from dishonour, for those who once looked up to him with respect now despised him in their hearts. He says that those whose fathers he would have disdained to have set with the dogs of his flock, opened their mouths against him; and whereas, when he stood in the street, princes were silent in his presence to listen to his wisdom, now among the basest of mankind he had become a song and a byword. As for his mistaken friends, he had grown so weary of them that he said, "O that ye would altogether hold your peace, and it would be your wisdom." Poor Job was sorely galled with the scorn poured on him at a time when he deserved both sympathy and honour, but yet his faith cries, "If I am more despised still, and forgotten as a dead man out of mind, yet will I trust in thee, my God."

Connected with all this, the afflicted patriarch must have felt much depression of spirit. Did he not say, "Even to-day is my complaint bitter: my stroke is heavier than my groaning. For God maketh my heart soft, and the Almighty troubleth me"? Those of us who are subject to depression of spirit find much that is congenial in the Book of Job, his music is in tune with our own. How bitterly does he wail at times! What wondrous insight has he into the mystery of sorrow! Though his grief has never been thoroughly weighed, nor his calamities laid in the balances together, yet have his woes been considered by thousands of mourners, and have ministered a wealth of consolation to them. Job does not exclude his despondencies from his resolves, nay, he mainly intends them, for these are in a special sense a man's own personal slaying, and he says, "Though he slay *me*,"—though my heart should break with anguish, pierced through with despondency, yet will I put my trust in God. I began by calling the supposition of our text a terrible one, and now I claim that I have shown it to be so, since it includes the coming upon us of all sorts of ills.

Listen yet again. *This supposition goes to the extreme of possibility*, if not beyond it, for it will be hard to find a case in which God has really slain any of his servants. The martyrs were slain for him, but not by him. To none of his children, save one, has the Lord been as Abraham was to Isaac when he unsheathed the knife to slay him. If it had been so, could we have been as the lamb beneath the sacrificial knife? The stones which slew Stephen, and the sword which slew James, were in the hands of cruel men, and not in the hands of God; but God himself is here supposed to slay us. Now, though he has not actually done so, we may enquire whether we could resign ourselves to him, even if he should take life and all with his own hand? Could we lie on the altar and not struggle? Do we hate even our own life also for love of him? What say we? Is our love stronger than death? God grant it may be so found.

But *this supposition goes further than matters ever will go.* Why, then, does the Psalmist suppose such a case? I answer because only by such suppositions can he express his faith to the full. Remember that psalm, "Therefore will not we fear, though the earth be removed, and though the mountains be carried into the midst of the sea." We are not expecting the earth to move nor the mountains to plunge into the ocean, but in order to express our confidence, we declare that even such a quaking would not affect the foundation of our faith. God himself meets his people in like manner, by saying, "The mountains shall depart, and the hills be removed; but my kindness shall not depart from thee, neither shall the covenant of my peace be removed." Child of God, you may suppose what never will occur, if you like, and project your soul by that supposition into depths of woe and grief, into which you will never actually come, and yet through divine grace you will resolve, "If it came even to that, still would I trust in him."

Though the text supposes what will not actually occur, yet *it is a just description of what often does occur as far as our conceptions go.* Have you never known what it is to be in your own conceptions slain by God? My heart has known it often. It is as death itself to feel all your religion melt away like the hoar frost of the morning, when the sun has risen; and all your joys in which you delighted flying away like birds when a man doth clap his hands. Have you never had to begin all over again, at the very alphabet of repentance and childlike faith, and find even that no easy work. Did you never know what it was to get your cup right full of what you thought was holy joy and sweet experience, and then for the Lord to turn it bottom upward and let you see that it was a mixture of self-conceit and sentimentalism, with thick dregs at the bottom of pride and falsehood? Can you say with David, "I have seen an end of all perfection"? Have you never been brought down from imaginary riches to bitter but honest poverty? Have you never thought you were becoming so wonderfully sanctified that you could scarcely lay a split sheet of tissue paper between you and perfection, and then on a sudden the Lord has laid you naked and made you loathe the sight of your inborn corruptions? You have been as a cup which bubbled at the top and frothed over, and the Lord has blown off the froth and made you see the black draught of your inward vileness. God has many ways of thus slaying in his children all that ought to die. Thus he kills the spiritual hypocrisy which is so common in us all. Our life seems at times to run all into puffballs and bloated fungi of self-glorying, we think that we are something when we are nothing, and then the Lord prunes us back to our real condition. Do you never know what it is to be thus slain? Ah, my brethren, at times our life is a long experience of the power of death. Do you not know what it is to say, "Is this prayer? Why, while I prayed my thoughts were perplexed, distracted, and wandering. Is this faith? Why, even on the most vital points my soul dares scarcely speak with confidence! Is this love?—love to Christ, which even while I exercise it accuses me on account of its lukewarmness and want of self-denying ardor. Can this be spiritual life? Life at which I blush and over which I mourn! Life which scarcely reaches so far as feeling, and when it does, soon subsides into insensibility!" Beloved brethren, I speak from experience, all this is a kind of slaying by which the Lord hides pride from men and keeps them from the snares of vain confidence. Has he not written, "I kill and I make alive, I wound and I heal"? In these times of wounding and killing, which are very common to the experience of some of the children of God, the only thing we can do is still to trust,—"Though he slay me, I will trust in him." Trust him though he sift out nine-tenths of thy hopes, burn up all thy experiences, grind thine evidences to powder, crush all thy realised sanctities, and sweep away all thy rests and refuses. Then, indeed, is the best time of all to exercise true faith.

Once more, *the grim supposition of the text, if ever it was realized by anybody it was realized by our Lord Jesus.* Our great covenant Head knows to the full what his members suffer. God did slay him, and glory be to his blessed name, he trusted God while he was being slain. "It pleased the Father to bruise him, he hath put him to grief;" yet from the lips of our dear Lord we hear no expressions of unbelief. Read the twenty-second Psalm, where he says, "Our fathers trusted in thee, they trusted in thee and thou didst deliver them, but I am a worm, and no man." Hear how he pleads with God, and specially listen to his dying words, where, though he says, "My God, my God, why hast thou forsaken me?" yet a few minutes after he cries, "Into thy hands I commit my spirit." What! into the hands of a God who had forsaken him and smitten him; did he commit himself into those hands? Yes, into those very hands; and herein we must follow in his steps. Though the Lord cut, hew, hack, tear, and grind us to powder, yet out of the dust, and the tears, and the blood of the conflict we must look up to him and say, "I trust thee still." Here is the patience of the saints! Here is the glory of faith! Blessed is the man who thus becomes more than a conqueror. I say it calmly, I would sooner be able to do as Job did, than to be one of yonder seraphim, who have never suffered, and consequently have never clung to a slaying God. I count it the grandest possibility of a created being that it should be able completely to yield itself up into the Creator's hand, and unwaveringly believing in the Creator's love, in hope believing against hope. Oh, royal word of a right royal soul, "Though he slay me, yet will I trust in him."

II. Secondly, we have before us A NOBLE RESOLUTION—"yet

will I trust in him." Job meant that he was confident that the
Lord was just, and though he did not feel that the sufferings
he was then enduring were sent upon him for his sins, yet he
never doubted the righteousness of God in so afflicting him.
His friends said, "You see, Job, you suffer more than anybody
else, therefore you must have been a hypocrite, for God will
not lay upon any man more than is just." "No," said Job, "I
have been upright before the Lord; and yet, on the other
hand, I do not accuse the Lord of injustice, I am sure he does
what is right, and I trust him as much as ever." There were
two things to which Job stuck very firmly—"Though he slay
me, yet will I trust in him, but I will maintain my own ways
before him"—that is, I will not admit that I have been a
hypocrite, for I have been sincerely obedient to him; nor will I
be driven to the other conclusion, that God is unjust in
afflicting me. Job did not understand the Lord's reasons, but
he continued to confide in his goodness. He set no terms or
limits to the Lord's action, but left all to his absolute will, and
was sure that whatever he might do it must be right. Should
death prevent all apparent possibility of making up to him all
his losses and woes, his faith o'erleaped the sepulchre, and
saw justice and mercy alive in the realms beyond, making all
things right in the end. Oh, it was grand thus to champion
almighty goodness in the teeth of death itself.

Now, dear brethren, you and I, if we are resting upon God
may say, "Whatever happens, though I may not be able to
understand God's dispensations to me any more than Job
understood God's dispensations towards him, yet I am quite
sure of this, that he will help me in my trouble, and I will,
therefore, cast myself upon him, believing that as my days my
strength shall be; or if he does not aid me in my trouble with
manifest help I will still trust that he will bring me out of it,
that if he seem to forsake for a while, yet it shall be said of me
as of Gad, "a troop shall overcome him, but he shall overcome
at the last."

If I should neither receive present help nor immediate
deliverance, yet I am persuaded that my good is designed by
my long trial, and that God is making the worst things work
out my everlasting benefit and his own glory; therefore will I
submit to his will, and expect in the end to see the
lovingkindness of the Lord. Yea, and if I should have neither
present help nor deliverance, nor see any immediate good

come of my affliction, yet will I repose myself upon God, for in some mysterious way or other I shall yet know that his providence was right and good; for he cannot err, his dealings must be wise; he cannot be unkind, his actions must be tender. Though the sharp edge of death itself invade me, I will hold to this belief, that thou, O Lord, doest all things right. If down to the sepulchre my steps must go, and through the gloomy valley's darkest shade my pilgrimage must wend, yet will I fear no evil, for thy rod and staff shall be my confidence, and I will be sure that he who bids me die will bid me live again; up from the grave my body shall yet rise, and in my flesh shall I see God. As for my spirit, though it pass through the death shade, it shall come forth into a brighter light, and in the eternity of glory it shall receive abundant recompense for the sorrows of the present time. This is the faith for us to hold at all times—"Though he slay me, yet will I trust in him."

Why, think you, was Job able to speak thus positively about his trusting God? Was it not because he knew God? "They that know thy name will put their trust in thee." If you would believe God you must know him. Those who are strangers to him cannot trust him. Oh, beloved, only think what God is! Sometimes when I am contemplating his being and character I feel as if I could leap for joy, and when I touch upon the theme in the pulpit I feel as if I could talk on for ever in his praise, and use the grandest, sweetest, richest words in human language to tell what a blessed God my God is. What! the Lord do wrong to any of us? Impossible! The Lord be unkind to us? The supposition cannot be endured for a single moment. After once knowing him we feel that all the goodness and kindness of fathers, mothers, brethren, children, husbands, wives, all put together, is only like one single drop of sweetness compared with that ocean full of honey which is to be found in his infinite love. Besides, we have not only his attributes to trust to, but his past actions to us. Did my Lord forgive me all my sin? and after that will he ever be unkind to me? Did he lay down his life for me upon the accursed tree, and can I dream that he will desert me? Have I looked into the wounds of my dying Saviour, and shall I ever murmur if he should multiply pains and sufferings and losses and crosses to me? God forbid. Such love as his forbids all fear. Did you ever lean on the Bridegroom's arm? Have you ever sung like the bride in the canticle, "His left hand is under my head, and his right arm doth embrace me"? Did he ever stay you with flagons and comfort you with apples while your soul was sick with too much delight; and after all that will you indulge hard thoughts of him? Oh no, till the day break and the shadows flee away, we cannot think hardly of him who has dealt so kindly with us. His ways must be right; such wondrous acts of love as his have proved to us beyond all question that he is love, essential love, and cannot, therefore, do us an ill turn.

Beside this, we know the relationship in which he stands to us. It has been said that you cannot trust an enemy, and it has been equally well added you cannot trust a reconciled enemy: suspicion lingers long. But our God is no reconciled enemy, though he is sometimes represented as if he were so: he has loved us with an everlasting love; his is no friendship of yesterday, no passion which began to burn a month or two ago; but long ere the hills lifted up their heads he loved us. The bands of his fatherhood are upon us, and we can well commit ourselves into his hands.

Are any of us in great trouble this morning; then let us trust in the Lord now, for what else can we do? Suppose we give up trusting in him, to whom or whither should we go? If this anchor drags, what other holdfast can there be? Let us continue to trust our Lord, for he deserves it. He has never done aught that could justify us in doubting him. Has he ever been false to us? Ah, Judas, you sold your Master, but your Master never sold you. Ah, unbelieving heart, you have wandered from Jesus, but he never wandered from you. If you do not doubt him till you have cause for doubting him it will not be soon. Let us trust our God, for this is the sweetest comfort a man can have. This side heaven nothing can yield the afflicted man such support under trial as when he can fall back upon the strong love of God, and believe that the wisdom of God is overruling all. Nothing tends so to sanctify our trials, and produce good results from them, as faith in God. This is the Samson which finds honey in the lion. For a thousand reasons I would say, "Trust in the Lord at all times: ye people, pour out your hearts before him. God is a refuge for us." Say ye each one, "Though he slay me, yet will I trust in him!"

III. And, now, the last point is this, A SECRET APPROPRIATE-

NESS about it all.

There is a something about our Lord's slaying us which should help us to trust him. I would sooner the Lord should slay me with troubles and trials than let me alone in my sin. What saith the Scriptures? "If ye be without chastisement, whereof all are partakers, then are ye bastards and not sons, for what son is he whom the father chasteneth not?" I do not so much pity the children of God who have a cross to carry, I reserve my fears for those worldlings who are not in trouble as other men, neither plagued like other men. It would be very foolish for the afflicted one to say, "I am no child of God because he smites me": there would be more reason in the sinner's saying, "I am no child of God, for I have my portion in this life." Surely there is something in you which God loves, or else he would not be killing that which he hates. If he hates the sin in you, it is a good sign; for where do we hate sin most? Why, in those we love most. If you see a fault in a stranger, you wink your eye, and say but little, but in your own dear child you are deeply grieved to observe it. Where there is true love there is a measure of jealousy, and the more burning the love the more fierce the jealousy, especially on the part of Jesus Christ. Where he sees sin in those who are very dear to him, his fury burns not against them, but against their sin, and he will not stop until he has slain it. His rebukes are severe, not because of want of love, but because he loves them so much. An ungodly man met me some years ago when I was suffering, and said to me in a jeering way, "Ah, whom the Lord loveth he chasteneth, I see." I said, "Yes, it is his custom." "Ah," said he, "so long as I am without the chastisement I am very content to be without the love." Oh, it brought the red into my cheeks and the tears into my eyes, and I cried, "I would not change places with you for ten thousand worlds. If my God were to afflict me from head to foot I would bear it joyfully sooner than live a moment without his love." When the Lord flogs us we love him, and we would not leave him though the devil should bribe us with all the kingdoms of the earth and the glory of them. Our Father puts us sometimes into the black hole, and we are there crying bitterly under a sense of his wrath, but we love him still, and if anybody were to find fault with him we would be up at once and say "He is a good God, and blessed be his name."

Note again that *the slaying of the creature is the very condition in which faith was born,* and in which she delights to display her power. We are saved by passing from death unto life. As Noah was like a dead man out of mind shut up in the ark, and by this burial passed into the new world; and as in the ordinance of baptism we are in like figure buried with Christ that we may rise with him, so faith took her birth in the death of the creature at the time when the new life was breathed into us. When God is slaying all that is capable of death, and our new immortal life alone survives, faith feels as if her birthday had come over again and brought with it her native air.

Notice again, *it is at times when God is slaying us that our faith is being tested* whether it is true or not. When all the winds are fair how can you tell whether your barque would bear a storm? How much faith some of us have at times! Have you never felt as if you could fight seven devils with one hand? There was not a devil within seven miles when you were so bold; but when the smallest fiend has drawn near your courage has oozed out. We are like an old man whom I once knew, who said to me, "Here am I, eighty years old, and through the winter I often think, I wish I had a bit of mowing or reaping to do, for I feel quite young again; but as soon as harvest comes on, and I get down my old sickle, I have not done much before I feel the old man is a very old man, and had better leave that work alone." Slaying times let us know whether our strength is real strength, and whether our confidence is true confidence, and this is good, for it would be a great pity for us to be stocked with heaps of sham faith, and fictitious grace, and ready-made holiness. Some of my friends talk as if they had holiness enough for a dozen people, but I am afraid if they were tried as some of us are they would find they had not half enough for one. This is the benefit of trial— it lets us see what is gold and what is tinsel, what is fact and what is fiction. Alas, how much religious fiction is abroad at this time!

Note further, that *slaying times are the most favourable for trusting God.* I have been putting a little riddle to myself. Here it is. Is it easier to trust God when you have nothing, or when you have all things? Is it easier to say, "Though he slay me, I will trust in him," or to say, "Though he make me alive, I will trust in him"? Will you think it over? Shall I help you?

Here is a man without a farthing in the world; his cupboard is bare, his flocks are cut off from the field, and his herds from the stall; is it hard for that man to trust in God? If you say so I will not dispute with you. But here is another man who has a bank full of gold, his meadows are covered with flocks and herds, his barns are ready to burst with corn, and his trade prospers on all hands. Now, sirs, is it easy for that man to trust God? Do you say "Yes"? I say "No." I say that he has a very hard task indeed to live by faith, and the probabilities are that when he says, "I trust God," he is trusting his barn or his bank. All things considered, it occurs to me that it is easier to trust God in adversity than in prosperity, because whatever trust there is in adversity is real trust, but a good deal of the faith we have in prosperity is a kind of trust which you will have to take upon trust, and whether it is faith or not is a matter of serious question. Sirs, where is the room for faith when you can see already all that you want? A full barn has no room for faith if she be any bigger than a mouse; but in an empty barn faith has scope and liberty. When the brook Cherith is dried up, when the poor widow has nothing left but a handful of meal and a little oil, then there is room for the prophet to exercise faith. Oh, brethren, it is well to go into action with clear decks. In the name of God, with double-shotted guns full of strong faith you can let the world and the flesh and the devil know what faith is; but while your deck is all hampered with comforts and visible resources faith can scarce stir a hand or move a gun. "Though he slay me,"— well, that means everything is gone, only breath enough left me just to exist; and now, my Lord, thou art all in all to me. Now can I say, "Whom have I in heaven but thee; there is none upon the earth that I desire beside thee."

Once more, *these slaying times* are very desirable occasions, because they *allow the child of God to show that he is not a mercenary professor*, held to Christ by a cupboard love. If God were always to prosper us the world would say, "These Christians follow their God as stray dogs follow those who give them bones, but they have no sincere love." When the Lord falls a whipping us, and we love him all the more, then they cannot say but what we are faithful, nor can they deny the work of grace in our souls. Oh, you that are Christians as long as it is pleasant to be Christians, you who make your love to Christ depend upon your feeling happy,—what despicable beings you are. Our Lord wants not such base disciples, but such as can say, "If I lose all I have, still I love thee, O my Saviour: thy sweet love is so precious that if death were threatened me I would still choose thee to be my all in all." Love desires opportunities for proving her disinterestedness, and such is the opportunity of the text.

There are seeking souls here this morning, and I daresay they have said, "Mr. Spurgeon has been describing great faith, we shall never get to that." I have been thinking, dear souls, what kind of a man is most like a little child. Is it not a very old man? What kind of faith is most like new-born faith? Why, the ripest and most advanced faith. My text is very old faith: "Though he slay me, yet will I trust in him," but the very first faith I had in Christ—I remember it well—was just like it. I thought he would destroy me, I could not see how he could do otherwise, and yet be a just God. I thought he must strike me down if I went to him. He seemed to stand with a drawn sword in his hand, but I felt "Well, if he does slay me, I had better die by his hand than remain his enemy;" and I went to him. I was like the boy who ran away from his home and dared not return, because he feared his father would flog him. He was out all night, shivering, cold, and wet, and had nothing to eat all day. By the time he got to the next evening, such was his dread of being alone all through another night, that he said to himself, "I would sooner feel my father's rod than lie here," and so he went home, and was received with tenderness. So with me. I thought if I went to the Lord, I should have to smart for it, but I concluded I would rather smart than be as I was, and so I went to him, and found I was safe. O poor souls, come to Jesus Christ in that fashion. Say—

> "I can but perish if I go,
> I am resolved to try;
> For, if I stay away, I know,
> I must for ever die.
> But if I die with mercy sought,
> When I the king have tried;
> That were to die, delightful thought,
> As sinner never died."

Say, "If I go to hell, I will trust Christ; if I am cast away for ever, I will trust Christ:" and that cannot be, for "he that believeth in him is not condemned." God grant you true faith, for Jesus' sake. Amen.

10

Concerning the Consolations of God

"Are the consolations of God small with thee? Is there any secret thing with thee?" Job 15:11

These are the words of Eliphaz, one of those three friends of Job who blundered dreadfully over his case. Their words are not to be despised; for they were men in the front rank for knowledge and experience. Eliphaz says, "With us are both the grayheaded and very aged men, much elder than thy father." Their errors were not the superficial mistakes of fools, but the profound reasonings of men of light and leading. Their utterances are, at least, equal to anything our own learned men may have to say on the same problem. However wrong Eliphaz may have been in reference to Job—and in reference to him his remarks were grossly unjust—yet many of them are correct in themselves, and may usefully be applied to our own hearts. Inasmuch as Eliphaz, in this verse, teaches no doctrine, but only asks two searching questions, he cannot mislead us; but he may do us good service. May God the Holy Spirit enable us so to consider these questions that we may be profited thereby!

The text is in the form of a question, and its sense I shall endeavour to bring out by other questions, each of which will have a practical relation to ourselves. The passage in the original has proved hard to translate; but I think that in four questions I can set forth the essence of the meanings which have been found therein.

If we are indeed believers in the gospel, and are living near to God, our consolation should be exceeding great. Passing through a troubled world, we have need of consolations; but these are abundantly provided by our God, and their influence upon us should be exceeding great. We ought not to be unhappy; for we have joy urged upon us by the precept, "Rejoice in the Lord alway"; and that precept is in substance often repeated. It is both the duty and the privilege of Christians to be of good cheer; if we are not glad, even amid our trials, there is a reason for it, and we shall do well, at this time, to use the text as a candle by which to search out that reason. "Are the consolations of God small with thee? is there any secret thing with thee?"

I. Our first question follows the interpretation given by most authorities: "DO YOU REGARD THE CONSOLATIONS OF GOD AS SMALL?" Do you judge that the comforts of faith are insignificant? "Are the consolations of God too small for thee?"

I would ask you, first, *Do you think religion makes men unhappy?* Have you poisoned your mind with that invention of the enemy? Have you made yourself believe that godliness consists in morbid self-condemnation, despondency, apprehension, and dread? If so, permit me to warn you that there are many popular errors, and that, in this case, "common fame is a common liar." Do you find in the preacher, and the members of his church, any confirmation of this silly assertion? We can personally assure you that the joys of religion are by no means meagre in our case. We beseech you not to let a groundless prejudice blind your eyes to the truth. I will hope that, like the Bereans, you are of a noble spirit, and will examine that which is told you.

Is not your verdict different from that of those who have tried godliness for themselves? Do you not know that many, for the joy they have found, in the love of Christ, have renounced all sinful pleasures, and utterly despised them? They were once fascinated with the world, but they tasted higher joys, and shook off the spell. He that drinks of the river of the water of life will count the streams of sin to be foul and brackish, and will no more drink thereof. Many a believer for the joy that is set before him has, in the service of God, encountered much ridicule, endured severe losses, and borne great hardships; and has done so with delight. Have you not also remarked, in many afflicted Christians, a peace which you yourself do not know? Have you not observed their patience under adversity? They have been poor, but perfectly content; they have been sick, and yet cheerful; racked with pain, and yet joyous. Under the apprehension of surgical operations, have you not seen them happily resigned? Have you ever seen one of them die? How often have we heard them singing in their death-throes, which have been to them death joys! Is it not a fact which cannot be disputed, that faith in our Lord Jesus has uplifted the sorrowful, and has rendered others supremely happy? This joy has sprung entirely from their hope in Christ, their communion with God, their delight in the truth revealed in Holy Scripture. Have we not among us in Christian fellowship many notable proofs that

> "Tis religion which can give,
> Sweetest pleasure while we live"?

Therefore, my questioning friend, it behoves you to look into this matter, and not to remain under the impression that the consolations of God are small. Those whose experience asserts that the joys of religion are great are not foolish or disreputable persons: give due weight to their witness, and believe that the consolations of God are precious beyond expression. Amid many pains and afflictions, I can personally assure you that it is a blessed thing to trust in the Lord.

Will you follow me a while as I ask you, *Upon consideration, will you not amend your judgment?* What are these consolations *of God?* The more you know of them, the more ground will you see for believing that they must be great. They are the "consolations *of God.*" If God himself deigns to comfort men, will he not greatly cheer them? Knowing human sorrow, and stepping from the height of his glory to comfort it, is it conceivable that he will labour in vain? Do you think that the All-sufficient cannot provide consolation equal to the affliction? The consolations we speak of are applied by the Spirit of God; and to prove how earnestly he performs his work, he has taken the name of "Comforter." Will the Comforter, the Holy Ghost, think you, come to any human heart with insufficient consolations? Will he trifle with our griefs? Can it be that he does not know how to give sunlight when our day is dark with sorrow? Think not so. Moreover, the Lord Jesus Christ, the Eternal Son of God, is the substance of those consolations. He is called "The consolation of Israel." Can a man have Christ to be his portion, and yet be poor? Can a man have Jesus for his joy, and yet be weighed down with sadness? Might he not well ask, "Why art thou cast down, O my soul?" I cannot for a moment dream of a joyless Christ.

See again, my friend, these consolations of God deal with the source of sorrow. Whence came the curse, but from the sin of man? Jesus has come to save his people from their sins. Those thorns and thistles which now rend our flesh are not the natural fruits of the earth as God created it. Sin sowed all these. The consolations of God deal with sin. As for the guilt which we have incurred, and the inevitable punishment, both are removed by pardon full and free. Jesus bore the guilt of sin, and put it all away by his death upon the cross; and, in consequence, sin can be blotted out. Is not this the grandest of all consolations—the consolation of God? When we lay hold on Jesus, and receive forgiveness, affliction may remain, but sin is gone for ever; and hence the affliction itself loses its bitterness. Sin reigning in the heart is the death of peace; but the dethronement of the usurper is provided for, and hence another divine consolation. Until we get the mastery over evil, we must be uncomfortable; but the consolations of God assure us of a new heart and a right spirit, and of a power supreme and divine, which enters the nature of the believer, and subdues, destroys, and at last annihilates the propensity to sin. Is not this a rich and rare consolation? Comfort which left us under the power of evil would be dangerous comfort; but comfort which takes away both the guilt and the power of sin is glorious indeed. Dream not that it can be small!

Remember, too, that the consolations of God reveal to us a reason for the sorrow when it is allowed to remain. There is a needs-be that we are in heaviness. "We know that all things work together for good to them that love God, to them who are the called according to his purpose." If suffering be a fire, the consolations of God assure us that it is a refining fire, which only consumes our dross. Do you not think that the comfortable fruits of righteousness, which are brought forth in those believers who are exercised by trial, are the source of great comfort to the afflicted of the Lord?

> "Since all that I meet shall work for my good,
> The bitter is sweet, the medicine is food."

Another reflection sweetly cheers the heart of the tried one during his tribulation, namely, that he has a comrade in it. We are not passing through the waters alone. We have a fellow-sufferer, of whom we read, "In all their affliction he was afflicted." Our Lord drank long ago of that cup whereof we sip. He knows the sting of treachery, the stab of calumny, the spit of scorn; for he was "in all points tempted like as we are." Many of us have found this to be an eminent comfort. Do you not think it must be so? Has not many a man, at the sound of another's voice, been cheered in the darkness of the night when pursuing a dangerous way? Has not the presence of a stronger and wiser one acting as guide been quite enough to remove all dread? If the Son of God be with us, surely there is an end of every sort of fear. Does he not use this as his own note of cheer, saying, "Fear thou not; for I am with thee?"

Besides, "the consolations of God" lie also in the direction of compensations. You have the rod; yes, but this is the small drawback to heavenly sonship, if drawback indeed it be. You have become a son of God, and "what son is there whom his father chasteneth not?" You are an heir of God, joint heir with Jesus Christ; and in accepting heirship will you not cheerfully take the cross therewith, seeing it is part of the entail? It is true that you have special sorrow; but then you have the royal nature to which that sacred sorrow is a witness. God has given to you a nature that wars against evil: hence these tears! Would you be of the seed of the serpent, and have your meat as plentiful as dust? Would you not far rather be of the seed of the woman, and have your heel bruised? What is the bruising of the heel compared with the eternal dominion to which that seed is predestinated? Compensations abound in every case of trouble. You have lost your child, but you believe in the resurrection. You will die yourself, it may be; but you shall rise again from the dust. You have lost your property; but you are an heir of all things in Christ Jesus. You have been persecuted; but in this you rejoice as a partaker of the sufferings of Christ. The compensations of the covenant of grace are so overflowing that we call our troubles "light afflictions, which are but for a moment," and they work out for us a far more exceeding and eternal weight of glory.

Besides, there is one consolation, with which I finish; not because I have completed my list, but because time does not permit me to enlarge: there is the consolation that you are on your journey home, and that every moment you are coming closer to the eternal rest. When we once reach heaven, we shall forget the trials of the way. An hour with our God will make up for a life of pain. You languish on that bed; but if you languish into immortality, you will no more remember your anguish. When your head wears the crown and your hand waves the palm, you will count it all joy that you were thought worthy to be persecuted for Christ's sake.

O sirs, we have the best of it! Whatever trouble may come to us as Christians, so much more of joy comes with it, that we have the best of the bargain. We give up drops of poisonous delight, but we dive into rivers of ineffable joy. The Christian's joy far excels the best that earth can afford. Grace is the dawn of glory. Faith brings heaven down to us, while love bears us up to heaven. Celestial fruits are gathered upon earthly ground by those who look up for the manna. Let us begin the song which with sweeter voices we shall continue, world without end—"Unto him that loved us and laved us in his own blood, be glory for ever!"

Still I fear there are some to whom it appears as if the joys of religion and the consolations of God were small. Let them correct their mistake; for the truth is far otherwise.

II. But now a second question comes up, which will come home to many Christian people. HAVE THESE CONSOLATIONS BEEN SMALL IN THEIR EFFECT UPON YOU? Have these consolations, though great in themselves, been small in their influence *upon you?*

I will begin my examination by putting to one disciple this question: *Have you never very much rejoiced in God?* Have you always possessed a little, and but a very little, joy? Are you one of those who are only up to the ankles in the river of grace? Why is this? Dear friend, you are believing upon a slender scale; you are living on a low plane. Why is it so? You hope you are saved, but it is by the skin of your teeth; you hope you are a child of God, but you are not very sure about it; and, consequently, you get very little joy out of it. This is mischievous. Whence comes it? Is it *ignorance?* Do you not know enough of the great doctrines of the gospel, and of the vast privileges of the redeemed? It may be so. We have heard of persons in Australia who walked habitually over nuggets of gold. We have heard of a bridge being built with what seemed common stones, but it contained masses of golden ore. Men did not know their wealth. Is it not a pity that you should be poor in comfort, and yet have all this gold of consolation at your foot? You have, lying within the leaves of your Bible, cheques for millions, and yet you have scarcely a penny to spend. What a pity! Is it *listlessness?* Have you never felt desirous to know the best of the Christian life? Have you never had the sacred ambition to gain all the blessings which are provided in the covenant of grace? It is wonderful how indifferent some people can be: they can fret when within reach of unutterable joy! I have heard of a person who walked some seven hundred miles to see the Falls of Niagara. When he was within seven miles, he thought he heard the roar of the cataract, and he called to a man working in the fields, and said, "Is that the roar of Niagara?" The man answered, "I don't know, but I guess it may be. What if it is?" With surprise, the good man said, "Do you live here?" "Born and bred here," the man answered. "And yet you don't know whether that thundering noise is from the waterfall?" "No, stranger," said he, "I don't care what it is. I have never seen those Falls. I look after my farm." No doubt there are many within hail of heaven's choicest joys who have never cared to know them. They hope they are saved, but they don't care for great joy. They use their spade and their hoe, and dig their potatoes; but Niagara is nothing to them. Many look well to this life, but do not arouse themselves to gain present spiritual joy. Oh, sad, that you should be so much a Christian, that we should not wish to question that you are converted, and yet you are half-asleep, and self-content! You labour under the notion that those good people who rejoice in the Lord are enthusiasts, or else you say to yourself, "It would be presumption on my part to aspire to have the same joy." What nonsense! Go in for everything that God can give you. If you are his child, nothing in his house is denied you. He saith to you, "Son, thou art ever with me, and all that I have is thine." Do not you, like the elder brother, complain that you have served him all these years, and yet he never gave you enough to make you merry with your friends.

But it may be, dear friend, that you once did joy and rejoice. Well, then, *is it of late that you have lost these splendid consolations, and come down to feel them small with you?* I suggest to you that you observe what alteration you have made of late. Is it that you have more business, and have grown more worldly? You cannot get out to prayer-meetings now, nor to week-night services. "No," you say, "I cannot; and if you knew what I have to do, you would not blame me." Just so, a little while ago you had not so much to do; but you chose to load yourself with an extra burden, knowing that you would not be able to get so much of spiritual food as aforetime. Somewhere in that line you will find the reason why your joy has declined. If anybody said to me, "The days are darker now than they used to be," I should remember that the sun is still the same. Perhaps my friend has not lately cleaned his windows; or he has not drawn up his blinds; and that is why he thinks there is less light. It is very possible to be much more in the dark than you need to be. The gloom may be in the eyes rather than in the heavens. May I suggest a little looking at home, that you may see why your former blessedness is gone?

Do you reply to me that you do use the means of grace? *Do the outward means fail to bring you the consolation they once did?* To what means do you refer? Are you as much in prayer as ever? and is prayer less refreshing than it used to be? Do you read the Scriptures as you formerly did, with the same regularity, attention, and devotion? Do you no longer draw the waters of comfort from these wells of salvation? Do you really go on hearing the Word as you once did, with the same hunger for it, and love to it, and yet do you find it unsatisfactory to you? I must again remind you that these things have not altered in themselves; for the ministry is the same to other saints, the Scriptures must be the same, and the mercy-seat is not removed. The fault is not in these, but in yourself. Surely, dear friend, some evil thing within you has curdled the milk of blessing, and stopped the flow of joy. Search yourselves, I pray you, if the consolations of God are small with you. He has not forgotten to be gracious, neither has he ceased to hear prayer and to speak to his servants through his sacred Word. You shut the door from within; he bars it not from without.

I may come near to your experience if I ask—*Do you revive occasionally, and then relapse?* I think I hear you say, "Oh, yes; I sometimes can clap my hands; for I feel delighted while hearing the gospel. I could shout Hallelujah, I do so rejoice. I am for a time up in the stirrups." But you come down again just as readily. Why is this? Surely, you are in a very changeful frame, and live by feeling rather than by principle. Are not the grounds of comfort always the same? If a promise is true this morning, it will be true this afternoon; and if it is a real source of comfort to you this afternoon, it ought to be a comfort to you on Monday and all the other days of the week. If the feast does not alter, and yet it does not satisfy you as it once did, you must be ill, some fever or other disease is upon

you. Haste away to the Great Physician of souls, and say to
him, "Lord, search me and try me, and see what evil thing
there is in me, and make me right, that I may again be
satisfied with heavenly food." It is childish to be so changeful.
Grow in grace, and be rooted in faith.

*Does the cause of your greater grief lie in a trial to which you
do not fully submit?* I think I hear you admit that you faint
under your load. "If thou faint in the day of adversity, thy
strength is small." But he giveth more grace. Get it. Are you
impatient? Do you kick against the pricks? Do you feel that
you can endure no longer? Since you are impatient, do you
wonder that you are unhappy? Since you walk contrary to
God, do you wonder that he walks contrary to you? Do not
find fault with his consolations; find fault with your own
rebellious heart. When a child rebels against his father, it is
not likely that his father's love will be a source of much
comfort to him. Dear friend, the Lord help you to get rid of
impatience, and you will be rid of anguish. Take the cup, and
drink it, and say, "Not as I will, but as thou wilt"; and an
angel will appear unto you strengthening you. As it was with
your Lord in a similar case, so shall it be with you. Are you
alarmed at what may yet come? Do you dread the future?
Well, if you will import trouble from the future, blame not the
consolations of God; for he has told you that "the morrow shall
take thought for the things of itself. Sufficient unto the day is
the evil thereof." He has never taught you to pray, "Give me
to-morrow my daily bread": he has limited you and pegged
you down to this, "Give us this day our daily bread." Will you
not be content to live by the day? Walking with him who is the
God of Eternity, you may leave days and years to him; and let
one day at a time be enough for you.

It may be that while you are thus without the enjoyment of
divine consolation, *Satan is tempting you to look to other
things for comfort.* I pray you, touch not the wine-cup, if this
be placed before you as a means of consolation. A dark hour is
often the crisis in the history of a man of God: if he can
weather this storm he will have fair sailing. Satan will now be
very busy to get you to act hastily, or wickedly. It will be
whispered to you, "Put your pen to that accommodation bill.
Borrow, though you cannot pay. It may be wrong, but you can
put it right afterwards." I pray you, do not dream of any
means of help which you cannot lay before God. How often

have men in offices of trust been tempted to handle money, for just a little while, and then to put it back again! I beseech you, shake this viper off your hand into the fire, for it is a viper. Better suffer anything than do wrong. Keep in the furnace till God bids you come out of it. Shadrach, Meshach, and Abednego, when they found themselves walking safely in the midst of the flames, and saw Nebuchadnezzar standing at the mouth of the furnace, did not leap out to assail the tyrant. Not they: they stayed till they came out with honour. Brother, seek not consolation in policy, in trickery, in falsehood. Do not even seek it in overhaste. Many a man who has run before the cloud has had to slink back again. Many a man who has taken a knife to carve for himself, has cut his fingers. Do not be tempted to think that you can find better comforts than God can give you. Look not to man, but let your expectation be in God alone. If you have despised the consolations of God by setting them below your own efforts, you cannot expect that they should be sweet to your taste. Amend this and you will be happy. Your lack of comfort lies not in the consolations themselves, but in your own heart. Pray God the Holy Spirit to revive the work of grace in your soul, and that being done, either the trouble will grow lighter, or your back will be stronger to bear the burden.

III. Our third question is this—Since the consolations of God appear so small to you, HAVE YOU ANYTHING BETTER TO PUT IN THEIR PLACE? Perhaps this is what Eliphaz meant when he said, "Is there any secret thing with thee?" He seemed to say to Job, "We cannot tell you anything. You will not hear us. Have you some wonderful discovery of your own? Have you some secret cordial, some mystic support, some unknown joy? Have you discovered a balm of greater efficacy than ours, a cure-all for your sorrow?" Let me ask you a similar question. If God's gospel fails you, what will you do?

Have you found out a new religion with brighter hopes? I do not think you have, for the prognostications of modern thought are dreary enough! Moreover, I have been informed by those who know most about it, that the theology of the future has not yet crystallized itself sufficiently to be defined. As far as I can see, it will take a century or two before its lovers have licked it into shape; for they have not yet settled what its shape is to be. While the grass is growing, the steed is starving. The new bread is baking: the arsenic is well mixed within it; but the oven is not very hot, and the dough is not turned into loaf yet. I should advise you to keep to that bread of which your fathers ate, the bread which came down from heaven. Personally I am not willing to make any change, even if the new bread were ready on the table; for new bread is not very digestible, and the arsenic of doubt is not according to my desire. I shall keep to the old manna till I cross the Jordan, and eat the old corn of the land of Canaan. Are you hopeful of finding comfort in new speculations? Is that the "secret thing"? Then you feed upon the wind.

Are you hoping to find comfort in the world? Will you be happy if you manage to get that position? if you pass that examination? if you save so much money? I beseech you, do not play the fool: there is no consolation in all this. Did you ever read a little book called "The Mirage of Life," published by the Tract Society? It ought to convince anybody that there is no satisfaction to be found in the greatest worldly success; for it shows us millionaires, statesmen, and princes all dissatisfied. But I need not refer to any book; observe for yourselves. The richest men have often been the most miserable, and those who have succeeded best in rising to places of honour have been worn out in the pursuit, and disgusted with the prize. Wealth brings care, honour earns envy, position entails toil, and rank has its annoyances. One of our richest men once said, "I suppose you fancy I am happy, because I am rich. Why, a dozen times in a year, and oftener, some fellow threatens to shoot me if I do not send him what he wants. Do you suppose that this makes me a happy man?" Believe me, the world is as barren of joy as the Sahara. Vain is the hope of finding a spring of consolation in anything beneath the moon. Seek the kingdom of God, and his righteousness.

Or, *do you conclude that you are strong-minded enough to bear all the difficulties and trials of life without consolation?* Well, friend, I will not discuss the point. I have found that persons who think themselves strong in mind are generally strong in the head. Yet I would remind you that the strongest are not too strong for life's battle. There never was a wise man yet who thought he was wise. This world has enough of woe in it to test all the wisdom you are likely to possess. For my own part, I feel very diffident, and would be glad of all the consolations heaven can give me. I suspect that you are as I

am, and will not be able to play the man without help from
God.

*Do you say that what can't be cured must be endured, and
you will keep as you are?* This is a poor resolve for a man to
come to. If there is better to be had, why not seek it? Do you
mean to abide in the sad state into which you have fallen? Are
you content to be discontented? Have you had a child of your
own? Have you seen it go wrong, and get itself into trouble,
and then resolve not to confess it, but to make itself appear a
martyr and fret? You wished to put it right, and cheer it into
obedience; but it would not get out of the sulks. What did you
do with it? I suppose, in the long run, you had to leave it to
have its sulk out, and you thought to yourself, "Silly child!
How miserable you make yourself, and all for nothing. You
might be as happy as your brothers and sisters; but if you
must sulk, you must." Some believers are of this sort. Because
they had a serious loss, they must needs rob themselves of
communion with God. Because they have endured terrible
bereavement, they bereave themselves of their Lord. Because
they are not well, they fret themselves into worse health.
Some are only satisfied when they are in the depths of
misery. I know some whose wretchedness is chronic: like
polar bears, they are only at home in the ice. You smile, and
well you may; but then you should also weep, if this is your
case. You should cry, "O Lord, put me right with thyself! I
cannot be content to be always repining and lamenting! If
there are consolations to be had in thee, let me have them
now. I know there is no consolation anywhere else. To whom
should I go? Thou alone hast the words of eternal life! There
is no secret thing with me, my God, upon which I can rely. I
must have thy consolation, or I shall have no comfort!"

IV. Here comes the most practical question of all, and with
this I close. If it be so, that you have hitherto found heavenly
consolations to have small effect with you, and yet have
nothing better to put in their place, IS THERE NOT A CAUSE
FOR YOUR FAILURE? Will you not endeavour to find it out?

Dear friends, you that seek to be right, you that desire to be
full Christians, and yet cannot rejoice in God, at least not
often, nor greatly, *is there not some sin indulged?* A child of
God may go on with a sin unwittingly, and that for years; and
all the while that sin may be causing a dreadful leakage in his
joy. You cannot be wrong in life, and thought, and word,

without a measure of joy oozing away. Take a good look at yourself, and examine your life by the light of Scripture, and if you find that you have been doing something wrong unawares, or for which you have made an unworthy excuse, away with the evil! Away with it at once! When this Achan is stoned, and the accursed thing is put away, you will be surprised to find what joy, what comfort will immediately flow into your soul.

Next, *may there not have been some duty neglected?* We are not saved by good works; but if any Christian omits a good work, he will find it injurious to his peace. Many Christian people never get into the clear light of full assurance, because they do not obey their conscience upon every point. I pray you, never quarrel with conscience, for it will have the best of it with you—if you have a conscience. If you go contrary to conscience, there will be trouble inside the little kingdom of your soul, as sure as you are alive. "Oh, but I have always been intending to do it." That makes it the greater sin that you have not done it, for evidently you knew your Lord's will. Have you considered that any wilful omission of duty is not one sin, but many? It is your duty to do it now; it is a sin that you have not done it already. It will be your duty to do it to-morrow; it will be another sin if you omit it to-morrow. How often the omission creates a new sin I cannot tell; but as surely as you rob God of obedience, sin will rob you of comfort. If you neglect obedience to the precept, you cannot have the comfort of the promise. Get that matter seen to at once, there's a dear friend! Omitted duty is like a little stone in the sole of your shoe. It is small, and some say it is a non-essential matter; but it is just because it is so small that it can do so much mischief. If I had a great pebble in my boot, I should be sure to get it out; but a tiny stone may remain, and blister me, and lame me. Get out the little stones, or they will hinder your travelling to heaven.

Again, *may there not be some idol in your heart?* That is a very searching suggestion. If the consolations of God are small with you, may you not have set up something in the place of God—a lover, a wife, a husband, a child, a friend, learning, honour, wealth? I need not mention the many forms taken by our idols. It is very easy to set up an image of jealousy. A thing in itself harmless and even lovely, may grievously provoke the Lord through our heart going after it.

Brother, sister, is it so? Do you love anything as you love God?
I suggest that you should at once cry—

> "The dearest idol I have known,
> Whate'er that idol be,
> Help me to tear it from thy throne,
> And worship only thee."

If you do not remove the idol from its throne, if God loves you,
he will make your Dagon fall and be broken. If you want to
lose that which is the object of your comfort and delight, love
it too much. This is a sort of unwilful murder which good
people can perform upon their children and their friends.
Idolize and destroy. Love the creature more than the Creator,
and it may be necessary that they should be taken from you
altogether.

But, beloved, if you do not enjoy the consolations of God, do
you not think it is because *you do not think enough of God?* I
am ashamed of myself that I do not live more with my God.
How little time do we spend with him! We think about his
work rather than himself. Even in the Scriptures we look
more to the words than to God speaking by the words. We
criticize a phrase when we should be drinking in the spirit of
the revelation, and so be getting near to God. If we are cold, is
it not because we do not sit in the sun? If we are faint, is it not
because we do not feed on him whose flesh is meat indeed?
How would a fish fare if it left the water? How can we prosper
if we leave our God, who is the element of our life? Say with
David, in the psalm we sang just now:

> "Like as the hart for water-brooks,
> In thirst doth pant and bray;
> So pants my longing soul, O God,
> That come to thee I may."

And then you will not long be disquieted, for you will go on to
sing:

> "For yet I know I shall him praise,
> Who graciously to me,
> The health is of my countenance,
> Yea, mine own God is he."

If any of you have not the joy of the Lord which you once
possessed, is it not possible that *when you used to have it you
grew proud?* "Jeshurun waxed fat and kicked." He will have to

be starved a bit to bring him to his senses. Ah! I have known a child of God so happy in the Lord, so useful and so blessed in every way, that he began to think he was something out of the common. He grew very sublime. As to the poor brethren around him, he could hardly put up with them—they were more dead than alive; they were weaklings, foolish men, mere babes, and so on. He saw a poor tried believer looking out of one of the windows of Doubting Castle, and instead of helping him out, he bullied him so much for being there at all that the poor prisoner was more shut up than ever. Look at him! He is a fine fellow! *He* never had sad doubts; *he* never felt anxious fears. Not he! You remind me, my dear brother, of the fat cattle mentioned in Ezekiel, of whom the prophet says that they thrust with side, and with shoulder, and pushed all the diseased with their horns till they had scattered them. "Therefore thus saith the Lord God unto them; behold, I, even I, will judge between the fat cattle and between the lean cattle." The Lord will not have you condemn the weak and sneer at the feeble. You may yet be such yourselves. His consolations will be small with you if his people are small with you. If you do not care for the little ones who believe in him, neither will he be quick to comfort *you*. Be humble. Take the lowest place. If you will lie low before the Lord, he will lift you up; but if you lift up yourself, God will throw you down.

I will close by saying that one of the worst causes of disquietude is unbelief. *Have you begun to distrust?* Do you really doubt your God? Then I do not wonder that the consolations of God are small with you. Here is the rule of the kingdom—"According to your faith, so be it unto you." If you doubt God, you will get but little from him. He that wavereth may not expect to receive anything of the Lord. Strong faith may have what it wills; but when your doubts master your faith, prayer cannot prevail. Few are the dainties from the King's table which come to the dish of mistrust. What do you doubt? Do you question the Word of God? Has the Lord said more than the truth will warrant? Do you think so? Will you dare to throw such a handful of mud upon the veracity of God? His truth is one of his crown jewels; would you take it away? Do you distrust his power? Do you think he cannot comfort you? Do you imagine that he cannot make you ride upon the high places of the earth? Do you think that he cannot put a new song into your mouth, and make you rejoice in his name from morning to night? Wherefore should you doubt his power to make you joyful in his house? Do you doubt the Lord's wisdom? Do you think the Holy Spirit cannot meet your case, and provide comfort suitable for your distress? Surely, you cannot have fallen into this base suspicion! Or, do you doubt the Lord's presence? Do you think that he is too far off to know you and help you? He is everywhere present, and he knows the way that you take.

Come and trust the Lord. Come, beloved, whether you be saint or sinner, come through the Lord Jesus, and fall down at Jehovah's feet and say, "Lord, my hope is in thee. I have no comfort elsewhere; but I know thy comforts are not small. Comfort me, I pray thee, in Christ Jesus." If you would have that prayer answered, listen to these words of the Lord Jesus: "Look unto me, and be ye saved, all the ends of the earth: for I am God, and there is none else." Though the tears be in your eyes, yet turn them to Christ crucified. Put your trust simply, immediately, wholly, and alone in him who died for you, and you shall go your way filled with consolation. God grant that it may be so, for Jesus Christ's sake. Amen.

11

Job's Sure Knowledge

"For I know that my Redeemer liveth..."   **Job 19:25**

I daresay you know that there are a great many difficulties about the translation of this passage. It is a very complicated piece of Hebrew, partly, I suppose, owing to its great antiquity, being found in what is, probably, one of the oldest Books of the Bible. Besides that, different persons have tried to translate it according to their own varying views. The Jews stiffly fight against the notion of the Messiah and his resurrection being found in this verse, while many Christian commentators see here everything that we can find in the New Testament, and translate the passage as though Job were as well instructed in this matter as we are now that Christ "hath brought life and immortality to light through the gospel." Others say that, while there is, no doubt, a reference to the person and the resurrection of Christ, yet it is not so vivid as some seem to think.

Personally, I am quite satisfied with the translation given in our Authorized Version; yet it has occurred to me that, possibly, Job himself may not have known the full meaning of all that he said. Imagine the patriarch driven into a corner, badgered by his so-called friends, charged by them with all manner of evils until he is quite boiling over with indignation, and, at the same time, smarting under terrible bodily diseases and the dreadful losses which he has sustained; and, at last, he bursts out with this exclamation, "I shall be vindicated one day; I am sure I shall. I know that my Vindicator liveth. I am sure that there is One who will vindicate me; and if he never clears my name and reputation as long as I live, it will be done afterwards. There must be a just God, in heaven, who will see me righted; and even though worms devour my body until the last relic of it has passed away, I do verily believe that, somehow, in the far-off ages, I shall be vindicated." He throws his faith forward to some tremendous era which he anticipates, and he declares that there will be found then, as he believes there is alive even now, a Goel, a Kinsman, an Avenger, who will stand up for him, and set right all this wrong. He cannot conceive that God will permit such gross injustice to be done as for a man, who has walked as he has walked, to be brought so low, and then to be stung with such unfounded accusations; he is positive that there must be a Vindicator for him somewhere, and he appeals to that last dread tribunal, which he dimly sees in the far-off future, and he believes that someone will be found to stand up successfully for him there.

If that be the case, you will see that Job was driven, perhaps beyond his former knowledge, by his very pains and trials. He may but dimly have perceived a future state, but his condition revealed to him the necessity for such a state. He felt that, if the righteous suffer so much in this life, often apparently without any just cause, and if the wicked prosper, then there must be another state in which God will set right the wrongs of this, and rectify the apparent inequalities of his providence here. Job realized that; and, possibly, his deep griefs may have been the channel of another revelation to him, namely, that there was a mysterious Divine Being, concerning whom that dark prophecy had been handed down from the garden of Eden itself, "The Seed of the woman shall bruise the serpent's head." He felt sure that, for those who were wronged as he had been, there must be an Advocate provided. He had before complained that there was no Umpire—no "Daysman"—to stand between them both; but now he asks for an Advocate, and he feels that there must be one, yea, he knows that there is, and he declares that, somewhere or other, there is an Advocate who will, some day or other, set right all that concerns him, let things go now as they may. So, possibly, Job was seeing more than he had ever seen before of that mysterious One who pleads the cause of those who are oppressed, and shows himself strong, on their behalf, at the right hand of God.

I am not going to enter into any discussion of the matter, but shall use the passage in the full Evangelical sense. Job may have known all that we now know concerning Christ, for he may have had special revelations and manifestations. We do not find all that we know in his Book, yet he may have meant all that I shall say in this discourse. If he did not mean it, I trust that we shall, under the gracious guidance of the Holy Spirit.

I. I shall speak first upon this point,—JOB HAD A TRUE FRIEND AMID MISTAKEN FRIENDS.

These men were miserable comforters, but Job had a real Comforter, they were estranged from him, but he had a true Friend left; so he said, "I know that my Goel liveth." That is the Hebrew word; I suppose you all know that it means the person nearest akin to him, who, because he was nearest akin, was bound to take up his cause. If a man was slain by misadventure, the goel pursued the one who had slain him, and endeavoured to avenge his death. If a person fell into debt, and was sold into slavery because of the debt, his goel, if he was able, had to redeem him; and hence we get the word "redeemer." Or if estates became mortgaged through poverty, it was the duty of the next of kin to redeem them, if possible; so again we get the idea of redeemer. But the word "goel" is more comprehensive than the word redeemer, so we will begin with its first meaning.

Job, in the midst of his false friends, had *One whom he called his kinsman.* "I know," he said, "that my Kinsman liveth." We interpret that word "Kinsman" as meaning our Lord Jesus Christ, and we sing,—

> "Jesus, our Kinsman and our God,
> Arrayed in majesty and blood,
> Thou art our life, our souls in thee,
> Possess a full felicity."

I want you, just now, to think of Jesus Christ as your Kinsman if you are really in him, for he is indeed the nearest akin to you of any,—bone of your bone, and flesh of your flesh. "Forasmuch then as the children are partakers of flesh and blood, he also himself likewise took part of the same." Now, your own flesh and blood, as you call them, are not so near to you in real kinship as Jesus is; for, often, you will find flesh and blood near akin by birth but not by sympathy. Two brothers may be, spiritually, very different from one another, and may not be able to enter into each other's trials at all; but this Kinsman participates in every pang that rends your heart; he knows your constitution, your weakness, your sensitiveness, the particular trial that cuts you to the quick, for in all your afflictions he was afflicted. Thus he is nearer to

you than the nearest of earthly kin can possibly be, for he
enters more fully into the whole of your life; he seems to have
gone through it all, and he still goes through it all in his
constant sympathy with you.

Christ's kinship with his people is to be thought of with
great comfort because it is voluntary. We have some, perhaps,
who are akin to us, yet, who wish they were not. Many a time,
when a rich man has poor relations, he is half-ashamed of the
kinship between them, and wishes that it did not exist.
Shame upon him for thinking so! But our Lord Jesus Christ's
relationship to us is no accident of birth; it was voluntarily
assumed by him. He would be one with us because he loved
us; nothing could satisfy him till he had come to this earth,
and been made one flesh with his Church. "For this cause," it
is said concerning marriage, "shall a man leave his father and
mother, and shall be joined unto his wife, and they two shall
be one flesh. This is a great mystery," said Paul; "but I speak
concerning Christ and the Church." And, verily, so was it with
Christ, as the poet sings,—

> "'Yea,' saith the Lord, 'with her I'll go
> Through all the depths of care and woe;
> And on the cross will even dare
> The bitter pangs of death to bear.'"

This he did because he would be one flesh with his people,
and that is a very near kinship which comes as close as that,
and which willingly does so,—not by force; but by voluntary
choice.

And, further, this is a kinship of which Jesus is never
ashamed. We have known or heard of the prosperous man
who has been ashamed of his poor old mother, and of the
educated young man who has looked down with scorn upon
the very father who has toiled and slaved in order to give him
the advantages of such an education. It is disgraceful that
there should ever be such ingrates; but it is written
concerning our great Kinsman, "He that sanctifieth and they
who are sanctified are all of one; for which cause he is not
ashamed to call them brethren." He declares to the whole
universe, concerning those persecuted ones, those who are
ridiculed as being fools, "They are my brethren." The Prince of
glory, whose fingers are adorned with stars of light like rings
of priceless value, calls the poor bedridden woman, who is a

child of God, his sister, and calls the humble, toiling, labouring man, who walks with him, his brother; and he is not ashamed to do so. Think, beloved, with intensest gratitude, of this great Kinsman of yours, who is so near of kin to you,—voluntarily near of kin, and not ashamed to own the kinship.

Remember, too, that your Kinsman liveth in this respect,— that he will always be your Kinsman. The closest ties of earthly relationship must, to a great extent, end in death, for there are no husbands and wives, as such, in heaven. There cannot be, "for in the resurrection they neither marry, nor are given in marriage, but are as the angels of God in heaven." There are other ties, of a spiritual kind, that will far outshine the best of bonds that linked us together here; but, when all other ties are broken, Jesus will always be our Kinsman, our Brother. We shall find the fraternal relationship better understood, more fully enjoyed, and more clearly manifested up there than it ever can be here. When all other relationships are growing dim, this blessed eternal kinship will shine out the more brightly. So I want all of you, who truly love the Lord Jesus Christ, to interpret my text in this way: "I know that my Kinsman liveth," and to feel how honoured you are to have such a Kinsman as Christ is. Ruth was highly privileged in having such a kinsman as Boaz, who was not content for her to glean in his fields, but who took her as his wife; and your great Kinsman intends that you should be betrothed unto him for ever, and he will bring you to his heavenly home at the marriage supper of the Lamb.

There was a second meaning to the word goel, arising out of the first,—*Job's Kinsman would become his Vindicator.* It was the kinsman's duty to defend the rights of his needy relative, so Job intended here to say, "I know that my Vindicator liveth;" and the Lord Jesus Christ is the Vindicator of his people from all false charges. It is not easy for Christians to live in this world without being slandered and misrepresented; certainly, those of us who live in the full blaze of public life can hardly utter a word without having it twisted, and tortured, and misconstrued. We are often represented as saying what we loathe even to think; yet we must not be surprised at that. The world loves lying,—it always has done so, and it always will. Even in private life you may meet with similar cruel treatment; there are some of

God's best children who lie under reproach by the year together. The very things which they would not tolerate for a moment are laid to their charge, and they are thought to be guilty of them, and even good people hold up their hands in pious horror at them, though they are perfectly innocent all the while. Well, beloved, ever remember that your Vindicator liveth. Do not be too much concerned to clear your own character; above all, do not attempt to vindicate yourself in a court of law, but say to yourself, "I know that my Vindicator liveth." When he cometh, "then shall the righteous shine forth as the sun in the kingdom of their Father." His people may be under a cloud now; but, when he appeareth, the cloud shall break, and their true glory shall be seen. The greater the obloquy under which any of us have unjustly lived on earth, the greater will be the joy and the honour which will be vouchsafed to us in the day when Christ shall clear our character from all the shameful aspersions that have been brought against us. All will be cleared up in that day, so leave the accusations alone, knowing that your Vindicator liveth.

There is another most comforting thought,—that our Vindicator will clear us from true charges as well as false ones. As for the false charges, what do they matter? It is the true ones that really concern us: can Christ clear us from them? Yes, that he can. Remember how the apostle John writes, "If any man sin, we have an Advocate with the Father, Jesus Christ the righteous." You see, it is not merely, if we have been said to sin when we did not, but if we really sin, "we have an Advocate with the Father." O blessed Advocate, how dost thou clear thy people of the sin which they have actually committed? Why, in this way; he took it upon himself,—the awful load of their guilt,—and suffered the full penalty for it. So there he stands before the eternal throne, to plead their cause; and, as he does so, he says, "Those sins, committed by my people,—I have taken them upon myself, and suffered in the room, and place, and stead of all who will believe in me." O thou blessed Kinsman, how glorious art thou in thy grace, in that thou hast so completely undertaken our cause that thou hast been made sin for us, that we might be made the righteousness of God in thee! Yes, beloved, Jesus will plead the merit of his precious blood and his spotless righteousness; and, before that powerful pleading, our sins and our transgressions shall sink beneath the flood, and shall not be remembered against us any more for ever.

In that day, too, our Vindicator will defend us against all the accusations of Satan. Our great adversary often assails and attacks us here, and the Lord says to him, as he did concerning Joshua the high priest, "The Lord rebuke thee, O Satan; even the Lord that hath chosen Jerusalem rebuke thee!" We may tell the devil, when we stand foot to foot with him, and are sore beset, that our Vindicator liveth, and we may quote to him that grand promise, "The God of peace shall bruise Satan under your feet shortly," because our Vindicator, who is to bruise the serpent's head, still liveth. The old serpent may nibble at your heel for a while, as he did at your Master's, but you, in the strength of your Lord, shall bruise his head; and whatsoever other adversary of your soul there may be, at any time, rest you in quiet confidence. Even if that adversary is permitted to prevail over you for a while, say unto him, "Rejoice not against me, O mine enemy: when I fall, I shall arise; when I sit in darkness, the Lord shall be a light unto me."

So you have two meanings of the word goel,—my Kinsman, my Vindicator, liveth. I hope you who are greatly tempted and tried, and you who are persecuted and oppressed, will catch that second meaning, and commit your cause unto God. "Dearly beloved, avenge not yourselves, but rather give place unto wrath; for it is written, Vengeance is mine; I will repay, saith the Lord." Be slow to anger; fret not yourselves because of the wicked man that prospereth in his evil way, and think not of being revenged upon your oppressors. In patience and quietness possess your souls, knowing that your time of vindication will surely come, for your Vindicator liveth.

Then the third meaning of the word goel certainly is redeemer, so Job could say, "*I know that my Redeemer liveth.*" As I have already said, the next of kin, in the process of vindicating his poor kinsman, was accustomed to redeem him from bondage, or to redeem any part of his estate that might be under mortgage. So, let us next think of how the Lord Jesus Christ hath redeemed us from bondage. Having broken the law of God, we were in bondage to that law; we had received the spirit of bondage again to fear. But we, who have believed in Jesus, our Kinsman, can say that he hath redeemed us from the curse of the law, being made a curse for us, and that we are no longer in bondage. We were also in bondage under sin, as Paul wrote, "I am carnal, sold under sin;" but Christ has come, and broken the power of sin in us, so that its reigning power is subdued; and though it still striveth to get the mastery, and often maketh us to groan within ourselves, even as Paul did, yet do we, with him, thank God, who giveth us the victory, through Jesus Christ our Lord.

There are two redemptions,—redemption by price and redemption by power, and both of these Christ hath wrought for us;—by price, by his sacrifice upon the cross of Calvary; and by power, by his Divine Spirit coming into our heart, and renewing our soul. Ought we not unceasingly to bless the Lord who hath redeemed us from under the law, having paid the penalty for the commands which we had broken, and who hath also redeemed us from the power of sin? "I know that my Redeemer liveth," then I know that I am a free man; for if the Son makes us free, then are we free indeed. I know that he paid the price for my soul's eternal redemption, then may my soul continually exult in him, and rejoice in the liberty wherewith he hath made me free.

But, as I have already reminded you, the redeemer was also accustomed to redeem the estate as well as the person of his kinsman. We had lost everything. Father Adam had put everything under a heavy mortgage, and we could not even meet the interest on it; but the whole estate is unmortgaged now, even to paradise itself. Does someone ask, "Is there not any mortgage even upon paradise?" I answer,—No; for Christ said to the dying thief, "Today shalt thou be with me in paradise;" so it is clear that he has entered paradise, and claimed it on his people's behalf. Jesus Christ hath said, in the words of the psalmist, "I restored that which I took not away." Bankrupt debtors, through the Lord's sovereign grace, you are no longer under any liabilities because of your sin if Christ be accepted by you as your Goel and Redeemer. He hath restored to you the estates which your first father, Adam, had lost; and he hath made you heirs of God, and joint-heirs with Jesus Christ, through the wondrous redemption which he wrought for you upon the cross of Calvary.

Suck the honey, if you can, out of these three glorious truths, and you will be able to do so in proportion as you can personally use the words of the text, "'I know that my Redeemer liveth.' I know that he lives who will vindicate my character, and rectify my wrongs. I know, too, that he lives who hath redeemed me from sin and hell; and even though I die, I know that he will redeem me from the power of the grave, and that he will enable me to say, 'O death, where is thy sting? O grave, where is thy victory?'" Dwell on the remembrance that you have such a Divine Helper, and then let us pass on to another thought, at which I will only briefly hint as I proceed to another part of my theme.

II. The second point is this,—JOB HAD REAL PROPERTY AMID ABSOLUTE POVERTY.

Job had lost everything,—every stick and stone that he possessed, he had lost his children, and he had lost his wife, too, for all practical purposes, for she had not acted like a wife to him in his time of trial. Poor Job, he had lost everything else, but he had not lost his Redeemer. Notice, he does not say, "I know that my wife and my children live;" but he says, "I know that my Redeemer liveth." Ah! "my Redeemer,"—he has not lost him, so he has the best of all possessions still left. Looking up to him, by faith, with the tears of joy standing in his eyes, he says, "Yes, he is my Redeemer, and he still lives; I accept him as mine, and I will cling to him for ever." Can you, beloved friends, not merely rejoice in Christ as *the* Redeemer, but also as *your* Redeemer? Have you personally accepted him as your Redeemer? Have you personally trusted him with your soul, wholly and really; and do you already feel, in your own heart, a kinship to this great Kinsman, a trust in this great Vindicator, a reliance upon his great redemption? Another man's redemption is of no value to my soul; the sweetness lies in the little word *"my"*—*"my* Redeemer." Luther used to say that the marrow of the gospel is found in the pronouns, and I believe it is: *"my* Redeemer." Say, with me, each one of you for himself or herself,—

> *"My* faith would lay her hand
> On that dear head of thine,
> While like a penitent I stand,
> And there confess *my* sin."

> *"My* soul looks back to see
> The burdens thou didst bear,
> When hanging on the cursed tree
> And hopes *her* guilt was there."

If you really do rely upon Christ's atoning sacrifice, and so

take him as your Redeemer, you may not only hope your guilt
was there, but you may know that it was. There, poor man,
you may not have a penny in your pocket, but if you can truly
say, "my Redeemer," you are infinitely better off than a
millionaire who cannot say that. Thou, who knowest not
where thou wilt have a lodging to-night, if thou canst truly
say, "my Redeemer," thou needest not envy the very angels of
God, for, in this respect, thou art ahead even of them, for they
can call him "Lord", but not "Redeemer." He is not so near
akin to them as he is to thee, "for verily he took not on him
the nature of angels; but he took on him the seed of
Abraham." He took your nature and mine, beloved, for Christ
became a man. So Job had something real and valuable left
even when he had lost all his property.

III. Thirdly, Job seems to lay stress upon the word "liveth":
"I know that my Redeemer *liveth*." This teaches us that JOB
HAD A LIVING KINSMAN AMID A DYING FAMILY.

All his children were dead. We cannot easily estimate the
full force of that blow upon the patriarch's heart. The loss of
one child is a very painful event, even when the child is a very
little one, and the parents have many others left; but it is a
far worse bereavement when the children, who are taken
away, are grown up, as Job's were. They were evidently a
very united family, who used to meet in each other's houses
for mutual fellowship. They seem to have been a very happy
family, and they were certainly a family under very gracious
influences, for Job was accustomed, after their days of
festival, to offer sacrifices for them, lest they should have
sinned against the Lord. Altogether, it was a fine family,—
seven sons and three daughters;—and now they were all gone
at once! To lose all one's family at once, like that, is a heavy
stroke that none can measure but those who have felt it. All
were gone,—the whole ten at once! That was sad for poor Job,
but it was most blessed that he was able to say, "Though my
children are all dead, 'I know that my Redeemer liveth.' He is
not dead, and in him I find more than all that I have lost."

Look at your Lord, dear friend, if you are mourning, just
now, the loss of loved ones, and see whether he is not better to
you than ten sons and daughters. See whether there is not, in
his heart, room enough for that affection, which has been so
rudely snapped, to grow again. The tendrils of your soul want
something to cling to, and to twist around; then let them

twine around him. Rejoice that he lives in a dying world. If
you walk through the cemetery, or stand by the open grave,
how blessedly these words seem to fall upon your spirit, like
the music of angels, "These are dead, but 'I know that *my
Redeemer liveth*,'—liveth on, liveth in power, liveth in
happiness, liveth with a life which he communicates to all
who trust him. He lives, and therefore I shall live with him.
He lives, and therefore the dead, who are in him, shall live for
ever." O blessed truth!

You will yourself die soon, dear friend; no, I must correct
myself, you will not *die*, for it is not death for one who knows
the Saviour to die. You will fall asleep in him, one of these
days, at the very hour that God has appointed; and when you
open your eyes, it will not be in the narrow death-chamber,
you will not be on the bed of sickness. Methinks you will be
startled to find yourself amid such new surroundings. "What
is this I hear?" you will say. "Such music as this has never
charmed me before, and what is that I see?" But you will not
need to enquire, for you will know *that* face at once. You
knew, while on earth, that Jesus still lived; but you will know
it better then, when you lay aside these heavy optics that do
but dim our sight, and get into the pure spirit state, and then
see HIM. Oh, the bliss of that first sight of Christ! It seems to
me as if that would gather up an eternity of delight into a
single moment; that first glimpse of him will be enough to
make us swoon away with excessive rapture. I do verily think
that some saints, whom I have known, have done just that,—
swooned away with the excess of joy that they have felt in
their departing moments. I have, sounding in my ears just
now, the voice of a dear brother, by whose bedside I sat for a
little while before I came to this service. He said to me, "I
shall be home to-night, pastor. I wanted to see your face once
more before I went; but I shall be home to-night, and see the
face of Jesus." I hope you will all be prepared to die after that
fashion. The godly old negro said, "Our minister is dying full
of life." That is the way to die,—full of life. Because Jesus
lives, we shall live also, and we may well die full of life
because of our union to him.

IV. The last thought I want to leave with you is this, JOB
HAD ABSOLUTE CERTAINTY AMID UNCERTAIN AFFAIRS.

He said, "I *know* that my Redeemer liveth." Why, Job, I
should have thought you would not have known anything for

certain now. I should not have liked to insure Job's sheep, and oxen, and asses, and camels, or the houses in which his children met together to feast. Nothing seemed to be certain with Job but uncertainty; yet there was one thing, concerning which he felt that he could put his foot down firmly, and say, "'I *know.*' The winds may rage, and the tempests roar, but they cannot shake this rock. 'I know.' 'I know.' 'I know.'" Beloved, is everything uncertain with you in this world? Of course it is, for it is so with everybody. But does it appear to be more uncertain with you than it does with anybody else? Does your business seem to be slipping away, and every earthly comfort be threatening to disappear? Even if it is so, there is, nevertheless, something that is certain, something that is stable,—Jesus your Redeemer lives. Rest on him, and you will never fail. Let your faith in him be firm, and confident; you cannot be too fully established in the belief that Jesus, who once died, has left the grave, to die no more, and that you, in him, must also live eternally. Something may be wrong with you, for the next few days or weeks, but all is right with you for ever, and "all's well that ends well." There may be some rough water to be crossed between here and the fair havens of eternal felicity, but all is right there for ever and ever. There may be losses and crosses, there may be tossings and shipwrecks, but all is right for ever with all who are in Christ Jesus. "Some on boards, and some on broken pieces of the ship,"—but all who are in Christ Jesus shall escape "safe to land." There are uncertainties innumerable, but there is this one certainty: "Israel shall be saved in the Lord with an everlasting salvation: ye shall not be ashamed nor confounded world without end." Spring on this rock, man! If you are struggling in the sea, just now, and waves of sin and doubt beat over you, leap on to this rock,—Jesus lives. Trust the living Christ; and, because he lives, you shall live also. I could cheerfully take my place with Job, if I might be able to say as confidently as he did, "I know that my Redeemer liveth;" and if you, as a poor sinner, are trusting wholly and only in Christ, then he is your Redeemer, and you are saved for ever. If he is the only hope that you have, and you cling to him as the limpet clings to the rock, then all is right with you for ever, and you may know that he is your Redeemer as surely as Job knew that he was his. The Lord bless you, for Jesus Christ's sake! Amen.

12

I Know That My Redeemer Liveth

"For I know that my redeemer liveth, and that he shall stand at the latter day upon the earth: And though after my skin worms destroy this body, yet in my flesh shall I see God: Whom I shall see for myself, and mine eyes shall behold, and not another; though my reins be consumed within me."   **Job 19:25-27**

The hand of God has been upon us heavily this week. An aged deacon, who has been for more than fifty years a member of this Church, has been removed from our midst; and a sister, the beloved wife of another of our Church-officers, a member for nearly the same term of years, has fallen asleep. It is not often that a church is called to sorrow over the departure of two such venerable members—let not our ears be deaf to such a double admonition to prepare to meet our God. That they were preserved so long, and upheld so mercifully for so many years, was not only a reason of gratitude to them, but to us also. I am, however, so averse to the preaching of what are called *funeral sermons,* that I forbear, lest I appear to eulogise the creature, when my only aim should be to magnify the grace of God.

Our text deserves our profound attention; its preface would hardly have been written had not the matter been of the utmost importance in the judgment of the patriarch who uttered it. Listen to Job's remarkable desire: "Oh that my words were now written! oh that they were printed in a book! That they were graven with an iron pen and lead in the rock for ever!" Perhaps, hardly aware of the full meaning of the words he was uttering, yet his holy soul was impressed with a sense of some weighty revelation concealed within his words; he therefore desired that it might be recorded in a book; he has had his desire, the Book of books embalms the words of Job. He wished to have them graven on a rock; cut deep into it with an iron pen, and then the lines inlaid with lead; or he would have them engraven, according to the custom of the ancients, upon a sheet of metal, so that time might not be able to eat out the inscription. He has not had his desire in that respect, save only that upon many and many a sepulchre those words of Job stand recorded, "I know that my redeemer liveth." It is the opinion of some commentators that Job, in speaking of the rock here, intended his own rock-hewn sepulchre, and desired that this might be his epitaph; that it might be cut deep, so that ages should not wear it out; that when any asked, "Where does Job sleep?" as soon as they saw the sepulchre of the patriarch of Uz, they might learn that he died in hope of resurrection, resting upon a living Redeemer. Whether such a sentence adorned the portals of Job's last sleeping-place we know not; but certainly no words could have been more fitly chosen. Should not the man of patience, the mirror of endurance, the pattern of trust, bear as his memorial this golden line, which is as full of all the patience of hope, and hope of patience, as mortal language can be? Who among us could select a more glorious motto for his last escutcheon? I am sorry to say that a few of those who have written upon this passage cannot see Christ or the resurrection in it at all. Albert Barnes, among the rest, expresses his intense sorrow that he cannot find the resurrection here, and for my part I am sorry for him. If it had been Job's desire to foretell the advent of Christ and his own sure resurrection, I cannot see what better words he could have used; and if those truths are not here taught, then language must have lost its original object, and must have been employed to mystify and not to explain; to conceal and not to reveal. What I ask, does the patriarch mean, if not that he shall rise again when the Redeemer stands upon the earth? Brethren, no unsophisticated mind can fail to find here what almost all believers have here discovered. I feel safe in keeping to the old sense, and we shall this morning seek no new interpretation, but adhere to the common one, with or without the consent of our critics.

In discoursing upon them I shall speak upon three things. First, *let us, with the patriarch, descend into the grave and behold the ravages of death.* Then, with him, *let us look up on high for present consolation.* And, still in his admirable company, let us, in the third place, *anticipate future delights.*

I. First of all then, with the patriarch of Uz, LET US DESCEND INTO THE SEPULCHRE.

The body has just been divorced from the soul. Friends who loved most tenderly have said—"Bury my dead out of my sight." The body is borne upon the bier and consigned to the silent earth; it is surrounded by the earthworks of death. Death has a host of troops. If the locusts and the caterpillars be God's army, the worms are the army of death. These hungry warriors begin to attack the city of man. They commence with the outworks; they storm the munition, and overturn the walls. The skin, the city wall of manhood, is utterly broken down, and the towers of its glory covered with confusion. How speedily the cruel invaders deface all beauty. The face gathers blackness; the countenance is defiled with corruption. Those cheeks once fair with youth, and ruddy with health, have fallen in, even as a bowing wall and a tottering fence; those eyes, the windows of the mind whence joy and sorrow looked forth by turns, are now filled up with the dust of death; those lips, the doors of the soul, the gates of Mansoul, are carried away, and the bars thereof are broken. Alas, ye windows of agates and gates of carbuncle, where are ye now? How shall I mourn for thee, O thou captive city, for the mighty men have utterly spoiled thee! Thy neck, once like a tower of ivory, has become as a fallen column; thy nose, so lately comparable to "the tower of Lebanon, which looketh toward Damascus," is as a ruined hovel; and thy head, which towered like Carmel, lies low as the clods of the valley. Where is beauty now? The most lovely cannot be known from the most deformed. The vessel so daintily wrought upon the potter's wheel, is cast away upon the dunghill with the vilest potsherds. Cruel have ye been, ye warriors of death, for though ye wield no axes and bear no hammers, yet have ye broken down the carved work; and though ye speak not with tongues, yet have ye said in your hearts, "We have swallowed her up, certainly this is the day that we have looked for; we have found, we have seen it." The skin is gone. The troops have entered into the town of Mansoul. And now they pursue their work of devastation; the pitiless marauders fall upon the body itself. There are those noble aqueducts, the veins through which the streams of life were wont to flow, these, instead of being rivers of life, have become blocked up with the soil and wastes of death, and now they must be pulled to pieces; not a single relic of them shall be spared. Mark the muscles and sinews, like great highways that penetrating the metropolis, carry the strength and wealth of manhood along —their curious pavement must be pulled up, and they that do traffic thereon must be consumed, each tunnelled bone, and curious arch, and knotted bond must be snapped and broken. Fair fabrics, glorious storehouses, costly engines, wonderful machines—all, all must be pulled down, and not one stone left upon another. Those nerves, which like telegraphic wires connected all parts of the city together, to carry thought and feeling and intelligence—these are cut. No matter how artistic the work might be,—and certainly we are fearfully and wonderfully made, and the anatomist stands still and marvels to see the skill which the eternal God has manifested in the formation of the body—but these ruthless worms pull everything to pieces, till like a city sacked and spoiled that has been given up for days to pillage and to flame, everything lies in a heap of ruin—ashes to ashes, dust to dust. But these invaders stop not here. Job says that next they consume his reins. We are wont to speak of the heart as the great citadel of life, the inner keep and donjon, where the captain of the guard holdeth out to the last. The Hebrews do not regard the heart, but the lower viscera, the reins, as the seat of the passions and of mental power. The worms spare not; they enter the secret places of the tabernacle of life, and the standard is plucked from the tower. Having died, the heart cannot preserve itself, and falls like the rest of the frame—a prey to worms. It is gone, it is all gone! The skin, the body, the vitals, all, all has departed. There is nought left. In a few years ye shall turn up the sod and say, "Here slept so-and-so, and where is he now?" and ye may search and hunt and dig, but ye shall find no relic. Mother Earth has devoured her own offspring.

Dear friends, why should we wish to have it otherwise? Why should we desire to preserve the body when the soul has gone? What vain attempts men have made with coffins of lead, and wrappings of myrrh and frankincense. The embalming of the Egyptians, those master robbers of the worm, what has it done? It has served to keep some poor shrivelled lumps of mortality above ground to be sold for curiosities, to be dragged away to foreign climes, and stared upon by thoughtless eyes. No, let the dust go, the sooner it dissolves the better. And what matters it how it goes! If it be devoured of beasts, if it be swallowed up in the sea and become food for fishes! What, if plants with their roots suck up the particles! What, if the fabric passes into the animal, and from the animal into the earth, and from the earth into the plants, and from the plant into the animal again! What, if the winds blow it along the highway! What, if the rivers carry it to the waves of ocean! It is ordained that somehow or other it must be all separated—"dust to dust, ashes to ashes." It is part of the decree that it should all perish. The worms or some other agents of destruction must destroy this body. Do not seek to avoid what God has purposed; do not look upon it as a gloomy thing. Regard it as a necessity; nay more, view it as the platform of a miracle, the lofty stage of resurrection, since Jesus shall surely raise again from the dead the particles of this body, however divided from one another. We have heard of miracles, but what a miracle is the resurrection! All the miracles of Scripture, yea even those wrought by Christ, are small compared with this. The philosopher says, "How is it possible that God shall hunt out every particle of the human frame?" He can do it: he has but to speak the word, and every single atom, though it may have travelled thousands of leagues, though it may have been blown as dust across the desert, and anon have fallen upon the bosom of the sea, and then have descended into the depths thereof to be cast up on a desolate shore, sucked up by plants, fed on again by beasts, or passed into the fabric of another man,—I say that individual atom shall find its fellows, and the whole company of particles at the trump of the archangel shall travel to their appointed place, and the body, the very body which was laid in the ground, shall rise again.

I am afraid I have been somewhat uninteresting while tarrying upon the exposition of the words of Job, but I think very much of the pith of Job's faith lay in this, that he had a clear view that the worms would after his skin destroy his body, and yet that in his flesh he should see God. You know we might regard it as a small miracle if we could preserve the bodies of the departed. If, by some process, with spices and gums we could preserve the particles, for the Lord to make those dry bones live, and to quicken that skin and flesh, were a miracle certainly, but not palpably and plainly so great a marvel as when the worms have destroyed the body. When the fabric has been absolutely broken up, the tenement all pulled down, ground to pieces, and flung in handfuls to the wind, so that no relic of it is left, and yet when Christ stands in the latter days upon the earth, all the structure shall be brought together, bone to his bone—then shall the might of Omnipotence be seen. This the doctrine of the resurrection, and happy is he who finds no difficulty here, who looks at it as being an impossibility with man but a possibility with God, and lays hold upon the omnipotence of the Most High and says, "Thou sayest it, and it shall be done!" I comprehend thee not great God; I marvel at thy purpose to raise my mouldering bones; but I know that thou doest great wonders, and I am not surprised that thou shouldst conclude the great drama of thy creating works here on earth by re-creating the human frame by the same power by which thou didst bring from the dead the body of thy Son Jesus Christ, and by that same divine energy which has regenerated human souls in thine own image.

II. Now, having thus descended into the grave, and seen nothing there but what is loathsome, LET US LOOK UP WITH THE PATRIARCH AND BEHOLD A SUN SHINING WITH PRESENT COMFORT.

"I know," said he, "that my Redeemer liveth." The word "Redeemer" here used, is in the original "goel"—kinsman. The duty of the kinsman, or goel, was this: suppose an Israelite had alienated his estate, as in the case of Naomi and Ruth; suppose a patrimony which had belonged to a family, had passed away through poverty, it was the goel's business, the redeemer's business to pay the price as the next of kin, and to buy back the heritage. Boaz stood in that relation to Ruth. Now, the body may be looked upon as the heritage of the soul —the soul's small farm, that little plot of earth in which the soul has been wont to walk and delight, as a man walketh in his garden or dwelleth in his house. Now, that becomes alienated. Death, like Ahab, takes away the vineyard from us who are as Naboth; we lose our patrimonial estate; Death sends his troops to take our vineyard and to spoil the vines thereof and ruin it. But we turn round to Death and say, "I know that my Goel liveth, and he will redeem this heritage; I have lost it; thou takest it from me lawfully, O Death, because my sin hath forfeited my right; I have lost my heritage through my own offence, and through that of my first parent Adam; but there lives one who will buy this back." Brethren, Job could say this of Christ long before he had descended upon earth, "I know that he liveth;" and now that he has ascended up on high, and led captivity captive, surely we may with double emphasis say, "I know that my Goel, my Kinsman liveth, and that he hath paid the price, that I should have back my patrimony, so that in my flesh I shall see God." Yes, my hands, ye are redeemed with blood; bought not with corruptible things, as with silver and gold, but with the precious blood of Christ. Yes, heaving lungs and palpitating heart, ye have been redeemed! He that redeemed the soul to be his altar has also redeemed the body, that it may be a temple for the Holy Ghost. Not even the bones of Joseph can remain in the house of bondage. No smell of the fire of death may pass upon the garments which his holy children have worn in the furnace.

Remember, too, that it was always considered to be the duty of the goel, not merely to redeem by price, but where that failed, to redeem by power. Hence, when Lot was carried away captive by the four kings, Abraham summoned his own hired servants, and the servants of all his friends, and went out against the kings of the East, and brought back Lot and the captives of Sodom. Now, our Lord Jesus Christ, who once has played the kinsman's part by paying the price for us, liveth, and he will redeem us by power. O Death, thou tremblest at this name! Thou knowest the might of our Kinsman! Against his arm thou canst not stand! Thou didst once meet him foot to foot in stern battle, and O Death, thou didst indeed tread upon his heel. He voluntarily submitted to this, or else, O Death, thou hadst no power against him. But he slew thee, Death, he slew thee! He rifled all thy caskets, took from thee the key of thy castle, burst open the door of thy dungeon; and now, thou knowest, Death, thou hast no power to hold my body; thou mayest set thy slaves to devour it, but thou shalt give it up, and all their spoil must be restored. Insatiable Death, from thy greedy maw yet shall return the multitudes whom thou hast devoured. Thou shalt be compelled by the Saviour to restore thy captives to the light of day. I think I see Jesus coming with his Father's servants. The chariots of the Lord are twenty thousand, even thousands of angels. Blow ye the trumpet! blow ye the trumpet!

Immanuel rides to battle! The Most Mighty in majesty girds on his sword. He comes! He comes to snatch by power, his people's lands from those who have invaded their portion. Oh, how glorious the victory! No battle shall there be. He comes, he sees, he conquers. The sound of the trumpet shall be enough; Death shall fly affrighted; and at once from beds of dust and silent clay, to realms of everlasting day the righteous shall arise.

To linger here a moment, there was yet, very conspicuously in the Old Testament, we are informed, a third duty of the goel, which was to avenge the death of his friend. If a person had been slain, the Goel was the avenger of blood; snatching up his sword, he at once pursued the person who had been guilty of bloodshed. So now, let us picture ourselves as being smitten by Death. His arrow has just pierced us to the heart, but in the act of expiring, our lips are able to boast of vengeance, and in the face of the monster we cry, "I know that my Goel liveth." Thou mayest fly, O Death, as rapidly as thou wilt, but no city of refuge can hide thee from him; he will overtake thee; he will lay hold upon thee, O thou skeleton monarch, and he will avenge my blood on thee. I would that I had powers of eloquence to work out this magnificent thought. Chrysostom, or Christmas Evans could picture the flight of the King of Terrors, the pursuit by the Redeemer, the overtaking of the foe, and the slaying of the destroyer. Christ shall certainly avenge himself on Death for all the injury which Death hath done to his beloved kinsmen. Comfort thyself then, O Christian; thou hast ever living, even when thou diest, one who avenges thee, one who has paid the price for thee, and one whose strong arms shall yet set thee free.

Passing on in our text to notice the next word, it seems that Job found consolation not only in the fact that he had a Goel, a Redeemer, but that this Redeemer liveth. He does not say, "I know that my Goel *shall live*, but that he *lives*,"—having a clear view of the self-existence of the Lord Jesus Christ, the same yesterday, to-day, and for ever. And you and I looking back do not say, "I know that he *did live*, but he *lives* to-day." This very day you that mourn and sorrow for venerated friends, your prop and pillar in years gone by, you may go to Christ with confidence, because he not only lives, but he is the source of life; and you therefore believe that he can give forth out of himself life to those whom you have committed to the

tomb. He is the Lord and giver of life originally, and he shall
be specially declared to be the resurrection and the life, when
the legions of his redeemed shall be glorified with him. If I
saw no fountain from which life could stream to the dead, I
would yet believe the promise when God said that the dead
shall live; but when I see the fountain provided, and know
that it is full to the brim and that it runneth over, I can
rejoice without trembling. Since there is one who can say, "I
am the resurrection and the life," it is a blessed thing to see
the means already before us in the person of our Lord Jesus
Christ. Let us look up to our Goel then who liveth at this very
time.

Still the marrow of Job's comfort it seems to me lay in that
little word "My." "I know that MY Redeemer liveth." Oh, to get
hold of Christ! I know that in his offices he is precious. But,
dear friends, we must get a property in him before we can
really enjoy him. What is honey in the wood to me, if like the
fainting Israelites, I dare not eat. It is honey in my hand,
honey on my lip, which enlightens mine eyes like those of
Jonathan. What is gold in the mine to me? Men are beggars in
Peru, and beg their bread in California. It is gold in my purse
which will satisfy my necessities, purchasing the bread I
need. So, what is a kinsman if he be not a kinsman to me? A
Redeemer that does not redeem me, an avenger who will
never stand up for my blood, of what avail were such? But
Job's faith was strong and firm in the conviction that the
Redeemer was his. Dear friends, dear friends, can all of you
say, "I know that *my* Redeemer liveth." The question is simple
and simply put; but oh, what solemn things hang upon your
answer, "Is he MY Redeemer?" I charge you rest not, be not
content until by faith you can say, "Yes, I cast myself upon
him; I am his, and therefore he is mine." I know that full
many of you, while you look upon all else that you have as not
being yours, yet can say, "*My* Redeemer is mine." He is the
only piece of property which is really ours. We borrow all else,
the house, the children; nay, our very body we must return to
the Great Lender. But Jesus, we can never leave, for even
when we are absent from the body we are present with the
Lord, and I know that even death cannot separate us from
him, so that body and soul are with Jesus truly even in the
dark hours of death, in the long night of the sepulchre, and in
the separate state of spiritual existence. Beloved, have you

Christ? It may be you hold him with a feeble hand, you half think it is presumption to say, "He is my Redeemer;" yet remember, if you have but faith as a grain of mustard seed, that little faith entitles you to say, and say now, "I know that my Redeemer liveth."

There is another word in this consoling sentence which no doubt served to give a zest to the comfort of Job. It was that he could say, "I KNOW"—"I KNOW that my Redeemer liveth." To say, "I hope so, I trust so," is comfortable; and there are thousands in the fold of Jesus who hardly ever get much further. But to reach the marrow of consolation you *must* say, "I KNOW." Ifs, buts, and perhapses, are sure murderers of peace and comfort. Doubts are dreary things in times of sorrow. Like wasps they sting the soul! If I have any suspicion that Christ is not mine, then there is vinegar mingled with the gall of death. But if I know that Jesus is mine, then darkness is not dark; even the night is light about me. Out of the lion cometh honey; out of the eater cometh forth sweetness. "I know that my Redeemer liveth." This is a brightly-burning lamp cheering the damps of the sepulchral vault, but a feeble hope is like a flickering smoking flax, just making darkness visible, but nothing more. I would not like to die with a mere hope mingled with suspicion. I might be safe with this but hardly happy; but oh, to go down into the river knowing that all is well, confident that as a guilty, weak, and helpless worm I have fallen into the arms of Jesus, and believing that he is able to keep that which I have committed to him. I would have you, dear Christian friends, never look upon the full assurance of faith as a thing impossible to you. Say not "It is too high; I cannot attain unto it." I have known one or two saints of God who have rarely doubted their interest at all. There are many of us who do not often enjoy any ravishing ecstacies, but on the other hand we generally maintain the even tenour of our way, simply hanging upon Christ, feeling that his promise is true, that his merits are sufficient, and that we are safe. Assurance is a jewel for worth but not for rarity. It is the common privilege of all the saints if they have but the grace to attain unto it, and this grace the Holy Spirit gives freely. Surely if Job in Arabia, in those dark misty ages when there was only the morning star and not the sun, when they saw but little, when life and immortality had not been brought to light,—if Job before the coming and advent still could say, "*I know*," you and I should not speak less positively. God forbid that our positiveness should be presumption. Let us try ourselves, and see that our marks and evidences are right, lest we form an ungrounded hope; for nothing can be more destructive than to say, "Peace, peace, where there is no peace." But oh, let us build for eternity, and build solidly. Let us not be satisfied with the mere foundation, for it is from the upper rooms that we get the widest prospect. Let us pray the Lord to help us to pile stone on stone, until we are able to say as we look at it, "Yes, I *know*, I KNOW that my Redeemer liveth." This, then, for present comfort to-day in the prospect of departure.

III. And now, in the third and last place, as THE ANTICIPATION OF FUTURE DELIGHT, let me call to your remembrance the other part of the text. Job not only knew that the Redeemer lived, but he anticipated the time when he should *stand in the latter day upon the earth.* No doubt Job referred here to our Saviour's first advent, to the time when Jesus Christ, "the goel," the kinsman, should stand upon the earth to pay in the blood of his veins the ransom price, which had, indeed, in bond and stipulation been paid before the foundation of the world in promise. But I cannot think that Job's vision stayed there; he was looking forward to the second advent of Christ as being the period of the resurrection. We cannot endorse the theory that Job arose from the dead when our Lord died, although certain Jewish believers held this idea very firmly at one time. We are persuaded that "the latter day" refers to the advent of glory rather than to that of shame. Our hope is that the Lord shall come to reign in glory where he once died in agony. The bright and hallowed doctrine of the second advent has been greatly revived in our churches in these latter days, and I look for the best results in consequence. There is always a danger lest it be perverted and turned by fanatical minds, by prophetic speculations, into an abuse; but the doctrine in itself is one of the most consoling, and, at the same time, one of the most practical, tending to keep the Christian awake, because the bridegroom cometh at such an hour as we think not. Beloved, we believe that the same Jesus who ascended from Olivet shall so come in like manner as he ascended up into heaven. We believe in his personal advent and reign. We believe and expect that when both wise and foolish virgins shall slumber;

in the night when sleep is heavy upon the saints; when men shall be eating and drinking as in the days of Noah, that suddenly as the lightning flasheth from heaven, so Christ shall descend with a shout, and the dead in Christ shall rise and reign with him. We are looking forward to the literal, personal, and actual standing of Christ upon earth as the time when creation's groans shall be silenced for ever, and the earnest expectation of the creature shall be fulfilled.

Mark, that Job describes Christ as *standing*. Some interpreters have read the passage, "he shall stand in the latter days against the earth;" that as the earth has covered up the slain, as the earth has become the charnel-house of the dead, Jesus shall arise to the contest and say, "Earth, I am against thee; give up thy dead! Ye clods of the valley cease to be custodians of my people's bodies! Silent deeps, and you, ye caverns of the earth, deliver, once for all, those whom ye have imprisoned!" Machpelah shall give up its precious treasure, cemeteries and graveyards shall release their captives, and all the deep places of the earth shall resign the bodies of the faithful. Well, whether that be so or no, the posture of Christ, in standing upon the earth, is significant. It shows his triumph. He has triumphed over sin, which once like a serpent in its coils had bound the earth. He has defeated Satan. On the very spot where Satan gained his power Christ has gained the victory. Earth, which was a scene of defeated goodness, whence mercy once was all but driven, where virtue died, where everything heavenly and pure, like flowers blasted by pestilential winds, hung down their heads, withered and blighted—on this very earth everything that is glorious shall blow and blossom in perfection; and Christ himself, once despised and rejected of men, fairest of all the sons of men, shall come in the midst of a crowd of courtiers, while kings and princes shall do him homage, and all the nations shall call him blessed. "He shall stand in the latter day upon the earth."

Then, at that auspicious hour, says Job, "In my flesh I shall see God." Oh, blessed anticipation—"I shall see God." He does not say, "I shall see the saints"—doubtless we shall see them all in heaven—but, "I shall see *God*." Note he does not say, "I shall see the pearly gates, I shall see the walls of jasper, I shall see the crowns of gold and the harps of harmony," but "I shall see God;" as if that were the sum and substance of

heaven. "In my flesh shall I see *God*." The pure in heart shall
see God. It was their delight to see him in the ordinances by
faith. They delighted to behold him in communion and in
prayer. There in heaven they shall have a vision of another
sort. We shall see God in heaven, and be made completely like
him; the divine character shall be stamped upon us; and
being made like to him we shall be perfectly satisfied and
content. Likeness to God, what can we wish for more? And a
sight of God, what can we desire better? We shall see God,
and so there shall be perfect contentment to the soul and a
satisfaction of all the faculties. Some read the passage, "Yet, I
shall see God in my flesh," and hence think that there is here
an allusion to Christ, our Lord Jesus Christ, as the word
made flesh. Well, be it so, or be it not so, it is certain that we
shall see Christ, and He, as the divine Redeemer, shall be the
subject of our eternal vision. Nor shall we ever want any joy
beyond simply that of seeing him. Think not, dear friend, that
this will be a narrow sphere for your mind to dwell in. It is
but one source of delight, "I shall see God," but that source is
infinite. His wisdom, his love, his power, all his attributes
shall be subjects for your eternal contemplation, and as he is
infinite under each aspect, there is no fear of exhaustion. His
works, his purposes, his gifts, his love to you, and his glory in
all his purposes, and in all his deeds of love—why, these shall
make a theme that never can be exhausted. You may with
divine delight anticipate the time when in your flesh you shall
see God.

But I must have you observe how Job has expressly made
us note that it is in the same body. "Yet, *in my flesh* shall I see
God;" and then he says again, "whom I shall see for myself,
and mine eye shall behold and not another." Yes, it is true
that I, the very man standing here, though I must go down to
die, yet I shall as the same man most certainly arise and shall
behold my God. Not part of myself, though the soul alone
shall have some view of God, but the whole of myself, my
flesh, my soul, my body, my spirit shall gaze on God. We shall
not enter heaven, dear friends, as a dismasted vessel is
tugged into harbour; we shall not get to glory some on boards,
and some on broken pieces of the ship, but the whole ship
shall be floated safely into the haven, body and soul both
being safe. Christ shall be able to say, "*All* that the father
giveth to me shall come to me," not only all the persons, but

all of the persons—each man in his perfection. There shall not
be found in heaven one imperfect saint. There shall not be a
saint without an eye, much less a saint without a body. No
member of the body shall have perished; nor shall the body
have lost any of its natural beauty. All the saints shall be all
there, and all of all; the same persons precisely, only that
they shall have risen from a state of grace to a state of glory.
They shall be ripened; they shall be no more the green blades,
but the full corn in the ear; no more buds but flowers; not
babes but men.

Please to notice, and then I shall conclude, how the
patriarch puts it as being a real personal enjoyment. "Whom
mine eye shall behold, and not another." They shall not bring
me a report as they did the Queen of Sheba, but I shall see
Solomon the King for myself. I shall be able to say, as they did
who spake to the woman of Samaria, "Now I believe, not
because of thy word who did bring me a report, but I have
seen him for myself." There shall be personal intercourse with
God; not through the Book, which is but as a glass; not
through the ordinances; but directly, in the person of our Lord
Jesus Christ, we shall be able to commune with the Deity as
a man talketh with his friend. "Not another." If I could be a
changeling and could be altered, that would mar my comfort.
Or if my heaven must be enjoyed by proxy, if draughts of bliss
must be drunk for me, where were the hope? Oh, no; for
myself, and not through another, shall I see God. Have we not
told you a hundred times that nothing but personal religion
will do, and is not this another argument for it, because
resurrection and glory are personal things? "Not another." If
you could have sponsors to repent for you, then, depend upon
it, you would have sponsors to be glorified for you. But as
there is not another to see God for you, so you must yourself
see and yourself find an interest in the Lord Jesus Christ.

In closing let me observe how foolish have you and I been
when we have looked forward to death with shudders, with
doubts, with loathings. After all, what is it? Worms! Do ye
tremble at those base crawling things? Scattered particles!
Shall we be alarmed at these? To meet the worms we have the
angels; and to gather the scattered particles we have the voice
of God. I am sure the gloom of death is altogether gone now
that the lamp of resurrection burns. Disrobing is nothing now
that better garments await us. We may long for evening to

undress, that we may rise with God. I am sure my venerable friends now present, in coming so near as they do now to the time of the departure, must have some visions of the glory on the other side the stream. Bunyan was not wrong, my dear brethren, when he put the land Beulah at the close of the pilgrimage. Is not my text a telescope which will enable you to see across the Jordan; may it not be as hands of angels to bring you bundles of myrrh and frankincense? You can say, "I know that my Redeemer liveth." You cannot want more; you were not satisfied with less in your youth, you will not be content with less now. Those of us who are young, are comforted by the thought that we may soon depart. I say comforted, not alarmed by it; and we almost envy those whose race is nearly run, because we fear—and yet we must not speak thus, for the Lord's will be done—I was about to say, we fear that our battle may last long, and that mayhap our feet may slip; only he that keepeth Israel does not slumber nor sleep. So since we know that our Redeemer liveth, this shall be our comfort in life, that though we fall we shall not be utterly cast down; and since our Redeemer liveth, this shall be our comfort in death, that though worms destroy this body, yet in our flesh we shall see God.

May the Lord add his blessing on the feeble words of this morning, and to him be glory for ever. Amen.

"Grave, the guardian of our dust!
Grave, the treasury of the skies!
Every atom of thy trust
Rests in hope again to rise.
Hark! the judgment trumpet calls;
Soul, rebuild thy house of clay,
Immortality thy walls,
And Eternity thy day."

13

Delight in the Almighty

"For then shalt thou have thy delight in the Almighty, and shalt lift up thy face unto God." **Job 22:26**

The Lord said unto Eliphaz and his friends, "Ye have not spoken of me the thing that is right, as my servant Job hath"; and therefore we must always regard what they said with careful discrimination. They were wise men according to their light, but they were quite at sea in their judgment of Job. However, in this particular verse Eliphaz declared that which is taught in many other parts of Holy Scripture, and we may profit by his utterance. God grant that by his Spirit we may fully experience the joys described in the words before us.

Eliphaz and his friends had judged Job from their own point of view, making their own experience to be the standard. They themselves, had prospered, and therefore they inferred that if a man served God he must necessarily prosper in worldly things; and that if he did not succeed as they had done, he must have been guilty of great crimes. Though they could not discover any actual fault in Job, they concluded without further evidence that he must have been a hypocrite, and have acted oppressively to his servants, or have been unmindful of the claims of the poor, or in some other way have brought upon himself the wrath of God. It never entered their mind that so terrible a sickness and such a list of dreadful calamities could have befallen any man except as a punishment for special sin. They inferred virtue from prosperity, and sin from adversity. Unrighteous and cruel logic! At once false and brutal! It renders men at once false witnesses and Pharisees; condemning the innocent because of their sorrows, and flattering themselves because of their ease. To judge according to outward circumstances has been the tendency of men in all times; even David could not

understand how it was that the wicked were so free from
troubles, while all the day long he was himself plagued, and
chastened every morning. A right principle lay at the bottom
of this wonder; for, indeed, the Lord will reward the good and
will punish the wicked; but a great mistake is made when we
suppose that this life is the time for meting out rewards and
punishments. God will, undoubtedly, when the time shall
have fully come, discharge the full vials of his wrath upon the
ungodly, but the present is a period of longsuffering, wherein
the wicked spread themselves like a green bay tree. Except
God's mercy shall lead them to repentance, they are in the
same wretched condition as bullocks which are being fattened
for the slaughter. Who envies them? The ungodly have their
portion in this life; they increase in riches; their eyes stand
out with fatness, they have more than heart can wish. As for
the children of God, it often happeneth that gall and
wormwood are mingled with their drink: waters of a full cup
are wrung out to them. We must not judge according to the
sight of the eyes, or according to present conditions, or we
shall make gross mistakes. The richest may be the most
wicked, and the poorest may be the most gracious; those who
suffer least may deserve to suffer most, and those who are
most afflicted in this life may have the highest glory in the life
to come.

I suspect that Eliphaz and his friends had enjoyed smooth
sailing. How should they judge the man who had done
business amid tempests? Their mental life was not disturbed
by great conflicts; they had not gone deeply into things, nor
searched to the bottom of spiritual matters; they had no
knowledge of their own hidden corruptions, and had endured
but little of the rod of chastisement, and, consequently, they
had been at ease. Their mistake was that they sat in
judgment upon another who was more tried than themselves,
and condemned him for being in sore distress. Their own
serenity led them to judge the troubled one very harshly. This
ought not to be. If any of us are inclined thus to judge and
condemn, it is time that we put this mischievous spirit far
from us. If we judge others, others will judge us. Two can
always play at that evil game. I remember a company of
terribly despondent believers who were for years a severe
scourge to their happier brethren. Having a deep sense of
their inward corruptions, being sorely tempted of the devil,

and having only a weak and trembling faith, they tyrannized over others who were more happy than themselves. They judged that those who were not as much tempted as themselves did not exhibit the spot of God's children. None were more bitter than these humble people in denouncing those who had not been as much humbled as themselves. Those who did not sit in the dust, and groan to the same tunes as themselves, they judged to be very dubious Christians, and took care to scald them with that kind of hot pity which is not much different from contempt. This was as wrong as wrong can be. It is not to be endured that the sick should make themselves the standard of health, that dwarfs should set up to be the models of manhood. These worthy people set up a standard marked in very black ink, and those who did not come up to so much grief and so much unbelief, they set aside as very questionable members of the divine family. This is manifestly vicious; but it is equally evil when judgments are pronounced from the other side. For persons in good health, whose livers act well, who have abundance of this world's good, and very little care and trial, who have not often had to stand by the grave and weep because the arrows of death have struck their dearest ones, who have never known what it is to be wounded in spirit,—for these to set up their standard and condemn the weak and the sad, is a crime against the Lord. To say,—If you do not believe as firmly as we do, if you do not rejoice as we do, if you are not as sensible of sanctification as we are, you are not in Christ at all, is a piece of arrogance very grievous to the Spirit of the Lord. Oh, my strong brother, listen to one who knows by experience the heaviness of a child of sorrow. Who made thee a ruler in Israel? God's children always play the fool when they play the judge; they are never in order when they act as if they were the head of the family of grace. The Father knows all his children. All who observe carefully will also know that while some are strong in the Lord and in the power of his might, others are weak in faith and mere babes in grace. These little ones are not one jot the less precious in the sight of the great Father than the more fully grown ones. Let none of the strong cattle push the weak cattle with horn and with shoulder; for when the weak ones complain unto God he will regard them, and will avenge them upon the proud. If thou be strong, God keep thee so, and make thee stronger; but use not thy strength for treading down the weak. If thou be weak, the Lord strengthen thee, and deliver thee from this malady; but do not envy the strong, and begin to speak lightly of those who excel thee. The more of light, the more of joy, the more of holy confidence, the more of faith, the more glory to God: therefore covet these things earnestly as among the best gifts. May the Holy Ghost help us to attain to the highest degree of grace; but may he ever prevent us from judging our brethren. Here was the fault of Eliphaz. He was right in many of his statements, but he was wrong in his ungenerous application of them to holy Job.

I want this morning, as God shall help me, to lead you up to the pastures on the hill tops. I pray that I may help you to a higher and joyful experience in the things of God, whilst I shall speak, first, of *a desired position* towards God,—"Then shalt thou have thy delight in the Almighty, and shalt lift up thy face unto God"; and secondly upon the question—*when can this happy experience be realized?* "Then," says the text, and, therefore, there is such a time when we can have delight in the Almighty and lift up our face unto God.

I. First, HERE IS A DESIRED POSITION TOWARDS GOD.

Many men forget God: he is no object of delight to them, for they ignore his existence, and they would even think it a great relief if it could be proved that there were no God,—no God to observe them, no God to record their misdeeds, no God to call them to judgment, no God to punish them for their iniquities. Let us pity the multitudes who claim to be happy without God; for it is the last extreme of depravity when, blotting out God from his soul, a man obtains a wretched comfort as the consequence of his folly. To be without God is to be without rest in the present and without hope for the future.

Great numbers of men go a stage further: they believe in God, they cannot doubt that there is a Most High God who judgeth the children of men; but their only thought towards him is that of dread and dislike. They do not want to hear of him: if the things of God are forced upon their attention they are soon weary of such distasteful themes, for they only look upon God as a just and terrible Judge, who will certainly punish them for their transgressions. It is woe to them even to think of the great God. Though this dread of God and this neglect of God cannot deliver them out of his hands, yet they find a kind of comfort in it. As we are told of the ostrich—I know not whether it be true or not—that when it cannot escape the hunter it buries its head in the sand so as not to see its pursuer; so these foolish persons blind their own eyes, and thus produce a foolish security of heart. They think of God with dread, dismay, despondency, and despair. I am grieved to add that this principle even tinctures the thoughts of true friends of God: for when they bow before God it is not only with the reverence of a loving child, but with the terror of a slave; they are afraid of him who should be their exceeding joy. Their view of God is incorrect, for it is not such as the Spirit of adoption would give them. They are really trusting in him and in the great propitiation which he has set forth, but they have not come to know him under that blessed term which our Saviour puts into our mouth when he bids us say, "Our Father, which art in heaven." Such trembling ones are still under the spirit of bondage, which causes them to fear, as condemned persons dread the executioner. They stand like Israel trembling at the foot of Sinai; they have not come unto Mount Zion and to the blood of sprinkling, which speaketh better things than that of Abel. God is still to them exceeding terrible, so that they fear and quake. Even though they are his children, they are not able to lift up their faces unto their own Father. They haunt the outer courts of the sanctuary, but into the most holy place they do not dare to enter: they see the smoke of the burnt-offering, but they have not learned to feed upon it, and so to have happy communion with God. These people may be safe, but they are not happy: they may be saved from sin, but not from sorrow. Faith, if it were stronger, would effectually slay and bury servile fear.

Let us meditate upon what is here meant by *delighting in the Almighty*. The man who experiences this delight is glad *that there is a God*. That atheistic philosophy which makes the whole world to be a chance production which grew of itself, or developed itself by some innate force, is a very dreary piece of fiction to the man who delights himself in the Almighty. I tremble at any teaching, religious or scientific, which seems to place God further off than we have believed him to be. To draw him nearer to me, and myself nearer to him, is the innermost longing of my soul. Do you not feel the same? I know you do if you have a child-like spirit towards him. We delight to see God in the shadow of every passing

cloud, in the colouring of every opening flower, in the glitter
of every dewdrop, in the twinkling of every star. The Lord is
personally at work in all the processes of nature, and natural
laws are simply the Lord's usual method of operation. Our
God is so near us that in him we live, and move, and have our
being. At this spring tide, in the fragrance of the flowers and
the song of birds, we perceive God everywhere present,
renewing the face of the year. Beloved, the thought of God is
to the souls of those who know and love him the most
delightful that can cross the mind. To put God away from us
is injury to our happiness, as well as treason to our duty; but
to get nearer and clearer views of his omnipresence, his
omniscience, his omnipotence, is to increase the joy of our
heart.

To go a step further, the delight of the believer in his God is
a delight in God *as he really is*; for there are in the world
many false gods of men's own manufacture. Remember that
your own thoughts of what God is are far from being correct
unless they are drawn from his own revelation. This sacred
book is infallible, but not our thoughts; and wherein we differ
from God as he has revealed himself we differ from the truth.
It is as easy to make an idol out of your own thought as it is
for the Hindoo to make a god of the mud of the Ganges. There
is but one God revealed in Holy Scripture, and in nature, and
in providence: his name is Jehovah, the God of Abraham, of
Isaac, and of Jacob, who has still further declared himself as
the God and Father of our Lord and Saviour Jesus Christ. He
is God in undivided unity of essence, in the trinity of his
persons, Father, Son, and Holy Spirit. With all our souls we
worship and adore him. Just as God appears in Holy
Scripture we are to delight in him; regarding him as love, as
mercy, as long-suffering, as justice, as power, as purity, as all
goodness and greatness in one. The characteristic which
seems to cause most delight to perfect saints in heaven is not
love alone, nor mercy alone, but that which comprehends
grace and mercy, and much more; I mean holiness. This is the
perpetual cry of the seraphim, "Holy, holy, holy, Lord God of
Sabaoth." The holiness of God, or, if you will, the wholeness of
God, the completeness of God, the perfection of God, is the
delight of all believers. We would not tone down a single
attribute, we would not disturb the equilibrium of the divine
perfections; but we delight in God in all those aspects of his

character which are mentioned in his Holy Word.

Further, he that delights in God delights not only in God as he is, but *in all that God does*, and this is a higher attainment than some have reached. "It is the Lord," said one of old, "let him do what seemeth him good." Too many would call God to their bar, and hold a trial upon what he does with men in this life, and with the wicked in the world to come. Far other was the spirit of the apostle when he said, "Nay, but, O man, who art thou that repliest against God? Shall the thing formed say to him that formed it, Why hast thou made me thus?" Concerning any event we simply ask,—Has God done it? Then we bow before his decree, and say no more; for what he has done must be right and wise. When the Lord afflicts us, and hides the reason from our eyes, let us not contend with him; but if we cannot go further, let us be silent before him; even as was the afflicted man of God of whom we read, "Aaron held his peace." Better still will it be if we can complete our confidence, and say with Job, "The Lord gave, and the Lord hath taken away, and blessed be the name of the Lord." He that delighteth in the Almighty will delight in him even though he smart beneath his hand, and will bless him even when his dispensations are killing ones: as said the patriarch of Uz, "Though he slay me, yet will I trust in him."

Practically put, this delight in the Almighty *shows itself in the Christian when nothing else remains to him.* If he be stripped of everything, he cries, "The Lord is my portion." When the cupboard is bare, and the garments are worn out, and poverty stares the man in the face, he says, "My God is such a satisfactory and all-sufficient portion that I am rich and increased in goods while possessing nothing but my God." The same is true when such a man is surrounded with every earthly comfort, for he still feels, "The Lord is my portion." The saint begs vehemently of his God that he may not have his portion in this life. If God were to multiply his stores beyond his power to count them, he would be dissatisfied unless in all these he saw his Father's covenant love. One saint, who suddenly became poor, was still as happy as ever, for he said, "When I had abundance, I saw God in all things, and now that I have lost my property I see all things in God." These are equally blessed states of mind. It were well to combine them, and see God in all things, and all things in God, at the same time! So it should be with the believer.

"Why," saith he, "these earthly comforts never were my delights; these were not my daily manna, but only little staybyes for the time; sips of sweetness while I pass through the barren wilderness." The Lord was and is my chief portion, my well of comfort, the rock of my salvation. If we make props of our outward joys, we shall fall when they are taken away; but if we rest wholly upon the foundation of divine love, altogether apart from external things, we shall never be moved. Happy is the Christian who can practically enjoy delight in the Almighty by making him to be his all in all, all the day, and every day.

You will see this delight in God exhibiting itself in frequent meditations upon God. Such a man has pleasure in being alone with God, and his sweetest occupation is meditation upon the years of the right hand of the Most High. He finds in holy contemplation pastures large and green, in which his soul doth feed and lie down.

> "My God, thou art mine, what a comfort divine!
> What a blessing to know my Jesus is mine."

These happy meditations very soon show themselves in words. The man that delights in the Almighty delights to speak about him. That which is in the well will before long come up in the bucket, and that which is in the heart will soon display itself in the tongue. Is there any conversation more elevating, more consoling, more strengthening, than conversation about the Lord our God? And when you go home from such society do you not feel it sweet to fall asleep with the savour of it upon your lips? Is not holy converse infinitely better than all the mirth and merriment of the world's amusements? Here is something to feed upon, something solid, something real; saints delight to contribute to such conversation and to receive instruction from it.

"Delight thyself in the Lord." This will give you pleasure in the midst of pain. Do you know what it is to have many aches, and sufferings, and, perhaps, a throbbing head, and yet to feel that you have another self which has no pains, because it dwells in God, where all is calm and quiet? You felt that it would be a great mercy to be released from this painful life; and yet you have not raised the question with your God, but have waited his good pleasure. Faith has made you feel, "Wherever I am, whatever I feel, so long as God is near me,

and his sweet love fills my bosom, I will greatly rejoice and
triumph in the God of my salvation."

This will show itself in your life, for it will be a pleasure to
do anything to exalt the name of God. It will gild your
ordinary conversation with heavenly splendour, if in it you
adorn the doctrine of God your Saviour in all things. You will
march to heaven beneath the spell of celestial music, and the
bliss of the glorified will stimulate your spirits, when you can
feel that all is for God, and that God is all in all to you. This is
to delight yourself in the Almighty. God give us to get into
that state, and to keep there till we leap to heaven, and are in
that state.

I call your attention to the special name by which Eliphaz
describes the ever-blessed God: he says, "Delight thyself in
the Almighty." Is it not singular that he should choose a term
descriptive of omnipotence as the paramount cause of the
believer's delight? God is love, and I can readily understand
how one might delight himself in God under that aspect; but
the believer is taught to delight himself in God as strong and
mighty. What a mercy it is that there is a power that makes
for righteousness!—that at the back of all these wars and
confusions, and behind all sin and false doctrine, there is an
infinitely powerful God! During the last few weeks you have
felt an intense joy in the omnipotence of God. You have
whispered to your forebodings,—"It is all right. The Almighty
is not paralyzed, his arm is not shortened: the Lord reigneth."
Brethren, the pendulum swings to and fro, advancing and
retreating, but yet there is a real progress made: you cannot
see it by watching the pendulum, but up higher on the face of
the clock there is evidence of an onward march, and of a
coming hour. The kingdom of God is coming; righteousness
shall prevail. Delight also in the fact that Jehovah is almighty
in mercy—mighty to save. He can forgive the greatest sin; he
can change the hardest heart; he can help us to fight out unto
victory the sternest of our battles against unrighteousness; he
is stronger than sin and Satan; for all power dwells with him.
When you look at this phase of it, and think of his dear Son
exalted on high to give repentance and remission of sins, you
may indeed delight in the Almighty Redeemer, as "able also
to save them to the uttermost that come unto God by him."
Surely, when you see omnipotence linked with righteousness
and mercy, you will delight yourself in the Almighty.

Think also of the Lord's almightiness in the matter of the keeping, preserving, defending, and perfecting of all his people. The sheep of his pasture shall not perish; for the good Shepherd is omnipotent to smite the roaring lion who would devour them. None that trust in him shall ever be ashamed or confounded, world without end. All the elect are well secured within the fold of Jesus, neither shall any pluck them out of his hand. Delight yourselves in the Almighty; for all the power of God is enlisted on the side of the believer. To me, I confess, it is an intense joy that he is almighty to carry out every one of his eternal purposes. Jesus shall not fail nor be discouraged. That which Jehovah hath willed shall be; in the unfolding of the great roll of history it shall be found that it tallies exactly with the divine purposes and immutable decrees. He that sitteth on the flood reigneth King for ever and ever. Hallelujah! Hallelujah! Hallelujah! Let our hearts delight that the Lord God Omnipotent reigneth already, and let us pray that in yet a further sense his kingdom may come, as come it will. Let us delight ourselves in the Almighty, linking that word to every other attribute, and rejoicing that he has almighty love, omnipotent grace. Again let us say "Hallelujah!"

Now, let us turn with intense satisfaction to the other expression used by Eliphaz: *"Thou shalt lift up thy face unto God."* What does it mean? Does it not mean, first, joy in God? When a man hangs his head down he is unhappy: it is the attitude of misery; but oh, when our thoughts of God are changed, and our relationship to God is different, we lift up our faces and sun our countenances in the light of God's favour. The face of God in his Anointed is toward the believer, and therefore the believer's face is toward the Most High. He hath said, "Seek ye my face," and how can we seek his face but with our own faces? "Look unto me, and be ye saved, all the ends of the earth," is the divine call; and the believer looks to God with intense joy, knowing that in him is his salvation.

Does it not signify, also, that this man is reconciled to God, and clear before him? How can he look up who is guilty? Guilt makes a man hang his head. "Conscience doth make cowards of us all"; but oh, my brothers, when the atoning sacrifice has come with all its power to us, when we are washed in the blood of the Lamb, and we are clean every whit, then we lift up our face unto God. In that tremendous day when heaven and earth shall flee before the face of the Judge, we shall be bravely calm, fearing no word of doom, because we are cleansed by the atoning sacrifice, and justified by the righteousness in which we put our trust. What a blessed thing to lift up one's face unto God in confidence towards him through Christ Jesus!

Does not our text indicate fearlessness? Fear covers her face, and would fain hide herself altogether, even though to accomplish concealment the rocks must fall upon her. That sacred bravery which the Holy Spirit breathes into the child of God makes him cry, "Abba, Father," and, in the spirit of adoption he lifts up his face unto God.

May it not also signify expectation? "I will lift up mine eyes unto the hills, from whence cometh my help." "My expectation is from him," says David. Oh, to lift one's face toward God, looking for deliverance, safety, and rest, and expecting both grace and glory from his right hand!

Brethren, I am talking very simply of things well known to me, and yet I cannot convey to you a sense of the joy of a face uplifted unto God. You must feel it for yourselves, by lifting up your own faces. Some of you poor creatures cannot lift up your faces unto God by reason of despondency; but we pray that you may yet do so. If you have ever looked unto the Lord through the glass of the atonement you will then be able to lift up your faces towards him with a calm delight. As for you who are God's own people, and yet go through the world in bondage, I charge you, cry unto the Lord to change your condition, and fill you with his joy, for then your faces will shine in the light of his face.

I am sure that he who has this delight in God, and this lifting up of the face towards God, is a man that has wonderful peace with regard to the past: the past is forgiven, its iniquity covered, for the Lord has looked in love upon him. The man who walks in happy communion with God has a wonderful peace with regard to the present. "Is it well with thee?" Exceedingly well. God loves me, and I love him; I am brought into fellowship with him by Christ Jesus my Lord, and we are friends, with a friendship which is secured by mutual delight and sealed by covenant engagements, so that it can never cease to be. Such a man has peace with regard to the future. He has no fear of evil tidings; his heart is fixed, trusting in the Lord. He is not afraid of coming dangers in

life, nor of the pangs of death, nor the terrors of judgment.
When you delight in the Lord, nothing can disturb the
unbroken current of your joy. The sublime serenity of the
heavens which arch above your head enters into your own
spirit when the Lord who made the heavens dwells in your
heart. Strive after this sacred peace: delight in the Almighty,
and lift up your faces unto God.

II. I must close by noticing our second point, and that is,
WHEN CAN WE REALIZE THIS? I have not confidence enough in
Eliphaz to make his answer to the question the only one that
I shall give you: I must give you something fuller and better
than was known to him.

First, a man can realize all this *when he knows that he is
reconciled to God.* What is God's way of effecting recon-
ciliation between a sinner and himself? Every sinner is under
the curse of the broken law; for it is written, "Cursed is every
one that continueth not in all things which are written in the
book of the law to do them." No one of us has continued in the
perfect observance of the whole law, and therefore God's
righteous verdict is against us. The only way of escape from
the curse is through the glorious Son of God, who took our
nature, and was made a curse for us, as it is written, "Cursed
is every one that hangeth on a tree." He stood in our room and
stead, bore the punishment due to our guilt, and thus became
a curse on our behalf. All the sacrifices of the Jews were types
of this: they were fingers of light pointing to the one all-
sufficient sacrifice. That sacrifice the Lord has accepted for
men, and he has set forth the Lord Jesus to be the
propitiation for our sins, and not for ours only, but for the sins
of the whole world; so that whosoever believeth in Jesus
Christ, God's appointed sacrifice, is set free from sin, and
being set free from sin he can then delight in the Almighty,
and lift up his face unto God.

Yet even this could not effect our delight in God unless
there was something else; so there must be, in the next place,
a renewed nature. Our old nature will never delight in God.
The carnal mind is enmity against God, it is not reconciled to
God, neither indeed can be; it is an alien from the life of God,
and an alien it will always be. So, then, ye must be born
again: but when a man is born again of the Spirit of God, and
receives a new nature, that new nature delights in the
Almighty. There is an old nature in us which fights against

God still; but the new nature, which is of divine origin, cries
after God as a child after its mother; it lives in God as fish live
in the sea; God is its element, its life, its all-in-all. So,
beloved, if you have been both reconciled and renewed; if you
have felt the power of the blood of Jesus and the power of the
Holy Ghost begetting in you a new nature, then you can
delight yourselves in God.

In addition to this, you will delight in God much more fully
when *the Spirit beareth witness with your spirit* that you are
born of God. The spirit of sonship is the spirit of delight in
God. What son is afraid to behold his father's face? A loving
child suns himself in his father's smile. How have I seen little
children clambering up their father's knees, and looking into
his face, and saying, "What a dear face it is!" This is a faint
picture of our joy in God through Jesus Christ, by whom also
we have received the atonement. What would some of you
give to see the dear face of that dear father who was taken
from you years ago! I can understand Cowper saying of his
mother's picture,

> "Oh, that those lips had language!"

Oh, that our departed ones could speak to us again; but our
heavenly Father ever lives; and never let it be said that we
dare not lift up our faces unto him. We look up, and say in our
darkest moments,

> "For yet I know I shall Him praise,
> Who graciously to me,
> The health is of my countenance,
> Yea, mine own God is He."

I cannot tell you the inexpressible sweetness of that last line
to my soul. Thousands of times it has fallen from my lips. If I
have nothing else I have a God, and my soul lays hold on him
as Jacob grasped the angel. I will not let him go. Whether he
bless me or do not bless me, still will I cling to him with
desperate resolve, and cry, "my Lord and my God." This God
is our God for ever and ever, he shall be our guide even unto
death.

To come to Eliphaz, and to conclude with him. We shall
delight ourselves in God, and lift up our face when we do as
Eliphaz here tells us. First, *when we live in communion with
him*. "Acquaint now thyself with him, and be at peace." If we

do not know God how can we delight in him? What delight can there be in an unknown God? Brothers, you are not half as happy as you might be, because you do not study this Book, wherein, as in a glass, you may see the face of Jehovah your God. Oh, that you knew more of his dear Son, for he that hath seen him hath seen the Father! Take God for thy daily company. "Acquaint now thyself with him." Great as he is, dare to be free with him. Though thou be but dust and ashes, yet, like Abraham, speak with him as a man speaketh with his friend, for as thou knowest thy God so shalt thou delight in him, and lift up thy face unto him.

Then, further, we must, if we are to know this delight, *lay up God's words in our hearts*—(verse 22). "Receive, I pray thee, the law from his mouth, and lay up his words in thine heart." Your neglected Bibles hide your God. When dust falls on the Scriptures dust falls on the eyes of those who have neglected them, and then they cannot behold the glory of the Lord God. The more of Scripture understood, fed upon, and received into the inward parts, the more will be your delight in God. You can have no pleasure in the speaker if you despise the word spoken: let it be to you as marrow and fatness.

There must be added to this delight in the word *a constant cleansing of the way*. "If thou return to the Almighty, thou shalt be built up, thou shalt put away iniquity far from thy tabernacles." God cannot manifest himself to us if we continue in sin. If you professing Christian people are as greedy and hard as other people in your dealings with the world, and if in your families you are as quarrelsome and untruthful as the ungodly, God cannot come to your tabernacles. There must be purification of life, or there cannot be fellowship with the Lord. "Blessed are the pure in heart, for they shall see God"; impurity of heart will cause blindness of the eyes as to spiritual things. Careful walking will bring joyful walking; but if you lose your purity you will lose your peace. If you are a child of God you cannot sin without feeling the rod: you must obey the Lord in order to enjoy the Lord. Walk in the footsteps of Christ, who did always the things which pleased the Father, and you will receive the joyful witness—"This is my beloved son!" Put away sin wherever you perceive it, and ask for grace to be helped to detect it in all its lurking places. Seek out the Babylonish garment and

the wedge of gold which Achan has hidden, or else the Lord
cannot abide with you. Get rid of your idols.

> "So shall your walk be close with God,
> Calm and serene your frame;
> So purer light shall mark the road
> That leads you to the Lamb."

In addition to this, there must be *a constant trust*. "Yea, the
Almighty shall be thy defense, and thou shalt have plenty of
silver." (See verse 25.) He who does not trust God cannot
delight in him. You cannot lift up your face to him while you
think him untrue. A childlike confidence is essential to a holy
joy. Let us throw ourselves upon God, as a swimmer casts
himself upon the water, that it may bear him up; let us trust
in God as a child trusts its mother, without the shadow of a
question. We sometimes know a great deal too much of what
we ought not to know. I see some of God's children very
anxious to feed upon the tree of the knowledge of good and
evil; but as for me, I am content with the tree of life. The old
serpent still persuades men to pluck forbidden fruit from that
evil tree. I know children of God who hold their hands to their
heads and cry, "Would God we had never read that sceptical
book, and never learned how to distrust the Lord!" Let the
time past suffice for the feeding of doubt. Let us eat no more
carrion, but feed upon the salted meat of the Word. Let us
quit the garlick of Egypt, and feed on the manna of heaven.
We do not want to know what the world believes or does not
believe, for the world lieth in the wicked one. We do not care
what may be the spirit of the age, for the spirit of the world in
all ages is the Prince of the power of the air, the spirit that
now worketh in the children of disobedience. Be it yours and
mine to come to Christ, to live on him, and to believe on him
with unstaggering faith; so shall we delight ourselves in God,
and lift up our faces to him.

Lastly, let us abide in *continual prayer*. Verse 27: "Thou
shalt make thy prayer unto him, and he shall hear thee, and
thou shalt pay thy vows." Want of prayer is a great want
indeed; slackness at the mercy-seat will soon take away the
spring and elasticity of our spiritual walk. If we are to have a
closer walk with God, we must have closer communion with
God in supplication.

Now, dear children of God, I have set all this before you, but what power can be in my word unless the Holy Ghost blesses it? I have watered this sermon with strong desires for the spiritual benefit of you all, and now I am mourning over the many who do not know anything at all about it. They are still devoid of the knowledge of God, and of all desire for him. I am very, very sorry for you. My heart pities you. We have heard of "the Bitter Cry" from the slums of London, and a bitter cry it well may be; but there is a poverty, compared with which mere want of bread is riches; there is a degradation, compared with which the low estate of the pauper is nobility itself. To live without your God—how terrible a death! You know not what joy means; you have not begun to spell the word "delight" until you have begun with God. True joy comes only from a true knowledge of the true God. Oh, sirs, if I had to die like a dog, I should wish to be a Christian, for the sake of the bird in the hand of present delight! If there were no hereafter, the immediate peace and joy of trusting my God are an overflowing reward. But there is a hereafter, and what will you ungodly ones do when that hereafter dawns upon you? You have done without God all your days, and God will do without you to all eternity. What terror lies in that fact! He will say, "Depart!" because you always did depart; he will decree your continuance in the path which you chose, and bid you keep on going away from him for ever. He will say, "He that is filthy, let him be filthy still," and what more dreadful doom can fall upon any one of you? O! ye immortal spirits, ye need an immortal God! O! ye, that cannot cease to be, ye need the Highest of all Beings in whom you may hide yourselves from ceaseless anguish. Trust in God, and then shall you be filled with infinite felicities, but not till then. God bring you to himself, that he may bring you to delight! May the uplifted Savior draw you and uplift you! May you begin the life of heaven by an immediate delight in the Almighty, and from that delight may you never cease! To him be glory for ever and ever. Amen.

14

Believers Tested by Trials

"Behold, I go forward, but he is not there; and backward, but I cannot perceive him: On the left hand, where he doth work, but I cannot behold him: he hideth himself on the right hand, that I cannot see him: But he knoweth the way that I take: when he hath tried me, I shall come forth as gold."   Job 23:8-10

Job, as we noticed in our reading, was at that time in very deep distress. I commend this fact to the notice of any here who are very sorely tried. You may be the people of God, and yet be in a terrible plight, for Job was a true servant of the Most High, yet he sat down among the ashes, and scraped himself with a potsherd because he was covered with sore boils, and, at the same time, he was reduced to absolute poverty. The path of sorrow has been trodden by thousands of holy feet; you are not the first one who could sit down, and say, "I am the man that hath seen affliction." You were not the first tried one, you are not the only one, and you will not be the last one. "Many are the afflictions of the righteous;" so let this be some comfort to you,—that you are one of the Lord's suffering children, one of those who have to pass through rough roads and fiery places in the course of their pilgrimage to heaven.

Job had to experience one trial which must have been very keen indeed, for it was brought about by his three choice friends, who were evidently men of mind and mark, for their speeches prove that they were by no means second-class men. Job would not have selected for his bosom friends any but those who were of high character, estimable in disposition, and able to converse with him upon high and lofty themes. Such, no doubt, those three men were; and I expect that, when Job saw them coming towards him, he looked for a store of comfort from them, imagining that they would at least sympathize with him, and pour out such consolations as their own experience could suggest, in order that he might be somewhat relieved. But he was utterly disappointed; these friends of his reasoned that there must be some extraordinary cause for such unusual distress as that into which Job had fallen. They had never seen wrong in him; but, then, he might be a very cunning man, and so have concealed it from them. As far as they had known him, he seemed to be a generous, liberal soul; but, perhaps, after all, he was one of those who squeeze the uttermost farthing out of the poor. They could not read his heart, so they put the worst construction upon his sorrows, and said, "Depend upon it, he is a hypocrite; we will apply caustic to him, and so we will test him, and see whether he really is what he professes to be. We will rub salt into his wounds by bringing various charges against him;" and they did so in a most horrible fashion. That is a cruel thing for anybody to do, and one that cuts to the quick. Possibly, some people, who used to court your company, and would not let you go down the street without bowing to you, now that your circumstances are changed, do not recognize you; or if they cannot help seeing you, they appear to have some distant recollection that, years ago, you were a casual acquaintance; or, peradventure, if they do speak in a kind, friendly way, though their words are smoother than butter, war is in their heart; though their words are softer than oil, yet are they drawn swords. You must be a bad man because you have come down in the world; it cannot be that you are the respectable person they thought you were, or you would not have lost your estate; for, in the estimation of some folk, to be respectable means to have a certain amount of cash. The definition was once given, in a court of law, that if a man kept a gig, it was proved by that fact that he was respectable. That is the way of the world; respect and respectability depend upon so much money; but the moment that is gone, the scene changes. The man is the same; ay, he may be a better and a nobler man without the money than with it; but it is only noble men who think so. It is only right-minded persons who judge not by the coat or the purse, but who say, with Burns,—

"A man's a man for a' that,—"

whatever may be his condition. Character is the thing to which we ought to look;—the man himself, and not merely his surroundings. But Job had to bear just that ignoble sort of scorn that some men seem to delight to pour upon the sorrows of others.

I want, first, to call your attention to *Job's desire in the time of his trouble.* It was his earnest desire to get to his God. Secondly, we will notice *Job's distress because he could not find him:* "Behold, I go forward, but he is not there; and backward, but I cannot perceive him." And, thirdly, we will consider *Job's consolation:* "He knoweth the way that I take: when he hath tried me, I shall come forth as gold."

I. First, then, notice JOB'S DESIRE IN THE TIME OF HIS TROUBLE.

He wanted his God; he did not long to see Bildad, or Eliphaz, or Zophar, or any earthly friend; but his cry was "Oh, that I knew where I might find HIM! that I might come even to his seat!" This is one of the marks of a true child of God,— that, even when God smites him, he still longs for his presence. If you get to the very back of all Job's calamities, you will see that God sent them; or, at least, permitted Satan to afflict him. "Yet," says Job, "I will not turn in anger against God because of this. 'Though he slay me, yet will I trust in him.' Let him do what he will with me, I will still seek to get near to him, and this shall be my heart's desire, 'Oh that I knew where I might find him!'" An ungodly man, if he has made any pretence of fellowship with God in his days of prosperity, forsakes him as soon as adversity comes; but the true child of God clings to his Father however roughly he may deal with him. We are not held captive to God by a chain of sweets, nor are we bought with cupboard love, nor bribed in any other way to love him; but now, because he first loved us, our heart hath loved him, and rested in him; and if cross providences and strange dealings come from the hand of the Most High, our cry shall not be, "Oh that we could get away from him!" but, "Oh that we knew where we might find him, that we might come even to his seat!" This is the mark of our regeneration and adoption,—that, whatever happens, we still cling to our God.

For, beloved friends, when a man is in trouble, if he can but get to God, in the first place, *he is quite sure of justice.* Men may condemn us falsely, but God never will. Our character may be cruelly slandered; and, doubtless, there have been good men who have lived for years under false accusations;—

but God knoweth the way that we take. He will be the
Advocate of his servants when their case is laid before the
heavenly Court of King's Bench. We need not be afraid that
the verdict will not be just: "Shall not the Judge of all the
earth do right?"

We know also that, if we can get to God, *we shall have
audience.* Sometimes, men will not hear us when we are
pleading for justice. "I do not want to hear a word you have to
say," says the man who is so prejudiced that he will not listen
to our plea. But there is an ear that no prejudice ever sealed;
there is a heart that is ever sympathetic towards the griefs of
a believer. You are sure to be heard, beloved, if you pour out
your heart before the God that heareth prayer. He will never
be weary of your cries; they may be poor, broken utterances,
but he takes the meaning of the sighs of his saints, he
understands the language of their groans. Go, then, to God
because you are sure of audience.

What is more, in getting near to God, a man is *sure to have
strength.* You notice how Job puts it: "Will he plead against
me with his great power? No; but he would put strength in
me." When once we get to realize that God is with us, how
strong we are! Then we can bear the burden of want or of
pain, or even the sharp adder's tongue of slander. The man
who has God with him is a very Samson; he may fling himself
upon a troop of Philistines, and smite them hip and thigh; he
may lay hold of the pillars of their temple, rock them to and
fro, and bring down the whole building upon them. I say not
that we shall work miracles, but I do say that, as our days, so
shall our strength be.

> "I can do all things, or can bear
> All sufferings, if my Lord be there."

And, once more, he who gets to his God is *sure of joy.* There
was never a soul, that was right with God, and that was
unhappy in the presence of God. Up yonder in glory, how
gladly they smile! How I would like to photograph their
beaming faces! What a group that would be,—of angel faces
bathed in everlasting light, and the faces of those redeemed
from among men, all radiant with celestial joy. What gives
them that gladness? It is because God is there that they are
so happy.

> "Not all the harps above,
> Can make a heavenly place,
> If God his residence remove,
> Or but conceal his face."

Just as the sun makes the landscape bright and fair, so does
the light of God's countenance make all his people glad. It
would not matter to a man whether he were in a dungeon or
a palace if he had the constant presence of God; I am not
speaking at random when I make that assertion. Read the
record of the martyr days of the Church, and you will
understand that the presence of God caused his persecuted
people to be the happiest in the whole world. No minstrels in
royal halls ever sang so sweetly as did the prisoners of the
Lord who were confined in deep, dark, underground
dungeons, where they could scarcely breathe. Nay, that is not
all; for some have been happy even on the rack. Think of
brave Lady Anne Askew sitting on the cold stones after the
cursed inquisitors had torn her poor feeble frame almost limb
from limb; and when they tempted her to turn from the faith,
she answered,—

> "I am not she that lyst,
> My anker to let fall,
> For every dryslynge mist;
> My shippe's substancyal."

Some who were tortured, not accepting deliverance, declared,
as in the case of Lawrence, that the gridiron was a bed of
roses, and that they never were so joyous as when their body
was being consumed in the fire,—every finger being like a
lighted candle,—for they were able even then to cry, "None
but Christ! None but Christ!" It is amazing how the presence
of God seems to be an anodyne that kills all pain;—an
uplifting, like an angel's wing, that bears upward one who,
without it, would be utterly crushed. The martyr is torn in
pieces, and full of agonies, and yet all his sufferings are
transformed, till they become sweet harmonies of intense
delight because God is with him. Oh! give me God, give me
God, and I care not what you withhold from me. "Whom have
I in heaven but thee? and there is none upon earth that I
desire beside thee."

II. The brightness of the first part of my subject will help to
make the second portion all the darker. We are now to

consider JOB'S DISTRESS,—the agony of a true child of God who cannot find his Father.

Your experiences are not all alike, brethren, and I do not want you to try to make them all alike. Some of you have very happy experiences, and very little spiritual trial. I am glad it is so; I only hope you will not be superficial, or conceited, or censorious of others. But there are some who know the darker paths in the heavenly pilgrimage, and it is to those that I specially speak just now. Dear friends, I pray you to remember that a man may be a true servant of God, and even an eminent and distinguished servant of God like Job, and yet he may sometimes lose the light of God's countenance, and have to cry out, "Oh that I knew where I might find him!" There are some special, superfine, hot-pressed Christians about, nowadays, who do not believe this. They say, "You ought to be joyous; you ought never to be depressed; you ought to be perfect;" all which is quite true, but it is a great deal easier to say so than to show how it is to be realized; and these brethren, who talk as if it were a very simple matter, like counting your fingers, may someday find that it is more difficult than they think, as some of us have sometimes done.

Job could not find his God; this is *apparently strange.* He was a specially good man, one who did what he could for all around him,—a very light in the city where he dwelt,—a man famous in all the country, yet in great trouble;—one might have thought that God would certainly comfort him. He has lost everything; surely, now the Lord will return to him, and be gracious unto him, and above all other times he will be cheered now with the presence of God. Yet it was not so. He was a man who valued the company of God, and who cried, "Oh that I knew where I might find him!" Yet he could not find him. It is passing strange; or, at least, it appears to be so.

Yet notice, next, that *it is essentially needful to some trials that God should with-draw the light of his countenance.* Our Lord Jesus Christ, with all the woes that he endured, could not have been made perfect through sufferings unless he had learnt to cry, "My God, my God, why hast thou forsaken me?" When God means to smite any child of his with the rod, he cannot do it with a smile. Suppose a father is chastening his son, and all the while is comforting him, where is the chastening? No; the very essence of the medicinal sorrow that is to do good to our souls will lie in our having to bewail the absence of the smile of God.

This is essential to our trial, but *it is greatly perplexing*. I do not know of anything that so troubles a Christian man as when he does not know where his God is. "God is everywhere," says one. I know he is, but yet there is a special presence which he manifests to his people, and sometimes it seems to them as if he were nowhere at all. So Job exclaimed, "Behold, I go forward, but he is not there; and backward, but I cannot perceive him." Tried children of God, you have had this experience; and it is very perplexing because, when you cannot find your God, you cannot make out why you are being troubled. An affliction that will talk is always a light one; but I dread most of all a dumb affliction, that cannot tell me why it has come. When I look around it, and ask, "Why is this?" and I cannot get an answer, that is what plagues me much. And when you cannot find God, you do not yourself know what to do; for, in losing him, you have lost your Guide. You are in a maze, and know not how to get out of it. You are like a man in a net; the more you pull, this way or that, the more you tighten the bonds that hold you prisoner. Where you hoped to have relieved yourself, you only brought yourself into further difficulties in another direction; and this bewilderment is one of the worst of sorrows.

The loss of God's presence is also *inexpressibly painful to a believer*. If you can live without God, I am afraid you will die without God; but if you cannot live without God, that proves that you are his, and you will bear me out in the assertion that this is the heaviest of mortal griefs,—to feel that God has forsaken you, and does not hear your prayer;—nay, does not seem even to help you to pray, so that you can only groan, "Oh that I knew where I might find him! . . . Behold, I go forward, but he is not there; and backward, but I cannot perceive him."

Then, dear friends, in closing what I have to say about this dark side of the subject, let me remind you that *it is marvelously arousing*, because the true child of God, when he finds that his Father has forsaken him for awhile, gets to be terribly unhappy. Then he begins to cry and to seek after God. Look at Job; he hunts for God everywhere,—forward, backward, on the left hand, on the right hand. He leaves no quarter unvisited; no part of the earth is left without being searched over that he might find his God. Nothing brings a real Christian to his bearings, and awakes all his faculties,

like the consciousness of his Lord's absence. Then he cries,
"My God, where art thou? I have lost the sense of thy
presence; I have missed the light of thy countenance." A man,
in such a case as this, goes to the prayer-meeting, in the hope
that other people's prayers may help to make his sad heart
happy again. He reads his Bible, too, as he has not read it for
months. You will also find him listening to the gospel with the
utmost eagerness, and nothing but the gospel will satisfy him
now. At one time, he could listen to that pleasant kind of talk
that lulls the hearers to slumber, but now he wants a heart-
searching ministry, and a message that will go right into him,
and deal faithfully with him; and he is not content unless he
gets it. Besides this, he is anxious to talk with Christian
friends of riper experience than his own; and he deals
seriously and earnestly with these eternal matters which,
before, he perhaps trifled with as mere technicalities. You see
a man, who once lived in the light of God's countenance, and
you will find him wretched indeed when the light is gone. He
must have his God.

III. Now, lastly, I want to speak, for a little while,
concerning THE TRIED BELIEVER'S CONSOLATION. It is a very
sweet consolation: "He knoweth the way that I take: when he
hath tried me, I shall come forth as gold."

God knows and understands all about his child. I do not
know his way, but he knows mine. I am his child, and my
Father is leading me, though I cannot see him, for all around
me it is so misty and dark. I can scarcely feel his hand that
grasps my little palm, so I cry to him, "Where art thou, my
Father? I cannot see my way; the next step before me
threatens to plunge me into imminent peril. I know nothing,
my Father, but thou knowest." That is just where knowledge
is of most use; it does not so much matter what you do not
know so long as God knows it, for he is your Guide. If the
guide knows the way, the traveller under his care may be
content to know but little. "He knoweth the way that I take."
There is nothing about you, my brother, which God does not
perfectly understand. You are a riddle to yourself, but you are
no riddle to him. There are mysteries in your heart that you
cannot explain, but he has the clue of every maze, the key of
every secret drawer, and he knows how to get at the hidden
springs of your spirit. He knows the trouble that you could not
tell to your dearest friend, the grief you dare not whisper in

any human ear.

I find that the Hebrew has this meaning, "He knoweth the way that is in me." God knows whether I am his child or not; whether I am sincere or not. While others are judging me harshly, he judges me truly; he knows what I really am. This is a sweet consolation; take it to yourself, tried believer.

Next, *God approves of his child.* The word "know" often has the meaning of approval, and it has that sense here. Job says "God approves of the way that I take." When you are in trouble, it is a grand thing to be able to say, "I know that I have done that which is right in the sight of God, although it has brought me into great trial. 'My foot hath held his steps, his way have I kept, and not declined.'" If you have a secret and sure sense of God's approval in the time of your sorrow, it will be a source of very great strengthening to your spirit.

But Job meant more than this. He meant that *God was considering him,—and helping him even then.* The fact that he knows of our needs guarantees that he will supply them. You remember how our Lord Jesus Christ puts this truth: "Take no thought, saying, What shall we eat? or, What shall we drink? or, Wherewithal shall we be clothed? for your heavenly Father knoweth that ye have need of all these things." Does he know all about our need? It is all right then; the Head of the house knows the need of all the members of his family, and that is enough, for he never yet failed to supply all the wants of those who depend upon him. When I need guidance, he will himself be my Guide. He will supply me when I lack supplies, he will defend me when I need defence, he will give me all things that I really require. There is an old proverb that says, "Where God is, nothing is lacking;" and it is blessedly true. Only remember that there is an ancient precept with a gracious promise attached to it, "Delight thyself also in the Lord; and he shall give thee the desires of thine heart." Believe it, and obey it, and you shall find it true in your case.

Furthermore, when Job says, "When he hath tried me, I shall come forth as gold," he comforts himself with the belief that *God times and manages all things,*—that his present distresses are a trial, by which God is testing him. A man who is like solid gold is not afraid to be tested. No tradesman is afraid to put into the scales that which is full weight; for, if it is weighed, it will be proved to be what he says it is. When the

inspector of weights and measures comes round, the
gentleman who does not like to see him is the man of short
weights and incorrect scales. He who knows he is upright and
sincere dares say even to the Lord, himself, "Search me, O
God, and know my heart: try me, and know my ways: and see
if there be any wicked way in me, and lead me in the way
everlasting." We do not profess to be perfect, but we dare
claim to be sincere, and he who is sincere is not afraid of
being tested and tried. Real gold is not afraid of the fire; why
should it be? What has it to lose? So Job seems to say, "I know
that God hath put integrity within my spirit, and now that he
is testing me, he will not carry the test further than, by his
grace, I shall be able to bear."

Lastly, Job's comfort was that *God secures the happy result
of trial.* He believed that, when God had tried him, he would
bring him forth as gold. Now, how does gold come out of the
crucible? How does a true Christian man come out of the
darkness and obscurity of missing his God for awhile? How
does he come out like gold? In the Hebrew, the word has an
allusion to the bright colour of the gold; so, when a Christian
is tried, is there not a bright colour upon him? Even though
he may have lost, for a while, the bright shining of God's
countenance, when that brightness returns, there is a lustre
about him which you cannot help seeing. He will speak of his
God in a more impressive way than he ever spoke before.
Examine the books that are most comforting to believers, and
that satisfy their souls, and you will find that the men who
wrote them were those who had been severely tried; and
when they came out of the fire, there was a brilliance upon
them which would not otherwise have been there. If you walk
in darkness, and see no light, believe that, when God hath
tried you, you shall come forth with the brightness of newly-
minted gold.

But brightness is of little value without preciousness, and
the children of God grow more precious through their trials;
and, being precious, they become objects of desire. Men desire
gold above almost everything else, yet the Lord has said, "I
will make a man more precious than fine gold; even a man
than the golden wedge of Ophir." There are some godly men
whose company we court, and some Christian women whose
society, when they talk of spiritual things, is worth a Jew's
eye to one that is in distress. Happy are they whom God has

passed through the fire, who become precious and desirable when they come out of it.

And they become honourable, too. "When he hath tried me," said Job, "even though my friends despise me now, when I come forth, they shall have different thoughts concerning me." They thought a great deal more of Job when God was angry with them, and would not restore them to his favour until the patriarch had prayed for them, than they thought of him when they went to find fault with him; and the day shall come to thee, true child of God, when those who now persecute thee, and look down upon thee, shall look up to thee. Joseph may be cast into the pit by his brethren, and sold into Egypt, but he shall yet sit on the throne, and all his father's sons shall bow before him.

Once more, you shall come out of the fire uninjured. It looks very hard to believe that a child of God should be tried by the loss of his Father's presence, and yet should come forth uninjured by the trial. Yet no gold is ever injured in the fire. Stoke the furnace as much as you may, let the blast be as strong as you will, thrust the ingot into the very centre of the white heat, let it lie in the very heart of the flame; pile on more fuel, let another blast torment the coals till they become most vehement with heat, yet the gold is losing nothing, it may even be gaining. If it had any alloy mingled with it, the alloy is separated from it by the fire, and to gain in purity is the greatest of gains. But the pure gold is not one drachma less; there is not a single particle of it that can be burnt. It is there still, all the better for the fiery trial to which it has been subjected; and thou, dear child of God, whatever may befall thee, shalt come out of the fire quite uninjured. Thou art under a dark cloud just now; but thou shalt come out into brightness, and thou shalt have lost nothing that was worth keeping. What is there that thou canst lose? When death comes, what wilt thou lose?

> "Corruption, earth, and worms,
> Shall but refine this flesh,
> Till my triumphant spirit comes
> To put it on afresh."

When we put on our new clothes, this body that shall have passed through God's transforming hand,—shall we be losers? No, we shall say, "What a difference! Is this my

Sabbath garment? The old one was dark and dingy, dusty and defiled; this is whiter than any fuller could make it, and brighter than the light." You will scarcely know yourselves, my brothers and sisters; you will know other people, I daresay; but I think you will hardly recognize yourselves when once you have put on your new array. You cannot really lose anything by death. You will not lose the eyes you part with for awhile; for, when Christ shall stand, at the latter day, upon the earth, your eyes shall behold him. You shall lose no faculty, no power, but you shall infinitely gain even by death itself; and that is the very worst of your enemies, so that you shall certainly gain by all the rest. Come then, pluck up courage, and march boldly on. Fear no ghosts, for they are but spectres, there is no reality about them.

Beloved, note well this closing word. *God is here.* You need not go forward to find him, or backward to hunt after him, or on the left to search for him, or on the right to see him. He is with his people still, as he said, "Lo, I am with you alway, even unto the end of the world." "Fear not: for I have redeemed thee. I have called thee by thy name; thou art mine. When thou passest through the waters, I will be with thee; and through the rivers, they shall not overflow thee: when thou walkest through the fire, thou shalt not be burned; neither shall the flame kindle upon thee."

Oh, seek him, then, every one of you, and God bless you all, for Christ's sake! Amen.

15

The Fair Portrait of a Saint

"My foot hath held his steps, his way have I kept, and not declined. Neither have I gone back from the commandment of his lips: I have esteemed the words of his mouth more than my necessary food." **Job 23:11-12**

Thus Job speaks of himself, not by way of vaunting, but by way of vindication. Eliphaz the Temanite and his two com-panions had brought distinct charges against Job's character: because they saw him in such utter misery they concluded that his adversity must have been sent as a punishment for his sin, and therefore they judged him to be a hypocrite, who under cover of religion had exercised oppression and tyranny. Zophar had hinted the wickedness was sweet in Job's mouth, and that he hid iniquity under his tongue. Eliphaz charged him with hardness of heart to the poor, and dared to say, "Thou hast taken a pledge from thy brother for nought, and stripped the naked of their clothing." This last from its very impossibility was meant to show the extreme meanness to which he falsely imagined that Job must have descended—how could he strip the naked? He was evidently firing at random. As neither he nor his companions could discover any palpable blot in Job upon which they could distinctly lay their finger, they bespattered him right and left with their groundless accusations. They made up in venom for the want of evidence to back their charges. They felt sure that there must be some great sin in him to have procured such extraordinary afflictions, and therefore by smiting him all over they hoped to touch the sore place. Let them stand as a warning to us never to judge men by their circumstances, and never to conclude that a man must be wicked because he has fallen from riches to poverty.

Job, however, knew his innocence, and he was determined not to give way to them. He said, "Ye are forgers of lies,

physicians of no value. O that ye would altogether hold your
peace! and it should be your wisdom." He fought the battle
right manfully; not, perhaps, without a little display of
temper and self-righteousness, but still with much less of
either than any of us would have shown had we been in the
same plight, and had we been equally conscious of perfect
integrity. He has in this part of his self-defence sketched a
fine picture of a man perfect and upright before God. He has
set before us the image to which we should seek to be
conformed. Here is the high ideal after which every Christian
man should strive; and happy shall he be who shall attain to
it. Blessed is he who in the hour of his distress, if he be falsely
accused, will be able to say with as much truth as the
patriarch could, "My foot hath held his steps, his way have I
kept, and not declined. Neither have I gone back from the
commandment of his lips; I have esteemed the words of his
mouth more than my necessary food."

I ask you, first, to inspect the picture of *Job's holy life,* that
you may make it your model. After we have done this, we will
look a little below the surface, asking the question, "How was
he enabled to lead such an admirable life as this? Upon what
meat did this great patriarch feed that he had grown so
eminent?" We shall find the answer in our second head, *Job's
holy sustenance*—"I have esteemed the words of his mouth
more than my necessary food." May he, who wrought in Job
his patience and integrity, by this our meditation teach us the
like virtues by the power of the Holy Ghost.

I. Let us sit down before this sketch of JOB'S HOLY LIFE: it
will well repay a meditative study.

Note, first, that *Job had been all along a man fearing God
and walking after the divine rule.* In the words before us he
dwells much upon the things of God—"his steps," "his way,"
"the commandment of his lips," "the words of his mouth." He
was pre-eminently one that "feared God and eschewed evil."
He knew God to be the Lord, and worthy to be served, and
therefore he lived in obedience to his law, which was written
upon his instructed conscience. His way was God's way; he
chose that course which the Lord commanded. He did not
seek his own pleasure, nor the carrying out of his own will:
neither did he follow the fashion of the times, nor conform
himself to the ruling opinion or custom of the age in which he
lived: fashion and custom were nothing to him, he knew no

rule but the will of the Almighty. Like some tall cliff which breasts the flood, he stood out almost alone, a witness for God in an idolatrous world. He owned the living God, and lived "as seeing him who is invisible." God's will had taken the helm of the vessel, and the ship was steered in God's course according to the divine compass of infallible justice and the unerring chart of the divine will. This is a great point to begin with; it is, indeed, the only sure basis of a noble character. Ask the man who seeks to be the architect of a great and honourable character this question—Where do you place God? Is he second with you? Ah, then, in the judgment of those whose view comprehends all human relationships you will lead a very secondary kind of life, for the first and most urgent obligation of your being will be disregarded. But is God first with you? Is this your determination, "As for me and my house, we will serve the Lord"? Do you seek first the kingdom of God and his righteousness? If so, you are laying the foundation for a whole or holy character, for you begin by acknowledging your highest responsibility. In this respect you will find that "the fear of the Lord is the beginning of wisdom." Whether the way be rough or smooth, uphill or down dale, through green pastures or burning deserts, let God's way be your way. Where the fiery cloudy pillar of his providence leads be sure to follow, and where his holy statutes command, there promptly go. Ask the Lord to let you hear his Spirit speak like a voice behind you saying, "This is the way, walk ye in it." As soon as you see from the Scriptures, or from conscience, or from providence, what the will of the Lord is, make haste and delay not to keep his commandments. Set the Lord always before you. Have respect unto his statutes at all times, and in all your ways acknowledge him. No man will be able to look back upon his life with complacency unless God has been sitting upon the throne of his heart and ruling all his thoughts, aims, and actions. Unless he can say with David, "My soul hath kept thy testimonies and I love them exceedingly," he will find much to weep over and little with which to answer his accusers.

We must follow the Lord's way, or our end will be destruction; we must take hold upon Christ's steps, or our feet will soon be in slippery places; we must reverence God's words, or our own words will be idle and full of vanity; and we must keep God's commands, or we shall be destitute of that

holiness without which no man shall see the Lord. I set not
forth obedience to the law as the way of salvation; but I speak
to those who profess to be saved already by faith in Christ
Jesus, and I remind all of you who are numbered with the
company of believers that if you are Christ's disciples you will
bring forth the fruits of holiness, and if you are God's children
you will be like your Father. Godliness breeds God-likeness.
The fear of God leads to imitation of God, and where this is
not so, the root of the matter is lacking. The scriptural rule is
"by their fruits ye shall know them," and by this we must
examine ourselves.

Let us now consider Job's first sentence. He says: *"My foot
hath held his steps."* This expression sets forth great
carefulness. He had watched every step of God, that is to say,
he had been minute as to particulars, observing each precept,
which he looked upon as being a footprint which the Lord had
made for him to set his foot in; observing, also, each detail of
the great example of his God; for in so far as God is imitable
he is the great example of his people, as he saith—"Be ye
holy, for I am holy": and again, "Be ye perfect, even as your
Father which is in heaven is perfect." Job had observed the
steps of God's justice, that he might be just; the steps of God's
mercy, that he might be pitiful and compassionate; the steps
of God's bounty, that he might never be guilty of churlishness
or want of liberality; and the steps of God's truth, that he
might never deceive. He had watched God's steps of
forgiveness, that he might forgive his adversaries; and God's
steps of benevolence, that he might also do good and
communicate, according to his ability, to all that were in
need. In consequence of this he became eyes to the blind and
feet to the lame; he delivered the poor that cried, and the
fatherless and him that had none to help. The blessing of him
that was ready to perish came upon him, and he caused the
widow's heart to sing for joy.

"My foot," he saith, "hath held his steps": he means that he
had laboured to be exact in his obedience towards God, and in
his imitation of the divine character. Beloved, we shall do well
if we are to the minutest point hourly observant of the
precepts and example of God in all things. We must follow not
only the right road, but his footprints in that road. We are to
be obedient to our heavenly Father not only in some things,
but in all things: not in some place but in all places, abroad

and at home, in business and in devotion, in the words of our lips and in the thoughts of our hearts. There is no holy walking without careful watching. Depend upon it, no man was ever good by chance, nor did anyone ever become like the Lord Jesus by a happy accident. "I put gold into the furnace," said Aaron, "and there came out this calf," but nobody believed him. If the image was like a calf it was because he had shaped it with a graving tool; and if it is not to be believed that metal will of itself take the form of a calf, much less will character assume the likeness of God himself, as we see it in the Lord Jesus. The pattern is too rich and rare, too elaborate and perfect, ever to be reproduced by a careless, half-awakened trifler. No, we must give all our heart, and mind, and soul, and strength to this business, and watch every step, or else our walk will not be close with God, nor pleasing in his sight. O to be able to say, "My foot hath held his steps."

Notice here that the expression has something in it of tenacity, he speaks of taking hold upon God's steps. The idea needs to be lit up by the illustration contained in the original expression. You must go to mountainous regions to understand it. In very rough ways a person may walk all the better for having no shoes to his feet. I sometimes pitied the women of Mentone coming down the rough places of the mountains barefooted, carrying heavy loads upon their heads, but I ceased to pity them when I observed that most of them had a capital pair of shoes in the basket at the top; and I perceived as I watched them that they could stand where I slipped, because their feet took hold upon the rock, almost like another pair of hands. Barefooted they could safely stand, and readily climb where feet encased after our fashion would never carry them. Many Orientals have a power of grasp in their feet which we appear to have lost from want of use. An Arab in taking a determined stand actually seems to grasp the ground with his toes. Roberts tells us in his well-known "Illustrations" that Easterns, instead of stooping to pick up things from the ground with their fingers, will take them up with their toes; and he tells of a criminal condemned to be beheaded, who, in order to stand firm when about to die, grasped a shrub with his foot. Job declares that he took hold of God's steps, and thus secured a firm footing. He had a hearty grip of holiness, even as David said, "I have stuck unto thy testimonies." That eminent scholar Dr. Good renders the passage, "in his steps will I *rivet* my feet." He would set them as fast in the footprints of truth and righteousness as if they were riveted there, so firm was his grip upon that holy way which his heart had chosen. This is exactly what we need to do with regard to holiness: we must feel about for it with a sensitive conscience, to know where it is, and when we know it we must seize upon it eagerly, and hold to it as for our life. The way of holiness is often craggy, and Satan tries to make it very slippery, and unless we can take hold of God's steps we shall soon slip with our feet, and bring grievous injury upon ourselves, and dishonour to his holy name. Beloved, to make up a holy character there must be a tenacious adherence to integrity and piety. You must not be one that can be blown off his feet by the hope of a little gain, or by the threatening breath of an ungodly man: you must stand fast and stand firm, and against all pressure and blandishment you must seize and grasp the precepts of the Lord, and abide in them, riveted to them. Standfast is one of the best soldiers in the Prince Immanuel's army and one of the most fit to be trusted with the colours of his regiment. "Having done all, still stand."

To make a holy character we must take hold of the steps of God in the sense of promptness and speed. Here again I must take you to the East to get the illustration. They say of a man who closely imitates his religious teacher, "his feet have laid hold of his master's steps," meaning that he so closely follows his teacher that he seems to take hold of his heels. This is a blessed thing indeed, when grace enables us to follow our Lord closely. There is his foot, and close behind it is ours; and there again he takes another step, and we plant our feet where he has planted his. A very beautiful motto is hung up in our infant class-room at the Stockwell Orphanage, *"What would Jesus do?"* Not only may children take it as their guide, but all of us may do the same, whatever our age. "What would Jesus do?" If you desire to know what you ought to do under any circumstances, imagine Jesus to be in that position, and then think, "What would Jesus do? for what Jesus would do that ought I to do." In following Jesus we are following God, for in Christ Jesus the brightness of the Father's glory is best seen. Our example is our Lord and Master, Jesus the Son of God, and therefore this question is but a beam from our guiding star. Ask in all cases—"What would Jesus do?" That unties the knot of all moral difficulty in the most practical way, and does it so simply that no great wit or wisdom will be needed. May God's Holy Spirit help us to copy the line which Jesus has written, even as scholars imitate their writing master in each stroke, and line, and mark, and dot. Oh, when we come to die, and have to look back upon our lives, it will be a blessed thing to have followed the Lord fully. They are happy who follow the Lamb whithersoever he goeth. Blessed are they in life and death of whom it can be said, as he was so were they also in this world. Though misunderstood and misrepresented, yet they were honest imitators of their Lord. Such a true-hearted Christian can say, "He knoweth the way that I take. He tried me, and I came forth as gold. My foot hath held his steps." Many a sorrow will you avoid if you keep close at your Master's heel. You know what came of Peter's following afar off; try what will come of close walking with Jesus. Abide in him, and let his words abide in you, so shall you be his disciples. You dare not trust in your works, and will not think of doing so, yet will you bless God that, being saved by his grace, you were enabled to bring forth the fruits of the Spirit, by a close and exact following of the steps of your Lord. Three things, then, we get in the first sentence, an exactness of obedience, a tenacity of grip upon that which is good, and a promptness in endeavouring to keep touch with God, and to follow him in all respects. May these things be in us and abound.

We now pass on to the second sentence. I am afraid you will say, "Spare us, for even unto the first sentence we have not yet attained." Labour after it then, beloved; forgetting the things that are behind except to weep over them, press forward to that which is before. May God give you those sensitive grasping feet which we have tried to describe: feet that take hold on the Lord's way, and may you throughout life keep that hold; for "blessed are the undefiled in the way, who walk in the law of the Lord."

The next sentence runneth thus: *"His way have I kept"*; that is to say, Job had adhered to God's way as the rule of his life. When he knew that such-and-such a thing was the mind of God, either by his conscience telling him that it was right, or by a divine revelation, then he obeyed the intimation and kept to it. He did not go out of God's way to indulge his own fancies, or to follow some supposed leader: to God's way he kept from his youth, even till the time when the Lord himself said of him, "Hast thou considered my servant Job, a perfect and an upright man, one that feareth God, and escheweth evil?" The Lord gave him this character to the devil, who could not deny it, and did not attempt to do so, but only muttered, "Doth Job serve God for nought? Hast thou not set a hedge about him and all that he hath?" When he uttered our text Job could have replied to the malicious accuser that, even when God had broken down his hedges and laid him waste, he had not sinned nor charged God foolishly. He heeded not his wife's rash counsels to curse God and die, but he still blessed the divine name even though everything was taken from him. What noble words are those: "Naked came I out of my mother's womb, and naked shall I return thither: the Lord gave, and the Lord hath taken away; blessed be the name of the Lord." Though bereft of all earthly comfort, he did not forsake the way of holiness, but still kept to his God.

Keeping to the way signifies not simply adherence, but continuance and progress in it. Job had gone on in the ways of God year after year. He had not grown tired of holiness, nor weary of devotion, neither had he grown sick of what men call straight-laced piety. He had kept the way of God on, and on, and on, delighting in what Coverdale's version calls God's "high street"—the highway of holiness. The further he went the more pleasure he took in it, and the more easy he found it to his feet, for God was with him and kept him, and so he kept God's way. "Thy way have I kept." He means that notwithstanding there were difficulties in the way he persevered in it. It was stormy weather, but Job kept to the old road; the sleet beat in his face, but he kept his way: he had gone that path in fair weather, and he was not going to forsake his God now that the storms were out; and so he kept his way. Then the scene changed, the sun was warm, and all the air was redolent with perfume, and merry with the song of birds, but Job kept his way. If God's providence flooded his sky with sunshine he did not forsake God because of prosperity, as some do, but kept his way kept his way when it was rough, kept his way when it was smooth. When he met with adversities he did not turn into a bye-road, but travelled the King's highway, where a man is safest, for those who dare to assail him will have to answer for it to a higher power. The high street of holiness is safe because the King's guarantee is given that "no lion shall be there, neither shall any ravenous beast go up thereon." The righteous shall hold on his way, and so did Job, come fair, come foul. When there were others in the road with him, and when there were none, he kept his way. He would not even turn aside for those three good men, or men who thought themselves good, who sat by the wayside and miserably comforted, that is to say, tormented him; he kept God's way, as one whose mind is made up and whose face is set like a flint. There was no turning him, he would fight his way if he could not have it peaceably. I like a man whose mind is set upon being right with God, a self-contained man by God's grace, who does not want patting on the back and encouraging, and who on the other hand does not care if he is frowned at, but has counted the cost and abides by it. Give me a man who has a backbone; a brave fellow who has grit in him. It is well for a professor when God has put some soul into him, and made a man of him, for if a Christian man is not a man as well as a Christian, he will not long remain a Christian man. Job was firm: a well-made character that did not shrink in the wetting. He believed his God, he knew God's way, and he kept to it under all circumstances from his first start in life even until that day when he sat on a dunghill and transformed it into a throne, whereon he reigned as among all mere men, the peerless prince of patience. Ye have heard of the patience of Job, and of this as one part of it, that he kept the way of the Lord.

Now, dear brethren, on this second clause let me utter this word of self-examination. Have we kept God's way? Have we got into it and do we mean to keep it still? Some are soon hot and soon cold; some set out for the New Jerusalem like Pliable, very eagerly, but the first slough of despond they tumble into shakes their resolution, and they crawl out on the homeward side and go back to the world again. There will be no comfort in such temporary religion, but dreadful misery when we come to consider it on a dying bed. Changeful Pliables will find it hard to die. O to be constant even to the end, so as to say, "My foot hath held his steps, his way have I kept." God grant us grace to do it, by his Spirit abiding in us.

The third clause is, *"And not declined,"* by which I understand that he had not declined *from* the way of holiness, nor declined *in* the way. First, he had not declined from it. He

had not turned to the right hand nor to the left. Some turn
away from God's way to the right hand by doing more than
God's word has bidden them do; such as invent religious
ceremonies, and vows, and bonds, and become superstitious,
falling under the bondage of priestcraft, and being led into
will-worship, and things that are not Scriptural. This is as
truly wandering as going out of the road to the left would be.
Ah, dear friends, keep to the simplicity of the Bible. This is an
age in which Holy Scripture is very little accounted of. If a
church chooses to invent a ceremony, men fall into it, and
practise it as if it were God's ordinance. Ay, and if neither
church nor law recognise the performance, yet if certain
self-willed priests choose to burn candles, and to wear all
sorts of bedizenments, and bow, and cringe, and march in
procession, there are plenty of simpletons who will go
whichever way their clergyman chooses, even if he should
lead them into downright heathenism. "Follow my leader" is
the game of the day, but "Follow my God" is the motto of a
true Christian. Job had not turned to the right.

Nor had he turned to the left. He had not been lax in
observing God's commandments. He had shunned omission as
well as commission. This is a very heart-searching matter; for
how many there are whose greatest sins lie in omission. And
remember, sins of omission, though they sit very light on
many consciences, and though the bulk of professors do not
even think them sins, are the very sins for which men will be
condemned at the last. How do I prove that? What said the
great Judge? "I was an hungered and ye gave me no meat, I
was thirsty and ye gave me no drink, sick and in prison and
ye visited me not." It was what they did not do that cursed
them, more than what they did do. So look ye well to it, and
pray God that you may not decline from the way of his
precepts, from Jesus who, himself, is the one and only way.

Furthermore, I take it Job means that he had not even
declined *in* that way. He did not begin with running hard and
then get out of breath, and sit by the wayside and say, "Rest
and be thankful;" but he kept up the pace, and did not decline.
If he was warm and zealous once he remained warm and
zealous; if he was indefatigable in service, he did not
gradually tone down into a sluggard, but he could say, "I have
not declined." Whereas we ought to make advances towards
heaven, there are many who are, after twenty years

profession, no forwarder than they were, but perhaps in a worse state. Oh, beware of a decline. We were accustomed to use that term years ago to signify the commencement of a consumption, or perhaps the effects of it; and indeed, a decline in the soul often leads on to a deadly consumption. In a spiritual consumption the very life of religion seems to ebb out by little and little. The man does not die by a wound that stabs his reputation, but by a secret weakness within him, which eats at the vitals of godliness and leaves the outward surface fair. God save us from declining. I am sure, dear friends, we cannot many of us afford to decline much, for we are none too earnest, none too much alive now; but this is one of the great faults of churches, so many of the members are in a decline that the church becomes a hospital instead of a barracks. Many professors are not what they were at first: they were very promising young men, but they are not performing old men. We are pleased to see the flowers on our fruit-trees, but they disappoint us unless they knit into fruit, and we are not satisfied even then unless the fruit ripens to a mellow sweetness. We do not make orchards for the sake of blossoms, we want apples. So is it with the garden of grace, our Lord comes seeking fruit, and instead thereof he often finds nothing but leaves. May God grant to us that we may not decline from the highest standard we have ever reached. "I would," said the Lord of the church of Laodicea, "that thou wert either cold or hot." Oh, you lukewarm ones, take that warning to heart. Remember, Jesus cannot endure you; he will spue you out of his mouth; you make him sick to think of you. If you were downright cold he would understand you; if you were hot he would delight in you; but being neither cold nor hot he is sick at the thought of you, he cannot endure you; and indeed, when we think of what the Lord has done for us, it is enough to make us sick to think that any one should drag on in a cold, inanimate manner in his service, who loved us, and gave himself for us.

Some decline because they become poor: they even stay from worship on that account. I hope none of you say, "I do not like to come to the Tabernacle because I have not fit clothes to come in." As I have often said, any clothes are fit for a man to come here in if he has paid for them. Let each come by all manner of means in such garments as he has, and he shall be welcome. But I do know some very poor professors

who, in the extremity of their anxiety and trouble, instead of
flying to God, fly from him. This is very sad. The poorer you
are, the more you want the rich consolations of grace. Do not
let this temptation overcome you, but if you are as poor as
Job, be as resolved as he to keep to the Lord's way and not
decline. Others fly from their religion because they grow rich.
They say that three generations never will come on wheels to
a dissenting place of worship, and it has proved to be sadly
true in many instances, though I have no cause to complain of
you as yet. Some persons when they rise in the world turn up
their noses at their poor friends. If any of you do so you will be
worthy of pity, if not of contempt. If you forsake the ways of
God for the fashion of the world you will be poor gainers by
your wealth. The Lord keep you from such a decline. Many
decline because they conform to the fashion of the world, and
the way of the world is not the way of God. Doth not James
say, "Know ye not that the friendship of the world is enmity
with God? Whosoever therefore will be a friend of the world is
the enemy of God." Others wander because they get into ill
company, among witty people, or clever people, or hospitable
people, who are not gracious people. Such society is
dangerous. People whom we esteem, but whom God does not
esteem, are a great snare. It is very perilous to love those who
love not God. He shall not be my bosom friend who is not
God's friend, for I shall probably do him but little service, and
he will do me much harm. May the grace of God prevent your
growing cold from any of these causes, and may you be able to
say, "I have not declined."

One more sentence remains: *"Neither have I gone back from
the commandment of his lips":* that is to say, as he had not
slackened his pace, so much less had he turned back. May
none of you ever go back. This is the most cutting grief of a
pastor, that certain persons come in among us, and even come
to the front, who after awhile turn back and walk no more
with us. We know, as John says, "They went out from us, but
they were not of us; for if they had been of us, they would no
doubt have continued with us; but they went out, that they
might be made manifest that they were not all of us"; yet
what anguish it causes when we see apostates among us and
know their doom. Take heed, brethren, lest there be in any of
you an evil heart of unbelief in departing from the living God.
Let Lot's wife be a warning. Season your souls with a

fragment of salt from that pillar, and it may keep you from corruption.

Remember that you can turn back, not only from all the commandments, and so become an utter apostate, but there is such a thing as backing at single commandments. You know the precept to be right, but you cannot face it; you look at it, and look at it, and look at it, and then go back, back, back from it, refusing to obey. Job had never done so. If it was God's command he went forward to perform it. It may be that it seems impossible to go forward in the path of duty, but if you have faith you are to go on whatever the difficulty may be. The negro was right who said, "Massa, if God say, 'Sam, jump through the wall'; it is Sam's business to jump, and God's work to make me go through the wall." Leap at it, dear friends, even if it seem to be a wall of granite. God will clear the road. By faith the Israelites went through the Red Sea as on dry land. It is ours to do what God bids us, as he bids us, when he bids us, and no hurt can come of it. Strength equal to our day shall be given, only let us cry "Forward!" and push on.

Here just one other word. Let us take heed to ourselves that we do not go back, for going back is dangerous. We have no armour for our back, no promise of protection in retreat. Going back is ignoble and base. To have had a grand idea and then to turn back from it like a whipped cur, is disgraceful. Shame on the man who dares not be a Christian. Even sinners and ungodly men point at the man who put his hand to the plough and looked back, and was not worthy of the kingdom. Indeed, it is fatal; for the Lord has said, "If any man draw back, my soul shall have no pleasure in him." Forward! Forward! though death and hell obstruct the way, for backward is defeat, destruction, despair. O God, grant us of thy grace that when we come to the end of life we may say with joy, "I have not gone back from thy commandment." The covenant promises persevering grace, and it shall be yours, only look ye well that ye trifle not with this grace.

There is the picture which Job has sketched. Hang it up on the wall of your memory, and God help you to paint after this old master, whose skill is unrivalled.

II. Secondly, let us take a peep behind the wall to see how Job came by this character. Here we note JOB'S HOLY SUSTENANCE, "I have esteemed the words of his mouth more than my necessary food."

First, then, *God spoke to Job*. Did God ever speak to you? I
do not suppose Job had a single page of inspired writing.
Probably he had not even seen the first books of Moses; he
may have done so, but probably he had not. God spoke to him.
Did he ever speak to you? No man will ever serve God aright
unless God has spoken to him. You have the Bible, and God
speaks in that book and through it; but mind you do not rest
in the printed letter without discerning its spirit. You must
try to hear God's voice in the printed letter. "God hath in
these last days spoken unto us by his Son"; but oh, pray that
this divine Son may speak by the Holy Ghost right into your
heart. Anything which keeps you from personal contact with
Jesus robs you of the best blessing. The Romanist says he
uses a crucifix to help him to remember Christ, and then his
prayers often stop at the crucifix, and do not get to Christ;
and in like manner you can make an idol of your Bible by
using the mere words as a substitute for God's voice to you.
The book is to help you to remember God, but if you stick in
the mere letter, and get not to God at all, you misuse the
sacred word. When the Spirit of God speaks a text right into
the soul, when God himself takes the promise or the precept
and sends it with living energy into the heart, this is that
which makes a man have a reverence for the word: he feels its
awful majesty, its divine supremacy, and while he trembles at
it he rejoices, and goes forward to obey because God has
spoken to him. Dear friends, when God speaks be sure that
you have open ears to hear, for oftentimes he speaketh and
men regard him not. In a vision of the night when deep sleep
falleth upon men God has spoken to his prophets, but now he
speaks by his word, applying it to the heart with power by his
Spirit. If God speaks but little to us it is because we are dull
of hearing. Renewed hearts are never long without a whisper
from the Lord. He is not a dumb God, nor is he so far away
that we cannot hear him: they that keep his ways and hold
his steps, as Job did, shall hear many of his words to their
soul's delight and profit. God's having spoken to Job was the
secret of his consistently holy life.

Then note, that *what God had spoken to him he treasured
up*. He says in the Hebrew that he had hid God's word more
than ever he had hidden his necessary food. They had to hide
grain away in those days to guard it from wandering Arabs.
Job had been more careful to store up God's word than to

store up his wheat and his barley; more anxious to preserve the memory of what God had spoken than to garner his harvests. Do you treasure up what God has spoken? Do you study the Word? Do you read it? Oh, how little do we search it compared with what we ought to do. Do you meditate on it? Do you suck out its secret sweets? Do you store up its essence as bees gather the life-blood of flowers, and hoard up their honey for winter food? Bible study is the metal that makes a Christian; this is the strong meat on which holy men are nourished; this is that which makes the bone and sinew of men who keep God's way in defiance of every adversary. God spake to Job, and Job treasured up his words.

We learn from our version of the text that *Job lived on God's word:* he reckoned it to be better to him than his necessary food. He ate it. This is an art which some do not understand—eating the word of the Lord. Some look at the surface of the Scriptures, some pull the Scriptures to pieces without mercy, some cut the heavenly bread into dice pieces, and show their cleverness, some pick it over for plums, like children with a cake; but blessed is he that makes it his meat and drink. He takes the word of God to be what is, namely, a word from the mouth of the Eternal, and he says, "God is speaking to me in this, and I will satisfy my soul upon it; I do not want anything better than this, anything truer than this, anything safer than this, but having got this it shall abide in me, in my heart, in the very bowels of my life, it shall be interwoven with the warp and woof of my being.

But the text adds that he esteemed it more than his necessary food. Not more than dainties only, for those are superfluities, but more than his necessary food, and you know that a man's necessary food is a thing which he esteems very highly. He must have it. What, take away my bread? says he, as if this could not be borne. To take the bread out of a poor man's mouth is looked upon as the highest kind of villainy: but Job would sooner that they took the bread out of his mouth than the word of God out of his heart. He thought more of it than of his needful food, and I suppose it was because meat would only sustain his body, but the word of God feeds the soul. The nourishment given by bread is soon gone, but the nourishment given by the word of God abideth in us, and makes us to live for ever. The natural life is more than meat, but our spiritual life feeds on meat even nobler than itself, for it feeds on the bread of heaven, the person of the Lord Jesus. Bread is sweet to the hungry man, but we are not always hungry, and sometimes we have no appetite; but the best of God's word is that he who lives near to God has always an appetite for it, and the more he eats of it the more he can eat. I do confess I have often fed upon God's word when I have had no appetite for it, until I have gained an appetite. I have grown hungry in proportion as I have felt satisfied: my emptiness seemed to kill my hunger, but as I have been revived by the word I have longed for more. So it is written, "Blessed are they that hunger and thirst after righteousness, for they shall be filled:" and when they are filled they shall continue to enjoy the benediction, for they shall hunger and thirst still though filled with grace. God's word is sweeter to the taste than bread to a hungry man, and its sweetness never cloys, though it dwells long on the palate. You cannot be always eating bread, but you can always feed on the word of God. You cannot eat all the meat that is set before you, your capacity is limited that way, and none but a glutton wishes it otherwise; but oh, you may be ravenous of God's word, and devour it all, and yet have no surfeit. You are like a little mouse in a great cheese, and you shall have permission to eat it all, though it be a thousand times greater than yourself. Though God's thoughts are greater than your thoughts, and his ways are greater than your ways, yet may his ways be in your heart, and your heart in his ways. You may be filled with all the fulness of God, though it seems a paradox. His fulness is greater than you, and *all* his fullness is infinitely greater than you, yet you may be filled with all the fullness of God. So that the word of God is better than our necessary food: it hath qualities which our necessary food hath not.

No more, except it be this: you cannot be holy, my brethren, unless you do in secret live upon the blessed word of God, and you will not live on it unless it comes to you as the word *of his mouth.* It is very sweet to get a letter from home when you are far away: it is like a bunch of fresh flowers in winter time. A letter from the dear one at home is as music heard over the water; but half a dozen words from that dear mouth are better than a score of pages of manuscript, for there is a sweetness about the look and the tone which paper cannot carry. Now, I want you to get the Bible to be not a book only but a speaking trumpet, through which God speaks from afar to you, so that you may catch the very tones of his voice. You must read the word of God to this end, for it is while reading, meditating, and studying, and seeking to dip yourself into its spirit, that it seems suddenly to change from a written book into a talking book or phonograph; it whispers to you or thunders at you as though God had hidden himself among its leaves and spoke to your condition; as though Jesus who feedeth among the lilies had made the chapters to be lily beds, and had come to feed there. Ask Jesus to cause his word to come fresh from his own mouth to your soul; and if it be so, and you thus live in daily communion with a personal Christ, my brethren, you will then with your feet take hold upon his steps; then will you keep his way, then will you never decline or go back from his commandments, but you will make good speed in your pilgrim way to the eternal city. May the Holy Ghost daily be with you. May every one of you live under his sacred bedewing, and be fruitful in every good word and work. Amen and amen.

16

A Vexed Soul Comforted

"...the Almighty, who hath vexed my soul."   **Job 27:2**

The word "who" was put into this verse by the translators, but it is not wanted; it is better as I have read it to you, "The Almighty hath vexed my soul." The marginal reading is perhaps a more exact translation of the original: "The Almighty hath embittered my soul." From this we learn that a good man may have his soul vexed; he may not be able to preserve the serenity of his mind. We think, and think rightly, that a Christian man should "glory in tribulations also," and rise superior to all outward afflictions; but it is not always so with us. There is a needs-be, sometimes, that we should be "in heaviness through manifold temptations." Not only are the temptations needed for the trial of our faith, but it is even necessary that we should be in heaviness through them. I hardly imagine that the most quiet and restful believers have always been unruffled; I can scarcely think that even those whose peace is like a river have always been made to flow on with calm and equable current. Even to rivers there are rapids and cataracts, and so, methinks, in the most smoothly flowing life, there must surely be breaks of distraction and of distress. At any rate, it was so with Job. His afflictions, aggravated by the accusations of his so-called friends, at least made the iron enter into his very soul, and his spirit was so troubled that he cried, "The Almighty hath embittered my soul."

It is also clear, from our text, that a good man may trace the vexation of his soul distinctly to God. It was not merely that Job's former troubles had come from God, for he had borne up under them; when all he had was gone, he had still blessed the name of the Lord with holy serenity. But God had permitted these three eminent and distinguished men, mighty in speech, to come about him, to rub salt into his wounds, and so to increase his agony. At first, too, God did not seem to help him in the debate, although afterwards he answered all the accusations of Job's friends, and put them to the rout; yet, for a time, Job had to stand like a solitary champion against all three of them, and against young Elihu, too; so he looked up to heaven, and he said, "'The Almighty hath embittered my soul.' There is an end of the controversy; I can see whence all my trouble comes."

Advancing a step further, we notice that, in all this, Job did not rebel against God, or speak a word against him. He swore by that very God who had vexed his soul. See how it stands here: "As God liveth, who hath taken away my judgment, and the Almighty, who hath vexed my soul." He stood fast to it that this God was the true God, he called him good, he believed him to be almighty; it never occurred to Job to bring a railing accusation against God, or to start aside from his allegiance to him. He is a truly brave man who can say with Job, "'Though he slay me, yet will I trust in him.' Let God deal with me as he will, yet he is good, and I will praise his name. What if he has vexed my soul? He hath a right to vex me, so I will not kick against the pricks. Let him grieve me, let him put gall and wormwood into my cup if so it shall please him; but still will I magnify his name, for he is good, and only good." Here is the strength of the saints, here is the glory which God getteth out of true believers,—that they cannot and will not be soured against their God.

Now go another step, and notice that this embittering of Job's soul was intended for his good. The patriarch was to have his wealth doubled, and he therefore needed double grace that he might be able to bear the burden. He was also to be a far holier man than he had been at the first; perfect and upright as he seemed to be, he was to rise a stage higher. If his character had been deficient in anything, perhaps it was deficient in humility. Truly, Job was no proud man, he was generous, and kind, and meek; but, possibly, he had a little too high a notion of his own character, so even that must be taken away from him. Other graces must be added to those he already possessed; he must have a tenderness of spirit which appears to have been lacking; he must become as gentle as a maid as he had been firm as a man of war; and, consequently, this bitterness of soul was meant to help him towards perfection of character. When that end was accomplished, all the bitterness was turned into sweetness. God made the travail of his soul to be forgotten by reason of the joy that came of it. Job no longer thought of the dunghill, and the potsherd, and the lost sheep, and the consumed camels; he only thought of the goodness of God who had restored everything to him again, and given him back the dew of his youth, and the freshness of his spirit.

Child of God, are you vexed and embittered in soul? Then, bravely accept the trial as coming from your Father, and say, "The cup which my Father hath given me, shall I not drink it?" "Shall we receive good at the hand of God, and shall we not receive evil?" Press on through the cloud which now lowers directly in your pathway; it may be with you as it was with the disciples on the Mount of Transfiguration, "they feared as they entered the cloud," yet in that cloud they saw their Master's glory, and they found it good to be there. Fear not, have confidence in God; all your sorrows shall yet end in joy, and the thing which you deplore to-day shall be the subject of to-morrow's sweetest songs. The Egyptians whom ye have seen to-day ye shall see no more for ever. Wherefore, be of good courage, and let your hearts be strengthened.

I am going to take the text right away from its connection; having explained it as it relates to Job, and those like to Job, I want to use it for the benefit of anyone else who can fitly use the expression, "The Almighty hath vexed my soul." My sermon will be like an archer's arrow; God knows where the heart is at which I am aiming. I draw the bow at a venture, the Lord will direct the bolt between the joints of the harness of the one it is intended to strike.

I. First, I shall speak upon A PERSONAL FACT. Many a person has to say, "The Almighty hath embittered my soul."

This happened to you, dear friend, perhaps, *through a series of very remarkable troubles*. Few persons were happier than Job, and few have found misfortunes tread so fast upon one another's heels. What were the troubles in your case? It may be that one child was taken away, and then another, and yet a third; or, perhaps, your infant was carried to the grave, to be soon followed by its dear mother, and you are left to mourn alone. Bereavement has followed bereavement with you until your very soul is embittered. Or it may be that there is one ill at home, and you fear that precious life cannot be preserved; your cup seems full of trembling. Or, possibly, you have had a series of disasters in business such as you could not have foreseen or prevented. It seems, indeed, to you as if no man ever was so unsuccessful, you have not prospered in anything; wherever you have put your hand, it has been like the hoof of the Tartar's horse which turns the meadow into a desert; nothing goes well with you. Perhaps you have desired to be a man of learning; you have worked very hard, and now your health is failing you, so that you cannot go through the examination for which you have been preparing. You would willingly die at your post if you had a hope of gaining the honour to which you aspire, but this is denied you; on the very doorstep of success, you are stopped; God seems to have embittered your life. Or you, of the tender heart, have been disappointed and rejected, and your love has been thrown away. Or you, of the energetic spirit, have been foiled and driven back a score of times, till you perceive that your attempts are fruitless. Or you, a man of true integrity, have been cruelly slandered, and you feel as if you could not bear up under the false charge that is in the air all around you. Ah, I know what that means! There are many like you, with whom the Almighty is dealing in all wisdom and goodness, as I shall have to show you.

It may be, however, that you have not had a succession of troubles, but you have had *one trial constantly gnawing at your heart.* It is only one, and that one you are half-ashamed to mention, for it seems so trifling when you try to tell it to another; but to you it is as when a wasp stings, and continues to sting, it irritates and worries you. You try patience, but you have not much of that virtue. You seek to escape from the trouble, but it is always boring into your very heart; it is only some one little thing,—not the devil, only a messenger of Satan, one of his errand boys, one of the small fry of trouble. You cannot make out how you can be so foolish as to let it worry you, but it does. If you rise up early, or if you sit up late, it is still there tormenting you; you cannot get rid of it, and you cry, "The Almighty hath embittered my soul." Time was when you would have laughed at such things, and put them aside with a wave of your hand; but now they follow you into business, they are with you at the desk, they come home with you, they go to bed with you, and they worry you even in your dreams.

Perhaps I have not yet hit the mark with you, my friend. It

is neither a succession of troubles nor yet any one trouble; in fact, you have no trouble at all in the sense of which I have been speaking. Your business prospers, you are in fine health, your children are about you, everyone holds you in good esteem; yet your very soul is embittered. I hope that it has become saddened *through a sense of sin.* At one time you did not think that there was any fault to be found with you; but you have had a peep in the looking-glass of the Word, the Spirit of God holding the candle; you have had a glimpse of yourself, and your inner life, and your condition before God, and therefore your soul is vexed. Ah, many of us have gone through that experience; and, wretched as it is, we congratulate you upon it, we are glad that it is so with you!

Is it more than a sense of sin? Is it *a sense of wrath* as well? Does it strike you that God is angry with you, and has turned his hand against you, and does this seem to loosen the very joints of your bones? Ah, this is a dreadful state of heart indeed,—to feel God's hand day and night upon you, till your moisture is turned into the drought of summer! Yet again I congratulate you on it; for the pilgrim path to Heaven is by Weeping Cross, the road to joy and peace is by the way of a sense of sin and a sense of the Lord's anger.

It may be that this is not exactly your case, but you are *restless and weary.* Somehow, you cannot be easy, you cannot be at peace. Someone recommended you to go to the play; but it seemed such a dull piece of stupidity, you came away worse than you went. Your doctor says that you must have a change of air. "Oh!" you cry, "I have had fifty changes of air, and I do not improve a bit." You are weary even of that in which you once delighted. Your ordinary pursuits, which once satisfied you, now seem to be altogether stale, flat, and unprofitable. The books that charmed your leisure have grown wearisome; the friends whose conversation once entranced you now seem to talk but idle chit-chat and frivolity.

Beside all that, there is *an undefined dread upon you.* You cannot tell exactly what it is like, but you almost fear to fall asleep, lest you should dream, and dreaming should begin to feel the wrath to come. When you wake in the morning, you are sorry to find that you are where you are, and you address yourself sadly to the day's business, saying, "Well, I will go on with it, but I have no joy in it all. 'The Almighty hath embittered my soul.'" This happens to hundreds, and they do

not know what it means, they cannot understand it; but I
hope that I may be privileged so to explain it that some may
have to say that never did a better thing happen to them than
when they fell into this state,—that never in all their lives did
they take so blessed a turning as when they came down this
darksome lane, and began to murmur, "The Almighty hath
embittered my soul."

II. From this personal fact of which I have spoken, I want to
draw AN INSTRUCTIVE ARGUEMENT, which has two edges.

The first is this. If the Almighty—note that word,
"Almighty"—has vexed your soul as much as he has, *how
much more is he able to vex it!* If he has embittered your life
up to the present point, and he is indeed almighty, what more
of bitterness may he not yet give you! You may go from being
very low in spirit to being yet more heavy even unto despair.
You may even come to be like Bunyan's man in the iron cage,
or like the demoniac wandering among the tombs. Remember
what God has done in the case of some men, and if he can do
that on earth, what can he not do in hell! If this world, which
is the place of mercy, yet contains in it men so wretched that
they would rather die than live, what must be the misery of
those who linger in a state of eternal death, and yet from
whom death for ever flies? O my God, when my soul was
broken as between the two great millstones of thy justice and
thy wrath, how my spirit was alarmed! But if thou couldst do
this to me here, what couldst thou not have done to me
hereafter if I had passed out of this world into the next with
sin unforgiven? I want everyone who is in sore soul-trouble to
think over this solemn truth, and consider what God can yet
do with him.

Now turn the argument the other way. If it be the Almighty
who has troubled us, *surely he can also comfort us.* He that is
strong to sink is also strong to save. If he be almighty to
embitter, he must also be almighty to sweeten. Draw, then,
this comfortable conclusion,—"I am not in such a state of
misery that God cannot lift me right out of it into supreme
joy." It is congenial to God's nature to make his creatures
happy. He delights not in their sorrow; but if, when he does
make them sorrowful, he can make life unendurable,—if his
anger can fill a man with terror so that he fears his own
footfall, and starts at his own shadow,—if God can do that on
the one hand, what can he not do on the other? He can turn

our mourning into music; he can take off from us the ashes and the sackcloth, and clothe us in beauty and delight. God can lift up thy head, poor mourner, sorrowing under sin and a fear of wrath. I tell thee, God can at once forgive thy sin, and turn away all his wrath, and give thee a sense of perfect pardon, and with it a sense of his undying love. Oh, yes, that word "Almighty" cuts both ways! It makes us tremble, and so it kills our pride; but it also makes us hope, and so it slays our despair. I put in that little piece of argument just by the way.

III. Now I come to my third point, which is more directly in my road; and that is this. Here is A HEALTHFUL ENQUIRY for everyone whose soul has been vexed by God.

The enquiry is, first, *is not God just in vexing my soul?* Listen. Some of you have long vexed him; you have grieved his Holy Spirit for years. Why, my dear man, God called *you* when you were but a boy! Or very gently he drew you while you were yet a young man; you almost yielded to the importunity of a dying friend who is now in heaven. Those were all gentle strokes, but you heeded them not, you would not return unto the Lord; and now, if he should see fit to lay his hand very heavily upon you, and vex you in his hot displeasure, have you not first vexed him, have you not ill-used him? If you would not come to him in the light, it is very gracious of him if he permits you to come in the dark. I do not wonder if he whips you to himself, seeing that you would not come when, like a father beckoning a little child, he smiled at you, and wooed you to him.

I might say to others, if God brings you to himself by a rough road, you must not wonder, for have not you many a time vexed your godly wife? When seeing friends who come to join the church, I am often struck with the way in which converts have to confess that, in former days, they made it very hard for their families. There are some men who cannot speak without an oath, and at the very name of Christ they begin to curse and to swear. They seem as if they hated their children for being good, and could not be too hard upon their wives because they try to be righteous in the sight of God. Well, if you vex God's people, you must not be surprised if he vexes you. He will give you a hard time of it, it may be; and if it ends in your salvation, I shall not need to pity you however hard it may be for you. There is one thing more you may say to yourself, and that is, "It is much better to get to heaven by a rough road than to go singing down to hell. O my God, tear me in pieces, but do save me! Let my conscience drive me to the very borders of despair, if thou wilt but give me the blood of Christ to quiet it. Only make sure work of my eternal salvation, and I will not mind what I have to suffer." I shall bless God for you, dear friend, and you will bless God for yourself, too, if you be but brought to him, even though you have to say, "The Almighty hath vexed my soul."

Another point of enquiry is this: *What can be God's design in vexing your soul?* Surely he has a kind design in it all. God is never anything but good. Rest assured that he takes no delight in your miseries; it is no pleasure to him that you should sit, and sigh, and groan, and cry. I mean that such an experience in itself affords him no pleasure, but he has a design in it; what can that design be? May it not be, first, to make you think of him? You forgot him when the bread was plentiful upon the table, so he is going to try what a hungry belly will do for you when you would fain fill it with the husks that the swine do eat. You forgot him when everything went merry as a marriage peal; it may be that you will recollect him now that your children are dying, or your father is taken away; these trials are sent to remind you that there is a God. There are some men who go on, by the space of forty years together, and whether there be a God or not, is a question which they do not care to answer; at least, they live as if there were no God, they are practically atheists. This stroke has come that you may say, "Yes, there is a God, for I feel the rod that he holds in his hand. He is crushing me, he is grinding me to powder; I must think of him."

It may be, too, that he is sending this trial to let you know that he thinks of you. "Ah!" you say, "I did not suppose that he thought of me; I thought that surely he had forgotten such an one as I am." But he does think of you, he has been thinking of you for many a day, and calling and inviting you to him, but you would neither listen nor obey; and now that he has come, he means to make you see that he loves you too well to let you be lost. You are having his blows right and left, to let you know that he thinks of you, and will not let you perish. When God does not care for a man, he flings the reins on to his neck, and says, "There! Let him go." Now see how the horses tear away; you need not lash them, they will go as though they had wings, and could fly. Leave a man to himself, and his lusts drag him posthaste to hell, he pants to destroy himself; but when God loves a man, he pulls him up, as you might pull your horse on to his haunches. He shall not do as he wills, the eternal God will not let him; in infinite mercy, he tugs at the rein, and makes the man feel that there is a mightier than he who will not let him ruin himself, but who will restrain him from rushing to his destruction. Am I speaking to any who are in this plight? Let them not kick against God, but rather be grateful that he condescends thus to meddle with their sinful souls, and check them in their mad career. I have spoken lately with some who were about to join this church, who, if friends had said, five or six months ago, that they would have been sitting on that chair talking to me about their souls, would have cursed them to their faces; yet they were obliged to come. The Lord had hold of them; they tried to break away, but he had them too firmly. They were served by my Lord and Master as a good fisherman will serve a salmon if once it takes his bait; he lets it run for a while, and then pulls it up a bit, and then lets it go again; but he brings it to land at last; and I have had the pleasure of seeing many sinners thus safely caught by Christ. It may be, dear friend, that the Almighty is vexing you to let you see that he loves you.

May it not be also for another reason,—that he may wean you entirely from the world? He is making you loathe it. "Oh!" you used to say, "I am a young man, and I must see life." Well, you have seen it, have you not? And do you not think that it is wonderfully like death and corruption? That which is called "London life" is a foul, loathsome, crawling thing, fit only for the dunghill. Well, you have seen it, and you have had enough of it, have you not? Perhaps your very bones can tell what you gained by that kind of life. "Oh!" you said, "but I must try the intoxicating cup." Well, what did you think of it the morning after you tried it? "Who hath woe? who hath sorrow? who hath contention? who hath babbling? who hath wounds without cause? who hath redness of eyes? They that tarry long at the wine; they that go to seek mixed wine." I saw a man of that kind in the street, the other day. Once, he was a most respectable man, who could consort with others, and be esteemed by them. Now he is dreadfully down at the heel. I think I saw a toe through each of his shoes, and he looked like the wretched being that he is. He shuffled from place to place as if he did not wish to be seen, and he did not lift himself up

until he got into the gin palace to take another draught of
hell-water; and then he seemed for a minute to be drawn
straight again by that which made him crooked. You know
the man; is he here to-night? Dear sir, have you not had
sufficient strong drink? God has let you have enough of it that
you may hate it from this hour, and flee away from it, never
to desire to go back to it again.

I heard, at Boulogne, the story of a Frenchman who had
been drinking heavily, and who threw himself into the
harbour. Some sailors plunged in, and rescued him. The man
was on the deck of a ship, and in a minute he broke away
from his keepers, and jumped in again. It was not pleasant to
be trying to save a madman again and again, yet they did get
him out, and took him down below; but he rushed on deck,
and jumped in a third time. A man there said, "You leave him
to me." So he jumped overboard, and seized hold of him, put
his head under the water, and held him there; when he
managed to get his head up again, his rescuer gave him
another ducking, and then another, till he just about filled
him up with water. He said to himself, "I will sicken him of it,
so that he will never jump in here again." He just diluted the
eau-de-vie the man had taken, and then he dragged him on
board ship, and there was no fear of his jumping overboard
any more. And I believe that, sometimes, the Lord acts like
that with men. He did so with me; he made sin to be
exceedingly bitter to my soul, till I loathed it; and it has often
given me a trembling even to think of those sins that then
were pleasurable to me. It is a blessed thing to be plucked out
of the water, and saved once for all, but a little of that sailor's
style of sousing the drunkard, a little of those terrors and
alarms that some of us felt, is not lost; and when the Lord
thus deals with sinners, it is with the design that they may
never want to go back to those sins any more. They have had
their fill of them, and henceforth they will keep clear of them.
It may be that the Almighty vexed some of you for this cause,
that you might thenceforth hate sin with a perfect hatred.

Do you say, my friend, that I have not been describing you?
You are still a gentleman, an excellent well-to-do man; you
have done nothing wrong in the way of vice, but still you
cannot rest. No; and God grant that you never may rest till
you come humbly to the Saviour's feet, confess your sin, and
look to him alone for salvation! Then you shall rest with that

deep "peace which passeth all understanding," which shall "keep your heart and mind by Christ Jesus" forever and ever.

I think I hear someone say (and with that I will finish), "As the Almighty hath vexed my soul, *what had I better do?* I thought, sir, when I came in here that I was a castaway; but I see that I am the man you are looking after. I thought that I was too wretched to be saved, but now I perceive that it is to the wretched that you are preaching. It is for the mourning, the melancholy, and the desponding; what had I better do?" Do? Go home, and shut your door, and have an hour alone with yourself and God. You can afford that time; it is Sunday night, and you do not want the time for anything else. That hour alone with God may be the crisis of your whole life; do try it!

"And when I am alone with God, what had I better do?" Well, first, tell him all your grief. Then tell him all your sin,—all you can remember. Hide nothing from him; lay it all, naked and bare, before him. Then ask him to blot it all out, once for all, for Jesus Christ's sake. Tell him that you can never rest till you are at peace with him. Tell him that you accept his way of making peace, namely, by the blood of the cross. Tell him that you are willing to trust his dear Son for everything now, and to accept salvation freely as the gift of sovereign grace. If you do so, you will rise from your knees a happy man, and, what is more, a renewed man; I will stand bondsman for God about this matter. If there be this honest confession, this hearty prayer, and this simple acceptance of Christ as your Saviour, the days of your mourning are ended, the daylight of your spirit shall be beginning, and I should not wonder if many of your present troubles come to an end; certainly, your heart-ache shall be ended, and ended at once. Oh, that you would accept my Saviour! Sometimes, when I am thinking about my hearers and my work, I seem to take God's part instead of yours, and to say, "O God, I have preached Christ to them; I have told them about thy dear Son, and how thy fatherly heart parted with him that he might die that men might live; yet they do not care for him. They will not have thy Son: they will not accept the pardon that Jesus bought." If the Lord were to say to me, "Then never go and say another word to them, they have so insulted me in refusing such a gift," I have at times felt as if I would say, "Lord, that is quite right; I do not want to have anything more to do with them as they treat thee so shamefully." But we have not reached that point yet, so once more I put it to you, have you not long enough delayed? Have you not long enough questioned? Have you not long enough turned away from the Saviour? And now that the arrows of God are sticking in you, will you not ask him to draw them out? Will you not plead that the precious blood of Christ may be balm to heal your wounds? Oh, come to him! In the name of Jesus of Nazareth, I beseech you, come! By amazing love and amazing pity, by wondrous grace that abounds over sin, come and welcome! Jesus said, "Him that cometh to me, I will in no wise cast out." Then, come unto him, and come now. Blessed Spirit, draw them; draw them now, for Jesus Christ's sake! Amen.

17

The Way of Wisdom

"There is a path which no fowl knoweth, and which the vulture's eye hath not seen: The lion's whelps have not trodden it, nor the fierce lion passed by it."   **Job 28:7-8**

In this chapter, Job is speaking of the hidden treasures that are to be found deep down in the bowels of the earth. The keen eyes of the vultures, though they see their prey afar off, have never seen the gold, and silver, and other precious metals which lie in the dark places of the earth; and the lions, especially the young lions hungering for their prey, though they will lie in wait in their lairs in the dens and caves of the earth, have never been able to descend into places so deep as those that are opened up by men who seek after gold and silver.

Yet, further on in the chapter, we notice that Job refers to the search after wisdom, and that he seems to say that, though men should explore the deep places of the earth with all the diligence of miners seeking gold and silver,—though they should exert all their mental force, as miners use all their muscular vigor,—and though they should employ all the machinery within their reach, as men do who pierce through the rocks in search of precious treasure,—yet it is not within the range of human labour and skill to attain unto wisdom. That can only be found by another and a higher method; it must come to us by revelation from God, for we cannot find it by our own efforts. I believe, therefore, that I am justified in using the expressions, which are found in my text in a spiritual sense; for I think that Job meant to teach us, not only what is true of the treasures hidden in the earth, but also something concerning the path of wisdom, which is altogether beyond the ken of the most piercing eye of reason or imagination.

I shall use the language of our text, first, *in reference to the way of God*, which is, in the highest sense, *the way of wisdom*; and then, secondly, *in reference to the path of the truly wise*, which is also, secondarily, the path of wisdom so far as mortal man can be wise, so far as he, who is born of a woman, can walk in the way of wisdom.

I. First, then, IN REFERENCE TO THE WAY OF GOD. His way, in dealing with men, is past our power to find out.

Think, first of all, of the way of God *in relation to predestination and free agency*. Many have failed to understand how everything, from the smallest event to the greatest, can be ordained and fixed, and yet how it can be equally true that man is a responsible being, and that he acts freely, choosing the evil, and rejecting the good. Many have tried to reconcile these two things, and various schemes of theology have been formulated with the object of bringing them into harmony. I do not believe that they are two parallel lines, which can never meet; but I believe that, for all practical purposes, they are so nearly parallel that we might regard them as being so. They *do* meet, but only in the infinite mind of God is there a converging point where they melt into one. As a matter of practical, everyday experience with each one of us, they continually melt into one; but, so far as all finite understanding goes, I do not believe that any created intellect can find the meeting-place. Only the Uncreated as yet knoweth this. It would be a very simple thing to understand the predestination of God if men were clay in the hands of the potter, and nothing more. That figure is rightly used in the Scriptures because it reveals one side of truth; if it contained the whole truth, the difficulty that puzzles so many would entirely cease. But man is not only clay, he is a great deal more than that, for God has made him an intelligent being, and given him understanding and judgment, and, above all, will. Fallen and depraved, but still not destroyed, are our judgment, our understanding, and our power to will; they are all under bondage, but they are still within us. If we were simply blocks of wood, like the beams and timbers in this building, it would be easy to understand how God could prearrange where we should be put, and what purpose we should serve; but it is not easy—nay, it is difficult, I venture to say that it is impossible for us to understand how predestination should come true, in every jot and little, fix everything, and yet that there should never be, in the whole history of mankind, a single violation of the will, or a single use of constraint, other than fit and proper constraint, upon man, so that he acts, according to his own will, just as if there were no predestination whatever, and yet, at the same time, the will of God is, in all respects, being carried out.

In order to get rid of this difficulty, there are some who deny either the one truth or the other. Some seem to believe in a kind of free agency which virtually dethrones God, while others run to the opposite extreme by believing in a sort of fatalism which practically exonerates man from all blame. Both of these views are utterly false, and I scarcely know which of the two is the more to be deprecated. We are bound to believe both sides of the truth revealed in the Scriptures, so I admit that, when a Calvinist says that all things happen according to the predestination of God, he speaks the truth, and I am willing to be called a Calvinist; but when an Arminian says that, when a man sins, the sin is his own, and that, if he continues in sin, and perishes, his eternal damnation will lie entirely at his own door, I believe that he also speaks the truth, though I am not willing to be called an Arminian. The fact is, there is some truth in both these systems of theology; the mischief is that, in order to make a human system appear to be complete, men ignore a certain truth, which they do not know how to put into the scheme which they have formed; and, very often, that very truth, which they ignore, proves to be, like the stone which the builders rejected, one of the headstones of the corner, and their building suffers serious damage through its omission.

Now, brethren, if I could fully understand these two truths, and could clearly expound them to you,—if I could prove to you that they are perfectly consistent with one another, I should be glad to do so, and to escape the censures which some people constantly pour upon those who are trying to preach the whole of revealed truth; but it is more than my soul is worth for me to attempt to alter and trim God's truth so as to make it pleasing to men. I preach it as I find it in God's Word; I am not responsible for what is in the Book, I am only responsible for telling out what I find there, as it is taught to me by the Holy Spirit. But mark this; to the mind of God, there is no difficulty concerning these two truths, though there is, to us, so much mystery and perplexity. It is all simple enough to him; he is omnipotent in the world of mind as well as in the world of matter; and he is omniscient, he knows everything, he foresees everything, so that there are no difficulties to him. I suppose that, if it will add to our happiness in heaven for us to understand this way of God, which as yet the vulture's eye hath never seen, he will reveal it to us; yet it may be that, even there, it will be of no practical use for us to understand it, but it will be better for us, even throughout eternity, still to continue as little children at our Heavenly Father's feet, believing a great deal which, even there, we cannot comprehend. Even in this life, I am as pleased not to know what God doth not tell me as I am to know what he reveals to me;—at least, if I am not, I ought to be, for that is the condition of a true disciple of Christ, to be inquisitive up to the point in which his Lord is com-municative, but to stay just there, and say, "If, my Master, thou hast anything to say to me, yet, in thy wisdom, thou knowest that I cannot bear it now, my ear is closed while thy tongue is still, and my heart asks for no more when thou tellest me that thou hast revealed enough." Believe me, brethren, there is a path, which God takes, which you cannot understand yet. You may look, and look, and look, as with an eagle's eye, but you may blind that eye by glaring at the sun; you may force your way, as with a lion's heart, into the deep mysteries of God, but you must beware lest you perish in the pit of controversy, or be taken, as in a net, in difficulties which you cannot break through. Doubting and enquiring man, be thou satisfied that God is infinitely above thee, and that thou canst no more comprehend him than thy hand can hold the ocean, or thy fingers grip the sun. If there were no mysteries in our holy faith, we might well believe that it was devised by men like ourselves; for, if men could fully understand it, men might have invented it; but as it is far beyond the comprehension of the mightiest human intellect, we recognize that it is the work of the infinite God. Infinite must his gospel and his truth be, because he is himself infinite; and dark and mysterious must his pathway sometimes be, though he himself dwells in light that is insufferable to mortal eyes. Finely does John Milton put this thought in his apostrophe to God,—

"Dark with excessive bright thy skirts appear."

Passing on to another illustration of the same great truth, I remind you that God is equally beyond our ken *in the accomplishment of the designs of his providence.* There are ways of God, in dealing with the human race, which are very perplexing to the judgment of such poor mortals as we are. We try to study a piece of history; and—especially if it is a short piece of history,—it appears to us all tangled and confused. A further research, over a longer period, will often explain what could not be understood in the shorter range of vision; but even history as a whole, from the Creation and the Fall until now, contains many strange puzzles to a man who believes that God is, through it all, working out his own glory, and that a part of his glory will consist in producing the highest amount of good to the greatest number of his creatures.

What a mass of mysteries meets us on the very threshold of human history. The serpent in the garden,—how and why came it to be there? And the devil in the serpent,—why was there a devil at all? And the evil that made the angel into a devil,—why was that permitted? And all the evil that has been since then,—why has it not been destroyed? We cannot answer any of these queries. The negro's question to the missionary, "If God is stronger than Satan, why does not he kill him?" is another enquiry which we cannot answer. Depend upon it, if it were, on the whole, best that the devil should be killed, he would be killed; and if it had been, after all, most for God's glory that there should be no evil, there would have been none. We do not know how and why certain things have happened, and we must be content not to know unless God reveals it to us.

All through history, God seems to be aiming at a certain mark, yet his arrow does not hit the target so far as you and I can judge. Often, he appears to do as the rifleman does, who knows that, if he sent the ball in a direct line to the target, he would miss it, so he makes allowance for certain deflections which will be caused by the force of attraction, by the wind, and various other opposing influences, and aims accordingly. God often proves that the nearest way to attain his end is to go round about; so, when he means to cleanse a man, he sometimes allows him first to get more foul; when he intends to clothe him, he first strips him naked; when he resolves to enrich him, he first makes him as poor as Lazarus at the rich man's gate, and, strange to say, when he means to make him alive, he kills him. God's modes of procedure, then, allow for deflection, and every other kind of influence, and are not to be understood by us. If you take the whole range of history, and look at it carefully, you will be obliged to feel that, if God has been working there, as we are quite sure he has, ordering all things with consummate wisdom, then his pathway through the world is one which no vulture's eye hath ever seen, and which no lion or lion's whelp hath ever travelled.

It may be that some of you are, at the present moment, complaining of a certain providential dealing of God with regard to you, and that you are thinking and saying that it must be an evil providence. Yet it is, all the while, one of the best things that has ever happened to you. That, over which you are now mourning, will give you good cause for singing in a little while. Probably, that tribulation, which fetches most tears from our eyes here, will be among the subjects of our choicest song in the eternal realms of joy. We need not know, and we cannot know, what God is doing, but we may be quite sure that he doeth all things well.

Very much is this the truth also in another respect, namely, *in the methods of his grace.* God will certainly save his chosen people; he will bring home all his lost children; but how strangely doth he deal with some of them! His pathway in grace no vulture's eye hath ever seen, and no lion or lion's whelp hath ever trodden. I have known him allow a child of his to go into sin after sin before he has saved him. A godly mother has anxiously prayed that her boy might be converted, but he has not been. He has grown up to manhood, and there has been much tender solicitude for him, and many prayers on his behalf; yet he has passed twenty, thirty, or forty years in sin, and has grown worse and worse. It did not seem as if all this could be according to God's grace, yet it was; for, in the mysterious providence of God, this man was brought low by sin, humbled by the iniquity which carried him into the far country, and led him to waste his substance in riotous living, and then, and not till then, did he come to God. His mother had gone to heaven, doubting whether her prayers for him would ever be heard; others who were anxious about him slept amidst the clods of the valley, not knowing, except by faith, that their supplications for him would be heard; and that man, because he had gone so far in sin, became the greater monument of the power of sovereign grace, was the better able to tell to others what God had done, was the more firmly bound to Christ, was the more ardent in Christ's service through the gratitude he felt, and became, for God's purposes, a better instrument than he would have been if he had been brought in before. John Bunyan, if he had not been among the chief of sinners, might never have been among the chief of saints. Had he never been what he was,— one of the worst men in the village,—he might never have preached as he did about "Jerusalem Sinners Saved," and might never have so boldly declared that the biggest sinners should receive the greatest mercy, and that God should be most glorified in their salvation.

I know that some people have turned this great truth to an evil purpose; for he, who looks at God's way, and sees the greatness of his grace, may, if he be wicked enough, draw the inference that he may continue in sin that grace may abound. Paul tells us plainly what the doom of such men will be: "whose damnation is just." A child of God draws no such evil inference as that from God's mercy; but he says, "After such love as that, how can I sin against the Lord?" So, in saving men, God traverses a path which no fowl knoweth, which the vulture's eye hath not seen, and the lion or the lion's whelp hath not trodden. God knoweth best how to time his gift of grace or his postponement of grace; he knoweth why he chooseth this man at this time and that man at that time; so let him do as seemeth good in his sight, for he always doeth right, and unto his name be praise for ever and ever.

Now, beloved, I am persuaded that this truth may also be applied to *the great things of God which are yet to come, in the latter days, and in the eternity of glory.* I do not often preach upon the Book of Revelation, nor upon the marvels that are to occur during the millennial period, or at the time of the ingathering of the Jews, and so on. I will tell you the reason why I do not, and I think it is a sufficient one, namely, that I do not understand these things. If I do not have clear views about these things, I will leave them alone until I have. I have often studied them, and I have never found anything so easy as the refuting of every view I have heard or read about the future, nor anything so difficult as to invent a view which somebody else could not refute. There are some great truths, about the future, that are clearly revealed,—such as the second coming of Christ, the flooding of the world with the gospel so that all flesh shall see the salvation of God, the ingathering of the Jews to Christ, if not to their own land, and so on; but as to the order of the various events, and the putting together of the various pieces of the puzzle I believe that my text is true that "there is a path which no fowl knoweth, and which the vulture's eye hath not seen; the lion's whelps have not trodden it, nor the fierce lion passed by it."

It is not easy to tell what Paul means in that wonderful passage, "Then cometh the end, when he shall have delivered up the kingdom to God even the Father...that God may be all in all." What new worlds may yet be created, what revolts there may be among fresh orders of creatures, how many orders of creatures there may yet be in the universe, and how great and comprehensive the vast dominions of Jehovah may be, we do not at present know; but we shall know all that we need to know in due time. It is enough for us now to know that our Bible is true, that Jesus Christ is our Saviour, and that we shall be with him where he is, and behold his glory, for ever and ever.

Why is there all this mystery? Is it not because God is so great? We can never gauge his greatness by our measuring line or plummet. We get utterly lost whenever we begin to estimate God's unsearchable greatness. Some of you have, perhaps, studied a little astronomy. You have begun to hear or read about the millions and millions of miles which some of the fixed stars are away from us, and yet, far beyond those, there may be others from which we are so distant that we are, comparatively speaking, quite near to those that now seem so far away. In trying to realize these wonders in the heavens, one feels as though the brain needed fresh faculties to enable it to grasp even that which the telescope reveals, yet all the starry worlds, which human eyes have gazed upon through the most powerful glass yet made, may only be like some tiny cove or bay upon the sea-shore of a universe which to us must be utterly boundless. Yet that universe, which we conceive to be boundless, is all known to the God who created and sustains it. We are utterly lost in the contemplation of the greatness of God's works; then how can we imagine that we can ever understand God who is infinitely greater than the greatest of the works of his hands?

Then, next, are not all these things mysteries to us because we are so little? I do not merely mean those of us who are feeble, and poor, and ignorant; but I mean the great divines, the doctors of the Sorbonne, the members of our Royal Societies, our D.D.'s, LL.D.'s, and all our most learned men,— all are fools compared with the wisdom of the Omniscient, all are feeble compared with the Almighty. I do not know how much a gnat understands, but I feel sure that a gnat understands a far larger proportion of what I know, than I can comprehend of what God knows. A fly on the dome of St. Paul's has a very imperfect idea of the greatness and glories of the cathedral, a still more incomplete idea of London, and a far more inadequate idea of England. Even if the fly knew England thoroughly, he would need to learn much more to enable him to understand the world,—and then there would be the sun,—and the sun himself is only like a tiny point of light compared with the greater worlds in God's universe. If the fly could comprehend all those worlds, he would still be no appreciable way towards understanding God. If you knew all that was to be known about a number of marbles that I had given to my sons to play with, that would not prove that you knew all about me; so, if we could understand everything about all the worlds that God has made, it would not prove that we could understand God himself. He is infinitely above our loftiest conception, and we are just nothing at all in comparison with him. You talk very loudly about your opinion, and your thoughts, and your conclusions,—ah! poor souls, the chattering of sparrows in the street is as much worthy to be called wisdom as the predilections of the most learned men among you apart from anything that they have been taught by God the Holy Spirit. All the wisdom that they have, which they have learned by themselves, is but varnished folly, and nothing more. Moreover, dear friends, the powers we possess are absolutely insignificant compared with God's. In trying to comprehend the Almighty, we are like a child, with a thimble, seeking to tell the size of the sea. We cannot, at our utmost, hold more than a thimbleful; and beside that, our thimble leaks. The powers that we have are warped and spoiled by sin and sinful influence. When we come into this world, our powers are very far from being fully developed; and as they are being developed, somebody or other comes along, and warps us with prejudice in our early youth; and as we grow older, we make other prejudices of our own, so that what we might know we sometimes do not care to know. Our scales also in which we try to weigh God, are not accurate. Instead of being true, they are all out of gear, and utterly unreliable as well as inadequate to such a task. Our faculties are so disordered and disarranged by all manner of surrounding circumstances that we cannot comprehend much about him who is incomprehensible even to the loftiest created intelligence. And, besides this, we have such a little time in which to learn about God. A child, going to school for five minutes, knows as much about Greek as we do about God in seventy years, apart from what he pleases to teach us by his Spirit.

Even with regard to God's dealings with his people, what mistakes they make in their judgments! No doubt, Protestantism in England was, upon the whole, greatly strengthened and more deeply rooted by the persecutions under cruel Queen Mary. Foxe's "Book of Martyrs" (which could not have been written had not the martyrs suffered and died,) is still, next to the Bible, the great master-gun of Protestantism. Yet many of the Protestants, who lived in Mary's day, must have felt that God had made an awful mistake in allowing that woman to sit upon the throne, and to do so much towards putting down the gospel of Christ by fire, and sword, and imprisonment. Yet they made a great mistake in judging by the few years of Mary's reign. God was judging more justly by the whole history of the land for hundreds of years to come. There is not much more wisdom in man's judgment of God than in the flies' fabled judgment of an elephant. It is said that a senate of flies once determined to form a judgment concerning an elephant, so one of them settled on the great creature's ear, and walked all round it, and then said that an elephant was a long flabby mass of flesh of a certain shape. Another fly had settled on one of the huge legs of the animal, and he said that an elephant was a tall column, something like the trunk of a cedar. One lit somewhere on the back, and he said that an elephant was a great moving plain, a sort of animal table-land. The flies could not agree upon any theory of what the creature was like; the fact was, that none of them had any clear idea of the whole elephant, but only a partial notion concerning the portion that they could manage to see. So, all that we can do, if we have fifty years in which to study the Scriptures, is to get some imperfect idea of a part of the great truth of God.

Yet some talk as if they knew all about it, like a man who says that he knows all about the Continent because he once landed at Boulogne for a few minutes, and then crossed the Channel again. Suppose that we have landed on the shores of knowledge, and that we have been there for fifty years, what is that compared with eternity? What shall I further say before I leave this point? First, let none of us despond because we do not know everything. Let no one say, "I am not God's child because my knowledge is so limited." A grain of grace is worth more than a ton of knowledge. If thou hast but a spark of true faith in Jesus Christ, it is better than a whole volcano full of worldly wisdom. Do not say, "I cannot be saved because I cannot understand all mysteries." Who but God can understand them? Be thankful that the way of salvation is not a mystery; it is this: "As Moses lifted up the serpent in the wilderness, even so must the Son of man be lifted up: that whosoever believeth in him should not perish, but have everlasting life." Are you puzzled about the doctrine of election? Do not ever fall into the mistake of imagining that nobody goes to heaven but those who understand that great truth. There are many there who disbelieved it while they were here below, though I think they rejoice in it now. It is not essential to salvation that you should understand that or any other difficult doctrine of the Scriptures. Dost thou believe in Jesus as thy Saviour? Then, go thy way, and rest assured that thou wilt in due time find thyself in heaven.

Again, let us never arraign God before our bar. It is a horrible thing for any man ever to say, "Well, if God acts like that, I do not see the justice of it." How dare you even hint that the Judge of all the earth is not just? He hath said, "I will have mercy on whom I will have mercy, and I will have compassion on whom I will have compassion;" so, do not you say, "It cannot be so." Is it so written in God's Word? Then it is so just because it is there. If God has said anything, it is not right for you to ask for an explanation of his reason for saying it, or to summon him to your judgment-seat. What impertinence is this! He must always do right; he cannot do wrong.

Some have staggered over the doctrine of eternal punishment, because they could not see how that could be consistent with God's goodness. I have only one question to ask concerning that or any other doctrine,—Does God reveal it in the Scriptures? Then, I believe it, and leave to him the vindication of his own consistency. I am sure that he will not inflict a pain upon any creature which that creature does not deserve, that he will never cause any sorrow or misery which is not absolutely necessary, and that he will glorify himself by doing the right, the loving, the kind thing, in the end. If we do not see it to be so, it will be none the less so because we are blind. The finger on the lip is the right attitude for us in the presence of things revealed by God, or wrought by God, as David said, "I was dumb, I opened not my mouth because thou didst it." If thou didst it, O Lord, there is no question about the rightness of it, for thou art supreme, and thou oughtest to be supreme! There is none like thee for goodness, for love, for wisdom. Thy will ought to be—so let it be—done on earth, as it is heaven, let it be done everywhere, for what thou doest is ever best.

II. I have not much time left for the second part of my discourse, which is IN REFERENCE TO THE TRULY WISE, that is, to those who are wise according to Job's declaration in the 28th verse of this chapter: "Behold, the fear of the Lord, that is wisdom; and to depart from evil is understanding." Concerning their path, we may truly say, that no fowl knoweth it, no vulture's eye hath seen it, no lion or lion's whelp hath trodden it.

First, *the entrance of the Christian into that path is beyond human knowledge.* Who can explain what it is to be born again? The very figure used by our Saviour implies a mystery. Our introduction into this world is shrouded in mystery, so is our introduction into the spiritual world,—the world of grace. Thou wilt never be able to explain, even though thou hast experienced it, how the Spirit of God creates a living soul, as it were, within the ribs of death, how he breathes into our soul the breath of spiritual life, so that we, who were enemies to God, become the new-born children in his family. This secret cannot be told by mortal man, for he does not know it; it is known to God alone.

And, next, *the walk of the Christian along that path is equally beyond human understanding.* How shall I tell you what it is to walk by faith? I have sometimes had, before my mind's eye, as it were, a vision. I thought I saw a great staircase, made of light. There appeared to be nothing solid or earthly about it. I was called to ascend this staircase. Beneath my feet there seemed to be nothing. Each step I stood upon appeared to be the last, yet I went on, on, on, up, up, up, till I was at a dizzy height, and I thought that a voice said to me, "Look up." I could see no other step; but, as fast as I ascended one tier, I was told still to go on, and fresh steps of light revealed themselves beneath my ascending feet. I trod upon the clouds, and found them to be granite. It seemed to be thin air and mist; to mortal men, it was nothing. They laughed at me for trusting to it; but, each time my foot went down upon the stair, I found it to be like the eternal hills that are never to be moved. When, in my vision, I had climbed, and climbed, and climbed, till I seemed to look down upon the stars, I still climbed on, and I understood that this is walking by faith,— going ever upward, seeing him who is invisible, depending upon him whom no mortal eye can see, but who is clearly recognized by our spiritual senses,—grasped by the hand of faith, seen by the eye of faith, heard by the ear of faith;— walking through a desert where there is no corn growing, yet daily gathering full supplies of heavenly manna;—standing by a rock in which there is no water, yet seeing the living floods leap forth to refresh the weary soul. This is walking by faith, and it is a great mystery.

I have known some, with eyes like a vulture's, who have said that they could live by reason. They always did that which they perceived to be best. They would never venture a step beyond where logic would lead them. Ah, sirs, your bleared eyes, which you think to be so keen, can never see the path of the Christian! Others have fancied that, to work themselves up into a high state of excitement and enthusiasm, is to lead a Christian life. Believe me, sirs, your vulture eye hath not seen this God-made path. Faith is reasonable, in the highest sense, for it reasons upon real truth, whereas mere human reason only reasons upon the semblance of truth. Some, who have no more spiritual knowledge than a lion's whelps, have said, "All you have to do is to persuade yourself that you are one of God's elect, and it is so." Ah, they know not the path of faith; and they who follow their lead will go down to destruction.

Another says, "I feel much that is good within myself, and I believe that I have strength enough, and wisdom enough, to find my way to heaven." Ah, thou mayest be strong as a fierce

lion, but thou knowest not the way of wisdom. That is the
very opposite way to thine. We, who walk by faith, have
nothing in ourselves to lean upon. Our very weakness is our
strength because it drives us to the Almighty. We have
nothing to rely upon except this,—that it is written that
"Christ Jesus came into the world to save sinners," and we
depend on him, and upon the oath and covenant of God, the
covenant that has been sealed with the precious blood of
Jesus, and there we rest. There are many imitations of this
faith, but the genuine article is as different from all the
imitations of it as the true coin of the realm is from the
counterfeit of the forger.

Once more, *the believer's trials are things which unrenewed
men cannot comprehend.* If some of us were to begin to tell the
ungodly all about our spiritual conflicts, they would think us
fools. If we were to describe to them our despair and our hope,
our rejoicings and our depressions, they would say, "You must
be mad to have such experiences." Just so; "there is a path
which no fowl knoweth," and no fool knoweth, and no unsaved
soul knoweth. Our desires, too, are beyond men's sight, and so
are our struggles with doubt, and our temptations, and trials.
Many a believer has been another Hercules, slaying a dragon,
and cleansing the Augean stables, yet it is all unrecognized
except by God, and by those who are themselves spiritual, for
the path of Christian victory is one that the lion's whelp
treads not.

So is it also with *the Christian's joys.* O brethren, I wish I
had time to talk about them! I could not get to the end of that
theme, for there are joys that we have, in which our spirit is
as cool and composed as at any other moment of our life, yet
those joys fill us with holy rapture, and sacred ecstasy, till we
feel that, whether in the body or out of the body, we cannot
tell, God knoweth. Then the head leans on the bosom of the
Saviour, and the lip of Christ is set to our soul's lip, and he
kisses us with the kisses of his mouth, and his love is better
than wine. I know that worldly men say, "Give us gold and
silver in abundance; fill our barns, and let our wine-vats burst
with new wine; give us all the good things of earth, and we
will be content." It is so, I know; but as for the Christian, he
says, "Whom have I in heaven but thee? and there is none
upon earth that I desire beside thee." When we have the love
of God shed abroad in our hearts by the Holy Ghost who is

given unto us, we get into a way of joy which is as far above all human joy as the path of the eagle, soaring among the Alps, is above that of the mole burrowing in the ground. There are many other equally high things about the way of a Christian which I have not time to mention. I will just refer to two other things. One is, *the path of communion with Christ.* We, who believe in Jesus, know what it is to walk with God. Ay, to walk with God, though he is a consuming fire;—to walk with Christ though he is the Judge of quick and dead. I have been as conscious of the presence of God as ever I have been of the presence of my child or of my friend. I have been as sure that I spoke with Christ, and emptied out my soul into his soul, and then received his heart's love into my heart, as I have been sure of any event in my whole history. I know what it is to receive sympathy from Christian men, but I also know what it is to have the sympathy of my Lord. I speak not now of things that are only occasional, and out of the ordinary course of our lives. To some of us, it has become a blessed habit to speak with Christ,—to speak, not merely into his ear, but right down into his heart, and to know that we have done so, and to act in a certain way because we have done so, and to have no other motive for the action than the fact that we have put the case before the Lord, and asked whether it was our duty to do this, and when we knew that it was, have risked everything because we were sure that God had bidden us take the step. Oh, the blessedness of living with God! You cannot imitate it; you cannot get near it; it is unapproachable to unrenewed men; it "is a path which no fowl knoweth, and which the vulture's eye hath not seen."

And it is so, lastly, *with regard to many a Christian's death.* In this matter also, "there is a path which the vulture's eye hath not seen." There are some of you, who have heard with your ears, and seen with your eyes, the wondrous man-ifestations at the deaths of some who were dear to you in life, and precious in death. Some of these have seen, in their departing moments, what no unaided human eye could ever have seen, and they have told us that they have heard words which it would not have been lawful for them to utter, and that they have enjoyed what it was impossible for human language ever to express; and while they have spoken, we have known that they spoke the truth, for the flash of their eye was supernatural, and the calm of their spirit, amidst racking pains, which naturally would depress, has been something sublime. We have felt, with regard to their death-bed, as Moses did with regard to the burning bush,—humble was the pallet, and humble was the patient who lay upon it; but, as the bush glowed with heavenly fire, that bed seemed to be bright with the presence of Deity, for God was there with his children, and Christ was there succouring the members of his mystical body; and we have marvelled, and been astonished, and have felt that we could put off our shoes from our feet, for the place whereon we stood was holy ground. Those of us, whose calling makes us familiar with the departure of believers, have often felt that there was a path for dying saints which biographers could not describe, which language could not picture, and of which memory has left but faint traces upon the tablets of our soul; but which, in itself, was something indescribable, unutterable, divine. May God grant to all of us the grace to know all this for ourselves! We can only know it by the illumination of the Divine Spirit; but that blessed Spirit illuminates all the souls that look to Jesus; indeed, their looking to Jesus is one effect of the divine illumination which they have already in part received. Oh, that each heart here may "lay hold on eternal life" by laying hold on the Saviour by faith, for then he will reveal to you the great mystery that the unsaved cannot comprehend, and he will say to you, as he said to Peter, "Blessed art thou, Simon Bar-jona, for flesh and blood hath not revealed it unto thee, but my Father which is in heaven." The Lord bless you, beloved friends, for Christ's sake! Amen.

18

Comfort for the Desponding

"Oh that I were as in months past..."   **Job 29:2**

For the most part the gracious Shepherd leads his people beside the still waters, and makes them to lie down in green pastures; but at times they wander through a wilderness, where there is no water, and they find no city to dwell in. Hungry and thirsty, their soul fainteth within them, and they cry unto the Lord in their trouble. Though many of his people live in almost constant joy, and find that religion's ways are ways of pleasantness, and all her paths are peace, yet there are many who pass through fire and through water: men do ride over their heads,—they endure all manner of trouble and sorrow. The duty of the minister is to preach to different characters. Sometimes we admonish the confident, lest they should become presumptuous; oftentimes we stir up the slumbering, lest they should sleep the sleep of death. Frequently we comfort the desponding, and this is our duty this morning-or if not to comfort them, yet to give them some exhortation which may by God's help be the means of bringing them out of the sad condition into which they have fallen, so that they may not be obliged to cry out for ever— "Oh that I were as in months past!"

At once to the subject. A *complaint;* its *cause and cure;* and then close up with an *exhortation* to stir up your pure minds, if you are in such a position.

I. First, there is a COMPLAINT. How many a Christian looks on the past with pleasure, on the future with dread, and on the present with sorrow! There are many who look back upon the days that they have passed in the fear of the Lord as being the sweetest and the best they have ever had, but as to the present, it is clad in a sable garb of gloom and dreariness. They could wish for their young days over again, that they might live near to Jesus, for now they feel that they have wandered from him, or that he has hidden his face from them, and they cry out, "Oh that I were as in months past!"

1. Let us take distinct cases one by one. The first is the case of a man who has *lost the brightness of his evidences,* and is crying out, "Oh that I were as in months past!" Hear his soliloquy:—"Oh that my past days could be recalled! Then I had no doubt of my salvation. If any man had asked for the reason of the hope that was in me, I could have answered with meekness and with fear. No doubt distressed me, no fear harassed me; I could say with Paul, 'I know whom I have believed,' and with Job, 'I know that my Redeemer liveth;'

> 'My steady soul did fear no more
> Than solid rocks when billows roar.'

I felt myself to be standing on the rock Christ Jesus. I said—

> 'Let cares like a wild deluge come,
> And storms of sorrow fall;
> Sure I shall safely reach my home,
> My God, my heaven, my all'

But ah! how changed it is now! Where there was no cloud it is *all* cloud; where I could read my 'title clear,' I tremble to read my damnation quite as clearly. I hoped that I trusted in Christ, but now the dark thought rises up, that I was a hypocrite, and had deceived myself and others. The most I can attain to, is—'Methinks I will hope in him still; and if I may not be refreshed with the *light* of his countenance, still in the *shadow* of his wings will I trust.' I feel that if I depart from him there is no other Saviour; but oh! what thick darkness surrounds me! Like Paul of old, there have been days and nights wherein neither sun, nor moon, nor stars have appeared. I have lost my roll in the Arbour of Ease; I cannot now take it out of my breast, and read it to console me on my journey; but I fear that when I get to the end of the way they will deny me entrance, because I came not in by the door to receive his grace and know his love, but have been deceived, have taken carnal fancies for the workings of the Spirit, and have imputed what was but natural conviction to the work of God the Holy Ghost."

This is one phase, and a very common one. You will meet many who are crying out like that—"Oh that I were as in months past!"

2. Another phase of this great complaint, which it also very frequently assumes, is one under which we are lamenting— not so much because our evidences are withered as because we *do not enjoy a perpetual peace of mind as to other matters.* "Oh" says one, "Oh that I were as in months past; for then whatever troubles and trials came upon me, were less than nothing. I had learned to sing,—

> 'Father, I wait thy daily will;
> Thou shalt divide my portion still;
> Give me on earth what seems thee best,
> Till death and heaven reveal the rest.'

I felt that I could give up everything to him; that if he had taken away every mercy I could have said,—

> 'Yea, if thou take them all away,
> Yet will I not repine;
> Before they were possessed by me,
> They were entirely thine.'

I knew no fear for the future. Like a child on its mother's breast I slept securely; I said, 'Jehovah-jireh, my God will provide;' I put my business into his hands; I went to my daily labour; like the little bird that waketh up in the morning, and knoweth not where its breakfast is to come from, but sitteth on the spray, singing,—

> 'Mortal, cease from toil and sorrow
> God provideth for the morrow;'

as was I. I could have trusted Him with my very life, with wife, with children, with everything; I could give all into his hands, and say each morning, 'Lord, I have not a will of my own, or if I have one, still, thy will be done; thy wish shall be my wish; thy desire shall be my desire.' But 'oh that I were as in months past!' How changed am I now! I begin fretting about my business; and if I lose now but a five pound note, I am worried incessantly, whereas, if it were a thousand before, I could have thanked the God who took it away as easily as I could the God that gave it to me. Now the least thing disturbs me. The least shadow of a doubt as to some calamity that may befall me, rests on my soul like a thick cloud. I am perpetually self-willed, desiring always to have just what I wish. I cannot say I can resign all into his hands; there is a certain something I could not give up. Twined round my heart there

is an evil plant called self-love. It has twisted its roots within
the very nerves and sinews of my soul. There is something I
love above my God. I cannot give up all now: but 'oh that I
were as in months past!' For then my mercies were real
mercies, because they were God's mercies. "Oh," says he,
"'that I were as in months past!' I should not have had to bear
such trouble as I have now; for though the burden might have
pressed heavily, I would have cast it on the Lord. Oh! that I
knew the heavenly science of taking the burdens off my own
shoulders, and laying them on the Rock that supports them
all! Oh! if I knew how to pour out my griefs and sorrows as I
once did! I have been a fool, an arrant fool, a very fool, that I
should have run away from that sweet confidence I once had
in the Saviour! I used then to go to his ear, and tell him all my
griefs.

> 'My sorrows and my griefs I poured,
> Into the bosom of my God;
> He helped me in the trying hour,
> He helped me bear the heavy load.'

But now, I foolishly carry them myself, and bear them in my
own breast, Ah!

> 'What peaceful hours I then enjoyed!'

Would that they would return to me."

3. Another individual perhaps is speaking thus concerning
his enjoyment in the house of God and the means of grace.
"Oh," says one, "in months past, when I went up to the house
of God, how sweetly did I hear! Why, I sat with my ears open,
to catch the words, as if it were an angel speaking; and when
I listened, how at times did the tears come rolling down my
cheeks! and how did my eyes flash, when some brilliant
utterance, full of joy to the Christian, aroused my soul! Oh!
how did I awake on the Sabbath morning, and sing,

> 'Welcome, sweet day of rest,
> That saw the Lord arise;
> Welcome to this reviving breast,
> And these rejoicing eyes!'

And when they sang in the house of God, whose voice was so
loud as mine. When I retired from worship, it was with a light
tread; I went to tell my friends and my neighbours what
glorious news I had heard in the sanctuary. Those were sweet

Sabbaths. And when the prayer-meetings came round, how was I found in my place! and the prayers *were* prayers indeed to my spirit; whoever I heard preach, provided it was the gospel, how did my soul feed and fatten under it! for I sat at a very banquet of joy. When I read the Scriptures they were always illuminated, and glory did gild the sacred page, whene'er I turned it over. When I bent my knee in prayer, I could pour my soul out before God, and I loved the exercise; I felt that I could not be happy unless I spent my time upon my knees; I loved my God, and my God loved me. But oh! how changed now! 'Oh that I were as in months past!' I go up to God's house; it is the same voice that speaks, the same man I love so much, still addresses me; but I have no tears to shed now; my heart has become hardened even under his ministry; I have few emotions of joy; I enter the house of God as a boy goes to school, without much love to it, and I go away without having my soul stirred. When I kneel down in secret prayer, the wheels are taken off my chariot, and it drags very heavily; when I strive to sing, all I can say is, 'I would but cannot' 'Oh that I were as in months past!' when the candle of the Lord shone round about me!"

I trust there are not many of you who can join in this; for I know ye love to come up to the house of God. I love to preach to a people who feel the word, who give signs of assent to it—men and women who can afford a tear now and then in a sermon—people whose blood seems to boil within them when they hear the gospel. I don't think *you* understand much of the phase I am describing; but still you may understand a little of it. The word may not be quite so sweet and pleasant to you as it used to be; and then you may cry out—"Oh that I were as in months past!"

4. But I will tell you one point which perhaps may escape you. There are some of us who lament extremely that *our conscience is not as tender as it used to be*; and therefore doth our soul cry in bitterness, "Oh that I were as in months past!" "When first I knew the Lord," you say, "I was almost afraid to put one foot before another, lest I should go astray; I always looked before I leaped; if there were a suspicion of sin about anything, I faithfully avoided it; if there were the slightest trace of the trail of the serpent on it, I turned from it at once; people called me a Puritan; I watched everything; I was afraid to speak, and some practices that were really allowable

I utterly condemned; my conscience was so tender, I was like a sensitive plant; if touched by the hand of sin, my leaves curled up in a moment; I could not bear to be touched I was so tender; I was all over wounds, and if any one brushed against me I cried out; I was afraid to do anything, lest I should sin against God. If I heard an oath, my bones shook within me; if I saw a man break the Sabbath, I trembled and was afraid; wherever I went, the least whisper of sin startled me; it was like the voice of a demon when I heard a temptation, and I said with violence, 'Get thee behind me, Satan,' I could not endure sin; I ran away from it as from a serpent; I could not taste a drop of it. But 'Oh that I were as in months past.' It is true, I have not forsaken his ways; I have not quite forgotten his law; it is true, I have not disgraced my character, I have not openly sinned before men, and none but God knoweth my sin; but oh! my conscience is not what it once was. It did thunder once, but it does not now. O conscience! conscience! thou art gone too much to sleep; I have drugged thee with laudanum, and thou art slumbering, when thou oughtest to be speaking! Thou art a watchman; but thou dost not tell the hours of the night as thou once didst. O conscience! sometimes I heard thy rattle in my ears, and it startled me; now thou sleepest, and I go on to sin. It is but a little I have done; still, that little shows the way. Straws tell which way the wind doth blow; and I feel that my having committed one little sin, evidences in what way my soul is inclined. Oh! that I had a tender conscience again! Oh! that I had not this rhinoceros conscience, which is covered over with tough hide, through which the bullets of the law cannot pierce! Oh! that I had a conscience such as I used to have! 'Oh that I were as in months past!'"

5. One more form of this sad condition. There are some of us, dearly beloved, who *have not as much zeal for the glory of God and the salvation of men as we used to have*. Months ago, if we saw a soul going to destruction, our eyes were filled with tears in a moment; if we did but see a man inclined to sin, we rushed before him with tears in our eyes, and wished to sacrifice ourselves to save him; we could not walk the street, but we must be giving somebody a tract, or reproving some one; we thought we must be for ever speaking of the Lord Jesus; if there were any good to be done, we were always first and foremost in it: we desired by all means to save some, and

we did think at that time that we could give up ourselves to death, if we might but snatch a soul from hell. So deep, so ardent was our love to our fellowmen, that for the love we bore Christ's name, we would have been content to be scoffed at, hissed at, and persecuted by the whole world, if we might have done any good in it. Our soul was burning with intense longing for souls, and we considered all things else to be mean and worthless. But ah! now souls may be damned, and there is not a tear; sinners may sink into the scalding pit of hell, and not a groan; thousands may be swept away each day, and sink into bottomless woe, and yet not an emotion. We can preach without tears; we can pray for them without our hearts. We can speak to them without feeling their necessities; we pass by the haunts of infamy—we wish the inmates better, and that is all. Even our compassion has died out. Once we stood near the brink of hell, and we thought each day that we heard the yellings and howlings of the doomed spirits ringing in our ears; and then we said, "O God, help me to save my fellow-men from going down to the pit!" But now we forget it all. We have little love to men; we have not half the zeal and energy we once had. Oh! if that be your state, dearly beloved; if you can join in that, as your poor minister, alas! can do in some measure, then may we well say, "Oh that I were as in months past!"

II. But now we are about to take these different characters, and tell you the CAUSE AND CURE.

1. One of the causes of this mournful state of things is *defect in prayer:* and of course the cure lies somewhere next door to the cause. You are saying, "Oh that I were as in months past!" Come, my brother; we are going into the very root of the matter. One reason why it is not with you as in months past is this: you do not pray as you once did. Nothing brings such leanness into a man's soul as want of prayer. It is well said that a neglected closet is the birth-place of all evil. All good is born in the closet, all good springeth from it; there the Christian getteth it; but if he neglecteth his closet, then all evil comes of it. No man can progress in grace if he forsakes his closet. I care not how strong he may be in faith. It is said that fat men may for a time live on the flesh they have acquired; but there is not a Christian so full of flesh that he can live on old grace. If he waxes fat he kicks, but he cannot live upon his fat. Those who are strong and mighty in

themselves cannot exist without prayer. If a man should have the spiritual might of fifty of God's choicest Christians in himself, he must die, if he did not continue to pray. My brother, cannot you look back and say, "Three or four months ago my prayers were more regular, more constant, more earnest than they are now; but now they are feeble, they are not sincere, they are not fervent, they are not earnest?" O brother, do not ask anybody what is the cause of your grief; it is as plain as possible; you need not ask a question about it. There is the cause. And where is the remedy? Why, in more prayer, beloved. It was little prayer that brought you down; it is great prayer that will lift you up. It was lack of prayer that brought you into poverty, it must be increase of prayer that will bring you into riches again. Where no oxen are the crib is clean. There is nothing for men to eat where there are no oxen to plough; and where there are no prayers to plough the soil, you have little to feed upon. We must be more earnest in prayer. Oh! beloved, might not the beam out of the wall cry against us? Our dusty closets might bear witness to our neglect of secret devotion; and that is the reason why it is not with us as in months past. My friends: if you were to compare the Christian to a steam-engine, you must make his prayers, fed by the Holy Spirit, to be the very fire which sustains his motion. Prayer is God's chosen vehicle of grace, and he is unwise who neglects it. Let me be doubly serious on this matter, and let me give a home-thrust to some. Dear friend, do you mean what you say, and do you believe what you say—that neglect of prayer will bring your soul into a most hazardous condition? If so, I will say no more to thee; for thou wilt easily guess the remedy for thy lamentable cry, "Oh that I were as in months past!" A certain merchant wishes that he were as rich as he used to be:—he was wont to send his ships over to the gold country, to bring him home cargoes of gold; but ne'er a ship has been out of port lately, and therefore can he wonder that he has had no cargo of gold? So when a man prayeth he sends a ship to heaven, and it comes back laden with gold; but if he leaves off supplication, then his ship is weather-bound and stays at home, and no wonder he cometh to be a poor man.

2. Perhaps, again, you are saying, "Oh that I were as in months past!" not so much from your own fault as from *the fault of your minister*. There is such a thing, my dear friends,

as our getting into a terribly bad condition through the
ministry that we attend. Can it be expected that men should
grow in grace when they are never watered with the streams
that make glad the city of our God? Can they be supposed to
wax strong in the Lord Jesus, when they do not feed on
spiritual food? We know some who grumble, Sabbath after
Sabbath, and say they can't hear such and such a minister.
Why don't you buy an ear-trumpet then? *Ah! but I mean, that
I can't hear him to my soul's profit.* Then do not go to hear
him, if you have tried for a long while and don't get any profit.
I always think that a man who grumbles as he goes out of
chapel ought not to be pitied, but whipped, for he can stay
away if he likes, and go where he will be pleased. There are
plenty of places where the sheep may feed in their own
manner; and every one is bound to go where he gets the
pasture most suited to his soul. But you are not bound to run
away directly if your minister dies, as many of you did before
you came here. You should not run away from the ship
directly the storm comes, and the captain is gone, and you
find her not exactly sea-worthy; stand by her, begin caulking
her, God will send you a captain, there will be fine weather
by-and-bye, and all will be right. But very frequently a bad
minister starves God's people into walking skeletons, so that
you can tell all their bones; and who wonders that they starve
out their minister, when they get no food and no nutriment
from his ministrations. This is a second reason why men
frequently cry out, "Oh that I were as in months past!"

3. But there is a better reason still, that will come more
home to some of you. *It is not so much the badness of the food,
as the seldomness that you come to eat it.* You know, my dear
friends, we find every now and then that there is a man who
came twice a day to the house of God on the Sabbath. On the
Monday night he was busy at work; but his apron was rolled
up, and if he could not be present all the while, he would come
in at the end. On the Thursday evening he would, if possible,
come to the sanctuary, to hear a sermon from some gospel
minister, and would sit up late at night and get up early in
the morning, to make up the time he had spent in these
religious exercises. But by-and-bye he thought, "I am too
hard-worked; this is tiring; it is too far to walk." And so he
gives up first one service, and then another, and then begins
to cry out, "Oh that I were as in months past!" Why, brethren

you need not wonder at it. The man does not eat so much as he used to do. Little and often is the way children should be fed, though I have given you a great deal this morning. Still, little and often is a very good rule. I do think, when people give up week-day services, unless it is utterly impracticable for them to attend them, farewell to religion. "Farewell to practical godliness," says Whitfield, "when men do not worship God on the week-day!" Week-day services are frequently the cream of all. God giveth his people pails full of milk on the Sabbath; but he often skims off the cream for the week-day. If they stay away, is it wonderful that they have to say, "Oh, that I were as in months past!" I do not blame you, beloved; I only wish to "stir up your pure minds by way of remembrance." A very plain fellow that is—is he not? Yes, he always tells you what he means, and always intends to do so. Stand to your colours, my men! Keep close to the standard if you would win the battle! And when there seems to be the slightest defection, it is simply our duty to exhort you, lest by any measure ye depart from the soundness of your faith.

4. But frequently this complaint arises from *idolatry*. Many have given their hearts to something else save God, and have set their affections upon the things of earth, instead of the things in heaven. It is hard to love the world and love Christ; it is impossible: that is more. But it is hard not to love the creature; it is hard not to give yourself to earth; I had almost said, it is impossible not to do that; it is difficult, and only God can enable us; he alone can keep us with our hearts fully set on him. But mark: whenever we make a golden calf to worship, sooner or later it will come to this,—we shall get our golden calf ground up and put into our water for us to drink, and then we shall have to say, "He hath made me drunken with wormwood." Never a man makes an idol for himself to worship but it tumbles down on him and breaks some of his bones. There was ne'er a man yet who departed to broken cisterns to find water, but instead thereof he found loathsome creatures therein, and was bitterly deceived. God will have his people live on him, and on none else; and if they live on anything else but him he will take care to give them of the waters of Mara, to embitter their drink, and drive them to the Rock of purest streams. Oh, beloved, let us take care that our hearts are wholly his, only Christ's, solely Christ's! If they are so, we shall not have to cry out, "Oh that I were as in months past!"

5. We scarcely need, however, detail any more reasons. We will add but one more and that is the most common one of all. We have, perhaps, become *self-confident and self-righteous*. If so, that is a reason why it is not with us as in months past. Ah! my friends, that old rascal self-righteousness, you will never get rid of him as long as you live. The devil was well pictured under the form of a serpent because a serpent can creep in anywhere, though the smallest crevice. Self-righteousness is a serpent; for it will enter anywhere. If you try to serve your God, "What a fine fellow you are," says the devil. "Ah! don't you serve your God well! You are always preaching. You are a noble fellow." If you go to a prayer meeting, God gives you a little gift, and you are able to pour out your heart. Presently there is a pat on the back from Satan. "Did not you pray sweetly? I know the brethren will love you; you are growing in grace very much." If a temptation comes, and you are able to resist it, "Ah!" says he at once, "you are a true soldier of the cross; look at the enemy you have knocked down; you will have a bright crown by-and-bye; you are a brave fellow!" You go on trusting God implicitly; Satan then says, your faith is very strong: no trial can overcome you: there is a weak brother, he is not half as strong as you are!" Away you go, and scold your weak brother, because he is not as big as you; and all the while Satan is cheering you up, and saying, "What a mighty warrior you are! so faithful—always trusting in God; you have not any self-righteousness." The minister preaches to the Pharisee: but the Pharisee is not fifty-ninth cousin to you; you are not at all self-righteous in your own opinion, and all the while you are the most self-righteous creature in existence. Ah! beloved, just when we think ourselves humble we are sure to be proud; and when we are groaning over our pride we are generally the most humble. You may just read your own estimate backwards. Just when we imagine we are the worst, we are often the best; and when we conceive ourselves the best, we are often the worst. It is that vile self-righteousness who creeps into our souls, and makes us murmur, "Oh that I were as in months past!" Your candle has got the snuff of self-righteousness upon it; you want to have that taken away, and then you will burn all right. You are soaring too high; you require something that will bring you down again to the feet of the

Saviour, as a poor lost and guilty sinner—nothing at all; then you will not cry any longer. "Oh that I were as in months past!"

III. And now, the closing up is to be an EXHORTATION.

An exhortation, first of all, to *consolation*. One is saying, "Oh! I shall never be in a more happy state than I now am in; I have lost the light of his countenance; he hath clean gone away from me, and I shall perish." You remember in John Bunyan's "Pilgrim's Progress," the description of the man shut up in the iron cage. One says to him, "Wilt thou never come out of this cage?" "No, never." "Art thou condemned for ever?" "Yes, I am." "Why was this?" "Why, I grieved the Spirit, and he is gone; I once thought I loved him, but I have treated him lightly and he has departed. I went from the paths of righteousness, and now I am locked up here, and cannot get out." Yes, but John Bunyan does not tell you that the man never did get out? There have been some in that iron cage that have come out. There may be one here this morning, who has been for a long while sitting in that iron cage, rattling the bars, trying to break them, trying to file them through with his own little might and strength. Oh! dear friend, you will never file through the iron bars of that terrible cage; you will never escape by yourself. What must you do? You must begin to sing like the bird in the cage does; then the kind master will come and let you out. Cry to him to deliver you; and though you cry and shout, and he shutteth out your prayer, he will hear you by-and-bye; and like Jonah you shall exclaim in days to come, "Out of the belly of hell I cried unto the Lord, and he heard me." You will find the roll under the settle, although you have dropped it down the Hill of Difficulty; and when thou hast it thou will put it in thy bosom again, and hold it all the more tightly, because thou hast lost it for a little season.

> "Return, O wanderer, return,
> And seek an injured Father's face;
> Those warm desires that in thee burn,
> Were kindled by reclaiming grace."

And now another exhortation, not so much to console you as to stir you up more and more to seek to be what you ought to be. O Christian men and women, my brethren and sisters in the faith of Jesus Christ! How many there are of you who are content just to be saved, and merely to enter heaven. How many do we find who are saying "Oh! if I can but just get in at the door—if I can simply be a child of God!" and they carry out their desires literally; for they are as little Christian as possible. They would have moderation in religion! But what is moderation in religion? It is a lie; it is a farce. Doth a wife ask her husband to be moderately loving? Doth a parent expect his child to be moderately obedient? Do you seek to have your servants moderately honest? No! Then how can you talk about being moderately religious? To be moderately religious is to be irreligious. To have a religion that does not enter into the very heart and influence the life, is virtually to have no religion at all. I tremble sometimes, when I think of some of you who are mere professors. Ye are content ye whitewashed sepulchres; because ye are beautifully whitened ye rest satisfied, without looking at the charnel-house beneath. How many of you make clean the outside of the cup and platter; and because the church can lay nothing to your charge, and the world cannot accuse you, you think the outside of the cup will be sufficient. Take heed! take heed! The judge will look at the inside of the cup and platter one day; and if it be full of wickedness he will break that platter, and the fragments shall for ever be cast about in the pit of torment. Oh! may God give you to be real Christians! Waxen-winged professors! ye can fly very well here; but when like Icarus, ye fly upwards, the mighty sun of Jesus shall melt your wings, and ye shall fall into the pit of destruction. Ah! gilded Christians, beautifully painted, varnished, polished, what will ye do when ye shall be found at last to have been worthless metal? When the wood, hay, and stubble shall be burned and consumed, what will ye do if ye are not the genuine coin of heaven, if ye have not been molten in the furnace, if ye have not been minted from on high? If ye are not real gold, how shall ye stand the fire in that "great and terrible day of the Lord?" Ah! and there are some of you who *can* stand the fire, I trust. You are the children of God; but, beloved, do I charge you wrongfully when I say, that many of us know that we are the children of God, but we are content to be as little dwarf children; we are always crying out, "Oh that I were as in months past!" That is a mark of dwarfishness. If we are to do great things in the world we must not often utter this cry. We must often be singing,—

"I the chief of sinners am; but Jesus died for me;"

and with cheerful countenance we must be able to say that we "know whom we have believed." Do you wish to be useful? Do you desire to honour your Master? Do you long to carry a heavy crown to heaven, that you may put it on the Saviour's head? If you do—and I know you do—then seek above all things that your soul may prosper and be in health—that your inner-man may not be simply in a living state, but that you may be a tree planted by the rivers of water, bringing forth your fruit in your season, your leaf never withering, and whatsoever you do prospering. Ah! do you want to go to heaven, and wear a starless crown there—a crown that shall be a real crown, but that shall have no star upon it, because no soul has been saved by you? Do you wish to sit in heaven with a dress of Christ's on, but without one single jewel that God has given you for your wages here below? Ah! no; methinks you wish to go to heaven in full dress, and to enter into the fullness of the joy of the Lord. Five talents well improved, five cities; and let no man be satisfied with his one talent merely, but let him seek to put it out at interest; "for unto him that hath shall be given, and he shall have abundance."

And finally, to many of you what I have preached about has no interest whatever. Perhaps you may say, "'Oh that I were as in months past!' for then I was quite well and a jolly fellow was I. Then I could drink with the deepest drinker anywhere. Then I could run merrily into sin, but I cannot now. I have hurt my body. I have injured my mind. It is not with me as it used to be, I have spent all my money. I wish I were as I used to be!" Ah! poor sinner, thou hast good reason to say, "Oh that I were as in months past!" But wait four or five months, and then you will say it more emphatically, and think even to day better than that day. And the further you go on, the more you will wish to go back again; for the path to hell is down, down, down, down—always down—and you will be always saying, "Oh that I were as in months past!" Thou wilt look back to the time when a mother's prayer blessed thee, and a father's reproof warned thee—when thou wentest to a Sabbath-school, and sattest upon thy mother's knee, to hear her tell thee of a Saviour; and the longer the retrospect of goodness, the more that goodness will pain you. Ah! my friends, ye have need to go back, some of you. Remember how far ye have fallen—how much ye have departed. But oh! ye need not turn back! Instead of looking back and crying, "Oh that I were as in months past!" say something different. Say, "Oh that I were a new man in Christ Jesus" It would not do for you to begin again in your present state; you would soon be as bad as you now are; but say, "Oh that I were a new man in Christ Jesus; oh that I might begin a new life!" Some of you would like to begin a new life—some of you reprobates, who have gone far away! Well, poor mortal, thou mayest. "How?" sayest thou. Why, if thou art a new man in Christ Jesus thou *wilt* begin again. A Christian is as much a new man as if he had been no man at all before; the old creature is dethroned, he is a new creature, born again, and starting on a new existence. Poor soul! God can make thee a new man. God the Holy Spirit can build a new house out of thee, with neither stick nor stone of the old man in it; and he can give thee a new heart, a new spirit, new pleasures, new happiness, new prospects, and at last give thee a new heaven. "But," says one, "I feel that I want these things; but may I have them?" Guess whether you may have them, when I tell you—"This is a faithful saying, and worthy of all acceptation, that Jesus Christ came into the world to save sinners." It does not say it is worthy of *some* acceptation, but it is worthy of *all* the acceptation you will ever give it. If you now say, "Jesus came into the world so save sinners, I believe he did! I know he did; he came to save *me*," you will find it "worthy of all acceptation." You say still, "But will he save *me*?" I will give you another passage: "Whosoever cometh unto me I will in no wise cast out." Ah! but I do not know whether *I* may come! "Whosoever," it saith. "*Him* that cometh unto me I will in no wise cast out." "Whosoever will, let him come," it is written. Dost thou will? I only speak to such as will, who know their need of a Saviour. Dost thou will? Then God the Holy Spirit says, "Whosoever will let him come, and take the water of life freely."

> "The feeble, the guilty, the weak, the forlorn,
> In coming to Jesus shall not meet with scorn;
> But he will receive them, and bless them, and save
> From death and destruction, from hell and the grave."

and he will lift them up to his kingdom of glory. God so grant it; for his name's sake.

19

Job's Regret and Our Own

"Oh that I were as in months past, as in the days when God preserved me; When his candle shined upon my head, and when by his light I walked through darkness; As I was in the days of my youth, when the secret of God was upon my tabernacle." **Job 29:2-4**

If Job here refers to the temporal prosperity which he had lost, we cannot condemn him for his complaint, neither can we commend him. It is but the expression of a natural regret, which would be felt by any man who had experienced such great reverses. But there is everywhere in the expressions which he uses such a strain of spirituality, that we are inclined to believe that he had more reference to the condition of his heart than to the state of his property. His soul was depressed; he had lost the light of God's countenance; his inward comforts were declining, his joy in the Lord was at a low ebb, this he regretted far more than anything besides. No doubt he deplored the departure of those prosperous days when, as he words it, his root was spread out by the waters, and the dew lay all night upon his branch; but, much more did he bemoan that the lamp of the Lord no more shone upon his head, and the secret of God was not upon his tabernacle. As his spiritual regrets are far more instructive to us than his natural ones, we will turn all our attention to them. We may, without violence, appropriate Job's words to ourselves; for I fear that many of us can with great propriety take up our wailing and mourn for the days of our espousals, the happy days of our first love. I shall have to trouble you with many divisions this morning; but I shall be brief upon each one, and I hope that our thoughts may be led onward, and rendered practically serviceable to us, by the blessing of God's Spirit.

I. Let us begin by saying, that regrets such as those expressed in the text are and ought to be very BITTER. If it be the loss of spiritual things that we regret, then may we say from the bottom of our hearts, "Oh that I were as in months past."

It is a great thing for a man to be near to God; it is a very choice privilege to be admitted into the inner circle of communion, and to become God's familiar friend. Great as the privilege is, so great is the loss of it. No darkness is so dark as that which falls on eyes accustomed to the light. The poor man who was always poor is scarcely poor, but he who has fallen from the summit of greatness into the depths of poverty is poor indeed. The man who has never enjoyed communion with God knows nothing of what it must be to lose it; but he who has once been pressed upon the Saviour's bosom will mourn, as long as he liveth, if he be deprived of the sacred enjoyment. The mercies which Job deplored in our text are no little ones. First, he complains that he had lost the consciousness of divine *preservation*. He says, "Oh that I were as in months past, as in the days when God preserved me." There are days with Christians when they can see God's hand all around them, checking them in the first approaches of sin, and setting a hedge about all their ways. Their conscience is tender, and the Spirit of God is obeyed by them; they are, therefore, kept in all their ways, the angels of God watching over them, lest they dash their foot against a stone. But when they fall into laxity of spirit, and walk at a distance from God, they are not so preserved. Though kept from final and total apostasy, yet they are not kept from very grievous sin; for, like Peter who followed afar off, they may be left to deny their Master, even with oaths and cursings. If we have lost that conscious preservation of God, which once covered us from every fiery dart; if we no longer abide under the shadow of the Almighty, and feel no longer that his truth is our shield and buckler, we have lost a joy worth worlds, and we may well deplore it with anguish of heart.

Job had also lost divine *consolation*, for he looks back with lamentation to the time when God's candle shone upon his head, when the sun of God's love was as it were in the zenith, and cast no shadow; when he rejoiced without ceasing, and triumphed from morning to night in the God of his salvation. The joy of the Lord is our strength, the joy of the Lord is Israel's excellency; it is the heaven of heaven, it is heaven even upon earth; and, consequently, to lose it, is a calamity indeed. Who that has once been satisfied with favour, and full of the blessing of the Lord, will be content to go into the dry and thirsty land, and live far off from God? Will he not rather cry out with David, "My soul thirsteth for God; when shall I come and appear before God?" Surely his agonising prayer will be, "Restore unto me the joy of thy salvation, and uphold me with thy free Spirit." Love to God will never be content if his face be hidden. Until the curtain be drawn aside and the King's face be seen through the lattices, the true spouse will spend her life in sighing; mourning like a dove bereaved of its mate.

Moreover, Job deplored the loss of divine *illumination*. "By his light," he says, "I walked through darkness," that is to say, perplexity ceased to be perplexity; God shed such a light upon the mysteries of providence, that where others missed their path, Job, made wise by heaven, could find it. There have been times when, to our patient faith, all things have been plain. "If any man will do his will, he shall know of the doctrine;" but, if we walk far off from God, then, straightway, even the precious truth of God is no more clear to us, and the dealings of God with us in providence appear to be like a maze. He is wise as Solomon who walks with God, but he is a very fool who trusts his own understanding. All the wit that we have gathered by observation and experience will not supply us with sufficiency of common sense, if we turn away from God. Israel, without consulting God, made a league with her enemies; she thought the case most plain when she entered into hasty alliance with the Gibeonites, but she was duped by cunning because she asked not counsel of the Lord. In the simplest business we shall err, if we seek not direction from the Lord; yet, where matters are most complicated, we shall walk wisely, if we wait for a voice from the oracle, and seek the good Shepherd's guidance. We may bitterly lament, therefore, if we have lost the Holy Spirit's light. If now the Lord answereth us not, neither by his word, nor by his providence, if we wander alone, crying, "Oh that I knew where I might find him," we are in an evil case, and may well sigh for the days, when by his light we walked through darkness.

Moreover, Job had lost divine *communion*: so it seems, for he mourned the days of his youth, when the secret of God was upon his tabernacle. Who shall tell to another what the secret of God is? Believing hearts know it, but they cannot frame to pronounce aright the words that could explain it, nor can they convey by language what the secret is. The Lord manifests himself unto his people as he doth not unto the world. We could not tell the love passages that there are between believers and their Lord; even when they are set to such sweet music as the Song of Solomon, carnal minds cannot discern their delights. They cannot plough with our heifer, and therefore they read not our riddle. As Paul in heaven saw things which it were unlawful for a man to utter, so the believer sees and enjoys in communion with Christ what it would not only be unlawful but impossible for him to tell to carnal men. Such pearls are not for swine. The spiritual discerneth all things, but he himself is discerned of no man. Now, it is a high privilege, beyond all privileges, to enter into familiar intercourse with the Most High, and the man who has once possessed it, and has lost it, has a bitterer cause for regret than if, being rich, he had lost his wealth; or being famous, he had lost esteem; or being in health, he were suddenly brought to the bed of languishing. No loss can equal the loss of thee, my God! No eclipse is so black as the hiding of thy face! No storm is so fierce as the letting forth of thine indignation! It is grief upon grief to find that thou art not with me as in the days of old. Wherever, then, these regrets do exist, if the men's hearts are as they should be, they are not mere hypocritical or superficial expressions, but they express the bitterest experiences of our human existence. "Oh that I were as in months past" is no sentimental sigh, but the voice of the innermost spirit in anguish, as one who has lost his firstborn.

II. But, secondly, let me remind you that these regrets are NOT INEVITABLE; that is to say, it is not absolutely necessary that a Christian man should ever feel them, or be compelled to express them. It has grown to be a tradition among us, that every Christian must backslide in a measure, and that growth in grace cannot be unbrokenly sustained. It is regarded by many as a law of nature, that our first love must grow cold, and our early zeal must necessarily decline. I do not believe it for a moment. "The path of the just is us the shining light, which shineth more and more unto the perfect day;" and were we watchful and careful to live near to God, there is no reason why our spiritual life should not continuously make progress both in strength and beauty. There is no inherent necessity in the divine life itself compelling it to decline, for is it not written, "It shall be in him a well of water, springing up unto everlasting life;" "out of his belly shall flow rivers of living water." Grace is a living and incorruptible seed that liveth and abideth for ever, and there is nowhere impressed upon the divine life a law of pining and decay. If we do falter and faint in the onward path, it is our sin, and it is doubly sinful to forge excuses for it. It is not to be laid upon the back of some mysterious necessity of the new nature that it should be so, but it is to be brought as a charge against ourselves. Nor do outward circumstances ever furnish a justification to us if we decline in grace; for, under the worst conditions, believers have grown in grace: deprived of the joys of Christian fellowship, and denied the comforts of the means of grace, believers have nevertheless been known to attain to a high-degree of likeness to Christ Jesus: thrown into the midst of wicked companions, and forced to hear, like righteous Lot, the filthy conversation of the ungodly, yet Christian men have shone all the brighter for the surrounding darkness, and have been able to escape from a wicked and perverse generation. Certain is it, that a man may be an eminent Christian, and be among the poorest of the poor: poverty need not, therefore, make us depart from God; and, it is equally certain, that a man may be rich, and for all that may walk with God and be distinguished for great grace. There is no lawful position of which we may say, "It compels a man to decline in grace."

And, brethren, there is no period of our life in which it is necessary for us to go back. The young Christian, with all the strength of his natural passions, can by grace be strong and overcome the Wicked One; the Christian in middle life, surrounded with the world's cares, can prove that "this is the victory which overcometh the world, even our faith." The man immersed in business may still be baptised of the Holy Ghost. Assuredly, old age offers no excuse for decline: "they shall still bring forth fruit in old age; they shall be fat and flourishing; to show that the Lord is upright." No, brethren, as Christ said to his disciples, when they would fain have sent the multitude away to buy meat, "they need not depart;" so would he say to the whole company of the Lord's people, "ye need not depart;" there is no compulsion for decline in grace." Your sun need not stand still, your moon need not wane. If you cannot add a cubit to your spiritual stature, at any rate, it need not decrease. There are no reasons written in the book of your spiritual nature why you, as a believer, should lose fellowship with God, and, if you do so, take blame and shame to yourself, but do not ascribe it to necessity. Do not gratify your corruptions by supposing that they are licensed to prevail occasionally, neither vex your graces by conceiving that they are doomed to inevitable defeat at a certain season. The spirit that is in us lusteth to evil, but the Holy Spirit is able to subdue it, and will subdue it, if we yield ourselves to him.

III. But, now, I am compelled to say that the regrets expressed in our text are exceedingly COMMON, and it is only here and there that we meet with a believer who has not had cause to use them. It ought not to be so, but it is so. How grievously often will the pastor hear this among the other bleatings of the sheep: "Oh that I were as in months past, as in the days when God preserved me:"

> "What peaceful hours I then enjoy'd,
> How sweet, their memory still;
> But they have left an aching void,
> The world can never fill."

The commonness of this lamentation may be somewhat accounted for, by the universal tendency to undervalue the present and exaggerate the excellence of the past. Have you never noticed this in natural things, we are prone to cast a partial eye upon some imaginary "good old times?" It is gone, and therefore it was good; it is here, and therefore it is dubious. In the middle of the summer, we feel that the heat is so relaxing that a frost would be the most delightful thing conceivable; we love, we say, the bracing air of winter; we are sure it is much healthier for us: yet, usually, when winter arrives, and the extreme cold sets in, we are all most anxious for the advent of spring, and we feel that somehow or other the frost is more trying to us than the heat. Personally, I met with an illustration of this tendency the other day. I went down a steep cliff to the sea shore, and during the descent every step tried my weak knees, and I felt that going down hill was the most difficult travelling in the world. Soon I had to return from the sands, and climb the steep path again; and, when I began to pant and puff with the difficult ascent, I changed my opinion, and felt that I would a great deal sooner go down than come up. The fact is that whatever is with us we think to be the worse, and whatever was with us we conceive to be the better. We may, therefore, take some discount from our regrets; for, peradventure, were we more conscious of the benefit of the present state, and did we make less prominent the difficulty of it, we should not sigh to be as we were in months past.

Then, again, regrets may in some cases arise from a holy jealousy. The Christian, in whatever state he is, feels his own imperfection much, and laments his conscious shortcomings. Looking back, he observes with joy the work of grace in his soul, and does not perhaps so readily recollect the then existing deficiencies of nature; hence, he comes to think that the past was better than the present. He is afraid of backsliding, and therefore he jealously fears that he is so; he is so anxious to live nearer to God, so dissatisfied with his present attainments, that he dares not believe that he advances, but fears that he has lost ground. I know this in my own experience, for when lying sick I have frequently lamented that pain has distracted my mind, and taken off my attention from the word of God, and I have longed for those seasons of health when I could read, meditate, and study with pleasure; but, now that I have risen up from the sick bed, and am growing strong again, I frequently look back to the long nights and quiet days spent in my sick chamber, and think that it was better with me then than now, for now I am apt to be cumbered with much serving, and then I was shut in with God. Many a man is really strong in Christ; but, because he does not feel all the juvenile vivacity of his early days, he fears that spiritual decrepitude has come upon him. He is now far more solid and steadfast, if not quite so quick and impulsive; but, the good man in his holy jealousy marks most the excellencies of his juvenile piety, and forgets that there were grave deficiencies in it; while, in his present state, he notes the deficiencies, and fears to hope that he possesses any excellencies. We are poor judges of our own condition, and usually err on one side or the other. All graces may not flourish at the same time, and defalcations in one direction may be more than balanced by advantages in another. We may be deeper in humility if we are not higher in delight. We may not glitter so much, and yet there may be more real gold in us. The leaf may not be so green, but the fruit may be more ripe. The way may be rougher, and yet be nearer heaven. Godly anxiety, then, may be the cause of many regrets which are, nevertheless, not warranted by any serious declension.

And, let me add, that very often these regrets of ours about the past are not wise. It is impossible to draw a fair comparison between the various stages of Christian experience, so as to give a judicious preference to one above another. Consider, as in a parable, the seasons of the year. There are many persons who, in the midst of the beauties of spring, say, "Ah, but how fitful is the weather! These March winds and April showers come and go by such fits and starts, that nothing is to be depended upon. Give me the safer glories of summer." Yet, when they feel the heat of summer, and wipe the sweat from their brows, they say, "After all, with all the full-blow of beauty around us, we admire more the freshness, verdure, and vivacity of spring. The snowdrop and the crocus, coming forth as the advance guard of the army of flowers, have a superior charm about them." Now it is idle to compare spring with summer; they differ, and have each its beauties. We are in autumn now, and very likely, instead of prizing the peculiar treasures of autumn, some will despise the peaceful Sabbath of the year, and mournfully compare you fading leaves to funeral sermons replete with sadness. Such will contrast summer and autumn, and exalt one above another. Now, whoever shall claim precedence for any season, shall have me for an opponent. They are all beautiful in their season, and each excels after its kind. Even thus it is wrong to compare the early zeal of the young Christian with the mature and mellow experience of the older believer, and make preferences. Each is beautiful according to its time. You, dear young friend, with your intense zeal, are to be commended and imitated; but very much of your fire I am afraid arises from novelty, and you are not so strong as you are earnest; like a newborn river, you are swift in current, but neither deep nor broad. And you, my more advanced friend, who are much tried and buffeted, to you it is not easy to hold on your way under great inward struggles and severe depressions, but your deeper sense of weakness, your firmer grasp of truth, your more intense fellowship with the Lord Jesus in his sufferings, your patience, and your steadfastness, are all lovely in the eyes of the Lord your God. Be thankful each of you for what you have, for by the grace of God you are what you are.

After making all these deductions, however, I cannot conceive that they altogether account for the prevalence of these regrets; I am afraid the fact arises from the sad truth that many of us have actually deteriorated in grace, have decayed in spirit, and degenerated in heart. Alas! in many cases, old corruptions have fought desperately, and for awhile caused a partial relapse. Grace has become weak, and sin has seized the occasion for attack; so that for a time the battle is turned, and Israel's banner is trailed in the mire. With many professors, I am afraid, prayer is neglected, worldliness is uppermost, sin has come to the front, nature leads the van, and grace and holiness are in the background. It should not be so, but I am afraid, ah, sadly afraid it is so.

IV. I will more fully speak upon this matter under the fourth head. Since these regrets are exceedingly common, it is to be feared that in some cases they are very sadly NEEDFUL. Now, let the blast of the winnowing fan be felt through the congregation. Behold, the Lord himself winnows this heap. Are there not many among us who once walked humbly with God, and near to him, who have fallen into carnal security? Have we not taken it for granted that all is well with us, and are we not settled upon our lees like Moab of old? How little of heart-searching and self-examination are practiced now-a-days! How little enquiry as to whether the root of the matter is really in us! Woe unto those who take their safety for granted, and sit down in God's house and say, "The temple of the Lord, the temple of the Lord are we." Woe unto them that are at ease in Zion. Of all enemies, one of the most to be dreaded is presumption. To be secure in a Christ is a blessing; to be secure in ourselves is a curse. Where carnal security reigns, the Spirit of God withdraws. He is with the humble and contrite, but he is not with the proud and self-sufficient. My brethren, are we all clear in this respect? Do not many of God's people also need to bemoan their worldliness? Once Christ was all with you, brethren; is it so now? Once you despised the world, and condemned alike its pleasures and its frowns; but now, my brethren, are not the chains of worldly custom upon you? Are you not many of you enslaved by fashion, and eaten up with frivolity? Do you not, some of you, run as greedily as worldlings after the questionable enjoyments of this present life? Ought these things to be so? Can they remain so and your souls enjoy the Lord's smile? "Ye cannot serve God and mammon." "If any man love the world, the love of the Father is not in him." You cannot be Christ's disciples, and be in fellowship with the ungodly. Come ye out from among them; be ye separate; touch not the unclean thing; then shall ye know right joyfully that the Lord is a Father to you, and that you are his sons and daughters. But, brethren, have ye gone unto Jesus without the camp, and do ye abide there with him? Is the line of your separation visible —ay, is it existing? Is there any separation at all? Is it not often the case that the professed people of God are mixed up with the sons of men so that you cannot discern the one from the other? If it be so with anyone of us, let him humble himself, and let him cry in bitterness, "Oh that I were as in months past."

Brethren and sisters, feel ye the breath of the winnowing fan again. How is it with you as to private prayer? Are there not believers, and we hope true believers too, who are lax in devotion? The morning prayer is brief, but alas! it is not fervent; the evening prayer is too often sleepy; ejaculations are few and far between; communion with heaven is distant, suspended, almost non-existent in many cases. Look ye to this, my brethren; let each man commune with his own heart, and be still. Think not of others just now, but let each one consider his ways. How is it with your love to the souls of sinners? There was a time when you would have done anything to bring a man to Christ, when any exertion you could have put forth would have been made spontaneously, without the need of incessant exhortations; are you as ready to speak for Jesus now as you once were? Do you watch to bring souls to him? Does the tear tremble in your eye, now, as it once did for lost souls, perishing without Christ? Alas, upon how many has a hardening influence operated. Ah, and this is true even of us, ministers. We have grown professional in our service, and now we preach like automatons, wound up for a sermon, to run down when the discourse is over, and we have little more care for the souls of men than if they were so much dirt. Trifles of criticism, fancies of speculation, or fopperies of oratory, fascinate too many who should be wise to win souls. God forgive us if we have fallen into so deplorable a state.

Ah, and how many of God's people must confess that their

conscience is not so tender now as it used be. The time was when, if you said half a word amiss, you would hide away to weep over it; when, in business, if there had been a little mistake, and anything that might be construed into want of integrity, you would have felt ashamed for a week that such a thing had happened; but now—ah, professors hear ye this— some of you can be dishonest and speak words that border on lasciviousness, and be as others are, yet your heart does not smite you, but you come to the communion table and feel you have a right to be there, and listen to the Word of God, and take comfort from it, when rather you should be ashamed and confounded.

Let me enquire whether there are not many of us whose zeal is almost gone? We once loved the Saviour intensely, and his cause we eagerly sought to serve, but now we take matters easily, and do not travail in birth for souls. Some rich men were wont to give most freely to the cause of God, but now covetousness has palsied the hand of generosity. Even poor Christians are not always so ready with their two mites as they were in better days. You were wont to labour, too, but that Sunday School class sees you no longer; no street preaching now; no tract distributing now; all forms of Christ's service you have renounced, for you fancy you have done enough. Alas, poor sluggard! Has the sun shone long enough? Has God given you your daily bread long enough? Oh, cease not working, brethren, till God ceases to be merciful to you. "On, on, on," "forward, forward, forward," is the very motto of the Christian life. Let none of us talk of finality, for we have not yet attained. Till life is over, our zeal should still glow, and our labours for Christ should multiply.

Are there not other signs of declension, that some of us might, with but a very slight examination, discover in ourselves? Is not brotherly love, in many Christians, very questionable? Have they not forgotten, altogether, the family ties which bind all Christians to one another? And, with brotherly love, has not love to the Gospel gone too, so that now with many, one doctrine is almost as good as another? If a man can talk well, and is an orator, they enjoy his ministry whether he advocates truth or error. Once they could go to the little meeting house, where Christianity was preached faithfully though in an uncouth style, but now they must have the help of organs or they cannot praise God; and there must

be millinery and genuflexions, or else they cannot pray to
him; and they must listen to oratory and elocution, or else
they cannot accept God's word. He is sickly who cannot dine
without made dishes and spiced meats, but he is a healthy
man of God who can eat heaven's bread and heaven's meat,
even when it is not served on a lordly dish. Might not many of
us blush, if we were to think how low our graces are, how
weak our faith, how few our good works, and our gracious
words with which we should bear testimony to his name. Yes,
in thousands of cases, Christians need not be stopped if they
were to commence this mournful cry, "Oh that I were as in the
days of my youth, when the secret of God was upon my
tabernacle."

V. But, I must pass on to observe that these regrets BY
THEMSELVES ARE USELESS. It is unprofitable to read these
words of Job, and say, "Just so, that is how I feel," and then
continue in the same way. If a man has neglected his
business, and so has lost his trade, it may mark a turn in his
affairs when he says, "I wish I had been more industrious;"
but if he abides in the same sloth as before, of what use is his
regret? If he shall fold his arms and say, "Oh that I had dug
that plot of land; oh that I had sown that field;" no harvest
will come because of his lamentations. Up, man, up and
labour, or you will have the sluggard's reward, rags and
poverty will still be your portion. If a man be in declining
health, if drunkenness and riot have broken down his
constitution, it may mark a salutary reform in his history if
he confesses his former folly; but if his regrets end in mere
expressions, will these heal him? I trow not. So neither will a
man, affected by spiritual decline, be restored by the mere
fact of his knowing himself to be so. Let him go to the beloved
physician, drink of the waters of life again, and receive the
leaves of the tree which are for the healing of the nations.
Inactive regrets are insincere. If a man really did lament that
he had lost communion with God, he would seek to regain it.
If he doth not seek to be restored he is adding to all his former
sins this of lying before God, in uttering regrets that he does
not feel in his soul.

I have known some, I fear who even satisfied themselves
with expressions of regrets. "Ah," say they, "I am a deep
experienced man, I can go where Job went; I can mourn and
lament as Job did." Remember, many have been on Job's

dunghill, who knew nothing of Job's God; many have imitated David in his sins, who never followed him in his repentance. They have gone from their sin into hell by the way of presumption, whereas David went from it to heaven by the road of repentance and forgiveness. Never let us, merely because we feel some uneasiness within, conclude that this suffices. If in the dead of the night you should hear thieves in your house, you would not congratulate yourself because you were awake to hear them. You would waive all such comfortable reflections till the rogues were driven out and your property was safe; and so, when you know things are amiss with you, do not say, "I am satisfied, because I know it is so." Up, man, and with all the strength that God's Holy Spirit can give you, strive to drive out these traitors from your bosom, for they are robbing your soul of her best treasures.

VI. Brethren, these regrets when they are necessary are very HUMBLING. Meditate now for a minute. Think, dear brother, what was thy position in thy happiest times, in those days that are now past. Had you any love to spare then? You were zealous; were you too zealous? You were gracious; were you too gracious? Nay, in our best estate, we were very far short of what we ought to be, and yet we have gone back from even that. It was a poor attainment at the best, have we fallen even from that. During the time we have been going back, we ought to have gone forward. What enjoyments we have lost by our wanderings! What progress we have missed! As John Bunyan well puts it, when Christian fell asleep and lost his roll, he had to go back for it, and he found it very hard going back, and, moreover, he had to go on again, so that he had to traverse three times the road he need only have travelled once, and then he came in late at the gates of the palace Beautiful, and was afraid of the lions, of which he would have had no fear had not the darkness set in. We know not what we lose, when we lose growth in grace.

Alas, how much the church has lost through us, for if the Christian becomes poor in grace, he lessens the church's wealth of grace. We have a common exchequer as a church, and every one who takes away his proportion from it robs the whole. Dear brethren, how accountable are many of us for the low tone of religion in the world, especially those of us who occupy the foremost ranks. If grace be at a low ebb with us, others say, "Well, look at so and so; I am as good as he." So

much in the church do we take the cue from one another, that
each one of us is in a measure responsible for the low state of
the whole. Some of us are very quick to see the faults of
others; may it not be that these faults are our own children?
Those who have little love to others generally discover that
there is little love in the church, and I notice that those who
complain of the inconsistencies of others, are usually the most
inconsistent persons themselves. Shall I be a robber of my
fellow Christians? Shall I be an injury to the cause of Christ?
Shall I be a comfort unto sinners in their sin? Shall I rob
Christ of his glory,—I, who was saved from such depths of sin,
—I, who have been favoured with such enjoyments of his
presence,—I, that have been on Tabor's top with him, and
seen him transfigured,—I, that have been in his banqueting
house, and have drunk out of the flagons of his love,—shall I
be so devoid of grace, that I shall even injure his children, and
make his enemies to blaspheme? Wretch that I am, to do this!
Smite your breast, my brother, if such has been your sin; go
home and smite your breast again, and ask God to smite it,
till, with a broken heart, you cry repentingly for restoration,
and then again go forth as a burning and a shining light, to
serve your Master better than before.

VII. These regrets then, are humbling, and they may be
made very PROFITABLE in many other ways. First, they show
us what human nature is. Have we gone back so far? O,
brethren, we might have gone back to perdition: we should
have done so, if it had not been for the grace of God. What a
marvel it is that God has borne with our ill manners, when he
might justly have laid the reins on our necks, and suffered us
to rush on in the road which we so often hankered after. See
you not, dear brethren, what a body of death we carry with
us, and what a terrible power it possesses? When you see the
mischief that corruption has already done, never trust
yourself, but look for new grace every day.

Learn again to prize what spiritual blessings yet remain. If
you have such bitter regrets for what you have lost, hold fast
what is still yours. Slip back no further, for if these slips have
cost you so much, take heed that they do not ruin you. To
continue presumptuous may be a proof that our profession is
rotten throughout: only a holy jealousy can remove the
suspicion of insincerity. Let your previous failings teach you
to walk cautiously for the future. Be jealous, for you serve a

jealous God. Since grey hairs may come upon you, here and there, and you may not know it, search, watch, try yourself day by day, lest you relapse yet more.

This should teach us to live by faith, since our best attainments fail us. We rejoice to-day, but we may mourn to-morrow. What a mercy it is that our salvation does not depend on what we are or what we feel. Christ has finished our salvation; no man can destroy what he has completed. Our life is hid with Christ in God, and is safe there; none can pluck us out of Jehovah's hands. Since we so frequently run aground, it is clear that we should be wrecked altogether, if we went to sea in a legal vessel with self for our pilot; let us keep to the good ship of free grace, steered by immutable faithfulness, for none other can bring us to the desired haven. But oh, let that free grace fill us with ardent gratitude. Since Christ has kept us, though we could not keep ourselves, let us bless his name, and, overwhelmed with obligations, let us rise with a solemn determination that we will serve him better than we have ever done before; and may his blessed Spirit help us to make the determination a fact.

VIII. So, to close; these regrets OUGHT NOT TO BE CONTINUAL: they ought to be removed, decidedly removed, by an earnest effort, made in God's strength, to get back to the position which we occupied before, and to attain something better still.

Dear brethren and sisters, if any of you desire now to come into the higher life, and to feel anew your first love, what shall I say to you? Go back to where you started. Do not stay discussing whether you are a Christian or not. Go to Christ as a poor guilty sinner. When the door to heaven seems shut to me as a saint, I will get through it as a sinner, trusting in the precious blood of Jesus. Come and stand again, as though all your sins were on you still, at the cross's foot, where still may be seen the dropping blood of the infinitely precious atonement. Saviour, I trust thee again: guilty, more guilty than I was before, a sinful child of God, I trust thee: "wash me throughly from mine iniquities, and purge me from my sin." You will never have your graces revived, unless you go to the cross. Begin life again. The best air for a man to breathe when he is sickly is said to be that of his birthplace: it was at Calvary we were born; it is only at Calvary we can be restored when we are declining. Do the first works. As a sinner, repair to the Saviour, and ask to be restored. Then, as a further means of health, search out the cause of your declension. Probably it was a neglect of private prayer. Where the disease began, there must the remedy be applied. Pray more earnestly, more frequently, more importunately. Or, was it a neglect of hearing the word? Were you enticed by novelty or cleverness away from a really searching and instructive ministry? Go back, and feed on wholesome food again: perhaps that may cure the disease. Or, have you been too grasping after the world? Brother, you loved God when you had but one shop, you have two now, and are giving all your time and thoughts to business, and your soul is getting lean. Man alive, strike off some of that business, for it is a bad business that makes your soul poor. I would not check industry or enterprise for a single moment; let a man do all he can, but not at the expense of his soul. Push, but do not push down your soul. You may buy gold too dear, and may attain a high position in this world at a cost which you may have to rue all your days. Where the mischief began, there apply the remedy. And oh, I urge upon you, and most of all upon myself, do not make excuses for yourselves; do not palliate your faults; do not say it must be so; do not compare yourselves among yourselves, or you will be unwise; but to the perfect image of Christ let your hearts aspire, to the ardour of your divine Redeemer, who loved not himself, but loved you; to the intense fervour of his apostles, who laid themselves upon the altar of God for his sake, for Christ's sake, and for yours. Aspire to this, and may we as a church live near to God, and grow in grace, then shall the Lord add to us daily of such as shall be saved.

There are some here who will say, "I do not comprehend this sermon: I have no cause to look back with regret. I have always been much the same as I am. I know nothing of religion." The day shall come when you will envy the least and most trembling believer. To you careless, Christless sinners, the day shall come when you will cry to the rocks for mercy, and beg them to conceal you from the eyes of him whom now you dare despise. I beseech you be not high minded, lift not up your horn on high, speak not so exceeding proudly, bow before the Christ of God, and ask him to give you the new life; for even if that new life have declined and become sickly, it is better than the death in which you dwell.

Go and seek grace of him who alone can give it, and he will grant it to you this day, for his infinite mercy's sake. Amen.

20

For the Sick and Afflicted

"Surely it is meet to be said unto God, I have borne chastisement, I will not offend any more: That which I see not teach thou me: if I have done iniquity, I will do no more.
Job 34:31-32

Even when addressing our fellow-men there should be a fitness about our speech; therefore Solomon represents the preacher as seeking out acceptable words, or words meet for the occasion. When we approach those who are high in authority this necessity becomes conspicuous, and therefore men who are petitioners in the courts of princes are very careful to order their language aright. Much more, then, when we speak before the Lord ought we to consider, as the text does, the meetness of our words. Some language must never be uttered in the divine presence, and even that which is allowed must be well weighed, and set forth with solemn humbleness. Hence Elihu does well to suggest in the text language that is "meet to be said unto God." May our lips ever be kept as by a watchful sentinel, lest they suffer anything to pass through them dishonourable to the Most High. In the divine presence—and we are always there—it is incumbent upon us to set a double watch over every word that comes from our mouth.

Remember that thought is speech before God. Thought is not speech to man, for men cannot read one another's thoughts until they are set forth by words or other outward signs, but God who reads the heart regards that as being speech which was never spoken, and he hears us say in our souls many things which were never uttered by our tongues. Beloved, there are thoughts which are not meet to be thought before the Lord; and it is well for us, especially those of us who are afflicted, to be very watchful over those thoughts, lest the Lord hear us say in our hearts things which will grieve his

Spirit, and provoke him to jealousy. O saints of God, since you never think except in the immediate presence of your heavenly Father, make a conscience of your every thought, lest you sin in the secret chambers of your being, and charge God foolishly. Elihu tells us what it would be proper for us to think and say, "It is meet to be said unto God, I have borne chastisement, I will not offend more: that which I see not teach thou me: if I have done iniquity, I will do no more."

We will use the text mainly at this time *in reference to those who are being chastened*; and afterwards we shall see if there is not teaching in it, even *to those who, at present, are not smarting under the rod.* Thirdly, *we shall find a word in our text to those who are not the children of God, and, therefore, know nothing of the smarting rod of fatherly correction.* Perhaps to them, also, God may speak through this text. Oh that his Holy Spirit may deign to do so.

I. But first, dear friends, let us commune together upon the text in its more natural application as addressed TO THE AFFLICTED. The instruction of the wise man is for them especially, and there are three duties here prescribed for them, or rather three privileges suggested, which they should pray the Holy Spirit to enable them to enjoy.

The first lesson is, *it is meet for them to accept the affliction which the Lord sends*, and to say unto God, "I have borne chastisement." We notice that the word "chastisement" is not actually in the Hebrew, though the Hebrew could not be well interpreted without supplying the word. It might exactly and literally be translated "I bear," or "I have borne." It is the softened heart saying to God, "I bear whatever thou wilt put upon me; I have borne it, I still bear it, and I will bear it, whatever thou mayest ordain it to be. I submit myself entirely to thee, and accept the load with which thou art pleased to weight me." Now, we ought to do this, dear friends, and we shall do it if we are right at heart. We should cheerfully submit, because no affliction from which we suffer has come to us by chance. We are not left to the misery of believing that things happen of themselves, and are independent of a divinely controlling power. We know that not a drop of bitter ever falls into our cup unless the wisdom of our heavenly Father has placed it there. We are not even left in a world governed by angels, or ruled by cherubim; we dwell where everything is ordered by God himself. Shall we rebel against the Most High? Shall we not let him do as seemeth good in his sight? Shall we not cover our lip in silence when we know that the evil is of the Lord? Shame upon us, if we be his children, if this be not the prevalent spirit of our mind—"It is the Lord, let him do what seemeth him good." Moreover, we should not only bear all things because the Lord ordains them, but because he orders all things for a wise, kind, beneficent purpose. He doth not afflict willingly. He takes no delight in the sufferings of his children. Whenever adversity must come it is always with a purpose; and, if a purpose of God is to be subserved by my suffering, would I wish to escape from it? If his glory will come of it, shall I not even crave the honour of being the agent of his glory, even though it be by lying passive and enduring in anguish. Yes, beloved, since we know that God can only grieve his regenerated creatures for some purpose of love, we should willingly accept whatever sorrow he pleases to put upon us. And we have his assurance, besides, that all things work together for our good. Our trials are not merely sent with a good object, but with an object good towards ourselves, a design which is being answered by every twig of our heavenly father's rod. "The cup which our Father hath given us, shall we not drink it?" It is healing medicine and not deadly poison, therefore let us put it to our lips without a murmur, ay, quaff it to its very dregs, and say, "Not as I will, but as thou wilt."

A constant submission to the divine will should be the very atmosphere in which a Christian lives. He should put an earnest negative upon his self-will by crying, "*Not* my will," and then he should with holy warmth beseech the Lord to execute his purpose, saying, "The will of the Lord be done." He should throw the whole vigour of his soul into the Lord's will, and exhibit more than submission, namely, a devout acquiescence in whatever the Lord appoints.

Beloved friends, we must not be content with bearing what the Lord sends, with the coolness which says, "It must be, and, therefore, I *must* put up with it." Such forced submission is far below a Christian grace, for many a heathen has attained it. The stolid stoic accepted what predestination handed out to him, and the Mahometan still does the same. We must go beyond unfeeling submission. We must not so harden our hearts against affliction as not to be affected by it. That chastisement which does not make us smart has failed of its end. It is by the blueness of the wound, says Solomon, that the heart is made better; and if there is no real blueness —if it be merely a surface bruise—little good will come of it. "For a season we are in heaviness," says the apostle, "through manifold trials," and not only the trial, but the heaviness which comes of it, is needful to us. God would not have his children become like the ox or the ass, which present hard skins to hard blows, but he would have us tender and sensitive. There is such a thing as despising the chastening of the Lord, by a defiant attitude which seems to challenge the Lord to draw a tear or fetch a sigh from us. Against this let us be on our guard.

Neither, on the other hand, are we to receive affliction with a rebellious spirit. It is hard for us to kick against the pricks, like the ox which, when goaded, is irritated, and strikes out and drives the iron into itself deeper than it went before. We can easily do this by complaining that God is too severe with us. In this spirit we may "take arms against a sea of troubles;" but by opposing we shall not end them, but increase their raging. By a proud murmuring spirit we only bring upon ourselves trial upon trial; "the Lord resisteth the proud," and a high spirit challenges his opposition.

Neither, dear friends, as believers in God, are we to despair under trouble, for that is not bearing the cross, but lying down under it. We are to take up our appointed burden, and carry it, and not sit down in wicked sullenness, and murmur that we can do no more. Some are in a very naughty frame of mind, their moody spirits mutter that if God will be so severe with them they must yield to it, but they have lost all heart, and all faith, and all they ask for is leave to die. A child of God must not repine. He has not yet "resisted unto blood, striving against sin"; and, if he had, still he should say, "Though he slay me yet will I trust in him." Since Jesus, the man of sorrows, never murmured, it ill becomes any of his followers to do so. We must in patience possess our souls. Perhaps you think it easier for me to say this than it would be to practise it; and yet, by Almighty grace, a saint can bear to the utmost of bearing, to the utmost of suffering he can suffer, to the utmost of loss he can lose, and even to the uttermost of death itself he can die daily, and yet triumph through the divine life, for God, that worketh in us to will and to do, is almighty, and makes our weakness strong.

The Christian, then, is not to treat the cross which God puts upon him in any such way as I have described, but he is to accept it *humbly*, looking up to God, and saying, "Much worse than this I might reckon to receive even as thy child; for the discipline of thine house requireth the rod, and well might I expect to be chastened every morning." The child of God should feel that it is in very faithfulness that the Lord afflicts him, and that every stroke has love in it. Anything over and above the lowest abyss of hell is a great mercy to us. If we had to lie ill for fifty years and scarcely have a minute free from pain, yet since the Lord has pardoned our sins, and accepted us in Christ Jesus, and made us his children, we should be grateful for every pang, and still continue to bless the Lord upon our beds, and sing his high praises in the midst of the fires. Humbly, therefore, as sinners deserving divine wrath, we are bound to accept the chastenings of the Lord.

We should receive chastisement *with meek submission*, presenting ourselves to God that he may do with us still as he has dealt with us—not wishing to start aside to the right hand or to the left: asking him, if it may be his will to remove the load, to heal the pain, to deliver us from the bereavement, and the like, but still always leaving ample margin for full resignation of spirit. The gold is not to rebel against the goldsmith, but should at once yield to be placed in the crucible and thrust into the fire. The wheat as it lies upon the threshing-floor is not to have a will of its own, but to be willing to endure the strokes of the flail that the chaff may be separated from the precious corn. We are not far off being purged from dross and cleansed from chaff when we are perfectly willing to undergo any process which the divine wisdom may appoint us. Self and sin are married, and will never be divorced, and till our self-hood is crushed the seed of sin will still have abundant vitality in it; but when it is "not I" but "Christ that liveth in me," then have we come near to that mark to which God has called us, and to which, by his Spirit, he is leading us.

But we ought to go farther than this. We should accept chastisement *cheerfully*. It is a hard lesson, but a lesson which the Comforter is able to teach us—to be glad that God should have his way. Do you know what it is sometimes to be very pleased to do what you do not like to do? I mean you would not have liked to do it, but you find that it pleases some

one you love, and straightway the irksome task becomes a
pleasure. Have you not felt, sometimes, when one whom you
very much esteem is sick and ill, that you would be glad
enough to bear the pain, at least for a day or two, that you
might give the suffering one a little rest? Would you not find a
pleasure in being an invalid for a while to let your beloved one
enjoy a season of health? Let the same motive, in a higher
degree, sway your spirit! Try to feel, "If it pleases God it
pleases me. If, Lord, it is *thy* will, it shall be *my* will. Let the
lashes of the scourge be multiplied, if so thou shalt be the
more honoured, and I shall be permitted to bring thee some
degree of glory." The cross becomes sweet when our heart is
so sweetened by the Spirit that our will runs parallel with the
will of God. We should learn to say, in the language of Elihu
"I have borne, I do bear, I accept it all." To be as plastic clay
on the potter's wheel, or as wax in the modeller's hand,
should be our great desire. That is the first business of the
sufferer.

*The next duty is to forsake the sin which may have
occasioned the chastisement.* "It is meet to be said unto God, I
have borne chastisement; *I will not offend anymore.*" There is
a connection between sin and suffering in every case. It would
be very wrong for us to suppose that every man who suffers is
therefore more guilty than others: that was the mistake of
Job's friends—a mistake too commonly made every day: but it
is right for the sufferer himself to judge his own case, by a
standard which *we* may not use toward him. He should say,
"Is there not some connection between this chastisement and
sin that dwelleth in me?" And here he must not judge himself
unrighteously, even for God, lest he plunge himself into
unnecessary sorrow. There are afflictions which come from
God, not on account of past sin, but to prevent sin in the
future. There are also sharp prunings which are intended to
make us bring forth more fruit: they are not sent because we
have brought forth no fruit, but because we are fruitful
boughs, and are worth pruning. "Every branch in me that
beareth fruit he purgeth it, that it may bring forth more
fruit." There are also afflictions which are sent by way of test,
and trial, and proof, both for God's glory and for the
manifestation of his power; as also for the comforting of
others, that trembling saints may see how weak and feeble
men can carry the heaviest cross for Christ's sake, and can

triumph under it. We are not to be sure that every sorrow
comes to us because of any sin actually committed; yet it will
be best for us to be more severe with ourselves than we
should think of being with others, and always to ask, "Is there
not some cause for this chastisement? May there not be
something of which God would rid me, or something which
has grieved *him* which has caused him to grieve *me*?"
Brothers and sisters, I charge you never be lenient with
yourselves. The best of us are men at the best, and at our best
we have much to mourn over in the presence of the Most
High. It is good to be always dissatisfied with ourselves, and
pressing forward to a something yet beyond; always praying
that in us Christ's likeness may be completely formed. Thorns
are often put in the nest that we may search for hidden evils.
"Are the consolations of God small with thee? Is there any
secret thing with thee?" Has there been a defeat at Ai? May
there not be an Achan in the camp? Has not a traitor
concealed in some secret place a goodly Babylonish garment
and a wedge of gold? Does not trial give a hint that there may
be something amiss? Beloved, I ask myself and I ask you to
look now, not only to your outward character, but to your
more private life and to your walk before God, and see if there
be not some flaw. Is there trouble in the family? Have you
always acted towards the children and the servants as you
should have done as a master and a father? Question
yourself. The child is grieving you. Have you, good mother,
always been as prayerful about that child as you should have
been? May not your chill's conduct to you be a fair reflection
of your own conduct towards your heavenly Father? I do not
mention any of these things to increase your grief, but in
order that you may put your finger on the evil which provokes
the Lord God, and may put it away. Have there been losses in
business? Are you sure, brother, that when you were making
money you always used it for God as you should? Were you a
good steward? Did you give the Lord his full portion—the
sacred tithe of all that you had? Or may you not have been too
selfish—and may not that be the cause why you must now be
reduced from wealth to comparative poverty? Is that so? Does
the affliction scourge your body? Then has there been
anything wrong with your habits? Has the flesh
predominated over the spirit? Has there been a failure of the
entire consecration of the vessel unto the Lord? Does the trial

occur in the person of some dear one? You may not be conscious of any wrong there, but still look, dear friends! Search the whole of your conduct as the spies searched Canaan of old. If your sin be glaring, there is little need of a chastisement to point it out to you, for you ought to see it without that: but there may be a secret sin between you and your Lord for which he has sent you chastisement, and after this you must raise a hue and cry. You know I do not mean that the Lord is punishing you for sin as a judge punishes a criminal, for he will not do that; since he has laid the punishment of sin upon Christ, and Christ has borne it as a matter of punitive justice. He, as a father, chasteneth his child, but never without a cause: I am urging you to see whether there may not be some cause for the present painful discipline. Never fall into the mistake of some who suppose that sin in God's children is a trifle. Why, if there is any place where sin is horrible it is in a child of God. Hence the text puts it, "I will not *offend* any more." Sin is an offensive thing to God, he cannot bear it. I should dislike a plague spot on anybody's face, but I should tremble to see it most of all upon my own child's face. Sin is more visible in a good man than in any other. I may drop a spot of ink upon a black handkerchief and never see it, but on a white one you will perceive it directly, and see it the more because of the whiteness of the linen which it defiles. You, child of God, know that just in proportion as you are sanctified—in proportion as you live near to God—sin will be grievous to the Most High. It is gloriously terrible to live near to God. I wonder if you understand me, all of you. To walk as a favoured courtier with a monarch is a very delicate matter. Favourites have to pick their steps; for though they stand near a king, they well know how soon they may fall from their high position. We serve a jealous God. That is a wonderful question, "Who among us shall dwell with the devouring fire? Who among us shall dwell with everlasting burnings?" God is that consuming fire. God is the everlasting burnings. Who among us shall dwell with him? The answer is, "He that hath clean hands and a pure heart, he shall dwell on high. His place of defence shall be the munitions of rocks": but it is only the man who is very jealous of himself who will be able to bear that fierce light which beats around the throne of God—that devouring flame which God himself is, as saith the apostle—"Even our God is a consuming fire." Caesar's wife must not only be without fault, but she must be above suspicion, and such must be the character of the child of God who, like Moses, lives in the inner circle—who stands on the mountain top—who knows what the peaks of Sinai mean, and what it is to be forty days in fellowship with the Most High.

Beloved friends, I urge upon you a very close search into what the transgression may be which has brought correction upon you, for it may be in you an offence which would scarcely be sin in anybody else. Another person might fall into your fault as a sin of ignorance, but since you know better the sin is all the blacker in you. The Lord will be sanctified in them that draw near unto him, and woe to them if they defile themselves.

The third lesson in the text to the afflicted clearly teaches them that *it is their duty and privilege to ask for more light.* The text says, "That which I see not teach thou me. If I have done iniquity, I will do no more." Do you see the drift of this? It is the child of God awakened to look after the sin which the chastisement indicates; and since he cannot see all the evil that may be in himself, he turns to his God with this prayer, "What I see not teach thou me."

Beloved friends, it may be that, in looking over your past life and searching through your heart, you do not see your sin, for perhaps it is where you do not suspect. You have been looking in another quarter. Your own opinion is that you are weak in one point, but possibly you are far weaker in the opposite direction. In nothing do men make more mistakes than concerning their own characters. I have known a brother confess that he was deficient in firmness, when, in my opinion, he was about as obstinate as any man I knew. Another man has said that be was always wanting in coolness, and yet I thought that if I needed to fill an ice-well, I had only to put him into it. Persons misjudge themselves. Unfeeling people say they are too sensitive, and selfish persons imagine themselves to be victims to the good of others. So, it may be, you have been looking in one quarter for the sin, while your fault lies in the opposite point of the compass. Pray, then, "Lord, search me and try me, and that which I see not teach thou me." Remember, brethren, that our worst sins may lurk under our holiest things. Oh, how these evils will hide away—not under the docks and nettles of the

dungheap—not they, but under the lilies and the roses of the
garden. In the cups of the flowers they lurk. They do not flit
through our souls like devils with dragons' wings; they fly as
angels of light, with wings tinted as the rainbow. They come
as sheep, and a very fat sort they seem to be, but they are
wolves in sheep's clothing. Watch, therefore, very carefully
against the sins of your holy things. In our holy things we are
nearer to God than at any other time, and hence such
defilement soonest brings upon us the stroke of our heavenly
Father's rod. Perhaps your sin is hidden away under
something very dear to you. Jacob made a great search for the
images—the teraphs which Laban worshipped. He could not
find them. No; he did not like to disturb Rachel, and Laban
did not like to disturb her either—a favourite wife and
daughter must not be inconvenienced. She may sit still on the
camel's furniture, but she hides the images there. Even thus
you do not like to search in a certain quarter of your nature;
it is a very tender subject—something you feel very grieved
about when anybody even hints at it: it is just there that the
sin is harboured. My brethren and sisters, let us be honest
with the Lord. Let us really wish to know where we are
wrong, and heartily long to be set right. Do you think we all
honestly want to know our errors? Are there not chapters of
the Bible which we do not like to read? If there are—if any
text has a quarrel with you, quarrel with yourself; but yield
wholly to the word of God. Is there any doctrine which you
almost think is a truth, but your friends do not believe it, and
they might, perhaps, think you heretical if you were to accept
it, and therefore you dare not investigate any further? Oh,
dear friends, let us be rid of all such dishonesty. So much of it
has got into the church that many will not see things that are
plain as a pikestaff. They will not see, for truth might cost
them too dear. They cover up and hide away some parts of
Scripture which it might be awkward for them to understand,
because of their connection with a church, or their standing in
a certain circle. This is hateful, and we need not wonder if
God smites the man who allows himself in it. Be true,
brother! You cannot deceive God. Do not try it. Ask him to
search you through and through. Let your desire be, "Refining
fire, go through my heart with a mighty flame that shall
devour everything like a lie, everything that is unholy,
selfish, earthly, that I may be fully consecrated unto the Lord

my God." This is the right way in which to treat our chastisements. "If I have done iniquity, I will do no more. That which I see not, teach thou me."

"Alas," says somebody, "we cannot say that we will do no more iniquity." Yes, we can *say* it a great deal more easily than we can practice it, and therefore it is a pity to say it except in the evangelical spirit, leaning entirely on the divine strength. He who says, "I will do no more iniquity" has there and then perpetrated iniquity if he has vowed in his own strength, for he has exalted himself into the place of God by self-confidence. Yet we must feel in our inmost hearts that we desire to depart from all iniquities. There must be an earnest and hearty intent that, as Paul shook off the viper into the fire, so will we, as God helps us, shake off the sin, whatever it may be, which brings us the trial, or that causes the Lord to take away the light of his countenance from us. Oh, how earnestly would I urge my dear tried brothers and sisters to seek after this excellent fruit of affliction. May it come to every one of us according as the affliction comes, that we may never miss the sweet fruit of this bitter tree. God bless you who are tried, and support you under your griefs; but, above all, may he sanctify you through tribulation, for that is the main point, and it little matters how sharp the flames if you are purified by the fire.

II. And now, briefly, I am going to use the text for THOSE OF US WHO MAY NOT HAVE BEEN AFFLICTED. What does the text say to us if we are not afflicted? Does it not say this—"If the afflicted man is to say 'I bear,' and to take up his yoke cheerfully, *how cheerfully ought you and I to take up the daily yoke of our Christian labor*"? Brother, sister, do you ever grow weary? Does the Sunday-school tax you too much? Is that Bible-class becoming somewhat a heaviness? That house-to-house visitation—has it become a drudgery? That distribution of tracts—is there a great sameness and tedium about it? Now look, my brother, look at yonder dear saint of God who has been for months upon his bed till the feathers have grown hard beneath him. He shifts from side to side but finds no ease—no sleep at night, no respite by day. Would you like to change places with him? Yet hear how he praises God amidst his many pains, and abundant weaknesses, and poverty. Do you prefer your lot to his? Well, then, in the name of everything that is good, accept your portion with joy, and throw your soul into the Lord's service. The great Captain might say to you, "What! tired of marching! I will send you back to the trenches, and let you lie there till you feel sick at heart of your inactivity. What! weary of fighting! You shall be put into the hospital with broken bones and made to lie there and pine, and see what you think of enforced inactivity." If I have any message to give from my own bed of sickness it would be this—if you do not wish to be full of regrets when you are obliged to lie still, work while you can. If you desire to make a sick bed as soft as it can be, do not stuff it with the mournful reflection that you wasted time while you were in health and strength. People said to me years ago, "You will break your constitution down with preaching ten times a week," and the like. Well, if I have done so, I am glad of it. I would do the same again. If I had fifty constitutions I would rejoice to break them down in the service of the Lord Jesus Christ. You young men that are strong, overcome the wicked one and fight for the Lord while you can. You will never regret having done all that lies in you for our blessed Lord and Master. Crowd as much as you can into every day, and postpone no work till to-morrow. "Whatsoever thy hand findeth to do, do it with thy might."

We have yet another remark for those that are strong. *Should not the favours of God lead us to search out our sins?* Chastisement acts like a black finger to point out our failures: ought not the love of God to do the same with its hand glittering with jewels? Lord, dost thou give me good health? Lord, dost thou spare my wife and my children to me? Dost thou give me of substance enough and to spare? Then, Lord, is there anything about me that might grieve thee? Do I harbour anything in my soul that might vex thy Spirit? Let thy love guide me that I may escape from these evils. It is a sweet text—"I will guide thee with mine eye. Be ye not as the horse, or as the mule, which have no understanding: whose mouth must be held in with bit and bridle, lest they come near unto thee." Your child only needs a glance of the eye, and he runs to you; but your horse and mule will not do that, you must put a bit into their mouths, and some of them must have very hard bits, and their mouths must be made very tender before they can be guided. You are men, do not be as the beasts are. Yet some of God's own children are very brutish. They will not obey his words, and so their God has to give them blows, for he will have his children obey him: if they will be drawn with cords of love so they shall be, but if they will not, they shall he driven with the rod. If you make yourselves horses and mules be will treat you like horses and mules, or you will have reason to think so; perhaps the best way to prevent you becoming altogether mulish is to treat you as if you were a mule, and so drive you out of it, by letting you see the effect of your folly. Let our mercies act as a sweet medicine, and then we shall not need bitter potions.

Once again. Do you not think that while enjoying God's mercy we should be anxious to be searched by the light of the love of God? Should we not wish to use the light of the divine countenance that we may discover all our sin and overcome it? I know some Christians who will not come to this point. They have an ugly temper, and they say, "Well, you know, that is constitutional." Away for ever with such wicked self-excusing. It is idle to say, "I cannot help it, it is my temperament." Your temperament will destroy you, as surely as you live, if the grace of God does not destroy your temperament. If such excuses were permitted there is no crime, however abominable, for which temperament might not be pleaded. Thieves, harlots, drunkards, murderers might all set up this justification, for they all have their evil temperaments. Do you find in the law that any sin is excused upon the ground that it is "constitutional?" Do you find anything in the example of Christ, or in the precepts of the gospel, to justify a man in saying, "I must be treated with indulgence, for my nature is so inclined to a certain sin that I cannot help yielding to it"? My brother, you must not talk such nonsense. Your first business is to conquer the sin you love best; against it all your efforts, and all the grace you can get must be levelled. Jericho must be first besieged, for it is the strongest fort of the enemy, and until it is taken nothing can be done. I have generally noticed in conversion that the most complete change takes place in that very point in which the man was constitutionally most weak. God's strength is made perfect in our weakness. "Well," cries one, "suppose I have a besetting sin, how can I help it?" I reply, if I knew that four fellows were going to beset me to-night on Clapham Common, I should take with me sufficient policemen to lock the fellows up. When a man knows that he has a besetting sin it is not for him to say, "It is a besetting sin and I cannot help it;" he must, on the other hand, call for heavenly assistance against these besetments. If you have besetting sins, and you know it, fight with them, and overcome them by the blood of the Lamb. By faith in Jesus Christ, besetting sins go to be led captive and they must be led captive, for the child of God must overcome even to the end. He is to be more than conqueror through him that has loved him. Let the love of God, then, lead you to search yourselves and say, "That which I see not teach thou me. If I have done iniquity, I will do no more."

III. The last remark I have to make is to THE UN-CONVERTED. Perhaps there are some here who are not the people of God, and yet they are very happy and prosperous. They have all that heart can wish, and as they hear me talk about God's children being chastened, they say, "I do not want to be one of them, if such is their portion." You would rather be what you are, would you? "Yes," say you. Hearken! We will suppose that we have before us a prince of the blood who will one day be a king. He has been doing something wrong, and his father has chastened him with the rod. There stands the young prince with the tears running down his cheeks; and over yonder is a street arab, who has no father that he knows of—certainly none that ever chastened him for his good. He may do what he likes—use any sort of language—steal, lie, swear, if he likes, and no one will chasten him. He stands on his head, or makes wheels in the streets, or rolls in the dirt, but no father ever holds a rod over him. He sees this little prince crying, and he laughs at him, "You don't have the liberty I do. You are not allowed to stand on your head as I do. Your father wouldn't let you beg for coppers by the side of the omnibuses as I do. You don't sleep under an arch all night as I do. I would not be you to catch that thrashing! I would sooner be a street-boy than a prince!" Your little prince very soon wipes his eyes, and answers, "Go along with you. Why, I would rather be chastened every day and be a prince and heir to a kingdom, than I would be you with all your fine liberty!" He looks down upon the ragged urchin with the greatest conceivable pity, even though he himself is smarting from the rod. Now, sinners, that is just what we think of you and your freedom from heavenly discipline. When you are merriest and happiest, and fullest of your joy, we would not be you for the world; when you have been electrified by that splendid spectacle at the theater, or have enjoyed yourself so much in a licentious dance, or, perhaps, in something worse, we would not be as you are. Take us at our worst—when we are most sick, most desponding, most tried, most penitent before God, we would not exchange with you at your best. Would we change with you, for all your mirth and sinful hilarity? No, *that* we would not! Ask the old woman in the winter time, who has only a couple of sticks to make a fire with, and has nothing to live upon but what the tender mercy of the parish allows her, ask her if she would change with Dives in his purple and fine linen. Look at her. She puts on an old red cloak to shelter her poor limbs, which are as full of rheumatism as they can be; the cupboard is bare, her poor husband lies in the churchyard, and she has not a child to come and see her. Ah, there she is. You say, "She is a miserable object." Here is the young squire in his top-boots, coming home from the hunt. He is standing in front of her. He might say to her, with all his large possessions and broad acres, "You would change with me, mother, would you not?" She knows his character, and she knows that he has no love to God, and no union to Christ, and therefore she replies, "Change with you? no, that I would not, for a thousand worlds."

> "Go you that boast of all your stores,
>   And tell how bright they shine;
> Your heaps of glittering dust are yours,
>   But my Redeemer's mine."

I have yet another word for you that fear not God. I wish you would reflect for a moment what will become of you one of these days. God loves his dear children very much: he loves them so much that Jesus died to save them, and yet he does not spare them when they sin, but he chastens them with the rod of men. Now, if he does so with his children, what will he do with you who are his enemies? If judgment begins at the house of God—if when his anger does but gently smoke it is so hot—what will it be when the winds of justice fan it to a furious flame? As when the fire sets the forests of the mountains burning, or as when the vast prairie becomes one sheet of fire, so shall it be in that dread day when God shall launch out all his vengeance against the sins of the ungodly. I beseech you, think of this. He spared not his own Son, but put

him to a cruel death upon the tree for the sins of others: will
he spare his enemies, think you, who have rebelled against
him, and rejected his mercy, when he visits them for their
own personal sins? "Beware, ye that forget God, lest he tear
you in pieces, and there be none to deliver you."

One only thought, for I must not send you away with that
terrible warning and no gospel encouragement. Learn a
lesson from the Lord's children. When his children are
chastened they submit, and when they submit they obtain
peace. Sinner, I pray you, learn wisdom; and if you have been
troubled of late, if you have had trials from God, yield to him,
yield to him. Old Master Quarles gives a quaint picture of a
man who is striking at an enemy with a flail. The person
assaulted runs right into the striker's arms, and so escapes
the force of the stroke, and Quarles adds the remark, "The
farther off the heavier the blow." Sinner, run in, run into
God's bosom to-night. Say "I will arise and go unto my
Father." God will not smite you if you come there. How can
he? The Lord says, "Let him take hold of my strength." When
that arm is lifted to scourge you, lay hold of it. Lay hold upon
that arm of strength as it is revealed in Jesus Christ, for in
him God hath made bare his holy arm in the eyes of all the
people. Hang on the arm that else might smite you. Trust in
the Lord, sinner, through Jesus Christ, the atoning sacrifice,
and you shall find peace with him. Ask him with humble
submission to put away the sin that has made you suffer, and
has nearly cost you your soul. Pray him to search you, and
find out the sin. Repent and believe the gospel. Forsake evil
and cling to the Saviour, the great Physician who heals the
disease of sin, and you shall live. Come now to your Father's
home. Those rags, that hungry belly, those swine and filthy
troughs, those citizens that would not help you, that blandest
of all citizens whose only kindness lay in degrading you lower
than you were before—all these are sent to fetch you home.
Believe it, soul, and say, "I will arise and go unto my Father,
and will say unto him, Father I have sinned"; and while you
are yet saying it you shall have the kiss of his love, the
embraces of his affection, the robe of his righteousness, and
the fatted calf of spiritual food, and there shall be merriment
concerning you, both on earth and in heaven. The Lord bless
you, for Jesus' sake. Amen.

21

Conceit Rebuked

"Should it be according to thy mind?"   **Job 34:33**

Elihu had thought that Job spoke too boastfully, and that there was too much of self about him, and, therefore, he reproved him by asking this question, "Should it be according to thy mind?" It is a question which, in the original, has a great wealth of meaning in it; and as the language of the Book of Job is extremely ancient, and very sententious, it is not easy to get the fulness of Elihu's meaning. But it has been said that, upon the whole, our translation not only gives the meaning of his enquiry, but also more of the meaning than can be conveyed in any other words, so that we may be perfectly satisfied with it, and may pray God the Holy Spirit to apply it to us; and if we have grown to be high and mighty, and have begun to criticize the way of God in dealing with us, this question may come to us very sharply, "'Should it be according to thy mind?' Should everything be arranged just to suit thy whims and wishes? Should everything in the world be fashioned according to thy taste, and the whole globe revolve just to serve thy turn, and please thy fancy? 'Should it be according to thy mind?'"

There are four things I am going to say concerning our text; and first, I shall ask, *Are there really any people in the world who think that everything should be according to their mind?* Then, secondly, I shall enquire, *what leads them to that notion?* Thirdly, I shall try to show you *what a mercy it is that they cannot have everything according to their mind;* and then, fourthly, I shall urge you *to keep this evil spirit in check,* so that, henceforth, you will not wish that things should be according to your mind.

I. Our first question has a measure of astonishment about it. ARE THERE REALLY ANY PEOPLE IN THE WORLD WHO WOULD HAVE EVERYTHING ACCORDING TO THEIR MIND? Oh yes, there are such people! I should not wonder if there are some of them here now; in fact, I question whether we have not, all of us, at times, drunk very deeply into this naughty, haughty spirit. If we have done so, may we be speedily delivered from it!

First, *there are some people who would have God himself according to their mind.* Now, as a matter of fact, all that I can know of God I must learn from God revealing himself to me. I cannot discover him by myself; he must unveil himself to me, and that he has done in Holy Scripture. All that he intends us to know about himself he has revealed in the written Word and in the Incarnate Word, his ever-blessed Son. But there are some people who get their idea of God out of themselves. You may have heard of the German philosopher who evolved the idea of a camel out of his own consciousness; at least, so he said. I do not think it was much like a camel when he had evolved it; but there are many persons who try to evolve the idea of God out of their own consciousness. It cannot be, they say, that certain statements in the Bible are true, because there is something or other, in their inner consciousness, that contradicts the Scriptural declarations. God, as they believe in him, is what they think he ought to be, not what he really is. And there are some, in these days, who have even gone so far as to reject the Old Testament altogether because its teaching concerning God does not meet the approval of their very marvellous minds. Practically, these people are idolaters, for an idolater is one who makes a god unto himself. The true worshipper of God— the accepted worshipper—is one who worships God as he is, and as he reveals himself in his Word; but there are many persons, who make a god out of their own thoughts. The teachers of the modern school of theology work in a kind of god-factory. The people in some heathen lands make their gods out of mud, but these men make their gods out of their own thought, their imagination, their "intellect." That is what they call it, though I am not sure that it is that organ which is at work in this instance. But when a man makes a god of thought, he is just as much an idolater as if he had made a god of wood or of gold. The true God—the God of Scripture— thus revealed himself to his ancient people, "I am the Lord thy God, which have brought thee out of the land of Egypt, out of the house of bondage." This God is our God, "the God of

Abraham, and the God of Isaac, and the God of Jacob," "the God of the whole earth shall he be called." Many a man refuses to accept this God as his; but I should like to ask him, "Should God be according to thy mind?" That would be a strange god indeed. Should he have no other attributes but such as thou wouldst give to him? Should his character and conduct be only such as thou canst comprehend and justify? Must there be nothing in him that shall puzzle thee? Are there to be no divine deeps that shall be beyond the reach of thy finite mind? Are there to be no heights beyond thy power to soar? That is what seems to be thy notion; and if there is anything that staggers thee a little, thou sayest, "I cannot believe it." If it were possible, thou wouldst eliminate from the character of God everything that is stern and terrible; though these attributes clearly appertain to the Most High as he has been pleased to reveal himself in Scripture. I beg you, dear friends, never to attempt to mould the character of God with the fingers of your own fancy. Worship him just as he is, though thou canst not comprehend him. Believe in him as he reveals himself, and never imagine that thou couldst, by making any change in him, effect an improvement in him. By toning down his justice, thou thinkest that thou art increasing his love; and, by denying his righteous vengeance, thou dost imagine that thou art honouring his goodness; but, instead of doing so by the removal of these things which alarm and annoy thee,—if thou couldst do so,—thou wouldst take away part of God's grandeur and strength which make his goodness and his mercy to shine so brightly as they now do. Leave God just as he is, remembering how he has said, "For as the heavens are higher than the earth, so are my ways higher than your ways, and my thoughts than your thoughts." The infinite God must be past finding out by the creatures whom he hath made. I confess that it is one of my greatest joys to find myself completely baffled when I am trying to comprehend the character of God. Sometimes, when I have tried to preach upon the Deity of Christ, I have been fairly staggered under the burden of that stupendous truth, and I have felt the utter uselessness and poverty of human language to describe our great and terrible yet loving Lord; and I have been glad to have it so; for, verily, God is altogether above our comprehension, and none of us can speak of him as he deserves to be spoken of; but never let us try in any way to diminish his glorious perfections.

A more common way of offending against God, and setting up our self-will, is by *quarreling with his providential dealings.* If anyone here is doing so, let me ask, "Should it be according to thy mind?" You look, sometimes, upon the arrangements of providence on a great scale in reference to the nations of the earth,—you see them at war with one another, and you note how slow is the progress of civil and religious liberty, and how few there are to rally in defence of right principles. Sometimes, you get greatly distressed about the general state of affairs, and you wish you could alter it; but the Lord looks down from his eternal throne, and he seems to say to you, "Should it be according to thy mind?" The world was wisely ordered by God before we were born, and it will be equally well ordered by him after we are dead. When Alexander Peden, the Covenanter, was dying, he sent for one of his brethren, a fellow-minister of the Word—James Renwick; and he bade him stand out in the room, and turn his back to his departing friend. When he had done so, Peden said to him, "I have looked at thee, and I perceive that thou are only a little man, and thou hast but feeble shoulders and weak legs." "Yes," replied Renwick, "that is true, but wherefore hast thou made that observation?" "Because," said Peden, "I perceive that thou canst not, after all, carry the whole world upon thy back; thou art not made for any such work as that;" and I may say of all of us who are here that we were not made to carry the world on our backs. Yet some of us attempt to play the part of Atlas, and not only try to carry the world, but seek to set the church right as well. We fancy that we can do that, poor worms that we are, but the Lord knows that we can do nothing of the kind. "He remembereth that we are dust," though we are apt to forget it ourselves. Well, beloved, after all, "should it be according to thy mind?" Wilt thou, like Jonah, sit pining, and mourning, and complaining? Does not the eternal Ruler understand the politics of nations, and the best way of governing the world, infinitely better than thou dost? Do not thou attempt to drive the horses of the sun; thy puny hands are unfit for so tremendous a task as that. Leave all things with God; they are ordered well so long as they are ordered by him.

Probably, however, it is with the minor providence that we more often quarrel when we are in an ill state of heart. You think that you would like to be rich, yet you are poor. "Should it be according to thy mind?" You would have liked to be healthy and strong, but you are weak and sickly, or you have a suffering limb that troubles you, and you sometimes think, "Mine is a very hard lot; I wish it could be altered." "Should it be according to thy mind?" Should the fashioning of thyself and thy circumstances have been left to thee? What thinkest thou? Possibly, you have recently sustained a great loss in business, and you cannot quite get over it. "Should it be according to thy mind?" Should providential circumstances have been arranged otherwise so as to suit thee? Should God have stopped the great machinery of the universe, and put it out of gear in order to prevent thee from losing a few pounds? "Should it be according to thy mind?"

Perhaps it is worse than that; a dear child has been taken away just when he had become most closely entwined around thy heart. Thou wouldst fain have kept him with thee; but was it right that he should go, or right that he should stay? Come now, there is a difference of opinion between thee and God, who is in the right? Should it be according to his mind, or according to thy mind? "Ah!" says someone else, "it is the mainstay of the home who has been taken away from us,—the husband, the father of the family." Well, though it is so, again I ask, concerning this bereavement, or any other trial that comes to you, "Should it be according to thy mind?" It should be sufficient for you to know that the Lord has permitted it, or actually performed it.

Should it be according to thy mind, or according to his mind? It is not easy, I know, to submit without murmuring to all that happens to us. I am probably touching very tender places in many who, at divers times and seasons, have really felt that God, in his providential dealings with them, had been unkind to them, or that, at least, he had been showing his kindness in a very strange way.

There are some, who carry this difference between them and God into another sphere; for *they do not approve of the gospel as it is taught in the Bible.* You know that the gospel, as revealed in the New Testament, is so simple that a child can understand it; and you may go and teach it to the poorest and the most illiterate, and many of them will leap at it, and grasp it at once. But there are others who think that it should be something which is much more difficult to understand, something which would need a higher order of intellect than the common people possess. Do you really think so, my dear sir? "Should it be according to thy mind?" Wouldst thou shut out the poor and the needy, and the illiterate, from the privileges of the gospel, and keep them to thyself, and to a few others who have been highly educated? Surely not. O brethren, if it were possible for us to preach a gospel that we had made obscure, or which could only be comprehended by the *élite* of society, we should soon have cause sadly to deplore before God that we had lost that simple, blessed, plain way of instruction which the wayfaring man, though a fool, can understand, and in which he need not err.

Many try to trim down the doctrines of grace. They would get rid of election if they could. Anything like the speciality of the atonement of Christ they cannot bear. The sweet and blessed doctrine of effectual calling they abhor, and they would fain make a gospel of their own. But should they want to do so? Is it not your duty and mine, brother, rather to try to find out what the gospel really is than to seek to make it what we consider it ought to be? "Should it be according to thy mind?" We have known some people take a text of Scripture, and because it did not square with the system in which they were brought up, they tried to cut it down to make it fit in with their notions; but, sirs, is not the gospel grander than any of our comprehensions of it? Are there not in it great truths that cannot be cut down to fit any system that the human mind can make? And ought we not to be thoroughly glad that it is so? For, surely, it is better that the gospel should be according to God's mind than that it should be according to the mind of Toplady, or the mind of Wesley, or the mind of Calvin, or the mind of Arminius! The mind of God is greater than all the minds of men, so let all men leave the gospel just as God has delivered it unto us.

Sometimes, this difference comes up *concerning the Church of Christ.* Some people do not like God's order of church-membership and church-government; they would like to see the world welcomed inside the church. They do not approve of the ordinances as they were instituted and observed by our Lord Jesus Christ; believers' baptism is peculiarly objectionable to them. Sometimes, they disapprove of God's ministers; they pick holes in the most useful of them; this man ought to be so-and-so, and that other man ought to be

something else. I can only ask again, with regard to the whole
matter, "Should it be according to thy mind?" Are you to make
the ministers, and to teach them what they are to preach? Are
they your servants or God's servants, and are they to deliver
their message in your way or in God's way? Let the question
be honestly considered, and then, perhaps, much of the
murmuring that is sometimes heard, and much of the discord
that often arises among professing Christians, would be
cleared away. For, surely, these things should not be
according to our mind; but we should let God appoint, and
equip, and send forth his own servants just as he pleases, and
not as we please. Christ must decide everything concerning
his own Church; he must be free to choose whom he likes to
be members of it, and to fashion his Church after his own
model.

II. Now, secondly, we are to enquire—WHAT LEADS PEOPLE
TO THINK THAT EVERYTHING SHOULD BE ACCORDING TO THEIR
MIND?

My answer is, first, that *there is a great deal of self-
importance in such a notion.* There are some people who seem
to fancy that they are the centre of the whole universe. The
times are always bad if they do not prosper. If the earth does
not so revolve as to bring grist to their mill, then the times
must be out of joint. But who are you, dear friend, that you
should suppose that for you suns rise and set, that for you
seasons change, and that God is to have respect to you, and to
nobody else? "Should it be according to thy mind?" Then, if so,
why not according to my mind also? And why not according to
the mind of another brother? And why not according to the
mind of yet another? But no, it is according to thy mind that
thou wouldst have it. Ah, does not this show what
overweening importance we attach to ourselves? We are mere
ephemera, creeping insects upon the bay-leaf of existence,—
here to-day, and gone to-morrow,—yet we suppose that all
things are to be ordered for our special benefit, and we
quarrel with God if we suffer even a little inconvenience.

This notion also arises from *self-conceit.* We really seem to
fancy that we could arrange things much better than they
now are; we would not dare plainly to say so, much less would
we be willing to write it; but we talk and feel as if it were
really so. If we only had had the ordering of things, we are
quite sure that they would not have happened as they have

done; but then, depend upon it, they would have happened wrongly if they had been other than they have been. "Should it be according to thy mind?" No; unless thou art self-conceited enough to put thy folly in comparison with the wisdom of God, thou knowest that it should not be according to thy mind.

Then there is *the spirit of murmuring* that so easily comes upon us; we have known some who really became slaves to that evil spirit. They complained of everything, nothing was right in their eyes; it was not possible, it seemed, even for God himself to please them. "Should it be according to thy mind?" How would it be possible to please one who is so changeable, so whimsical, so fanciful, as thou art? Poor simpleton; surely thou canst not think that such a thing should be.

But, oftentimes, this quarrel arises from *want of faith in God.* If we did but believe in him, we should see that all things are ordered well. If we did but trust in God as a loving child trusts in its father, we should feel safe enough at all times, and we should not want to have anything different from what it is. Have you never heard of the woman, who was in a great storm at sea, and terribly frightened? She saw her husband, who was the captain of the ship, perfectly composed even while the vessel was tossed about by the mighty billows, but he could not calm her troubled heart. So he drew a sword from its scabbard, and held it close to her breast. As he did so, he said to her, "Do you not tremble, my wife?" "No," she replied, "I am not in the least afraid." "But this sword is close to you." "I am not afraid of that," said she, "because it is in my husband's hand." "Well," said he, "is it not even so with this storm? Is it not in the hand of God; and if it be in his hand, why should we be alarmed?" So, if we have true faith in God, we shall accept whatever God sends us, and we shall not want to have things arranged according to our mind, but we shall quite agree with what his mind ordains.

So would it be, too, if you had *more love to God,* for love always agrees with that which its object delights in. So, dear friends, when we come to love God with a perfect heart, we are glad for God to have his way with us. If he wills that we should be sick, we would not wish to be otherwise. If he wills that we should be poor, we are willing to be poor, and if he wills that we should pass through a sea of trial, we would not wish to have a drop less than his blessed will appoints.

III. But now, thirdly, WHAT A MERCY IT IS THAT THINGS ARE
NOT ACCORDING TO OUR MIND! If they were, I wonder what
sort of world we should live in.

If things were according to our mind, *God's glory would be
obscured.* He knows what will best glorify him, and he has
been pleased to so arrange his providential dealings with men
that all shall glorify him to the highest possible degree. And,
beloved, if we were to alter anything of this, if we could altar
anything, it is evident that the glory of God would not be so
well promoted; so, "should it be according to thy mind" that
God should lose a measure of the glory that is due unto his
name? God forbid!

If it were according to our mind, *others could often have to
suffer.* At any rate, if things were arranged according to the
mind of some people, they would grind the poor in the dust,
and utterly crush them. If things were settled according to the
mind of man, we should often be in a terrible plight. Did not
David say to God, "Let us fall now into the hand of the Lord;
for his mercies are great: and let me not fall into the hand of
man"? When God is most grieved with his people, he never
deals with them in so harsh a manner as the ungodly would
deal with them if they had them in their power. Let us trust
in the Lord, my brethren, and thank him that he does not
allow things to be according to the mind of man, for it would
be terrible indeed for us then.

Here is another reflection. If things were according to our
mind, *we should have an awful responsibility resting upon us,*
because we should feel that, if anything went amiss, we
should be the cause of it. If we had the choosing of our
circumstances, and the details of all that happened to us, we
should straightway feel that we should be called to account
for everything by our fellow-men and by our own conscience.
But now that it is according to the mind of God, you have no
responsibility concerning it. If it be according to his will, it
must be that which is right, and that which is best; so let us
bless his name that all things are left at his disposal.

If things were according to our mind, I am afraid *our
temptations would soon be greatly increased;* for many who
are poor would speedily become rich, and they do not know
what the temptation of riches might be, nor the grace they
would need to resist it. And some, who are sick now, and are
praising God upon their sick-beds, if they were well, might

find much of their spirituality departing, and they might be thrown into a thousand troubles which they now escape in the quiet of their own room. Some of you are in a condition of life where you may not have many comforts; but, on the other hand, you are not subject to those trials which come to us who are prominent in public life. Be sure that you are in your right place if God put you there. "Should it be according to thy mind?" If so, thou wouldst have more temptations, and less grace;—more of the world, but less of thy Lord. So, thank him that it is not according to thy mind.

If it were according to our mind, *we should seldom know our own mind.* If a man could manage everything as he liked, he would not long like his own management. Unrenewed men, especially, are never satisfied. The way for a man to be happy is not to have his own will, but to sink his will in the will of God. Look at Solomon when he had his own way. At one time, he gave all his thoughts to grand buildings; and when he had built his palaces, he got quite tired, so he took to making gardens, and aqueducts, and fountains of water. When he had made them, he did not get much satisfaction out of them, so he gat him instruments of music, and singing men and singing women, but he was soon tired of them. Then he took to study, but he said, "Of making many books there is no end; and much study is a weariness of the flesh." He had whatever he chose to have, yet it was all vanity and vexation of spirit to him; and he never had what filled his soul till he came to rest alone in his God, which, we trust, he did in his old age. I do not know a more horrible endowment that a man could have than for God to say to him, "Everything shall be as you like to have it." He would probably be the most miserable and most dissatisfied person under heaven. "Should it be according to thy mind?" Ah, then, sin would go uncorrected in thee, for thou wouldst never have a mind to use the rod! Then thy dross would remain, for thou wouldst never have a mind to be put into the furnace. Should all things go with thee according to thine own will, then thy flesh would get the mastery over thee, and be pampered and indulged; thou wouldst be settled on thy lees, and not emptied from vessel to vessel, and thou wouldst bring upon thyself unutterable woe. O beloved, for this reason also it is a thousand mercies that things are not arranged according to the mind of even the best saint out of heaven except when his mind is brought into full subjection to the will of God.

"Should it be according to thy mind?" Then *there would be universal strife.* If this were the case, think what a terrible condition the Church of God, and the world, too, would soon be brought into, because, as I have already hinted, if it were according to your mind, why should it not be according to my mind, or according to the mind of every other body? Then, what chaos, what confusion there would be! How would the world be managed if you, and I, and fifty others, each one with a different mind from all the rest, must have it according to our minds? It would mean that the King of heaven must resign his throne, and give place to universal anarchy. It could not be; it would be impossible that such an arrangement should continue for an hour. We should have to go, in tears, before the Lord, and cry to him, "O Lord, come back, and reign over us, for we cannot get on without thee! Everything is going to destruction for want of an almighty will to manage it." Should it be according to thy mind?" No, Lord never let it be so except when thou hast made my mind to be filled with thy mind, and then it shall be well. "I always have my way," said a holy man. "How is that?" asked one who heard him, and the good man replied, "Because God's way is my way." "I always have my will," said another, and he gave a similar explanation, "because it is my will that God should have his will." When God's will gets to be your will, then it may be according to your mind; but not till then, thank God, not till then.

IV. So now, in the last place, dear friends, I am going to say to you, let us try, by the help of God's Holy Spirit, to CHECK THAT SPIRIT WHICH LEADS MEN TO THINK THAT ALL THINGS SHOULD BE ACCORDING TO THEIR MIND.

First, *because it is impracticable.* As I have already shown you, it is quite impossible that all things should be according to the mind of men so long as their mind is in its natural carnal state.

Again, *it is unreasonable* that it should be so. In a well-ordered house, whose will ought to be supreme? Should it not be the father's? Do you expect everything in your home to be ordered according to the will of your little boy? No, you know that you take a comprehensive view of all who are in the house, and all their concerns, and you are better able to judge than he is what is right. It would be very unreasonable for your child to say, "Everything is to be managed according to my will." If he were to talk like that, you would soon teach him better, I warrant you; and it is unreasonable to imagine that the Lord should make your will to be the rule of his dispensations. Do not cultivate a spirit which you cannot justify by any sensible and reasonable arguments.

In the next place, *it is un-Christlike.* "Should it be according to thy mind?" Why, if ever there was a Son of the great Father, according to whose mind things should be, it was our blessed Lord Jesus Christ; yet what did he say? "Not as I will, but as thou wilt." And as Jesus said, "Not as I will," is there one among us who shall dare to say, "Let it be as I will?" Will you not join your Elder Brother in that sweet resignation of all desire to be the ruler, in order that the great Father, who filleth all things, may have his way? If you wish to have all things according to your mind, you are not like Christ; for in all things he did the Father's will, and suffered the Father's will, too, and rejoiced in it. Let us pray the Holy Spirit to help us to do the same.

Once more, if we desire to have our own mind, *it is atheistic;* for a god without a controlling mind is no god, and a god, whose will was not carried out, would be no god. If you were to have your way in all things, you would be taking the place of God; do you not tremble at the very thought of it? His throne ill beseems you. Would you—

> "Snatch from his hand the balance and the rod,
> Rejudge his judgments, be the God of God"?

If you are truly converted, you shudder at the bare mention of such a thing as that. Yet, dear sister, was not that the spirit in which you came into this house? Did you not feel, "The Lord has dealt very hardly with me; I can scarcely be reconciled to him"? Oh, drop that rebellious spirit! Thou art but a poor, helpless creature, and he is God over all. Let his supreme will sweetly rule thy heart at this hour; and labour to get rid of that waywardness and that revolting from the Most High. I knew one, who was in mourning many, many years for a child; and a good Quaker said to her, "Friend, hast thou not forgiven God yet?" There are some to whom we might put the same question; and we have heard of some, who professed to be Christians, who, when they met with a very terrible reverse, said they never should understand it,—

meaning really that they should never acquiesce in the divine will about that loss. It must not be so with us. Whenever a child falls out with his father, the best thing he can do is to fall in again; for a sullen child, who is angry with his father, will have to come round if he has a wise father. The father will say to him, "My dear boy, there is one of us who must alter before we can be perfectly agreed; and I cannot, for I know I am in the right. It is you who must alter, and come round to my way of thinking." And if you have fallen out with God by wilfulness and stubbornness, he cannot come round to you, but you will have to come back to him. So yield to him at once; bow down before him,—your own Father in heaven, who loves you infinitely. Do you mean to say that you will keep up the quarrel with him? You began the dispute, and you know that you are in the wrong, and that he is right; so say, "It is the Lord; let him do what seemeth him good." Or if you cannot say as much as that, at least do what Aaron did in his great bereavement, "Aaron held his peace," or what David did when he said, "I was dumb, I opened not my mouth; because thou didst it." Oh, for that blessed silence which springs from acquiescence in the divine will!

I should like you to go further than that, however, and even to praise and bless the Lord for poverty, and pain, and bereavement. In heaven, among the sweetest notes of your song, will be those you sing over your trials here below. There was one who lost his eyesight, but he always praised God for that, for he said that he never saw till he was blind. I have heard of another, who had lost a leg, and he said that he never stood on the Rock of Ages till he had that leg amputated. We, who are branches of the true Vine, will have more of Christ's sharp pruning-knife than of anything else; but let us praise and bless God for it, and henceforth labour, by the Spirit's power, to chase out of our soul the idea that things should be according to our mind. Get away to thy room, and confess thy wilfulness and pride, dear brother, if thou hast fallen into that sad state. Ask the Lord to make thy soul even as a weaned child,—

> "Pleased with all the Lord provides,
> Weaned from all the world besides."

I know that I have been speaking to some who do not love the Lord. I wonder what it is that keeps them where they now are,—out of Christ. You want something to be altered, you say. Well, ask the Lord to alter you, for that is the alteration that is needed. The plan of salvation does not quite suit you. Well, there will never be another. Does not Jesus Christ please you? God will never lay another foundation for a sinner to build his hopes upon, so you had better be pleased with God's way, and build upon Christ Jesus, the sure foundation stone. We tell people, sometimes, that they had better not fall out with their living; and I can tell you, soul, that you had better not fall out with your salvation. God's way of saving you is the best conceivable way, and it is also the only way. He says that whosoever believeth on the Lord Jesus Christ shall not perish, but shall have everlasting life. May the Eternal Spirit bring you now to believe in the Lord Jesus; and if you do so believe, you shall be saved at once. But do not think that the plan of salvation will be altered to please you. It will not be made according to your mind. There is the gospel; have it or leave it, but alter it you cannot. May the Lord grant that you may accept it, and rejoice in it, for his dear Son's sake! Amen.

22

Songs in the Night

"But none saith, Where is God my maker, who giveth songs in the night?"   Job 35:10

Elihu was a wise man, exceeding wise, though not as wise as the all-wise Jehovah, who sees light in the clouds, and finds order in confusion; hence Elihu, being much puzzled at beholding Job so afflicted, cast about him to find the cause of it, and he very wisely hit upon one of the most likely reasons, although it did not happen to be the right one in Job's case. He said within himself, "Surely, if men are sorely tried and troubled, it is because, while they think about their troubles, and distress themselves about their fears, they do not say, 'Where is God my Maker, who giveth songs in the night?'" Elihu's reason is right in the majority of cases. The great cause of a Christian's distress, the reason of the depths of sorrow into which many believers are plunged, is simply this—that while they are looking about, on the right hand and on the left, to see how they may escape their troubles, they forget to look to the hills whence all real help cometh; they do not say, "Where is God my Maker, who giveth songs in the night?"

We shall, however, leave that inquiry, and dwell upon those sweet words, "God my Maker, who giveth songs in the night." The world hath its night. It seemeth necessary that it should have one. The sun shineth by day, and men go forth to their labours; but they grow weary, and nightfall cometh on, like a sweet boon from heaven. The darkness draweth the curtains, and shutteth out the light, which might prevent our eyes from slumber; while the sweet, calm stillness of the night permits us to rest upon the bed of ease, and there forget awhile our cares, until the morning son appeareth, and an angel puts his hand upon the curtain, undraws it once again, touches our eyelids, and bids us rise, and proceed to the labours of the day. Night is one of the greatest blessings men enjoy; we have many reasons to thank God for it. Yet night is to many a gloomy season. There is "the pestilence that walketh in darkness;" there is "the terror by night"; there is the dread of robbers and of fell disease, with all those fears that the timorous know, when they have no light wherewith they can discern different objects. It is then they fancy that spiritual creatures walk the earth; though, if they knew rightly, they would find it to be true that—

"Millions of spiritual creatures walk the earth
Unseen, both when we wake, and when we sleep,"—

and that at all times they are round about us, not more by night than by day. Night is the season of terror and alarm to most men; yet even night hath its songs. Have you never stood by the seaside at night, and heard the pebbles sing, and the waves chant God's praises? Or have you never risen from your couch, and thrown up the window of your chamber, and listened there? Listened to what? Silence—save now and then a murmuring sound, which seems sweet music then. And have you not fancied that you have heard the harps of gold playing in heaven? Did you not conceive that yon stars— those eyes of God, looking down on you, were also mouths of song, that every star was singing God's glory, singing as it shone its mighty Maker's well-deserved praise? Night hath its songs; we need not much poetry in our spirit to catch the song of night, and hear the spheres as they chant praises which are loud to the heart, though they be silent to the ear,—the praises of the mighty God, who bears up the unpillared arch of heaven, and moves the stars in their courses.

Man, too, like the great world in which he lives, must have his night. For it is true that man is like the world around him; he is himself a little world; he resembles the world in almost everything; and if the world hath its night, so hath man. And many a night do we have,—nights of sorrow, nights of persecution, nights of doubt, nights of bewilderment, nights of affliction, nights of anxiety, nights of ignorance, nights of all kinds, which press upon our spirits, and terrify our souls. But blessed be God, the Christian man can say, "My God giveth me songs in the night."

It is not necessary, I take it, to prove to you that Christian men have nights; for if you are Christians, you will find that *you* have them, and you will not want any proof, for nights will come quite often enough. I will, therefore, proceed at once to the subject; and notice, with regard to songs in the night, first, *their source,* God giveth them; secondly, *their matter,* —what do we sing about in the night? Thirdly, *their excellence* —they are hearty songs, and they are sweet ones; and fourthly, *their uses,* their benefits to ourselves and others.

I. First, songs in the night—WHO IS THE AUTHOR OF THEM? *"God,"* says the text, our "Maker, giveth songs in the night."

Any man can sing in the day. When the cup is full, man draws inspiration from it; when wealth rolls in abundance around him, any man can sing to the praise of a God who gives a plenteous harvest, or sends home a loaded argosy. It is easy enough for an Aeolian harp to whisper music when the winds blow; the difficulty is for music to come when no wind bloweth. It is easy to sing when we can read the notes by daylight; but he is the skilful singer who can sing when there is not a ray of light by which to read,—who sings from his heart, and not from a book that he can't see, because he has no means of reading, save from that inward book of his own living spirit, whence notes of gratitude pour forth in songs of praise. No man can make a song in the night himself; he may attempt it, but he will find how difficult it is. It is not natural to sing in trouble, "Bless the Lord, O my soul, and all that is within me bless his holy name," for that is a daylight song. But it was a divine song which Habakkuk sang when in the night he said, "Although the fig-tree shall not blossom," and so on, "yet I will rejoice in the Lord, I will joy in the God of my salvation." Methinks, on the margin of the Red Sea, any man could have made a song like that of Moses, "The horse and his rider hath he thrown into the sea;" the difficulty would have been to compose a song before the Red Sea had been divided, and to sing it before Pharaoh's hosts had been drowned, while yet the darkness of doubt and fear was resting on Israel's hosts. Songs in the night come only from God; they are not in the power of man.

But what does the text mean, when it asserts that God giveth songs in the night? We think we find two answers to the question. The first is, that usually in the night of a Christian's experience, *God is his only song.* If it be daylight in my heart, I can sing songs touching my graces, songs touching my sweet experiences, songs touching my duties, songs touching my labours; but let the night come, my graces appear to have withered; my evidences, though they are there, are hidden; now I have nothing left to sing of but my God. It is strange that, when God gives his children mercies, they generally set their hearts more on the mercies than on the Giver of them; but when the night comes, and he sweeps all the mercies away, then at once they each say, "Now, my God, I have nothing to sing of but thee; I must come to thee, and to thee only. I had cisterns once; they were full of water; I drank from them then; but now the created streams are dry, sweet Lord, I quaff no stream but thine own self, I drink from no fount but from thee." Ay, child of God, thou knowest what I say; or if thou dost not understand it yet, thou wilt do so by-and-by! It is in the night we sing of God, and of God alone. Every string is tuned, and every power hath its tribute of song, while we praise God, and nothing else. We can sacrifice to ourselves in daylight; we only sacrifice to God by night. We can sing high praises to ourselves when all is joyful; but we cannot sing praise to any save our God when circumstances are untoward, and providences appear adverse. God alone can furnish us with songs in the night.

And yet again, not only does God give the song in the night, because he is the only subject upon which we can sing then, but because *he is the only One who inspires songs in the night.* Bring me a poor, melancholy, distressed child of God; I seek to tell him precious promises, and whisper to him sweet words of comfort; he listeneth not to me, he is like the deaf adder, he heeds not the voice of the charmer, charm he never so wisely. Send him round to all the comforting divines, and all the holy Barnabases who ever preached, and they will do very little with him; they will not be able to squeeze a song out of him, do what they may. He is drinking the gall and wormwood; he says, "O Lord, I have eaten ashes like bread, and mingled my drink with weeping;" and comfort him as you may, it will be only a woeful note or two of mournful resignation that you will get from him; you will evoke no psalms of praise, no hallelujahs, no joyful sonnets. But let God come to his child in the night, let him whisper in his ear as he lies on his bed, and now you can see his eyes glisten in the night season. Do you not hear him say,—

> "'Tis Paradise, if thou art here;
> If thou depart, 'tis hell"?

I could not have cheered him: it is God that has done it; for God "giveth songs in the night." It is marvellous, brethren, how one sweet word of God will make many songs for Christians. One word of God is like a piece of gold, and the Christian is the gold-beater, and he can hammer that promise out for whole weeks. I can say myself, I have lived on one promise for weeks, and wanted no other. I had just simply to hammer the promise out into gold-leaf, and plate my whole existence with joy from it. The Christian gets his songs from God; God gives him inspiration, and teaches him how to sing: "God my Maker, who giveth songs in the night." So, then, poor Christian, thou needest not go pumping up thy poor heart to make it glad. Go to thy Maker, and ask him to give thee a song in the night; for thou art a poor dry well. You have heard it said that, when a pump is dry, you must pour water down it first of all, and then you will get some up. So, Christian, when thou art dry, go to thy God, ask him to pour some joy down thee, and then thou wilt get more joy up from thine own heart. Do not go to this comforter or that, for you will find them "Job's comforters" after all; but go thou first and foremost to thy Maker, for he is the great Composer of songs and Teacher of music, he it is who can teach thee how to sing.

II. Thus we have dwelt upon the first point; now turn to the second. WHAT IS GENERALLY THE MATTER CONTAINED IN A SONG IN THE NIGHT? What do we sing about?

Why, I think, when we sing by night, there are three things we sing about. Either we sing about the day that is over, or about the night itself, or else about the morrow that is to come. Those are all sweet themes, when God our Maker gives us songs in the night. In the midst of the night, the most usual method is for Christians to sing about *the day that is over.* The man says, "It is night now, but I can remember when it was daylight. Neither moon nor stars appear at present; but I recollect when I saw the sun. I have no evidences just now; but there was a time when I could say, 'I know that my Redeemer liveth.' I have my doubts and fears at this present moment; but it is not long since I could say with full assurance, 'I know that he shed his blood for me.' It may be darkness now; but I know the promises *were* sweet; I know I had blessed seasons in his house. I am quite sure of this, I used to enjoy myself in the ways of the Lord; and though now my path is strewn with thorns, I know it is the

King's highway. It was a way of pleasantness once, it will be a way of pleasantness again. 'I will remember the years of the right hand of the Most High.'" Christian, perhaps the best song thou canst sing, to cheer thee in the night, is the song of yestermorn. Remember, it was not always night with thee; night is a new thing to thee. Once thou hadst a glad heart and a buoyant spirit; once thine eye was full of fire; once thy foot was light; once thou couldst sing for very joy and ecstasy of heart. Well, then, remember that God who made thee sing yesterday has not left thee in the night. He is not a daylight God who cannot know his children in darkness, but he loves thee now as much as ever; though he has left thee for a little while, it is to prove thee, to make thee trust him better, and love and serve him more. Let me tell you some of the sweet things of which a Christian may make a song when it is night with him.

If we are going to sing of the things of yesterday, let us begin with what God did for us in past times. My beloved brethren, you will find it a sweet subject for song at times to begin to sing of electing love and covenant mercies. When thou thyself art low, it is well to sing of the Fountain-head of mercy, of that blessed decree wherein thou wast ordained unto eternal life, and of that glorious Man who undertook thy redemption; of that solemn covenant signed, and sealed, and ratified, in all things ordered well; of that everlasting love which, ere the hoary mountains were begotten, or ere the aged hills were children, chose thee, loved thee firmly, loved thee fast, loved thee well, loved thee eternally. I tell thee, believer, if thou canst go back to the years of eternity,—if thou canst in thy mind run back to that period before the everlasting hills were fashioned, or the fountains of the great deep were scooped out, and if thou canst see thy God inscribing thy name in his eternal Book,—if thou canst read in his loving heart eternal thoughts of love to thee, thou wilt find this a charming means of giving thee songs in the night. There are no songs like those which come from electing love, no sonnets like those that are dictated by meditations on discriminating mercy.

Think, Christian, of the eternal covenant, and thou wilt get a song in the night. But if thou hast not a voice tuned to so high a key as that, let me suggest some other mercies thou mayest sing of; they are the mercies thou hast experienced.

What, man! canst thou not sing a little of that blessed hour when Jesus met thee, when a blind slave thou wast sporting with death, and he saw thee, and said, "Come, poor slave, come with me"? Canst thou not sing of that rapturous moment when he snapped thy fetters, dashed thy chains to the earth, and said, "'I am the Breaker; I am come to break thy chains, and set thee free"? Though thou art ever so gloomy now, canst thou forget that happy morning when, in the house of God, thy voice was loud, almost as a seraph's voice, in praise, for thou couldst sing, "I am forgiven! I am forgiven; a monument of grace, a sinner saved by blood"? Go back, man; sing of that moment, and then thou wilt have a song in the night. Or, if thou hast almost forgotten that, then surely thou hast some precious milestone along the road of life that is not quite overgrown with moss, on which thou canst read some happy inscription of God's mercy towards thee. What! didst thou never have a sickness like that which thou art suffering now, and did he not raise thee up from it? Wast thou never poor before, and did he not supply thy wants? Wast thou never in straits before, and did he not deliver thee? Come, man! I beseech thee, go to the river of thine experience, and pull up a few bulrushes, and weave them into an ark, wherein thine infant faith may float safely on the stream. I bid thee not forget what God hath done for thee. What! hast thou buried thy diary? I beseech thee, man, turn over the book of thy remembrance. Canst thou not see some sweet hill Mizar? Canst thou not think of some blessed hour when the Lord met with thee at Hermon? Hast thou never been on the Delectable Mountains? Hast thou never been fetched from the den of lions? Hast thou never escaped the jaw of the lion, and the paw of the bear? Nay, O man, I know thou hast! Go back, then, a little way, to the mercies of the past; and though it is dark now, light up the lamps of yesterday, and they shall glitter through the darkness, and thou shalt find that God hath given thee a song in the night.

"Ay!" says one, "but you know that, when we are in the dark, we cannot see the mercies that God has given us. It is all very well for you to talk to us thus, but we cannot get hold of them." I remember an old experimental Christian speaking about the great pillars of our faith; he was a sailor, and we were then on board ship, and there were sundry huge posts on the shore, to which the vessels were usually fastened by throwing a cable over them. After I had told him a great many promises, he said, "I know they are good promises, but I cannot get near enough to shore to throw my cable around them; that is the difficulty." Now, it often happens that God's past mercies and lovingkindnesses would be good sure posts to hold on to, but we have not faith enough to throw our cable around them, so we go slipping down the stream of unbelief, because we cannot stay ourselves by our former mercies.

I will, however, give you something over which I think you can throw your cable. If God has never been kind to you, one thing you surely know, and that is, he has been kind to others. Come, now; if thou art in ever so great straits, surely there have been others in greater straits. What! art thou lower down than poor Jonah was when he went to the bottom of the mountains? Art thou worse off than thy Master when he had not where to lay his head? What! conceivest thou thyself to be the worst of the worst? Look at Job there, scraping himself with a potsherd, and sitting on a dunghill. Art thou as low as he? Yet Job rose up, and was richer than before; and out of the depths Jonah came, and preached the Word; and our Saviour Jesus hath mounted to his throne. O Christian, only think of what God has done for others! If thou canst not recollect that he has done anything for thee, yet remember, I beseech thee, what his usual rule is, and do not judge hardly of my God. You remember when Benhadad was overcome and fled, his servants said to him, "Behold now, we have heard that the kings of the house of Israel are merciful kings; let us, I pray thee, put on sackcloth on our loins, and ropes upon our heads, and go out to the king of Israel: peradventure he will save thy life. So they girded sackcloth on their loins, and put ropes on their heads, and said, Thy servant Benhadad saith, I pray thee, let me live." What said the king? "Is he yet alive? He is my brother." And truly, poor soul, if thou hadst never had a merciful God, yet others have had; the King of kings is merciful; go and try him. If thou art ever so low in thy troubles, look to the hills, from whence cometh thy help. Others have had help therefrom, and so mayest thou. Up might start hundreds of God's children, and show us their hands full of comforts and mercies; and they could say, "The Lord gave us these without money and without price; and why should he not give to thee also, seeing that thou too art the King's son?" Thus, Christian, thou

mayest get a song in the night out of other people, if thou
canst not get a song from thyself. Never be ashamed of taking
a leaf out of another man's experience book. If thou canst find
no good leaf in thine own, tear one out of someone's else; if
thou hast no cause to be grateful to God in darkness, or canst
not find cause in thine own experience, go to someone else,
and, if thou canst, harp God's praise in the dark, and like the
nightingale, sing his praise sweetly when all the world has
gone to rest; sing in the night of the mercies of yesterday.

But I think, beloved, there is never so dark a night but there
is something to sing about, even *concerning that night;* for
there is one thing I am sure we can sing about, let the night
be ever so dark, and that is, "It is of the Lord's mercies that
we are not consumed, and because his compassions fail not."
If we cannot sing very loudly, yet we can sing a little low tune,
something like this, "He hath not dealt with us after our sins,
nor rewarded us according to our iniquities." "Oh!" says one,
"I do not know where I shall get my dinner tomorrow; I am a
poor wretch." So you may be, my dear friend; but you are not
so poor as you deserve to be. Do not be mightily offended
about that; if you are, you are no child of God; for the child of
God acknowledges that he has no right to the least of God's
mercies, but that they come through the channel of grace
alone. As long as I am out of hell, I have no right to grumble;
and if I were in hell, I should have no right to complain, for I
felt, when convinced of sin, that never creature deserved to go
there more than I did. We have no cause to murmur; we can
lift up our hands, and say, "Night! thou art dark, but thou
mightest have been darker. I am poor, but if I could not have
been poorer, I might have been sick. I am poor and sick, yet I
have some friends left; my lot cannot be so bad but it might
have been worse." Therefore, Christian, you will always have
one thing to sing about, "Lord, I thank thee it is not all
darkness!" Besides, however dark the night is, there is always
a star or moon. There is scarcely a night that we have, but
there are just one or two little lamps burning in the sky, and
however dark it may be, I think you may find some little
comfort, some little joy, some little mercy left, and some little
promise to cheer thy spirit. The stars are not put out, are
they? Nay, if thou canst not see them, they are there; but
methinks one or two must be shining on thee, therefore give
God a song in the night. If thou hast only one star, bless God

for that one, and perhaps he will make it two; and if thou hast only two stars, bless God twice for the two stars, and perhaps he will make them four. Try, then, if thou canst not find a song in the night.

But, beloved, there is another thing of which we can sing yet more sweetly; and that is, we can sing of *the day that is to come*. Often do I cheer myself with the thought of the coming of the Lord. We preach now, perhaps, with little success; "the kingdoms of this world" have not yet "become the kingdoms of our God and of his Christ." We are labouring, but we do not see the fruit of our labour. Well, what then? We shall not always labour in vain, or spend our strength for nought. A day is coming when every minister of Christ shall speak with unction, when all the servants of God shall preach with power, and when colossal systems of heathenism shall tumble from their pedestals, and mighty, gigantic delusions shall be scattered to the winds. The shout shall be heard, "Alleluia! Alleluia! The Lord God Omnipotent reigneth." For that day do I look; it is to the bright horizon of Christ's second coming that I turn my eyes. My anxious expectation is, that the blessed Sun of righteousness will soon arise with healing in his wings, that the oppressed shall be righted, that despotism shall be cut down, that liberty shall be established, that peace shall be made lasting, and that the glorious liberty of the children of God shall be extended throughout the known world. Christian! if it is night with thee, think of the morrow; cheer up thy heart with the thought of the coming of thy Lord. Be patient, for you know who has said, "Behold, I come quickly; and my reward is with me, to give every man according as his work shall be."

One thought more upon that point. There is another sweet tomorrow of which we hope to sing in the night. Soon, beloved, you and I shall lie on our dying bed, and we shall not lack a song in the night then: and I do not know where we shall get that song, if we do not get it from the to-morrow. Kneeling by the bed of an apparently dying saint recently, I said, "Well, sister, the Lord has been very precious to you; you can rejoice in his covenant mercies, and his past lovingkindnesses." She put out her hand, and said, "Ah, sir! Do not talk about them now; I want the sinner's Saviour as much now as ever; it is not a saint's Saviour I want, it is still a sinner's Saviour that I need, for I am a sinner still." I found that I could not comfort her with the past; so I reminded her of the golden streets, of the gates of pearl, of the walls of jasper, of the harps of gold, of the songs of bliss, and then her eyes glistened; she said, "Yes, I shall be there soon; I shall see them by-and-by;" and then she seemed so glad. Ah, believer, you may always cheer yourself with that thought! Thy head may be crowned with thorny troubles now, but it shall wear a starry crown presently; thy hand may be filled with cares, it shall grasp a harp soon, a harp full of music. Thy garments may be soiled with dust now; they shall be white by-and-by. Wait a little longer. Ah, beloved! how despicable our troubles and trials will seem when we look back upon them! Looking at them here in the prospect, they seem immense; but when we get to heaven, they will seem to us just nothing at all; we shall talk to one another about them in heaven, and find all the more to converse about, according as we have suffered more here below. Let us go on, therefore; and if the night be ever so dark, remember there is not a night that shall not have a morning; and that morning is to come by-and-by. When sinners are lost in darkness, *we* shall lift up our eyes in ever lasting light. Surely I need not dwell longer on this thought. There is matter enough for songs in the night in the past, the present, and the future.

III. And now I want to tell you, very briefly, WHAT ARE THE EXCELLENCES OF SONGS IN THE NIGHT ABOVE ALL OTHER SONGS.

In the first place, when you hear a man singing a song in the night,—I mean in the night of trouble,—you may be quite sure it is a *hearty one.* Many of you sing very heartily now; I wonder whether you would sing as loudly if there were a stake or two in Smithfield for all of you who dared to do it. If you sang under pain and penalty, that would show your heart to be in your song. We can all sing very nicely indeed when everybody else sings; it is the easiest thing in the world to open our mouth, and let the words come out; but when the devil puts his hand over our mouth, can we sing then? Can you say, "Though he slay me, yet will trust in him"? That is hearty singing, that is real song that springs up in the night.

Again, the song we sing in the night will be *lasting.* Many songs we hear our fellow-creatures singing will not do to sing by-and-by. They can sing now rollicking drinking songs; but they will not sing them when they come to die. No; but the

Christian who can sing in the night, will not have to leave off his song; he may keep on singing it for ever. He may put his foot in Jordan's stream, and continue his melody; he may wade through it, and keep on singing still until he is landed safe in heaven; and when he is there, there need not be a pause in his strain, but in a nobler, sweeter song he may still continue singing the Saviour's power to save.

Again, the songs we warble in the night are those that show we have *real faith in God.* Many men have just enough faith to trust God as far as providence goes as they think right; but true faith can sing when its possessors cannot see, it can take hold of God when they cannot discern him.

Songs in the night, too, prove that we have *true courage.* Many sing by day who are silent by night, they are afraid of thieves and robbers; but the Christian who sings in the night proves himself to be a courageous character. It is the bold Christian who can sing God's sonnets in the darkness.

He who can sing songs in the night, proves also that he has *true love to Christ.* It is not love to Christ merely to praise him while every body else praises him; to walk arm in arm with him when he has the crown on his head, is no great thing to do. To walk with Christ in rags, is something more. To believe in Christ when he is shrouded in darkness, to stick hard and fast by the Saviour when all men speak ill of him and forsake him,—that proves true faith and love. He who singeth a song to Christ in the night, singeth the best song in all the world, for he singeth from the heart.

IV. I will not dwell further on the excellencies of night songs, but just, in the last place, SHOW YOU THEIR USE. Well, beloved, it is very useful to sing in the night of our troubles, first, *because it will cheer ourselves.* When some of you were boys, living in the country, and had some distance to go alone at night, do you not remember how you whistled and sang to keep your courage up? Well, what we do in the natural world, we ought to do in the spiritual. There is nothing like singing to keep up our spirits. When we have been in trouble, we have often thought ourselves to be well-nigh overwhelmed with difficulty; so we have said, "Let us have a song." We have begun to sing; and we have proved the truth of what Martin Luther says, "The devil cannot bear singing, he does not like music." It was so in Saul's day; an evil spirit rested on him, but when David played his harp, the

evil spirit went from him. This is usually the case; and if we
can begin to sing, we shall remove our fears. I like to hear
servants sometimes humming a tune at their work; I love to
hear a ploughman in the country singing as he goes along
with his horses. Why not? You say he has no time to praise
God; but if he can sing a song, surely he can sing a psalm, it
will take no more time. Singing is the best thing to purge
ourselves of evil thoughts. Keep your mouth full of songs and
you will often keep your heart full of praises; keep on singing
as long as you can, you will find it a good method of driving
away your fears.

Sing in trouble, again, *because God loves to hear his people
sing in the night.* At no time does God love his children's
singing so well as when he has hidden his face from them,
and they are all in darkness. "Ah!" says God, "that is true
faith that can make them sing praises when I do not appear
to them; I know there is faith in them, that makes them lift
up their hearts, even when I seem to withhold from them all
my tender mercies and all my compassions." Sing then,
Christian, for singing pleases God. In heaven we read that
the angels are employed in singing, be you employed in the
same way; for by no better means can you gratify the
Almighty One of Israel, who stoops from his high throne to
observe us poor, feeble creatures of a day.

Sing, again, for another reason; *because it will cheer your
companions.* If any of them are in the valley and in the
darkness with you, it will be a great help to comfort them.
John Bunyan tells us that, as Christian was going through
the valley, he found it a dreadful place; horrible demons and
hobgoblins were all about him, and poor Christian thought he
must perish for certain; but just when his doubts were the
strongest, he heard a sweet voice; he listened to it, and he
heard a man in front of him singing, "Yea, though I walk
through the valley of the shadow of death, I will fear no evil."
Now, that man did not know who was near him, but he was
unwittingly cheering a pilgrim behind. Christian, when you
are in trouble, sing; you do not know who is near you. Sing;
perhaps you will get a good companion by it. Sing! perhaps
there will be another heart cheered by your song. There is
some broken spirit, it may be, that will be bound up by your
sonnets. Sing! there is some poor distressed brother, perhaps,
shut up in the Castle of Despair, who, like King Richard, will

hear your song inside the walls, and sing to you again, and you may be the means of getting him ransomed and released. Sing, Christian, wherever you go; try, if you can, to wash your face every morning in a bath of praise. When you go down from your chamber, never go to look on man till you have first looked on your God; and when you have looked on him, seek to come down with a face beaming with joy,—carry a smile, for you will cheer up many a poor, wayward pilgrim by it. And when thou fastest, Christian, when thou hast an aching heart, do not appear to men to fast, appear cheerful and happy; anoint thy head, and wash thy face; be happy for thy brother's sake; it will tend to cheer him up, and help him through the valley.

One more reason, and I know it will be a good one for you. Try and sing in the night, Christian, for *that is one of the best arguments in all the world in favour of your religion.* Our divines nowadays spend a great deal of time in trying to prove the truth of Christianity to those who disbelieve it; I should like to have seen Paul trying that plan. Elymas the sorcerer withstood him; how did Paul treat him? He said, "O full of all subtilty and all mischief, thou child of the devil, thou enemy of all righteousness, wilt thou not cease to pervert the right ways of the Lord?" That is about all the politeness such men ought to have when they deny God's truth; we start with this assumption, that the Bible is God's Word, but we are not going to prove God's Word. If you do not believe it, we will bid you "Good-bye;" we will not argue with you. Religion is not a thing merely for your intellect to prove the greatness of your own talent; it is a thing that demands your faith. As a messenger of heaven, I demand that faith; if you do not choose to give it, on your own head be your doom. O Christian, instead of disputing, let me tell you how to prove your religion! Live it out! Live it out! Give the external as well as the internal evidence; give the external evidence of your own life. You are sick; there is your neighbour, who laughs at religion, let him come into your house. When he was sick, he said, "Oh! send for the doctor;" and there he was fretting, and fuming, and making all manner of noises. When you are sick, send for him; tell him that you are resigned to the Lord's will, that you will kiss the chastening rod, that you will take the cup, and drink it, because your Father gives it. You need not make a boast of this, or it will lose all its power: but do it because you cannot help doing it. Your neighbor will say, "There is something in such a religion as that." And when you come to the borders of the grave (he was there once, and you heard how he shrieked, and how frightened he was), give him your hand, and say to him, "Ah! I have a Christ who is with me now, I have a religion that will make me sing in the night." Let him hear how you can sing, "Victory, victory, victory," through him that loved you. I tell you, we may preach fifty thousand sermons to prove the gospel, but we shall not prove it half so well as you will through singing in the night. Keep a cheerful face, keep a happy heart, keep a contented spirit, keep your eye bright, and your heart aloft, and you will prove Christianity better than all the Butlers, and all the wise men who ever lived. Give them the "analogy" of a holy life, and then you will prove religion to them; give them the "evidences" of internal piety, developed externally, and you will give the best possible proof of Christianity. Try and sing songs in the night; for they are so rare that, if thou canst sing them, thou wilt honour thy God, and bless thy friends.

I have been all this while addressing the children of God, and now there is a sad turn that this subject must take; just a word or so, and then I have done. There is a night coming, in which there will be no songs of joy,—a night when a song shall be sung, of which misery shall be the subject, set to the music of wailing and gnashing of teeth; there is a night coming when woe, unutterable woe, shall be the theme of an awful, terrific *miserere*. There is a night coming for the poor soul, and unless he repent, it will be a night wherein he will have to sigh, and cry, and moan, and groan for ever. I hope I shall never preach a sermon without speaking to the ungodly, for oh, how I love them! Swearer, your mouth is black with oaths now; and if you die, you must go on blaspheming throughout eternity, and be punished for it throughout eternity! But list to me, blasphemer! Dost thou repent? Dost thou feel thyself to have sinned against God? Dost thou feel a desire to be saved? List thee! thou mayest be saved; thou mayest be saved. There is another; she has sinned against God enormously, and she blushes even now while I mention her case; dost thou repent of thy sin? Then there is pardon for thee; remember him who said, "Go, and sin no more." Drunkard! but a little while ago thou wast reeling down the street, and now thou repentest; drunkard, there is hope for thee. "Well," sayest thou, "what shall I do to be saved?" Let me again tell thee the old way of salvation; it is, "Believe on the Lord Jesus Christ, and thou shalt be saved." We can get no further than that, do what we will; this is the sum and substance of the gospel. "He that believeth and is baptized shall be saved." So saith the Saviour himself. Dost thou ask, "What is it to believe?" Am I to tell thee again? I cannot tell thee except that it is to look to Christ. Dost thou see the Saviour there? He is hanging on the cross; there are his dear hands, pierced with nails, fastened to a tree, as if they were waiting for thy tardy footsteps, because thou wouldst not come. Dost thou see his dear head there? It is hanging on his breast, as if he would lean over, and kiss thy poor soul. Dost thou see his blood, gushing from his head, his hands, his feet, his side? It is running after thee, because he well knew that thou wouldst never run after him. Sinner, to be saved, all thou hast to do is to look at that Man! Canst thou not do it now? "No," thou sayest, "I do not believe that will save me." Ah, my poor friend, try it, I beseech thee, try it; and if thou dost not succeed, when thou hast tried it, I will be bondsman for my Lord,—here, take me, bind me, and I will suffer thy doom for thee. This I will venture to say; if thou castest thyself on Christ, and he deserteth thee, I will be willing to go halves with thee in all thy misery and woe; for he will never do it; never, *never,* NEVER!

> "No sinner was ever empty sent back,
> Who came seeking mercy for Jesus's sake."

I beseech thee, therefore, try him, and thou shalt not try him in vain; but thou shalt find him "able to save them to the uttermost that come unto God by him;" and thou shalt be saved now, and saved for ever.

23

Rain and Grace-A Parallel

"Who hath divided a watercourse for the overflowing of waters, or a way for the lightning of thunder; To cause it to rain on the earth, where no man is; on the wilderness, wherein there is no man; To satisfy the desolate and waste ground; and to cause the bud of the tender herb to spring forth?"   Job 38:25-27

Job was an admirable man, but the Lord meant to make him still better. The best of men are but men at the best; and though Job was in a certain sense perfect, yet he was not perfectly perfect, there was a further stage beyond that which he had reached, else would he not have been tried as he was. But, because the Lord knew that there was something better for Job than he had already attained, he had to be subjected to extraordinary trial. He was such a valuable diamond that there had to be more cutting for him than a common stone. He was made of such good metal that he paid for being put into the furnace; there would come out something still more pleasing to the great Refiner if he cast that which was so precious into the most fervent heat. Hence it was that Job was so greatly tried; yet, after all his trials, it seemed as if he would miss their blessed result, for his three friends—the miserable comforters—appeared to be the marplots of the whole design. By their cruel, cutting, sarcastic observations, they irritated Job, so that it looked as if he would be harder instead of softer because of the fires. Sometimes, when a man knows that he is being unjustly and unfairly treated, he stiffens his back, and hardens himself, and influences which, by themselves, might have wrought great tenderness of spirit, are spoiled because something else is thrown in. Job was in this condition, and he therefore seemed to rise in his own estimation rather than to sink, as was desired, until at last the Lord ended the dispute by manifesting himself. Out of the whirlwind he spoke to Job, and bade him gird up his loins, and meet his Maker if he dared; then it was that Job was brought to his right position, and at the end he said, "I have heard of thee by the hearing of the ear: but now mine eye seeth thee. Wherefore I abhor myself, and repent in dust and ashes." Then Job realized the benefit of his affliction; but not till then. When the Lord revealed to Job his supremacy, his eternal glory, and in that light compelled him to see his own imperfection and nothingness, then the patriarch's trials became sanctified to him.

Our text is a part of God's challenge to Job. The Lord seemed to say, "If Job is indeed as great as he half thinks he is, let him see whether he can do what his Creator does." He is challenged about so slight a matter, apparently, as the sending of the rain. Does Job know how it is done? Can he explain all the phenomena? Our modern scientists tell us how rain is produced, and I suppose their explanation is the correct one; but they cannot tell us how it is that power is given to carry out what they call "the laws of nature," neither can they make the rain themselves; nor, if a drought were to continue till the nation was on the verge of famine, would they be able to cover the skies with blackness, or even to water a single acre of land. No; with all our explanations, it is still a great mystery, and it remains a secret with God how it is that he waters the earth with rain.

I am not going into that matter at this time; I intend to use the rain as an emblem of the grace of God, as it usually is in Scripture,—a figure of that blessed overflowing of the river of God's love which comes down to quench our thirst of sin, to refresh us, to enliven us, to fertilize us, to soften us, and to cleanse us. This matchless water of life has all sorts of uses, and God sends it, when he pleases, in abundant showers upon his own people according to that ancient word, "Thou, O God, didst send a plentiful rain whereby thou didst confirm thine inheritance, when it was weary." The Hebrew means, "Thou didst pour out blessings," as from a cornucopia, and so "Thou didst confirm thine inheritance, when it was weary." There are many here who are weary, they want to be refreshed, and they are praying to God to send a gracious shower, a copious distilling of his matchless grace upon their hearts and lives. I am going to preach upon this passage with the desire that, while I am speaking, such a blessing may come upon us, or that, at any rate, we may begin to pray for it.

I. My first point is that, AS GOD ALONE GIVETH RAIN, SO GOD ALONE GIVETH GRACE.

Jehovah asks of Job the question, "Who hath divided a watercourse for the overflowing of waters, or a way for the lightning of thunder; to cause it to rain on the earth?" It is God, and God only, who creates rain. We cannot make it, but he can and he does give it; and it is absolutely so with his grace. *The Lord must give it, or there will be none.* If it had not been for his eternal plan, whereby he purposed to give grace to the guilty, the whole race of mankind would have been left, like the fallen angels, without hope and without mercy. The angels that kept not their first estate, but rebelled against God, were given over to punishment, without any intimation whatever of redemption for them, or of any possibility of their restoration. God, who does as he wills with his grace which is most sovereign and free, passed over the fallen angels, and made his grace to light on insignificant and guilty men. And it has been after the same fashion in all history; if God has withholden the blessings of his grace from any of the nations, they have not been able to procure them for themselves. One lone light burned in Israel for hundreds of years, while the rest of the inhabitants of the earth were left in darkness; and the world, with all its wisdom, could not and did not find out God. Men, in their ignorance, set up idols almost as numerous as their worshippers, and in their blindness they went this way and that way, but always astray from God. "Every good gift and every perfect gift is from above, and cometh down from Father of lights," as certainly as the rain comes down from heaven. There is but one source of supply for grace, and that source is God himself. He giveth grace, and "he giveth more grace;" else there would be none whatever amongst the sons of men.

And, moreover, *it is God who finds the way by which his grace can come to men.* I will not enter into any elaborate explanations of my text; it signifies that God finds a way by which the rain comes down from the upper regions to water the thirsty fields. "Who hath divided a watercourse for the overflowing of waters?" Only God himself has made a channel for the rain; we could not have made it. So is it with his grace; otherwise, how could grace have come to man? How was it possible for the thrice-holy God to deal leniently with sinners

who had provoked him to anger? How could it be that the
Judge of all the earth, who must be just, should, nevertheless,
pass by transgression, iniquity, and sin? This is a problem
which would have perplexed a Sanhedrin of seraphim. If all
the mightiest intelligences that God has ever made had sat
together in solemn conclave for a thousand years, yet they
would not have been able to solve this problem,—How can
God be just, and yet the Justifier of the ungodly? Infinite
wisdom devised that matchless way of substitution, by which,
through the death of the Son of God, men might be saved.
There is the stamp of Divinity about that verse, "the
chastisement of our peace was upon him; and with his stripes
we are healed."

It is God who gives grace, and God who, in a divinely-
gracious way, has given his only-begotten and well-beloved
Son to be the channel through which grace can come down to
guilty men. Blessed be God for this; and let his name be
adored for ever.

Having thus resolved upon giving grace to men, and having
made a channel in which his grace might flow to men, let it
never be forgotten that *God now directs the pathway of all the
grace that comes into the world.* Our parallel, in the natural
world, is that, according to the original of our text, there is a
sort of canal, or trackway, made for every drop of water as it
descends from the heavens to the earth. There is not the most
minute particle of rain that is left to fall according to its own
fancy or will; each single drop of water, that is blown aslant
by the March wind, is as surely steered by God as are yonder
glorious stars revolving in their orbits. There is a purpose of
God concerning every solitary flake of snow and every single
portion of hail that comes down from heaven; all these are
ordered according to his eternal counsel and will. God alone
can arrange all this. It always seems to me to be a very
wonderful way in which the world is watered. If all the rain
were to pour upon us at once in a deluge, we should all he
drowned; but it comes down gently, drop by drop, and thus it
effects God's purpose much more surely than if it burst in one
tremendous waterspout destroying everything. God, by the
mysterious laws by which he governs inanimate matter, has
so planned it that the rain shall come in drops exactly of the
right size, such drops as shall hang upon a tiny blade of grass,
and scarcely shall bend it. See how the bright drops, like so

many diamonds, hang in myriads on the hedgerows, just the right size to hang there,—neither too large nor too little; so is it with the grace of God, it is given sovereignly and wisely.

I daresay some Christian people think that they would like to have, in their first five minutes after believing in Christ, all the grace they ever will have; but it cannot be so. I have often admired that expression of the apostle Paul, "In whom we have redemption through his blood, the forgiveness of sins, according to the riches of his grace; wherein he hath abounded toward us in all wisdom and prudence." God teaches us his will, but he does not teach us too much at a time. Have you never seen children, who have been put to school, so hardly driven by their masters, that they have been crippled mentally, and have never made the advance they ought to have made because they were overdriven at the first? I have met with this sort of thing spiritually; in several cases I have known, men and women have learned so much of the things of God in a short time that their reason has been most seriously jeopardized. I have often had to look at young converts, and almost to pray that they might not learn too much at once, for the deep things of God are so wonderful to a man who is just plucked out of the world that, if the cases of insanity through religion were much more frequent than they are, I should not be at all astonished. I wonder how any of us can bear what God has taught us already. If you could give eyesight to a man born blind, and then, in a moment, were to place him in the full blaze of the sun, it would be a serious danger to him; if he has been long in the darkness, he must see the light by degrees. In like manner, we ought to thank God that he does not deluge us at once with all the grace we ever shall have; but he gives it to us gently, as soft vernal showers which, in infinite wisdom, distil upon the thirsty earth.

So we have seen that God giveth grace, God finds a way of giving grace, and then God directs the way of his grace, and the measure and the manner of it; and he does it all in wisdom and prudence.

See, then, my dear friends,—I hope you all do,—*our absolute dependence upon God for all spiritual blessings.* A farmer may do all he likes with his ground, but he will never have a harvest if God withholds the rain. He may be the most skilful agriculturist who ever lived, but he can do nothing if the heavens above him are as brass. If he were to call in the most learned astronomer of the day, there is not one who, with his wand, could move the stars, or cause the clouds to open, and pour down rain upon the earth. If there were sore trouble in the land because farming was failing for lack of rain, if both Houses of Parliament were to be called together, and the Queen were to sit upon her throne of state, and they were unanimously to pass an act ordering the rain to fall, he that sitteth in the heavens would laugh, the Lord would have them in derision, for the key of the rain is in no hand but that of Jehovah. It is exactly so with the grace of God. You and I cannot command it. The presence of the most holy men in our midst would not of itself bring it. The most earnest preaching, the most Scriptural doctrine, the most faithful obedience to ordinances, would not make it necessary that we should receive grace. God must give it; he is an absolute Sovereign, and we are entirely dependent upon him.

To what does this fact drive us? It drives us to prayer. When we have done all that we can,—and surely we can scarcely pray if we have neglected anything that we can do,—but when we have done all that lies within our power as earnest-hearted Christian workers, then we must come to the Lord himself for strength, and unto the God of our salvation for all power. This has been said so many times that, when I say it again, someone may reply, "That is a mere platitude." Just so, and the mischief is that the Church is beginning to think it is only a platitude; but if we all felt that the most important thing for the Church of Christ to do, after she has borne her testimony to the world, is to pray, what a different state of things there would soon be! But now you know what they are doing in far too many places; they push the prayer-meeting up into a corner, and if there is anything to be put off, they give up the prayer-meeting. In some of our places of worship, we might search a long time for the prayer-meeting. It is somewhere in the back settlements, down in some small room which is too big for it even then. People plead that they cannot get out to the prayer-meeting; they will go out to a lecture, or to spend the evening for pleasure; but they do not care to go out when it is "only a prayer-meeting." Just so; and as long as that is the estimation in which professing Christians hold it, so long must we cease to expect showers of blessing from on high. The main thing is for the Church to pray. She knows that she is dependent upon her God; let her show it by crying day and night to him that he would send a blessing.

There is a big mill, with all its spindles and all its workers; I think I see it now as we speed along in the train through one of our Northern counties. It is all lit up to-night, and many busy hands are at work; but where is the power that makes those spindles move? In that little shed outside, where there is a man, with black hands, stirring the fire, and keeping up the pressure of steam. That is where the power is; and that is a picture of the prayer-meeting. It is the source of the Church's energy; and if public prayer be neglected, or if private prayer be slackened, or if family prayer be held back in any degree, we lose the power which brings the blessing; and this will be acknowledged when we come truly to know that all the power is of God, and that, as we cannot command a drop of rain, but must leave it in the hands of God, so we cannot command an ounce of grace,—if grace is to be so measured,—it must come from God, and from God alone.

II. Now, secondly, dear friends, notice in my text that, AS GOD GIVES RAIN, SO RAIN FALLS IRRESPECTIVE OF MEN: "Who hath divided a watercourse for the overflowing of waters, or a way for the lightning of thunder; to cause it to rain on the earth, where no man is; on the wilderness, wherein there is no man?"

I daresay you have often thought it strange that it should rain out at sea, where it cannot water a single furrow, or apparently benefit any human being. Is it not still more strange that the water should fall so abundantly on vast tracts of sand, and on plains that as yet have never been trodden by the foot of man, and on those lofty peaks, those virgin hills, where a human being has never yet been found? Men have a notion that nothing is good for anything if it is not good for them; but they are very foolish for thinking so. If what God does in providence is good for nothing but for a rat, it is not unwise for him to do it. He has other creatures to think of beside men, and he does think of them. The little fish in the sea, and the birds of the air, and even the worms in the earth, are remembered by the Most High; and, sometimes, that weather which we say is so bad is only bad because it is bad for us,—the rebels against God. It may have been given specially for the birds; and perhaps, sometimes, God thinks that it is better to have weather that is good for birds than good for men, for he has to provide for us all, and they at least have not sinned; and if he thinks of them, there is as much of mercy in the thought as when he thinks of us rebellious creatures. He makes it "to rain on the earth, where no man is."

Now the parallel in grace is this,—that *God's grace will come without any human observation.* If the grace of God comes to some of us, thousands will see it, for they will mark the working of his grace in our life and conversation. But there sits a dear friend, over yonder, so obscure that possibly only two or three will ever know anything that she does. Perhaps, my brother, only half-a-dozen are affected by your influence. Do you not rejoice that God, who makes the rain to fall where no man is, will make his grace to come to you, though nobody, or, at most, only two or three, may see it? I have delighted sometimes to wander into the middle of a wood, and get far away from all sound of the voices of fallen men, and then to spy out some little flower growing right amongst the big trees. The sun gets at it, somehow, for a few hours in the day, and in his golden beams that little flower rejoices; and as I have looked at it, and seen its beauty, I have remembered the words of the poet,—

"Full many a flower is born to blush unseen,"

and I have not at all agreed with him when he added,—

"And waste its sweetness on the desert air."

It is God's flower; God made it grow that he might look at it himself, and, therefore, its sweetness was not wasted, for God was there to appreciate and accept it. The most beautiful places in the world are, doubtless, places where men have never been. The most lovely gardens are those that God himself keeps, where no Adam has been placed to till the soil. His trees, untouched by the axe, and unpruned by the knife, grow gloriously: "The trees of the Lord are full of sap; the cedars of Lebanon, which he hath planted." My heart has rejoiced as I have thought of God walking among the great trees of the far-off West,—those mighty monarchs of the forest that seem to touch the stars,—walking among them when nobody was there but himself, looking at the works of his own hands, and admiring what he had made. Well, now, if you happen to be a solitary person, quite alone, one who will never make a noise in the world for all that God does for you; never mind about that. He causes it to rain on the earth, where no man is; and your obscurity shall not keep back the blessing.

So, you see, rain comes without human observation. And it also comes *without human co-operation,* for it often rains "where no man is." Therefore, no man helps God to send the rain. As to grace, it also often comes where there is no man to bring it. When a person has not heard a sermon, when he has been on the sea, far away from all means of grace, yet God has caused it to rain upon him. There is here to-night, I think, a brother, who left this country unimpressed by the gospel, who, nevertheless, when near the shores of Australia, sat down, and read a sermon which his wife had put into his box, and God met with him there. The Lord has many ways of proving that his grace descends upon men without any help from them, and that he can send it where he pleases by ways of his own. If the ordinary means should seem to fail, he can cause it to rain "where no man is."

Perhaps there is somebody here who is going right away from the usual means of grace. Possibly, dear friend, you are fretting to yourself as you think, "I shall never come to this place of worship again; perhaps I may never hear the gospel to my soul's comfort again." Suppose you are right away in the bush of Australia, God can send his grace to you there just as easily as he can send it here. If you are going to the backwoods of America or Canada, do not be afraid; the Lord is at home there. If you have to settle down in a log-hut, and are miles from any meeting of Christian people, be not dispirited or cast down; but, in your loneliness, sit and sing, and let this be a part of your song, "He maketh a way for the overflowing of waters, to cause it to rain on the earth, where no man is; on the wilderness, wherein there is no man." Wherefore be encouraged by this second thought.

III. I had many other things to say to you upon this point, but time fails, so I must notice, thirdly, that BOTH RAIN AND GRACE FALL WHERE WE MIGHT LEAST HAVE EXPECTED THEM: "To satisfy the desolate and waste ground."

Grace comes where there was no grace before. Where all was desert and waste, there comes the rain; and where all was graceless and godless, there comes the grace of God. *Grace*

comes where there is the greatest need of it. Here was a
dreadful place; it was waste; it was a wilderness; yet the rain
came there; and where there are men who feel themselves to
be just as dead and barren as a desert, grace will come even
there. The rain comes to wildernesses, and grace can come to
you, poor guilty sinners. If you have nothing with which to
entertain the grace, grace will bring its own company with it.
It will come into your empty heart, and make you one of the
"people prepared for the Lord." Grace waits not for men,
neither tarries for the sins of men. We call it prevenient
grace, because it comes before it is sought, and God bestows it
on a people who are utterly undeserving of it.

*Grace comes where, apparently, there is nothing to repay it
for coming.* When the rain falls on the wilderness, it does
seem as if no result could follow from its fall. What a mercy it
is that, when we have nothing to pay, God lavishes his mercy
upon us, and in due time we do repay him in the way he
expects. I do not suppose that many of you have ever seen the
great steppes of Russia; but I have been told that, for
thousands of miles, they are like our London streets, without
a single blade of anything green,—a horrible desolation; yet
after the snow has gone, and spring time comes in, and
summer with its wonderful heat, that plain is covered with
grass and with abundant flowers of the field; and the grass
continues until it is cut for use, and then the land returns to
just that same barren appearance which it wore before. It is
singular, is it not, that showers of rain and the warmth of the
sun should produce vegetation where, apparently, there
seemed to be none whatever?

Just so does the grace of God come to a sinner's heart, It is
all hard, dead, black, hopeless; but when the grace comes, it
brings life with it, and suddenly there spring up in the man
all manner of good works, and holy words, and gracious
thoughts, and everything that is sweet and pleasing in the
sight of God. And what is best of all, it continues to produce a
harvest that never dries up, and never does the soil return to
its former barrenness again. Wherefore, beloved, let us take
heart concerning the grace of God. If the rain comes where
there seems to be no argument in favour of its coming, so may
the grace of God come to you who have no right to it,—no
expectation of it,—no hope of it,—nay, are even filled with
despair concerning it. While you are sitting here, the Lord can

meet with you, and save you. Be of good comfort; to you is the gospel sent, saying, "Believe on the Lord Jesus Christ, and thou shalt be saved." Trust thy guilty soul with him, and thou, even thou, shalt receive the showers of love that come from God's right hand. There is nothing in the covenant of grace that shall be held back from you, even though you are the very worst and vilest one in this place, if you only trust the Saviour. Though you may write yourself down as most surely lost, and given up to barrenness, like the heath that is nigh unto burning, yet it shall not be so with you, God shall bless you, and that right early.

"Oh, if he does!" says one, "I will bless his name." Then that is one reason why he will do it, that you may bless his name. I have often told you of one who said, "If God saves me, he shall never hear the last of it." Well, that is the sort of people he likes to save,—people who, with glad heart and voice, will tell out, and tell out again, and tell out to all eternity that the Lord saved them,—even them. Remember the text of last Sabbath night, for it is just in the same key as the text of to-night: "He hath filled the hungry with good things; and the rich he hath sent empty away." He has caused it "to rain on the earth where no man is; on the wilderness, wherein there is no man; to satisfy the desolate and waste ground;" for it is to these waste grounds, these desolate places, that God specially looks with favour. If you are great in your own esteem, he will make you little; but if you are little, he will make you great. If you live by your own power, you shall be slain; but if you are slain, and dead beyond hope of recovery in yourself, you shall be made alive. You empty ones shall be filled; and you filled ones shall be emptied. You that are up shall be down; and you that are down shall be lifted up, for God turns things upside down; and when he comes to work, he effects marvellous changes in the condition of the hearts of men.

IV. Now I close by noticing, in the fourth place, that RAIN, WHEN IT COMES, IS MOST VALUED BY LIFE, for we read in our text, that it comes "to cause the bud of the tender herb to spring forth."

You may water a dead post as long as you like, yet nothing will come of it; but the tenderest, tiniest little herb, that has a bud fast shut, knows when the rain comes, and begins to develop its hidden power, and open its bud to the rain and to

the sun. That is why the grace of God comes, "to cause the
bud of the tender herb to spring forth." I hope that there is
here a good deal of budding life. The Lord has looked upon
you, and has made you feel uneasy; that is a bud. Oh, that the
uneasiness might open into full repentance! The Lord has
looked upon you, and he has given you desires. Oh, that the
grace of God may increase those desires till they shall open
into resolution and determination! The Lord has sent the dew
from on high upon your soul, dear friend, and you are
beginning to hope that there is salvation somewhere, and
perhaps for you. Oh, that the hope may open, like a bud that
has been shut up,—open into faith in Jesus Christ, so that
you shall say, "I will trust in him." All the buds everywhere
just now are trying to get out into the sunshine; they seem
bound up in gummy envelopes, but they are beginning to open
in the sunshine. I like to sit under the fir trees, and hear the
crack of the opening caused by the heat of the sun. You can
almost see the trees rejoicing that summer-time is coming. So
may you see young converts open when the grace of God is
displayed abundantly; they grow before your very eyes till,
sometimes, you are astonished at what the grace of God does,
with wise prudence, but yet with a sweet readiness, upon the
hearts of the sons of men.

How far have your buds developed? Have you begun to pray
a little? Oh, that your prayer might be more intense! I hope
that little bud of private prayer will grow till it comes to
family prayer,—so that you can pray with your wife and
children. You have been reading your Bible lately, have you?
Oh, thank God for that! Now I hope that bud of Bible-reading
will open into the daily habit of feeding upon the Word of God.
Go right through the Bible if you can. Pray to God to give you
a solid knowledge of its contents, that you may be rooted and
grounded in what his Spirit teaches you there. Some of you
have another sort of bud; you have been thinking of what you
can do for Christ. You thought you were converted, but you
have never done much for Christ. I do not use any whips, but
sometimes I am tempted to take a good long one to some of
those lazy folk who do nothing, and yet hope to go to heaven.
One says, "I think, my dear Pastor, that I must try to do
something for Christ." Well, that is a bud; may the grace of
God be so abundant that you will leave off trying, and get
actually to doing! "How am I to serve God?" said one to me,

the other day. I answered, "My dear brother, get at it. 'Whatsoever thy hand findeth to do, do it with thy might.' Don't come and ask me, for where there is so much to be done, the man is idle who asks, 'What am I to do?' Do the first thing that comes to hand." If a soldier in battle saw that the enemy was winning the day, he would not be hesitating, and asking, "Captain, what can I do?" He would kill the first fellow that came near, and so must you, in a spiritual sense. Do something for Christ. Oh, that this church might begin to open all its buds! May every little one become a thousand, and every small one a great multitude, to the praise of the glory of the grace of God! O you little ones, you hidden ones, you timid ones, you trembling ones, the grace of God is abundant! Open to receive it. See how the crocus, after having been long hidden beneath the soil, knows when the new year begins, and as soon as the sun smiles on the earth, it gently lifts up its golden cup; and is there anything more beautiful in all the world than the crocus cup when God fills that chalice with the light of heaven? What a depth of wonderful brightness of colour there is within it! All the crocus can do is to open itself; and that is all you can do,—just stand and drink in God's light. Open yourself to the sweet influences of the grace of God. The fair lilies of the garden toil not, neither do they spin; but yet they glorify God. How they seem to stand still and just show what God can do with them! They just drink in the light and heat, and then pour it all out again in silent, quiet beauty. Now you do just the same; let the purity of your life, like the purity of the lily, glorify the God who created it in you. So may his blessing rest upon you all, dear friends, for our Lord Jesus Christ's sake! Amen.

24

Job Among the Ashes

"I have heard of thee by the hearing of the ear: but now mine eye seeth thee. Wherefore I abhor myself, and repent in dust and ashes." **Job 42:5-6**

JEHOVAH had spoken, Job had trembled. The Lord had revealed himself, Job had seen him. Truly, God did but display the skirts of his robe, and unveil a part of his ways; but therein there was so much of ineffable glory, that Job laid his hand upon his mouth in token of his silent consent to the claims of the Everlasting One. God spoke to Job out of the whirlwind concerning the greatness of his power, the wonders of his workings, the splendour of his skill, the infinity of his wisdom. Carefully read that wonderful speech of the Most High to the trembling patriarch. I dare not call it poetry; for it rises as much above human poetry as the sublimest poetry stands above the poorest prose. It is simply a statement of facts, and these are mentioned in language of the simplest kind; but the overpowering glory of the utterance lies in the facts themselves. These sublime stanzas are spoken in the idiom of God. Those only know the peculiar style of the living God who have become familiar with the sacred word in spirit and in truth, and such persons can at once distinguish the speech of Jehovah from that of men. Read the divine address, that you may see how Jehovah caused the afflicted patriarch to feel him near.

In the confession which now lies before us, *Job acknowledges God's boundless power;* for he exclaims, "I know that thou canst do everything, and that no thought can be withholden from thee." He felt that whatever the Lord chose to think or desire he could at once accomplish. Job had a glimpse of that omnipotence of which the height and depth no mind can ever measure.

Job sees his own folly. He speaks like a man in a maze or a muse, and he says, "Who is he that hideth counsel without knowledge?" Look at the second verse of chapter thirty-eight, and you will see that he is quoting what God had said to him. The Lord's words are ringing in his ears, and in his anguish he repeats them, accepting them as justly applicable to himself. It is not far from being right with us when the words of God can fitly become our words. "The Lord answered Job out of the whirlwind, and said, Who is this that darkeneth counsel by words without knowledge?" And now Job replies, "I am that foolish one: I uttered that I understood not; things too wonderful for me, which I knew not." Job felt that what he had spoken concerning the Lord was in the main true; and the Lord himself said to Job's three friends, "Ye have not spoken of me the thing that is right, as my servant Job hath"; but under a sense of the divine presence Job felt that even when he had spoken aright, he had spoken beyond his own proper knowledge, uttering speech whose depths of meaning he could not himself fathom. Many a holy prophet has done this, for inspired men are described as those who "enquired and searched diligently; searching what, or what manner of time the Spirit which was in them did signify, when it testified beforehand the sufferings of Christ, and the glory that should follow." It is not the thoughts of the prophet which have been inspired of God so much as their words; for frequently they were moved to speak prophecies which were quite beyond their own understanding: in fact, my brethren, are not all the great mysteries of the faith above human thought? and may we not fearlessly assert that no inspired man has ever known all the depth of God's meaning treasured up in the words which he himself has been led by the Spirit of God to write? Hence I assert that there is a verbal inspiration, or no inspiration at all worthy of the name. Job, as he comes before us in the text, is impressed with his own folly. He had to a large degree spoken what he felt sure was true, but he now feels that he did not understand what he said; and he at the same time tacitly confesses that he may have said in his bitterness many an unwise and unseemly thing, and therefore he bows his head before the Lord his God, and confesses that he has darkened counsel by words without knowledge, and uttered things that he understood not.

Notwithstanding, *the man of God proceeds to draw near unto the Lord,* before whom he bows himself. Foolish as he confesses himself to be, he does not therefore fly from the supreme wisdom. Although he knows that he has babbled ignorantly, he does not therefore seek to hide away from the Lord, as Adam did when he sought the shade of the trees of the garden. No, he takes up the Lord's words again, and is emboldened by them to approach. Read the thirty-eighth chapter, third verse; the Lord there says, "Gird up now thy loins like a man: for I will demand of thee, and answer thou me." Like a man in a dream, Job accepts the invitation, and answers, "Hear, I beseech thee, and I will speak: I will demand of thee, and declare thou unto me." This was brave and wise action. Whatever Job might be or might not be, he was a firm believer in his God, and in every word which the Lord was pleased to speak. He held even to discouraging words with desperate tenacity, and even learned to find honey in words which roared like lions upon him. Hence, when he is humbled in the dust, he recollects that God had bidden him draw nigh to him; and albeit to his fears that bidding may have sounded like a challenge, yet to his faith it becomes an encouragement, and he in effect replies, "My God, I will venture to take thee at thy word. Thou biddest me come, and come I will. Dust and ashes though I be, I will do as thou dost allow me, and make my humble appeal to thee." Dear friends, it is altogether wrong to allow our sense of folly or of sin to drive us away from God; but it is altogether right when our humiliation draws us to the Lord, and our conscious need drives us to the throne of grace. The more foolish and sinful we are, the more urgent is our need to come to God, who alone can make us clean, and instruct us in the way of heavenly wisdom. I commend to you, therefore, God's servant Job, of whom I may say, whatever fault we may perceive in him, none of us could have behaved so gloriously as he did; unless, indeed, the Lord should give us like grace. The Lord led Job to find fault with himself, yet God himself does not complain of him, but even commends him. The three carping friends are commanded to bring a costly sacrifice, but this was not demanded from Job; and even when they brought their seven bullocks the Lord did not accept them till Job, whom they had condemned, had made intercession for them. Job bore away the palm from the conflict. So let us do as Job did, and make our approach unto the Lord in childlike confidence even when he seems to frown. Let us get where Job was when he said,

"Though he slay me, yet will I trust in him." When we bow
lowest before his throne, let not our humble bending have
anything of distance in it. Lowlier before thee, O Lord, would
we be; but at the same time our cry is, "Nearer to thee."

Thus we come to the text, having used the connection as a
step to its door. On the text I make three observations: first,
we have sometimes very vivid impressions of God. Job said, "I
have heard of thee by the hearing of the ear: but now mine
eye seeth thee." In the second place, *when we are favoured
with these clearer views of God, we have lowlier thoughts of
ourselves*—"wherefore I abhor myself"; and thirdly, *whenever
we are thus made lowly, our heart is filled with repentance:* "I
abhor myself, and repent in dust and ashes." May the Holy
Spirit aid us in this experimental meditation!

I. First, then, WE HAVE SOMETIMES VERY VIVID IMPRESSIONS
OF GOD. Job had long before *heard* of God, and that is a great
matter. I do not think he meant merely that he had heard
men speak of God, but that he had really, for himself, heard
God's voice. He had been a reverent believer in the teachings
of God, and an obedient servant to his commands: thus he had
really heard God. The man who can say this can say a great
deal. If God has ever been on speaking terms with you, you
have much cause for gratitude. It is clear that you are not
dead in sin, or if you were so when the Lord spoke to you, you
are now alive; for his voice causes the dead to live. If you have
heard God in the secret of your soul, you are a spiritual man;
for only a spirit can hear the Spirit of God: none can discern
the Lord but the man to whom he has given spiritual life. Job
had heard God, but now he has a more vivid apprehension of
him. It is sometimes said that one eye-witness is better than
ten ear-witnesses, and there is much truth in the saying:
certainly, facts perceived by the eye make a far more vivid
impression upon the mind than the same facts heard by the
ear. If we witness a sad scene of poverty it has far more effect
upon our heart than the most graphic description.
Wordpainting can never bring out the reality of a thing so
well as the actual sight of it. Of course, Job could not literally
see God, he does not mean to assert that he did; for "no man
hath seen God at any time"; but Job means that he now had a
view of God very much more clear than any which he had
obtained before; in fact, as much clearer as eyesight is more
clear than hearing.

Notice, that *in order to acquire this close vision of God affliction had overtaken him*. It was not till after he had scraped himself with the potsherd, nor till his friends had scraped him with something worse than potsherds, that Job could say, "Mine eye seeth thee." Not till every camel and every sheep had been stolen, and every child was dead, could the afflicted patriarch cry, "Now mine eye seeth thee." Happy is that man who in prosperity can hear the voice of God in the tinkling of the sheep-bells of his abundant flocks, can hear him in the lowing of the oxen which cover his fields, and in the loving voices of dear children around him. But, mark you! prosperity is a painted window which shuts out much of the clear light of God, and only when the blue, and the crimson, and the golden tinge are removed, is the glass restored to its full transparency. Adversity thus takes away tinge, and colour, and dimness, and we see our God far better than before, if our eyes are prepared for the light. The Lord had taken everything away from Job, and this paved the way to his giving him more of himself. In the absence of other goods the good God is the better seen. In prosperity God is *heard,* and that is a blessing; but in adversity God is *seen,* and that is a greater blessing. Sanctified adversity quickens our spiritual sensitiveness. Sorrow after sorrow will wake up the spirit, and it will infuse into it a delicacy of perception which, perhaps, does not often come to us in any other way. I purposely say, "perhaps"; for I believe that some choice saints are favoured to reach it by smoother ways; but I think they are very few. The most of us are of such coarse material that we need melting, ay, and braying as in a mortar before we attain to that sacred softness by which the Lord God is joyfully perceived. O child of God, if thou art to suffer as much as Job suffered, if thou gettest to see the Lord with a spiritually enlightened eye, thou mayest be thankful for the sorrowful process! Who would not go to Patmos if he might see the visions of John, and who would not sit on the dunghill with Job to cry with him, "Now mine eye seeth thee"?

Possibly, also, *helpful to this was Job's desertion by his friends*. Job's three friends! Ah me, I know their kindred! They were most devotedly attached to him, no doubt; and how warmly they proved it! They had met together with him, and said soft and sweet things to him in those days when he moved like a prince among the nobles of his people, and every

eye that saw him blessed him. But when they found him
sitting "down among the ashes," they had altered thoughts of
him. They suspected him; and though they knew nothing
against him, yet they perceived that he was not in the same
honour as before. Between a prince in ermine and the same
man in sackcloth there is, to some minds, a great difference.
Besides, the instinct of self-preservation leads men to hold off
from one who is sinking, lest they sink with him. After sitting
in silence for a week, these excellent men found it in their
hearts to assail him with their judicious observations. Here
and there they inserted nice little bits of cruelty, all meant for
his good. Was he not covered with sores? Was there not a
cause for all this? By this torture God delivered Job from
men: he was not likely after that to incur the curse which
comes through making flesh your arm. He was also
strengthened in personal independence of mind: he could
clearly see that his breath was in his own nostrils, and not in
other people's, and that he could stand alone by God's help,
ay, even stand against those eminent men who had contended
with him. Friends are all too apt to block out our view of our
best Friend. When gracious minds are driven from men, they
are drawn to God, and learn to sing with David, "My soul,
wait thou only upon God; for my expectation is from him." I do
not doubt therefore that the desertion and upbraiding
endured by Job from his friends, were a great help towards
his being able to say to the Lord his God, "Now mine eye seeth
thee." Eliphaz and Bildad and Zophar might have interposed
between Job and God, and their kindly help might have
placed Job under lasting obligations to them; but now he
looks alone to God, and honours him only.

Still, *before Job could see the Lord, there was a special
manifestation on God's part to him.* "Then the Lord answered
Job out of the whirlwind." God must really come and in a
gracious way make a display of himself to his servants, or else
they will not see him. Your afflictions will not of themselves
reveal God to you. If the Lord himself does not unveil his face,
your sorrow may even blind and harden you, and make you
rebellious. The desertion and unkindness of friends is, also,
no help to grace: its tendency is to sour and imperil your
piety, if it act out its natural influence: there must be a
special revealing of the Lord to our own souls before we shall
get such a clear apprehension of him as Job intended by the

words, "Now mine eye seeth thee." Read through the thirty-eighth chapter, and see how Jehovah declares his wisdom and his power: "Where wast thou when I laid the foundations of the earth? declare, if thou hast understanding. Who hath laid the measures thereof, if thou knowest? or who hath stretched the line upon it? Whereupon are the foundations thereof fastened? or who laid the corner stone thereof; when the morning stars sang together, and all the sons of God shouted for joy?" "Hast thou entered into the treasures of the snow? or hast thou seen the treasures of the hail?" "Canst thou bind the sweet influences of Pleiades, or loose the bands of Orion? Canst thou bring forth Mazzaroth in his season? or canst thou guide Arcturus with his sons?" Here was a marvellous field for thought. The Lord speaks in nature, and it is done. His glory is seen in heaven and earth, in the sea, and all deep places. God is, and there is none beside him. Yea, Jehovah is God alone.

Nor did the Lord fail to show to Job his justice, defying him to emulate it. See the fortieth chapter, eleventh and twelfth verses:—"Cast abroad the rage of thy wrath: and behold every one that is proud, and abase him. Look on every one that is proud, and bring him low; and tread down the wicked in their place." God is the supreme governor, and he beareth not the sword in vain; he is impartial and infallible, and none can disannul his judgment, or condemn his acts.

I need not tarry to say to you that all through that wonderful address of the Lord to his servant he is saying, in so many words, "I am God; but who art thou?" The Lord is proving that nothing is impossible to his power and his wisdom. He had, after all, not allowed his servant to sink out of his reach. He was always able to rescue him. You learn here, also, that God is not amenable to our judgment. He giveth no account of his matters. He makes Job feel that he is God, and then there is an end of the matter. No apology is made to Job, and no explanation is given him: he must bow in unreserved submission, and surrender unconditionally; and he does so.

Notice how by the Lord's first words Job was silenced, and could only whisper, "Behold I am vile, what shall I answer thee? I will lay mine hand upon my mouth. Once have I spoken; but I will not answer: yea, twice; but I will proceed no further." Thus far he worshipped; but he must yet go further, until he cries, "I abhor myself, and repent in dust and ashes."

II. We have now reached our second point—WHEN WE HAVE THESE VIVID APPREHENSIONS OF GOD, WE HAVE LOWLIER VIEWS OF OURSELVES.

Why are the wicked so proud? It is because they forget God. Why did Pharaoh dare to say, "Who is the Lord, that I should obey his voice?" It was because he did not know Jehovah; but after those ten plagues, he altered his tone, and cried out, "Intreat the Lord (for it is enough"). Even his great pride was forced to bow before Jehovah when judgments were let loose upon him. If men knew God, how it would change their thoughts and talk! If they could have even an indistinct idea "by the hearing of the ear," many of them would never be so irreverent as they now are, nor so lofty in their ideas of their own wisdom; but if they could "see" him as Job did, and behold his inexpressible glory, they would become far more meek and lowly.

Here let me observe that *God himself is the measure of rectitude,* and hence, when we come to think of God, we soon discover our own shortcomings and transgressions. Too often we compare ourselves among ourselves, and are not wise. A man says, "I am not so bad as many, and I am quite as good as such a one, who is in high repute." What if it be so? Dost thou judge thyself by other erring ones? Thy measuring line is false; it is not the standard of the sanctuary. If thou wouldest be right, thou must measure thyself with the holiness of God; God himself is the standard of perfect holiness, truth, love, and justice; and if thou fallest short of his glory, thou hast fallen short of what thou oughtest to be. When I think of this, self-righteousness seems to me to be a wretched insanity.

If you would know what God is, he sets himself before us in the person of his dear Son. In every respect in which we fall short of the perfect character of Jesus, in that respect we sin. There is no better description of sin that I know of than this: "Sin is any want of conformity to the law of God," and God's law is the transcript of his own mind. Wherein in any moral or spiritual respect, we fall short of the divine character, we to that extent fall into sin. No, my brethren, we cannot hear the ceaseless cry of the cherubim, "Holy, holy, holy, Lord God of Sabaoth," without at once sinking, sinking, sinking, till we abhor ourselves, and repent in dust and ashes. Permit me to suggest to each one here who has a high idea of himself, and has no sense of self-abhorrence, that such self-honour must arise from ignorance of God; for there is such an immeasurable distance between the perfection of God and our faultiness that our true position is that of penitent humility.

Our next reflection is this: *God himself is the object of every transgression,* and this sets sin in a terrible light. Sin frequently has our fellow-men as its object; but even then I am not incorrect in what I have said, for sins against our fellow-men are still sins against God. It would be well if we felt with David—"Against thee, thee only, have I sinned, and done this evil in thy sight." Think, then, of sin as an offence against God, committed in God's presence, committed while he is looking on. My beloved friends, in this light observe the wantonness of sin; for who could wish to offend against a perfectly holy and entirely loving God? If God is all he should be, why do we not agree with him? If in God we see every possible and conceivable good, why do we set up ourselves, our wills, our desires in opposition to him? He is so gracious towards man that he may be described by that one word "love"; and if it be so, why do we not love him with all our heart, and all our soul, and all our strength? Every shortcoming and every transgression, therefore, is a wanton offense against infinite goodness. If Jehovah were a tyrant, there might be some excuse for rebellion; but since he is infinitely just and loving, it is atrocious that his own creatures, ay, his own children, should offend against him.

Note, next, the impertinence of sin. How dare we transgress against God? O man, who art thou that rebellest against God? How darest thou to do to his face that which he forbids thee? How darest thou to leave undone in his very presence that which thy Lord commands thee to do? This makes sin a piece of presumption, a daring and glaring provocation of the Lord God. Thus it is evident that in the immediate presence of God sin doth like itself appear.

The fact that sin is levelled at God makes us bow in lowliness. Although some of us can hold our heads high among our fellow-men, and we can say, "I am neither a drunkard, nor a thief, nor a liar, neither have I offended against the laws of integrity and charity"; yet when we come before God, we perceive that we have not dealt towards him as we ought to have done. To him we have been thieves, robbing him of his glory. "Will a man rob God?" To him we

have been liars: we have dealt treacherously, and have
broken our promises. To him we have been ingrates; to him
we have been worse than brutes. Instead of equity, we have
dealt towards God iniquity. Instead of love, we have dealt out
enmity. The Lord has nourished and brought up children, and
they have rebelled against him. Even our holy things have
been defiled; our best tears need to be wept over, and our
truest faith is spoiled with unbelief. Oh, when we think of
this, we can understand why Job says, "Now mine eye seeth
thee. Wherefore I abhor myself."

Once more, *when God is seen with admiration, then of
necessity we are filled with self-loathing.* The more you
appreciate God, the more you will depreciate yourself. While
the thought of God rises higher, and higher, and higher, you
also will sink lower and lower in your own esteem. The word
used by Job, "I abhor myself," is a strong one. It might be
paraphrased thus, "I nauseate myself. I am disgusted with
myself. I cast forth from my soul every proud thought of
myself—cast it out from me as a sickening and intolerable
thing." Ah, dear friends, you have not seen God aright if your
abhorrence turns upon your fellow-men; but if the one man
you abhor is yourself, you are not mistaken! A sight of God
will make us regard our fellow-creatures with sympathy, as
involved in the same sin and misery as ourselves. As a
common danger in a sinking ship makes every man a brother
to his fellow, so a clear sense of our common guilt and ruin
will make us feel the brotherhood of man: but, on the other
hand, a sight of God will prevent our dreaming of personal
excellence, and will compel us to take the lowest room. Since
God is glorious in our eyes, we become ashamed. We adore
God, and in contrast, we abhor self.

Do you know what self-loathing means? Some of you do, I
know. And I am sure that in proportion as you truly love,
reverence, and worship God, in that proportion you are full of
abhorrence of self. You fine gentlemen, who hold your heads
so high that you can scarcely get through common door-ways,
you know nothing of this! You high and mighty ladies, who
cannot condescend to associate with any who are not of your
superior rank; and you purse-proud men, who expect all to
worship the golden calf which you have set up, you know
nothing about this. O you wonderfully wise men, you
intellectual persons, who so modestly dub yourselves

"thoughtful and cultured," you snuff out a poor evangelical believer as if he were an idiot; may the Lord give you an hour of Job's "I abhor myself," and then you will be bearable; but as you now are, you are a trial! While the dunghill is your proper place, you covet the throne of the Almighty; but he will not yield it to you: you would improve upon divine revelation, and revise infallible inspiration; but your boasting is vain. Oh that you had a manifestation of God, and then you would know yourselves! God grant it to you for his mercy's sake!

III. Thirdly, I have to show you that SUCH A SIGHT FILLS THE HEART WITH TRUE REPENTANCE. Job says, "I abhor myself, and repent in dust and ashes." The word "myself" has been added by the translators; and they could hardly have done otherwise. Job's expression, however, refers to all that had come out of himself, or had lurked within himself. He abhorred all that he had been doing and saying. He says, "I abhor, and repent in dust and ashes." What did he repent of? I think Job repented, first, of *that tremendous curse which he had pronounced upon the day of his birth*. It was terrific. See the third chapter. "Let the day perish wherein I was born, and the night in which it was said, There is a man child conceived. Let that day be darkness; let not God regard it from above, neither let the light shine upon it. Let it not be joined unto the days of the year, let it not come into the number of the months." He wished he had perished from the womb, that his birthcry had been his first and his last:—"For now should I have lain still and been quiet." Before God Job has to eat his bitter words. It is always a pity to say too much in moments of agony, because we may have to unsay that which escapes us. He would not curse God, but he did curse the day of his birth, and it was unseemly. Of this he unfeignedly repents.

Next, Job heartily repented of *his desire to die*. In the sixth chapter he expresses it as he did several times: he says, "Oh that I might have my request; and that God would grant me the thing that I long for! Even that it would please God to destroy me; that he would let loose his hand, and cut me off!" Do you wonder that he said this? Was ever man so tried? I do not wonder at all, even at his cursing the day of his birth, considering all the bodily pain and mental irritation which he was enduring at the time. I wonder that he played the man as well as he did; but still he must have looked back with deep regret upon his impatience. The last verses of the book run thus: "After this lived Job an hundred and forty years, and saw his sons, and his sons' sons, even four generations. So Job died, being old and full of days." This is the same man who begged to die. Elijah also said, "Let me die, I am not better than my fathers," and yet he never died at all. What poor creatures we are! What haste impatience breeds!

Job had to repent, next, of *all his complaints against God.* These had been very many. In the seventh chapter he turns to God and says, "I will speak in the anguish of my spirit; I will complain in the bitterness of my soul. Am I a sea, or a whale, that thou settest a watch over me? When I say, My bed shall comfort me, my couch shall ease my complaint; then thou scarest me with dreams, and terrifiest me through visions: so that my soul chooseth strangling, and death rather than my life. I loathe it; I would not live alway: let me alone; for my days are vanity. How long wilt thou not depart from me, nor let me alone till I swallow down my spittle?" Ah! poor Job had to swallow his murmuring as well as his spittle, for he repents of every rebellious thought. He complains of his having complained, and with self-abhorrence he repents in dust and ashes.

I do not doubt but what Job repented of *his despair.* The ninth and tenth chapters, and many other passages wherein Job speaks, are tinged with hopelessness. He felt as if God had left him a prey to the enemy; but this was not true. The Lord has never deserted any one of his people. There is not on record in all the history of the ages a case in which God has failed them that trust him. Has he not said, "I will never leave thee, nor forsake thee"? and he never has left nor forsaken any believer; yet Job evidently thought that he had done so, and he was greatly troubled.

Job had uttered *rash challenges of God.* In the ninth chapter, at the thirty-fourth verse, he says that there is no daysman between him and God, or else he would plead his cause: "Let him take his rod away from me, and let not his fear terrify me: then would I speak, and not fear him: but it is not so with me." This was wrong, and Job abhorred himself for having fallen into so ill a temper, and so little becoming in a man of God.

His critics goaded him by cruelly charging him with hypocrisy and wickedness, and Job vindicated himself with great earnestness, appealing to God, and saying, "Thou knowest that I am not wicked." This was true. The indignation of an honest heart cannot be blamed for speaking thus to men; but Job felt that he could not speak thus before the Lord. He could plead his innocence in the common courts of men, and there he could well enough defend himself; but when the matter came into the King's own court, he could not answer in the same strain, but felt compelled to plead guilty. Job has to retract all his pleadings and challenges. If the case is to be heard as "Jehovah *versus* Job," then Job yields the point unreservedly. Who is he that can contend with his Maker over a matter of holiness? We are wrong, God must be right!

Job had also to confess that his statements had been a darkening of wisdom by words without knowledge. Sometimes we say, "I perfectly understand *that;* I could clear up that mystery." We define this and define that to our brethren; but when we get into the presence of God, we find that our definitions are the proofs of our ignorance. "Vain man would be wise, though man be born like a wild ass's colt." Job drops his wisdom as well as his righteousness, although he was one of the wisest and holiest of men. While we see not God, we fancy that we can read all the riddles of his word; but when we behold him more nearly, we say with David, "So foolish was I, and ignorant: I was as a beast before thee." We are apt to judge the Lord by feeble sense instead of trusting him for his grace. This cometh of evil. In the presence of God Job bowed his head and repented of all his suspicions and mistrusts; and this is what we must do if, in the day of our sorrow, we have been petulant and unbelieving.

Let me pass on. According to our text, *repentance puts man into the lowest place.* He says, "I repent in dust and ashes." "Dust and ashes"—that signifies the dust-heap, or what in Scotland they call the "midden." Job had made dust and ashes his head-quarters. The dunghill, the refuse place, was now the spot which he felt to be fitted for him. Repentance puts us in a lowly seat. You have heard sometimes, I dare say, among the beautiful nothings of the modern school, the mention of "the dignity of human nature." Behold a throne for the "dignity of human nature." Yonder dust and ashes are for this proud royalty. The dust-heap is for human nature in its glory, when it has on its richest robes. When it takes its worst place, where is it? The lowest pit of hell, prepared for the devil and his angels, is the fit place for man when he has at last come to his true estate. I say that when man wears his best Sunday righteousness, he is even then only fit for the midden; and every man of God that has been brought to true repentance, owns that it is so. Alas! saith the man that sees his sinfulness, I should be a disgrace to any dust shoot; if I were cast away with the rotten refuse of the house, it might creep away from me, because my sin is a worse corruption than physical nature knows of, an insult even to the worm of decay, since in common putridity there is not the foul offense of moral evil. Repentance, you see, makes a man take the lowest place.

Next, note that *all real repentance is joined with holy sorrow and self-loathing.* I have read in the sermons of certain teachers that "Repentance is only a change of mind." That may be true; but what a change of mind it is! It is not such a change of mind as some of you underwent this morning when you said, "It is really too cold to go out," but afterwards you braved the snow, and came to the Tabernacle. Oh, no! repentance is a thorough and radical change of mind, and it is accompanied with real sorrow for sin, and self-loathing. A repentance in which there is no sorrow for sin will ruin the soul. Repentance without sorrow for sin is not the repentance of God's elect. If thou canst look upon sin without sorrow, then thou hast never looked on Christ. A faith-look at Jesus breaks the heart, both for sin and from sin. Try thyself by this test.

But, next, *repentance has comfort in it.* It is to my mind rather extraordinary that the Hebrew word, which is justly translated "repent," is also used in two or three places at least in the Old Testament to express comfort. Isaac, it is said, took Rebekah to his mother's tent, and was "comforted" after his mother's death." Here the word is the same as that which is here rendered "repent." Isaac's mind was changed as to the death of his mother. As, then, there is in the Hebrew word just a tinge of comfort, so in repentance itself, with all its sorrow, there are traces of joy. Repentance is a bitter-sweet or a sweet-bitter. After thou hast tasted it in thy mouth as gall, it will go down into thy belly, and be sweeter than honey and the honeycomb.

The door of repentance opens into the halls of joy. Job's repentance in dust and ashes was the sign of his deliverance.

God turned his wrath upon the three critics, but justified Job, and gave him the honourable office of intercessor on their behalf. Then "the Lord turned the captivity of Job when he prayed for his friends." "The Lord blessed the latter end of Job more than the beginning," and the turning point was that sitting down in the dust and ashes. When you are brought as low as you can be, the next turn must be upward. Down with you, then! Off with the feathers of your pride, and the finery of your self-righteousness! Down with you among the useless and worthless things! From that point you will ascend. The more crushed, humbled, exhausted, and near to death you are, the more prepared you are for God to raise you up.

Job was an unrivalled saint; none of us can compare with him; and if that perfect and upright man had to say, "I abhor myself," what will you and I say when we see God? We shall by-and-by behold him on the judgment-seat; how shall we endure it? If you have no righteousness but your own, you will stand naked to your shame in the day when the Lord appeareth. You self-righteous men, dare you go before God in your own righteousness? If you dare, I marvel at your presumption. Job dared not. He could stand up boldly before his accusers, but when before God he was in another attitude. When it comes to dying and appearing before the Most High, you that have no righteousness but one of your own spinning, what will you do? If God should take away your soul at once, could you dare to go before him in that fine character of yours, that wonderful morality, that large generosity? If you have any sense left, you dare not attempt such a thing.

What shall you and I do? Brethren, we are not afraid; for there is a righteousness of God which is given to us by faith through Jesus Christ. God himself cannot find any fault with his own righteousness; and if he gives me his own righteousness, even the righteousness of God which is by faith in Jesus Christ, which is to all and upon all them that believe, then I may hope to sit at last, not on the midden, but on the throne, rejoicing to find myself in Christ Jesus, crowned with a crown which I shall delight to cast at his feet. How happy are we if we can sing—

> "Jesus, thy blood and righteousness,
> My beauty are, my glorious dress;
> Midst flaming worlds, in these array'd,
> With joy shall I lift up my head"!

25

The Turning of Job's Captivity

"And the LORD turned the captivity of Job, when he prayed
for his friends: also the LORD gave Job twice as much as he
had before."   Job 42:10

Since God is immutable he acts always upon the same
principles, and hence his course of action in the olden
times to a man of a certain sort will be a guide as to what
others may expect who are of like character. God does not act
by caprice, nor by fits and starts. He has his usual modes and
ways. The psalmist David uses the expression, "Then will I
teach transgressors *thy ways*," as if God had well-known
ways, habits, and modes of action; and so he has, or he would
not be the unchangeable Jehovah. In that song of Moses the
servant of God, and the song of the Lamb, which is recorded
in the fifteenth chapter of the Revelation, we read, "Just and
true are thy ways, thou King of saints." The Lord has ways as
high above our ways as the heavens are above the earth, and
these are not fickle and arbitrary. These ways, although very
different if we view them superficially, are really always the
same when you view them with understanding. The ways of
the Lord are right, though transgressors fall therein by not
discerning them; but the righteous understand the ways of
the Lord, for to them he makes them known, and they
perceive that grand general principles govern all the actions
of God. If it were not so, the case of such a man as Job would
be of no service to us. It could not be said that the things
which happened aforetime happened unto us for an
ensample, because if God did not act on fixed principles we
could never tell how he would act in any fresh case, and that
which happened to one man would be no rule whatever, and
no encouragement whatever, to another. We are not all like
Job, but we all have Job's God. Though we have neither risen
to Job's wealth, nor will, probably, ever sink to Job's poverty,

yet there is the same God above us if we be high, and the
same God with his everlasting arms beneath us if we be
brought low; and what the Lord did for Job he will do for us,
not precisely in the same form, but in the same spirit, and
with like design. If, therefore, we are brought low to-night, let
us be encouraged with the thought that God will turn again
our captivity; and let us entertain the hope that after the time
of trial shall be over, we shall be richer, especially in spiritual
things, than ever we were before. There will come a turning
point to the growing heat of affliction, and the fire shall cool.
When the ebb has fallen to its lowest, the sea will return to its
strength; when mid-winter has come, spring will be near, and
when midnight has struck, then the dawning will not be far
away. Perhaps, too, the signal of our happier days shall be the
very same as that of the patient patriarch, and when we pray
for our friends, blessings shall be poured into our own
bosoms.

Our text has in it three points very clearly; firstly, *the Lord
can soon turn his people's captivity*: "The Lord turned the
captivity of Job." Secondly, *there is generally some point at
which he does this*: in Job's case he turned his captivity when
he prayed for his friends. And, thirdly, *believers shall never be
losers by God*, for he gave Job twice as much as he had before.

I. First, then, THE LORD CAN SOON TURN HIS PEOPLE'S
CAPTIVITY.

That is a very remarkable expression—"captivity." It does
not say, "God turned his poverty," though Job was reduced to
the extremity of penury, having lost all his property. We do
not read that the Lord turned his sickness, though he was
covered with sore boils. It does not say that he turned away
the sting of bereavement, reproach, and calumny, although
all those are included. But there is something more meant by
the word *captivity*. A man may be very poor, and yet not in
captivity, his soul may sing among the angels when his body
is on a dunghill, and dogs are licking his sores. A man may be
very sick, and yet not be in captivity; he may be roaming the
broad fields of covenant mercy though he cannot rise from his
bed; and his soul may never enjoy greater liberty than when
his body is scarcely able to turn from side to side. Captivity is
bondage of mind, the iron entering into the soul. I suspect
that Job, under the severe mental trial which attended his
bodily pains, was, as to his spirit, like a man bound hand and

foot and fettered, and then taken away from his native country, banished from the place which he loved, deprived of the associations which had cheered him, and confined in darkness. I mean that, together with the trouble and trial to which he was subjected, he had lost somewhat the presence of God; much of his joy and comfort had departed; the peace of his mind had gone, and the associations which he had formed with other believers were now broken: he was in all these respects like a lone captive. His three friends had condemned him as a hypocrite, and would not have association with him except to censure him, and thus he felt like one who had been carried into a far country, and banished both from God and man. He could only follow the occupation of a captive, that is, to be oppressed, to weep, to claim compassion, and to pour out a dolorous complaint. He hung his harp on the willows, and felt that he could not sing the Lord's song in a strange land. Poor Job! He is less to be pitied for his bereavements, poverty, and sickness than for his loss of that candle of the Lord which once shone about his head. That is the worst point of all when trouble penetrates to the heart. All the bullets in the battle, though they fly thick as hail, will not distress a soldier like one which finds a lodging in his flesh. "To take arms against a sea of troubles, and by opposing end them," is a grand and manly thing; but when that sea of trouble fills the cabin of the heart, puts out the fires of inward energy, washes the judgment from the wheel, and renders the pumps of resolution useless, the man becomes very nearly a wreck. "A wounded spirit who can bear?" Touch a man in his bone, and in his flesh, and yet he may exult; but touch him in his mind —let the finger of God be laid upon his spirit—and then, indeed, he is in captivity. I think the term includes all the temporal distress into which Job came, but it chiefly denotes the bondage of spirit into which he was brought, as the combined result of his troubles, his sickness, the taunts of his friends, and the withdrawal of the divine smile. My point is that God can deliver us out of that captivity; he can both from the spiritual and the temporal captivity give us a joyful release.

The Lord can deliver us out of spiritual captivity, and that very speedily. I may be addressing some, to-night, who feel everything except what they want to feel. They enjoy no sweetness in the means of grace, and yet for all the world they would not give them up. They used at one time to rejoice in the Lord; but now they cannot see his face, and the utmost they can say is, "Oh that I knew where I might find him!" It little matters that some live in perpetual joy, the triumphs of others cannot cheer a man who is himself defeated. It is idle to tell a distressed soul that it ought to rejoice as others do. What one ought to do and what one can do are sometimes very different, for how to perform that which we would we find not. In vain do you pour your glad notes into a troubled ear. Singing songs to a sad heart is like pouring vinegar upon nitre, the elements are discordant, and cause a painful effervescence. There are true children of God who walk in darkness and see no light; yea, some who are the excellent of the earth, nevertheless are compelled to cry aloud, "My God, my God, why hast thou forsaken me?" Throughout all time some of these have been in the church, and there always will be such, let our perfect brethren condemn them as they please. The Lord will always have his mourners, his church shall always have an afflicted and poor people in her midst. Let us all take warning, for we also may be tried and cast down ere our day is over; it may be that the brightest eye among us may yet be dimmed, and the boldest heart may yet be faint, and he that dwells nearest to his God at this moment may yet have to cry out in bitterness of soul, "O God, return unto me, and lift up the light of thy countenance upon me."

Therefore mark well this cheering truth, God can turn your captivity, and turn it at once. Some of God's children seem to think that to recover their former joy must occupy a long period of time. It is true, dear brother, that if you had to work your passage back to where you came from it would be a weary voyage. There would have to be most earnest searchings of heart and purgings of spirit, struggling with inbred lusts and outward temptations, and all that, if joy were always the result of inward condition. There must needs be a great deal of scrubbing and cleansing and furbishing up of the house, before you could invite your Lord to come, if he and you dwelt together on terms of law. But albeit, that all this cleansing and purifying will have to be done, it will be done far better when you have a sense of his love than it ever can be if you do it in order to make yourself fit for it. Do you not remember when first you sought him you wanted him to deal with you on the legal ground of making yourself better, and you prepared the house for him to come and dwell in it; but he would not come on such terms. He came to you just as you were, and when he came, he himself drove out the intruders which profaned the temple of your soul, and he dwelt with you, in order to perfect the cleansing. Now he will vouchsafe to you the conscious enjoyment of his presence on the same terms as at first, that is, on terms of free and sovereign grace. Did you not at that time admit the Saviour to your soul because you could not do without him? Was not that the reason? Is it not a good reason for receiving him again? Was there anything in you when you received him which could commend you to him? Say, were you not all over defilement, and full of sin and misery? And yet you opened the door, and said, "My Lord, come in, in thy free grace, come in, for I must have thee or I perish." My dear friend, dare you invite him now on other terms? Having begun in the Spirit, wouldst thou be made perfect in the flesh? Having begun to live by grace, wouldst thou go on to live by works? When thou wast a stranger, didst thou trust in his love, and now that thou art his friend, wilt thou appeal to the law? God forbid. O, brother, Jesus loves thee still, and in a moment he will restore thee. O, sister, Jesus would fain come back to thy heart again, and that in an instant. Hast thou never read that joyful exclamation of the spouse, "Or ever I was aware, my soul made me like the chariots of Ammi-nadib?" Why, can he not do the same with you now, and quicken and enspirit you even in a moment? After all, you are not worse than you were when he first visited you; you are not in so sorry a plight after all, as your first natural state, for then you were dead in trespasses and sins altogether, and he quickened you, and now, though you say you feel dead, yet the very expression proves that there is some life lingering in you. Did I not hear you say,

> "Return, O Sacred Dove, return,
> Sweet messenger of rest,
> I hate the sins that made thee mourn,
> And drove thee from my breast."

Why, friend, those sighs and groans are sweet to the Lord, and they would not have been in thee it he had not put them there; they are sure tokens that his grace has not been altogether taken from thee. Knowest thou not, O child of God, that the grace of God is intended to meet all thy sins after conversion as well as before conversion? Dost thou not know that the Lord loved thee of old, despite thy sins, and he loves thee still? Understandest thou not that the ground of thy salvation is not thy standing or thy character, but the standing of Christ before God, and the character and work of Christ in the presence of God? Believe thou firmly that still he loves thee, for so indeed he does. Cast thine eyes upon those dear wounds of his, and read his love still written there. Oh, unbelieving Thomas, do not put thy finger into thine own wounds, for that will not help thee, but place them in the wounds of Jesus. Come close to him, and thou shalt cry with ecstasy of spirit, "My Lord and my God." Well do I know what it is to feel this wondrous power of God to turn our captivity. When one is constantly engaged in ministry, it sometimes happens that the mind wanders, the spirit flags, and the energy is damped, yet, all in a minute, the Lord can quicken us into vigorous activity; the tow catches fire and blazes gloriously, when the Holy Spirit applies the fire. We have heard a hymn sung, and we have said, "I cannot join in that as I could wish," and yet, on a sudden, a mighty rushing wind has borne us away with the song right into heaven. The Lord does not take days, months, weeks, or even hours, to do his work of revival in our souls. He made the world in six days, but he lit it up in an instant with one single word. He said, "light be," and light was, and cannot he do the same for us, and chase away our gloom before the clock ticks again? Do not despair, nay, do not even doubt your God. He can turn your captivity as the streams in the south.

Beloved, *he can do the same as to our temporal captivity.* We do not often say much about temporals when we are preaching; I fear we do not say enough about them, for it is wonderful how the Old Testament is taken up with the narration of God's dealings with his people as to temporal things. Many people imagine that God has a great deal to do with their prayer-closet, but nothing to do with their store-closet; it would be a dreadful thing for us if it were so. Indeed, my brethren, we ought to see as much the hand of our Lord on the table in the kitchen when it is loaded as we do at the communion table, for the same love that spreads the table when we commemorate our Saviour's dying love, spreads the table which enables us to maintain the bodily life without

which we could not come to the other table at all. We must
learn to see God in everything, and praise him for all that we
have. Now, it may be I address some friend who has been a
great sufferer through pecuniary losses. Dear friend, the Lord
can turn your captivity. When Job had lost everything, God
readily gave him all back. "Yes," say you, "but that was a very
remarkable case." I grant you that, but then we have to do
with a remarkable God, who works wonders still. If you
consider the matter you will see that it was quite as
remarkable a thing that Job should lose all his property as it
was that he should get it back again. If you had walked over
Job's farm at first, and seen the camels and the cattle, if you
had gone into his house and seen the furniture and the
grandeur of his state—if you had seen how those who passed
him in the street bowed to him, for he was a highly respected
man, and if you had gone to his children's houses, and seen
the comfort in which they lived, you would have said, "Why,
this is one of the best-established men in all the land of Uz."
There was scarcely a man of such substance to be found in all
that region, and if somebody had foretold that he would in one
day lose all this property—all of it—and lose all his children,
why you would have said, "Impossible! I have heard of great
fortunes collapsing, but then they were built on speculations.
They were only paper riches, made up of bills and the like;
but in the case of this man there are oxen, sheep, camels, and
land, and these cannot melt into thin air. Job has a good
substantial estate, I cannot believe that ever he will come to
poverty." Why, when he went out into the gate where the
magistrates sat to administer justice, they rose up and gave
him the chief seat on the bench. He was a man whose flocks
could not be counted, so great were his possessions—
possessions of real property, not of merely nominal estate:
and yet suddenly, marvellously, it all took to itself wings and
disappeared. Surely, if God can scatter he can gather. If God
could scatter such an estate as that, he could, with equal ease,
bring it back again. But this is what we do not always see. We
see the destructive power of God, but we are not very clear
about the upbuilding power of God. Yet, my brethren, surely
it is more consonant with the nature of God that he should
give than take, and more like him that he should caress than
chastise. Does he not always say that judgment is his strange
work? I feel persuaded that it was strange work with God to

take away all Job's property from him and bring him into that deep distress; but when the Lord went about to enrich his servant Job again, he went about that work, as we say, *con amore*—with heart and soul. He was doing then what he delights to do, for God's happiness is never more clearly seen than when he is distributing the largesses of his love. Why can you not look at your own circumstances in the same light? It is more likely that God will bless you and restore to you than it was ever likely that he would chasten you and take away from you. He can restore you all your wealth, and even more.

This may seem to be a very trite observation, commonplace, and such as everybody knows, but, beloved, the very things that everybody knows are those which we need to hear, if they are most suitable to our case. Those old things which we did not care about in our prosperity are most valued when we are cast down by the terrible blows of tribulation. Let me then repeat the truism, the Lord who takes away can as easily restore. "The Lord maketh sore, *and bindeth up*; he woundeth, *and his hands make whole*. He killeth, *and he maketh alive*." Believe that he will put forth his right hand soon if the left has been long outstretched, and, if you can believe it, it will not be long before you will be able to say, he hath regarded the low estate of his servant. He hath lifted the poor from the dunghill and set him among princes, even the princes of his people. For the Lord putteth down the mighty from their seat, but he exalteth them that are of low degree. I leave with you this simple truth. The Lord can turn the captivity of his people. You may apply the truth to a thousand different things. You Sunday-school teachers, if you have had a captivity in your class, and no good has been done, God can change that. You ministers, if for a long time you have ploughed and sowed in vain, the Lord can turn your captivity there. You dear wives who have been praying for your husbands, you fathers who have been pleading for your children, and have seen no blessing yet, the Lord can turn your captivity in those respects. No captivity is so terrible but God can bring us back from it; no chain is so fastened but God can strike it off, and no prison-house is so strong but God can break the bars and set his servants free.

II. I pass on to our second remark, which is this. THERE IS GENERALLY SOME POINT AT WHICH THE LORD INTERPOSES TO

TURN THE CAPTIVITY OF HIS PEOPLE.

In Job's case, I have no doubt, the Lord turned his captivity, as far as the Lord was concerned, because *the grand experiment which had been tried on Job was now over.*

The suggestion of Satan was that Job was selfish in his piety—that he found honesty to be the best policy, and, therefore, he was honest—that godliness was gain, and therefore he was godly. "Hast thou not set a hedge about him and all that he hath?" said the old accuser of the brethren. The devil generally does one of two things. Sometimes he tells the righteous that there is no reward for their holiness, and then they say, "Surely, I have cleansed my heart in vain and washed my hands in innocency;" or else he tells them that they only obey the Lord because they have a selfish eye to the reward. Now, it would be a calamity if the devil could charge the Lord with paying his servants badly: it would have been an ill thing if the fiend had been able to say, "There is Job, a perfect and an upright man, but thou hast set no hedge about him. Thou hast given him no reward whatever." That would have been an accusation against the goodness and justice of God; but, as the devil cannot say that, he takes the other course, and says—"Thou hast set a hedge about him and all that he has; he serves thee for gain and honour; he has a selfish motive in his integrity." By God's permission the matter was tested. The devil had said, "Put forth now thy hand and touch his bone and his flesh, and he will curse thee to thy face." But Job had done no such thing. In his extremity he said, "The Lord gave and the Lord hath taken away, and blessed be the name of the Lord." God puts his servants sometimes into these experiments that he may test them, that Satan himself may know how true-hearted God's grace has made them, and that the world may see how they can play the man. Good engineers, if they build a bridge are glad to have a train of enormous weight go over it. You remember when the first Great Exhibition was built they marched regiments of soldiers, with a steady tramp, over the girders, that they might be quite sure that they would be strong enough to bear any crowd of men; for the regular tramp of well disciplined soldiers is more trying to a building than anything else. So our wise and prudent Father sometimes marches the soldiery of trouble right over his people's supports, to let all men see that the grace of God can sustain every possible pressure and load. I am sure that if any of you had invented some implement requiring strength you would be glad to have it tested, and the account of the successful trial published abroad. The gunsmith does not object to a charge being fired from the barrel at the proofhouse far greater than any strain which it ought ordinarily to bear; for he knows that it will endure the proof. "Do your worst or do your best; it is a good instrument; do what you like with it;" so the maker of a genuine article is accustomed to speak; and the Lord seems to say the same concerning his people. "My work of grace in them is mighty and thorough. Test it Satan; test it world; test it by bereavements, losses, and reproaches; it will endure every ordeal." And when it is tested, and bears it all, then the Lord turns the captivity of his people, for the experiment is complete.

Most probably there was, in Job's character, some fault from which his trial was meant to purge him. If he erred at all, probably it was in having a somewhat elevated idea of himself and a stern manner towards others. A little of the elder-brother spirit may, perhaps, have entered into him. A good deal that was sour came out of Job when his miserable comforters began to tease him—not a hundredth part as much as would come out of me, I warrant you, or, perhaps, out of you; but, still, it would not have come out if it had not been in. It must have been in him or otherwise all the provocation in the world would not have brought it out; and the Lord intended by his trials to let Job have a view of himself from another standpoint, and discover imperfections in his character which he would never have seen if he had not been brought into a tried condition. When through the light of trial, and the yet greater light of God's glorious presence, Job saw himself unveiled, he abhorred himself in dust and ashes. Probably Job had not humbled himself of late, but he did it then; and now, if any sort of selfishness lurked in him it was put away, for Job began to pray for his cruel friends. It would take a good deal of grace to bring some men to pray for such friends as they were. To pray for one's real friends, I hope, comes natural to us; but to pray for that Bildad and the other two, after the abominable things they had spoken and insinuated—well, it showed that there was a large amount of sweetness and light in Job's character, and abounding grace deep down in his soul, or he would scarcely have interceded for such ungenerous tramplers upon a fallen friend. Now, behold, Job has discovered his fault, and he has put it away, and the grand old man bows his knee to pray for men who called him hypocrite—to pray for men who cut him to the very soul. He pleads with God that he would look in mercy upon men who had no mercy upon him, but had pitilessly heaped all kinds of epithets upon him, and stung him in his tenderest places, just when they ought to have had pity upon him. His misery alone ought to have stopped their mouths, but it seems as if that misery egged them on to say the most cruel things that could possibly have been conceived—the more cruel because they were, all of them, so undeserved. But now Job prays for his friends. You see the trial had reached its point. It had evidently been blessed to Job, and it had proved Satan to be a liar, and so now the fire of the trial goes out, and like precious metal the patriarch comes forth from the furnace brighter than ever.

Beloved friends, the point at which God may turn your captivity may not be the same as that at which he turned Job's, for yours may be a different character. I will try and indicate, briefly, when I think God may turn your trial.

Sometimes he does so *when that trial has discovered to you your especial sin.* You have been putting your finger upon divers faults, but you have not yet touched *the* spot in which your greatest evil is concentrated. God will now help you to know yourself. When you are in the furnace you will begin to search yourself, and you will cry, "Show me wherefore thou contendest with me." You will find out three or four things, perhaps, in which you are faulty, and you will commit yourself to the Lord and say, "Give me grace, good Lord, to put away these evil things." Yes, but you have not come to the point yet, and only a greater trial will guide you to it. The anger of the Lord smokes against your house, not for this or that, but for another evil, and you have need to institute another search, for the images may be under the seat whereon a beloved Rachel sits. The evil in your soul may be just at the point where you think that you are best guarded against temptation. Search, therefore, and look, dear brother, for when the sin has been found out, and the Achan has been stoned, then the valley of Achor shall be a door of hope, and you shall go up to victory, the Lord going with you.

Perhaps, too, your turning point will be *when your spirit is broken.* We are by nature a good deal like horses that want breaking in, or, to use a scriptural simile, we are as "bullocks unaccustomed to the yoke." Well, the horse has to go through certain processes in the *menagé* until at last it is declared to be "thoroughly broken in," and we need similar training. You and I are not yet quite broken in, I am afraid. We go very merrily along, and yield to the rein in certain forms of service; but if we were called to other sorts of work, or made to suffer, we should need the kicking strap put on, and require a sharper bit in our mouths. We should find that our spirit was not perfectly broken. It takes a long time of pain and sickness to bring some down to the dust of complete resignation to the divine will. There is a something still in which they stick out against God, and of many it is true, "Though thou shouldest bray a fool in a mortar among wheat with a pestle, yet will not his foolishness depart from him." We have been brayed in that mortar, and with that pestle day after day, and week after week, and yet we are still foolish. When our soul shall cheerfully say, "Not as I will, but as thou wilt," then our captivity will be almost over, if not quite. While we cry, "It must not be so, I will not have it so," and we struggle and rebel, we shall only have to feel that we are kicking against the pricks, and wounding our foot every time we kick; but when we give up all that struggling, and say, "Lord, I leave it entirely with thee, thy will be done"—then will the trial cease, because there will be no necessity for it any longer. That is with some the culmination and turning point of trouble. Their Gethsemane ends when, like the Lord Jesus, they cry, "Nevertheless, not as I will, but as thou wilt."

Sometimes, again, trial may cease *when you have learned the lesson which it was intended to teach you, as to some point of gospel truth.* I think I have sometimes said that many truths of the gospel are like letters written with sympathetic ink. If you have ever had a letter written with that preparation, when you look at it you cannot see anything whatever: it is quite illegible. The proper thing to do is to hold the writing up to the fire. As it warms at the fire the acid writing becomes manifest, and the letters are before you. Many of God's promises need to be held before the scorching fires of adversity and personal trouble, and then we read the precious secret of the Spirit's consolation. You cannot see the stars in the day time upon the surface of the earth, but if you go down into a well you can, and when you go down the deep well of trouble it often happens that you see a beauty and lustre in the promise which nobody else can see, and when the Lord has brought you into a certain position in which you can see the glory of his grace as you never could have seen it anywhere else, then he will say, "It is enough; I have taught my child the lesson, and I will let him go."

I think, too, it may be with some of us that *God gives us trouble until we obtain a sympathetic spirit.* I should not like to have lived forty years in this world without ever having suffered sickness. "Oh," you say, "that would have been very desirable." I grant you it appears so. When I met with a man that never had an ache or a pain, or a day's sickness in his life, I used to envy him; but I do not now, because I feel very confident that he is a loser by his unvarying experience. How can a man sympathise with trouble that he never knew? How can he be tender in heart if he has never been touched with infirmity himself? If one is to be a comforter to others, he must know the sorrows and the sicknesses of others in his measure. It was essential to our Lord, and, certainly, what was essential to him is necessary to those who are to be shepherds of others, as he was. Now, it may be that by nature some of us are not very sympathetic; I do not think Job was: it is possible that though he was kind, and generous to the poor, yet he was rather hard, but his troubles taught him sympathy. And, perhaps, the Lord may send you trouble till you become softer in heart, so that afterwards you will be one who can speak a word in season to the weary. As you sit down by the bedside of the invalid, you will be able to say, "I know all the ins and outs of a sick man's feelings, for I have been sore sick myself." When God has wrought that in you, it may be he will turn your captivity.

In Job's case, the Lord turned his captivity *when he prayed for his friends.* Prayer for ourselves is blessed work, but for the child of God it is a higher exercise to become an intercessor, and to pray for others. Prayer for ourselves, good as it is, has just a touch of selfishness about it: prayer for others is delivered from that ingredient. Herein is love, the love which God the Holy Spirit delights to foster in the heart, when a man's prayers go up for others. And what a Christlike form of prayer it is when you are praying for those who have ill-treated you and despitefully used you. Then are you like

your master. Praying for yourselves, you are like those for
whom Jesus died; but praying for your enemies, you are like
the dying Jesus himself. "Father, forgive them, for they know
not what they do," has more of heaven in it than the songs of
seraphs, and your prayer when offered for those who have
treated you ill is somewhat akin to the expiring prayer of your
Lord. Job was permitted to take a noble revenge, I am sure
the only one he desired, when he became the means of
bringing them back to God. God would not hear them, he said,
for they had spoken so wrongly of his servant Job, and now
Job is set to be a mediator, or intercessor on their behalf: thus
was the contempt poured upon the patriarch turned into
honour. If the Lord will only save the opposer's soul through
your prayer, it will be a splendid way of returning bitter
speeches. If many unkind insinuations have been thrown out,
and wicked words said, if you can pray for those who used
such words, and God hears you and brings them to Jesus, it
will be such a triumph as an angel might envy you. My
brother, never use any other weapon of retaliation than the
weapon of love. Avenge not thyself in anywise by uttering
anything like a curse, or desiring any hurt or mischief to come
to thy bitterest foe, but inasmuch as he curses, overwhelm
him with blessings. Heap the hot coals of thy good wishes and
earnest prayers upon his head, and if the Lord give thee to
bring him to a state of salvation, he shall be praised, and thou
shalt have happiness among the sons of men.

Perhaps some of you are in trouble now because you cannot
be brought sincerely to pray for your enemies. It is a grievous
fault when Christian men harbour resentments; it is always a
sad sign when a man confesses, "I could not heartily pray for
So-and-so." I would not like to live an hour at enmity with any
man living, be he who he may; nor should any Christian man,
I think. You should feel that however treacherous,
dishonourable, unjust, and detestable the conduct of your
enemy may have been to you, yet still it is forgiven, quite
forgiven in your heart, and, as far as possible, forgotten, or
wherein remembered, remembered with regret that it should
have occurred, but with no resentment to the person who
committed the wrong. When we get to that state, it is most
probable that the Lord will smile upon us and turn our
captivity.

III. The last word I have to say—the third word—is this,

that BELIEVERS SHALL NOT BE LOSERS FOR THEIR GOD. God, in
the experiment, took from Job all that he had, but at the end
he gave him back twice as much as he had—twice as many
camels and oxen, and twice as many of everything, even of
children. I heard a very sweet remark about the children the
other day, for somebody said, "Yes, God did give him twice as
many children, because his first family were still his. They
were not lost but gone before." So the Lord would have his
people count their children that are gone to heaven, and
reckon them as belonging to the family still, as the child did
in Wordsworth's pretty poem, "Master, we are seven." And so
Job could say of his sons and daughters, as well as of all the
other items, that he had twice as many as before. True, the
first family were all gone, but he had prayed for them in the
days of their feasting, he had brought them together and
offered sacrifice, and so he had a good hope about them, and
he reckoned them as still his own. Tried brother, the Lord can
restore to you the double in temporal things if he pleases. If
he takes away he can as certainly give, and that right early.
He certainly can do this in spiritual things; and if he takes
away temporals and gives spirituals we are exceedingly great
gainers. If a man should take away my silver and give me
twice the weight in gold in return, should I not be thankful?
And so, if the Lord takes away temporals and gives us
spirituals, he thus gives us a hundred times more than he
takes away.

Dear brethren, you shall never lose anything by what you
suffer for God. If, for Christ's sake, you are persecuted, you
shall receive in this life your reward; but if not, rejoice and be
glad, for great is your reward in heaven. You shall not lose
anything by God's afflicting you. You shall, for a time, be an
apparent loser; but a real loser in the end you shall never be.
When you get to heaven you will see that you were a priceless
gainer by all the losses you endured. Shall you lose anything
by what you give to God? Never. Depend on it, he will be no
man's debtor. There dwells not in earth or heaven any man
who shall be creditor to the Most High. The best investment a
man makes is that which he gives to the Lord from a right
motive. Nothing is lost which is offered to the cause of God.
The breaking of the alabaster box of precious ointment was
not a wasteful thing, and he who should give to the Lord all
that he had would have made a prudent use of his goods. "He

that giveth to the poor lendeth to the Lord," and he that giveth to the Lord's church and to the Lord himself lays up his treasure in heaven, where it shall be his for ever.

Beloved, we serve a good Master, and if he chooses to try us for a little we will bear our trial cheerfully, for God will turn our captivity ere long.

In closing, I wish I could feel that this subject had something to do with you all, but it is not the case. Oh, no, there are some of you who have felt no captivity, but you have a dreadful captivity to come, and there is no hope of God's ever turning that captivity when once you get into it. Without God, without Christ, strangers from the commonwealth of Israel, you are in bondage until now, and there will ere long come upon you bondage that will never end. You cannot pray for your friends: you have never prayed for yourself. God would not hear you if you did pray for others, for, first of all, you must be yourself reconciled to him by the death of his Son. Oh, that you would mind these things and look to Jesus Christ alone for your salvation, for if you do he will accept you, for he has promised to cast out none who come to him. And then look at this: after all is right between God and your soul you need not fear what happens to you in the future, for, come sickness or health, come poverty or wealth, all is right, all is safe, all is well. You have put yourself into the hand of God, and wherever God may lift that hand you are still within it, and therefore always secure and always blessed; and, if not always consciously happy, yet you have always the right to be so, seeing you are true to God, and he delights in you. God bless you, and give you all salvation, for Jesus Christ's sake. Amen.

INDEX OF SERMONS FROM THE BOOK OF JOB

NPSP   New Park Street Pulpit 1855-1860
MTP   Metropolitan Tabernacle Pulpit 1861-1917